ALSO BY FERGUS M. BORDEWICH

Washington: The Making of the American Capital

*Bound for Canaan: The Underground Railroad
and the War for the Soul of America*

My Mother's Ghost

*Killing the White Man's Indian: Reinventing Native Americans
at the End of the Twentieth Century*

Cathay: A Journey in Search of Old China

AMERICA'S
GREAT
DEBATE

HENRY CLAY, STEPHEN A. DOUGLAS, AND THE
COMPROMISE THAT PRESERVED THE UNION

—◆—

FERGUS M. BORDEWICH

SIMON & SCHUSTER

New York   London   Toronto   Sydney   New Delhi

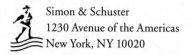
Simon & Schuster
1230 Avenue of the Americas
New York, NY 10020

Copyright © 2012 by Fergus M. Bordewich

First Simon & Schuster hardcover edition April 2012

SIMON & SCHUSTER and colophon are registered trademarks
of Simon & Schuster, Inc.

For information about special discounts for bulk purchases,
please contact Simon & Schuster Special Sales at
1-866-506-1949 or business@simonandschuster.com.

The Simon & Schuster Speakers Bureau can bring authors
to your live event. For more information or to book an event,
contact the Simon & Schuster Speakers Bureau at
1-866-248-3049 or visit our website at www.simonspeakers.com.

Designed by Joy O'Meara

Manufactured in the United States of America

10   9   8   7   6   5   4   3   2   1

Library of Congress Cataloging-in-Publication Data

Bordewich, Fergus M.
  America's great debate : Henry Clay, Stephen A. Douglas, and the compromise
that preserved the Union / Fergus M. Bordewich.
      p.   cm.
  Includes bibliographical references and index.
  1. Compromise of 1850. 2. Clay, Henry, 1777–1852. 3. Douglas,
Stephen A. (Stephen Arnold), 1813–1861.   4. United States—Politics and
government—1815–1861. 5. Slavery—United States—History—19th century.
6. United States—History—Civil War, 1861–1865—Causes. I. Title.
  E423.B73 2012
  973.6'4—dc23   2011029547
ISBN 978-1-4391-2460-4
ISBN 978-1-4391-4168-7 (ebook)

All photos not otherwise credited are courtesy of the Library of Congress.

For J.P.B.,
whose steadfast devotion
to the values of democracy embodies
the best tradition of American government

"The North Americans will spread out far beyond their present bounds. They will encroach again and again on their neighbors. New territories will be planted, declare their independence and be annexed! We have New Mexico and California! We will have Old Mexico and Cuba! The isthmus cannot arrest—nor even the St. Lawrence!! Time has all this in her womb."

—DEBOW'S REVIEW, 1848

"A dismemberment of this republic I now consider inevitable."

—ALEXANDER STEPHENS, 1850

"Wo to all the just and merciful in the land!"

—FREDERICK DOUGLASS, 1850

CONTENTS

———•◆•———

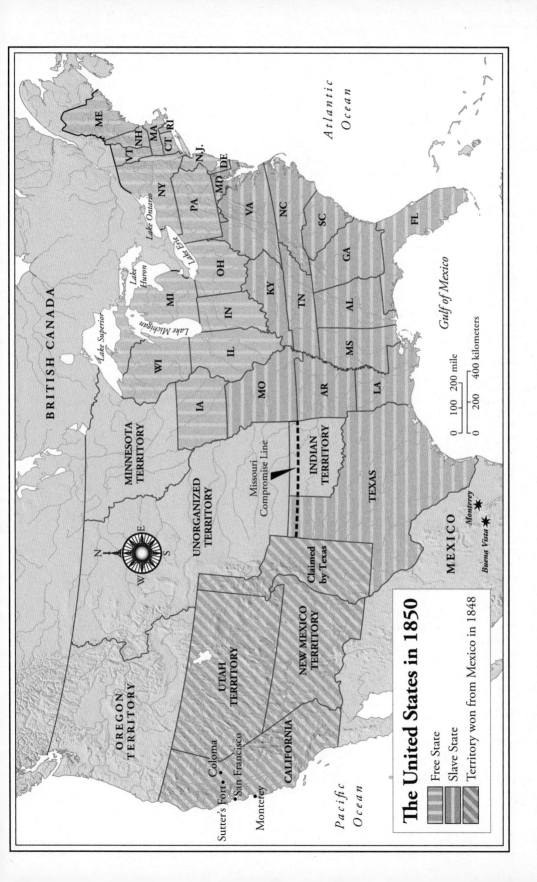

The United States in 1850

Free State
Slave State
Territory won from Mexico in 1848

OREGON TERRITORY

UTAH TERRITORY

CALIFORNIA

Sutter's Fort
Coloma
San Francisco
Monterey

NEW MEXICO TERRITORY

Claimed by Texas

MEXICO

Monterey
Buena Vista

TEXAS

INDIAN TERRITORY

Missouri Compromise Line

UNORGANIZED TERRITORY

MINNESOTA TERRITORY

BRITISH CANADA

IA
WI
IL
MO
AR
LA
MS
AL
TN
KY
IN
MI
OH
GA
SC
NC
VA
FL

PA
NY
MD
DE
N.J.
VT
ME
NH
MA
CT
RI

Lake Superior
Lake Michigan
Lake Huron
Lake Erie
Lake Ontario

Atlantic Ocean

Gulf of Mexico

Pacific Ocean

0   100   200 mile
0   200   400 kilometers

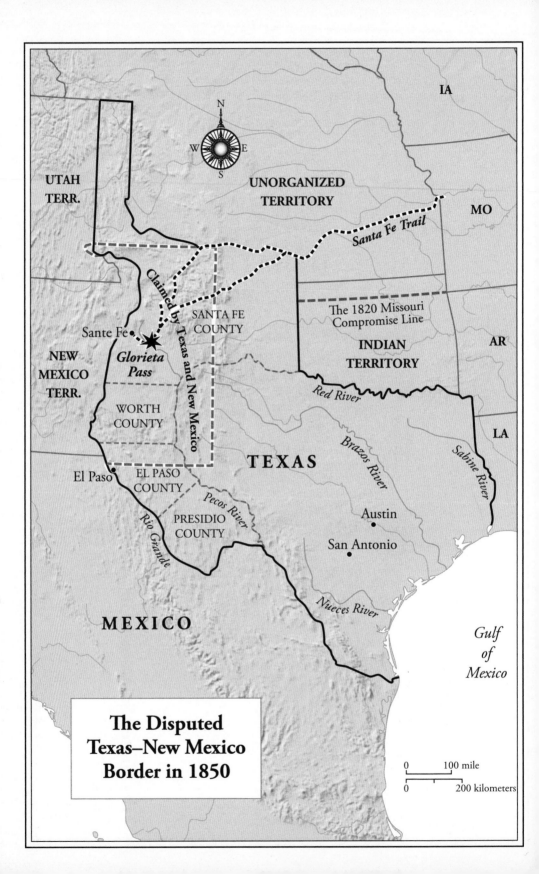

IA

UTAH
TERR.

UNORGANIZED
TERRITORY

MO

Santa Fe Trail

Claimed by Texas and New Mexico

SANTA FE
COUNTY

The 1820 Missouri
Compromise Line

Sante Fe

*Glorieta
Pass*

INDIAN
TERRITORY

AR

NEW
MEXICO
TERR.

WORTH
COUNTY

Red River

TEXAS

Brazos River

LA

Sabine River

El Paso

EL PASO
COUNTY

Pecos River

Austin

PRESIDIO
COUNTY

Rio Grande

San Antonio

MEXICO

Nueces River

Gulf
of
Mexico

The Disputed
Texas–New Mexico
Border in 1850

| 0 | 100 mile |
| 0 | 200 kilometers |

AMERICA'S
GREAT
DEBATE

PREFACE

———— •◆• ————

Some years ago, writing about the Underground Railroad, I came across a speech that was delivered by Daniel Webster in 1851 to conservative businessmen in upstate New York. Webster declared—he ranted, really—that the Fugitive Slave Law that had passed a few months earlier would be executed in every city of the North, and that all who dared oppose it were "traitors! traitors! traitors!" I was startled by his ferocity. Surely, he must have been misquoted, I thought. Hadn't he delivered one of the most ringing denunciations of slavery ever made, at Plymouth Rock, in 1820? Wasn't he from Boston, the very epicenter of the abolitionist movement? But it was no misquote. Webster, the "Godlike Daniel," as he was often called, made many such speeches that winter, and he did everything he could to see that the law was enforced. Wondering what had happened to Daniel Webster led me to the great congressional debate of 1850, which had produced not just the enactment of the Fugitive Slave Law, but beyond that, the stupendously ambitious compromise that its architects, Henry Clay and Stephen A. Douglas foremost among them, believed would bring sectional peace by ending the nation's deepening agony over slavery.

The radicals of the abolitionist underground were comfortable company for me. Their muscular idealism and their commitment to racial justice looked forward to the progressive social movements of the twentieth century. Despised outsiders in their own time, they stood for reforms that had become the modern mainstream. The political men of the climactic moment of the antebellum era, whose fears, passions, and certitudes collided dramatically in the debate of 1850, however, seemed much less comprehensible. Denizens of a political world that, even outside the South, was irreversibly shackled to slavery, *their* mainstream had utterly disappeared, scrubbed away by the wash of history. Questions nagged: How had the imperatives of slavery played out against the expanding landscape of America made possible by the nation's first imperial war in Mexico? How did the men (and they were all men) who led the nation rationalize slavery—how did they defend the morally indefensible—in order to keep the nation intact? How close had the United States actually come to war in 1850?

These questions formed the starting point for this book. They began to preoccupy me during a period when Congress was, and still is, considered by many Americans to be paralyzed and "broken." There are significant differences between the mid-nineteenth century and our own time, of course. In 1850, many Americans thought the United States was about to crack apart, and that little could (or, as far as some were concerned, even should) be done about it. And amid all the bellicose rhetoric that was hurled among the sectional contenders, it is virtually impossible to find an attack on government itself: Americans then, North and South, were immensely proud of its machinery, even when it seemed to malfunction. They admired "career politicians" as the very embodiment of democracy, rather than scorned them as an alien species. But there are also intriguing parallels.

As the year 1850 dawned, Congress seemed hopelessly crippled. Senators and congressmen met, debated, and fought in the long shadow of a bloody foreign war that had begun in a fever of patriotism and ended with a public sufficiently angry at its cost that they threw out the party that started the war and replaced it with one that had largely opposed it. Then as now, Congress contained men of extraordinary ability, as well as a leavening of self-serving opportunists and preening peacocks, sanctimonious ideologues and amoral realists, advocates of a forceful national government and fierce advocates of states' rights. Then as now, politicians jockeyed relentlessly for their own advantage and that of their parties. The closer I looked at the political struggle of that year, the more astonished I was that the country *didn't* disintegrate, and the more amazed I was that the mostly conservative, occasionally flamboyant, and sometimes genuinely inspired men of 1850 succeeded in drawing the nation back from the brink. More questions plucked at me: How did they do it? How did they make the paralyzed system finally work? What would a close examination of the debate reveal about the costs of unyielding partisanship? About the nature of compromise? About the human qualities that it took to bridge a divide that many Americans feared could not be crossed?

Something else intrigued me, too, the more I read through the records of the debate itself: never did American politicians speak to the nation more honestly, more persuasively, more provocatively, and more passionately, in language that was often so splendid that it nearly reached the level of poetry. The poll-tested, spin-doctored, shoddily argued, and grammatically challenged "messaging" that today passes for political communication is pathetic and often incoherent by comparison. It can be no surprise that many Americans have lost interest in politicians who have forgotten how much can be accomplished by the persuasive power of well-crafted English. In 1850, senators and congressmen who more often than not lacked college educations spoke from the barest of notes (or none at all) for hours on end, and were confident that their colleagues and the public would understand them, in speeches that were peppered with allusions to Shakespeare, the Bible, American history, British common law, and classical literature. They also said what they meant. Men who believed in slavery said so, as did those who hated it, no matter how much odium their words attracted. By listening in on the debate of 1850, we can learn much not only about what Americans thought about their new empire, about the profound ways in which slavery warped our political system, and about the creative craft of compromise, but also about how to talk politics to each other so that we actually listen.

Although this book is primarily about the events of 1850, it is in a larger sense about the genesis of the Civil War. It will be clear to anyone who unravels the debate of that year that the war was already under way in the psyches of many Americans, in their agonized struggle to respond to slavery. For many in the South secession had already taken place mentally and emotionally, while for others the sentiment of an indissoluble Union was hardening into an ideology for which they would soon be willing to fight and die.

Washington, D.C.
September 2011

PROLOGUE

———— ·✦· ————

On February 5, 1850, Henry Clay of Kentucky raised his long, creaky, seventy-two-year-old frame from behind his desk in the back row of the United States Senate to begin one of the most memorable speeches ever delivered in the chamber. As he looked out upon the expectant faces of his colleagues, the chamber's marble columns, and the crimson carpets and drapes that bestowed an ambience of regal dignity through the clouds of cigar smoke that filled the air, Clay knew that it was his last act in the great theater where he had played to rapt audiences for nearly half a century. "When my services are terminated in this body—and I hope that before the expiration of my present term they may be—my mission, so far as respects the public affairs of this world and upon earth, is closed, and closed, if my wishes prevail, forever," he told his fellow senators. Although he still projected his magnetic amalgam of moral gravity and sparkling wit, and still set female hearts beating, he was no longer regarded, as he had been for so many years, as a prince in waiting for the throne of the presidency. He felt, and was, an old man. Yet never had he felt more needed by the nation, and never had he offered more of himself to it than he did now. As he faced the Senate, he looked beyond it to a future he could not behold, hoping that what he said this day, and did in the weeks to come, would find its place in history. His mission, he said, was to offer a soothing balm for "this distracted and, at the moment, unhappy country," a permanent solution to the nation's most intractable problem of slavery, a compromise that would, perhaps, secure him a seat in the pantheon of luminaries where dwelt his beloved George Washington, and the rest of the Founding Fathers. If this was to be his last battle, he intended to go out like a cannonade.

The scene would be memorialized in countless paintings, engravings, and prints as if it were not the beginning but rather the climax of the remarkable debate, the longest in the body's history, which continued almost without interruption through most of 1850, and produced some of the most exciting events ever witnessed on its floor. The image is legendary: Clay, usually looking younger than his years, his body thrown back and his arm thrust forward in classic oratorical pose, senators pressing around him with stark attention, men and women—symbolically, all of America—crowding the colonnaded gallery, and soaring overhead a carved eagle as if it were Clay's own guardian totem. Many who were there remembered it as the greatest speech they had ever heard. Certainly, there were few moments in American history when it was felt that so much might turn on a single speech, or that the country's fate hinged on one man's persuasive ability to overcome rigidly held beliefs, and to change minds. Spectators had come to hear Clay from as far away as Baltimore and Philadelphia, and so dense was the crush on the Senate floor, it was said, that at least one female visitor was carried across the gallery by the human tide without her feet touching the ground.

"Never, on any former occasion, have I risen under feelings of such deep solicitude," Clay intoned, in the familiar high-pitched nasal drawl that had delivered countless speeches in village squares and wayside taverns since the days when Kentucky was still a wild frontier. "I have witnessed many periods of great anxiety, of peril, and of danger even to the country; but I have never before arisen to address any assembly so oppressed, so appalled, so anxious."

Clay had scarcely begun when he was interrupted by noisy tumult in the corridors outside the chamber. Crowds of latecomers were trying to push their way in, loudly complaining when the doorkeepers forced them back. Senators shouted for order until the sergeant-at-arms mobilized his men to shove the rowdiest intruders away from the door.

When Clay was finally able to resume, he delivered one of the most vivid and frightening rhetorical images of his career. The nation, he declared, had become like some kind of monstrous industrial hell full of "uproar, confusion and menace," the states like "twenty-odd furnaces in full blast in generating heat, and passion, and intemperance." (In fact, there were then thirty states.) The disintegration of the Union was an immediate possibility, he warned. He begged his fellow senators, those from both North and South, to "pause at the edge of the precipice, before the fearful and disastrous leap is taken into the yawning abyss below." His plan had three goals: to settle once and for all every question arising from the problem of slavery; to craft a compromise that required neither side to sacrifice any core principles; and to ask the opposing parties to make concessions, "not of principle," he again emphasized, but only "of feeling, of opinion." He would call upon both sections alike for mutual forbearance. What he asked of them would be neither easy nor painless, but unless they were able to overcome the rancorous distrust that increasingly drove them apart, the only possible outcome must be the ruin of all they held most dear.

The crisis that had led to this superlatively intense moment, and to the almost unbearable tension that gripped both the Senate and the nation, had begun four years earlier on the Rio Grande, with America's first unabashedly imperial war of conquest. Westward expansion had long been encoded in the nation's political genes. After the Revolutionary War, Americans poured over the Appalachian Mountains into the Ohio Country and the future states of the Deep South. In 1803, the Louisiana Purchase launched the nation's ambitions beyond the Missouri River to the Pacific Northwest. In 1812, jingos—Henry Clay among them— helped propel Americans into war with Britain by urging the annexation of Canada, a dream that was dispelled only after two failed invasions. Spain's holdings in Florida and along the Gulf Coast were purchased in 1819. That Canada and Texas both would eventually be absorbed by the United States was "as much the law of nature as that the Mississippi should flow to the sea," declared John Quincy Adams, who as secretary of state in the 1820s did much to set the nation on its course of empire. Texas, torn from Mexico and established as an independent republic, was, in fact, annexed in 1845, and the sprawling Oregon Territory the following year.

Much of this long westward march had taken place at rifle point, particularly when recalcitrant Indians were the targets. However, no American conflict before the Mexican War had cloaked so naked a conquest in such a shimmering mist of self-serving rhetoric. The war began with a calculated provocation. President James K. Polk of Tennessee, a cipher before his election in 1844, once in office revealed an unexpected skill at acquiring new real estate. Having engineered the acquisition of Texas, he readily embraced Texas's extravagant claim to everything that lay as far south as the Rio Grande, and as far west as distant Santa Fe. In the spring of 1846, Polk dispatched troops under Zachary Taylor, a coarse-grained veteran of the War of 1812, into disputed territory between the Nueces River and the Rio Grande. When the Mexicans fired on them, the United States, on May 13, declared war. Foreshadowing all too similar disclaimers in generations to come, the president disingenuously blamed the war on the Mexicans' "wanton violation of the rights of persons and property of our citizens," and reassured restive members of Congress that the United States was really the "aggrieved nation" reluctantly forced to defend itself against foreign attackers. War fever ran high, especially but by no means only in the South. "Let our arms now be carried with a spirit which shall teach the world that, while we are not forward for a quarrel, America knows how to crush, as well as how to expand!" trumpeted an impassioned Brooklyn newsman, Walt Whitman.

Feeding the fever was the surging popular belief that God and fate had predestined the United States for unlimited territorial growth. "It is a right such as that of the tree to the space of air and earth," asserted New York journalist John L. O'Sullivan, whose patriotic salvos in the *Demo-*

cratic Review inspired millions. "Away, away with all these cobweb tissues of rights of discovery, exploration, settlement, contiguity," he wrote, coining one of the most famous slogans in American history: expansion was "the fulfilment of our *manifest destiny* to overspread the continent allotted by Providence for the free development of our yearly multiplying millions." In article after article, O'Sullivan's marching prose pounded greed into glory: "More, more, more will be the unresting cry, till our national destiny is fulfilled and the whole boundless continent is ours." Conquest would deliver to the United States everything it desired. "We shall have it, we must have it, we will have it."

At the end of summer, Taylor crossed the Rio Grande. On September 24, he captured Monterrey, 170 miles south of the frontier, and in February 1847 defeated a Mexican army four times the size of his own at Buena Vista, in a victory that made famous both Taylor himself and a dashing planter named Jefferson Davis, whose red-shirted Mississippi Regiment played a decisive and widely publicized role in both battles. In September, the war's final chapter unfolded on the southern outskirts of Mexico City, when a second American army under Winfield Scott stormed the citadel of Chapultepec and seized the capital. Four months later, a humiliated and supine Mexico signed the Treaty of Guadalupe Hidalgo, yielding the entire northern third of its land area to the victors. With the stroke of a pen, the United States grew by 40 percent, adding 1.2 million square miles of largely unmapped prairie, deserts, and mountain ranges extending from the undefined borders of western Texas to the Pacific Ocean, and incorporating the future states of California, Arizona, New Mexico, Nevada, Utah, and parts of Oklahoma, Colorado, and Wyoming. "The Mississippi, so lately the frontier of our country, is now only its center," boasted President Polk, who, having provoked the war, now luxuriated in its success.

In the fifth decade of the nineteenth century, the United States was still molten, its ultimate shape and extent unformed and unpredictable. There was no certainty that it would become a bicoastal power, nor that once expansion began it would not continue on to swallow all of Mexico, Canada, Cuba, and the rest of the Caribbean. The war and its aftermath would fuel years of bitter debate over what the United States was to be, not only geographically, but also morally. Many in the Whig opposition saw the war as a threat to the country's fundamental republican ideals. "Of all the dangers and misfortunes which could befall this nation, I should regard that of its becoming a warlike and conquering power the most direful," Henry Clay told an audience at Lexington, where he lived in Kentucky. The United States was big enough already, he said: what need had it of more territory? "We have already, in our glorious country, a vast and almost boundless territory. Ought we not to be profoundly thankful to the Giver of all good things for such vast and beautiful land? Is it not the height of ingratitude to Him to seek by war and conquest, indulging in a spirit of rapacity, to acquire other lands, the homes and habitations of a large part of His common children?"

Clay's sometime ally and sometime rival, Daniel Webster, revolted at the acquisition of New Mexico, whose inhabitants, he claimed, were more depraved than even the inhabitants of the Sandwich Islands (Hawaii). Did they have any capacity at all to grasp even the rudiments of free government? "Not the slightest on earth!" And as for California, who wanted it? Apart from a few coastal villages, Webster scoffed, "all is wilderness and barrenness, and Indian country." Abolitionists, who considered the war no more than a scheme to acquire more territory for slavery, were positively volcanic in their fury. Frederick Douglass, the most famous black orator in the United States, denounced the conflict "as a murderous war—as a war against the free states—as a war against the interests of the workingmen of this country—and as a means of extending that great evil and damning curse, negro slavery. For my part," he added, in words that still have the power to shock, "I would not care if, tomorrow, I should hear of the death of every man who engaged in that bloody war in Mexico, and that every man had met the fate he went there to perpetrate upon unoffending Mexicans."

But sentiments such as these were mere whispers against the pounding surf of pro-war opinion. The ideology of Manifest Destiny fused with racial ideas that permeated the minds of Americans in all parts of the country. By the 1840s, popular theories of "scientific racism" comfortably rationalized both the institutional brutality of slavery and the bloody destruction of native societies as settlers moved steadily west. Mexicans, for their part, were widely derided as a mongrel race, corrupted by "ignorance, vice, bigotry and degradation," people of a "weaker blood," who would either benefit from enlightenment by American principles, or simply perish. Many Americans, South and North, believed the replacement of the "inferior races" by superior Anglo-Saxons was the fulfillment of a scientific law of nature that had been sanctified by divine intention. "Nations and races, like individuals, have each an especial destiny: some are born to rule and others to be ruled," wrote the dean of scholarly racists, Dr. Josiah Nott of Alabama. By this logic, hesitation was irresponsible, and war against Mexico not a land grab, but the fulfillment of racial destiny.

The war gained an empire, but in the process it burst the political sutures that had stitched together the body politic for a generation. Most Americans supported territorial expansion if for no other reason than that it was a means to acquire cheap land on which to settle. For slave-owning southerners, however, it was a strategy for survival. Slavery was growing at a phenomenal rate. Since 1800, the number of enslaved Americans had swollen from one million to more than three million, thanks in large part to the invention of the cotton gin in 1793, which had revolutionized slave-based plantation agriculture, propelling it westward a thousand miles from the Atlantic coast across Georgia, Alabama, Mississippi, and Louisiana, to Texas. By 1845, slave-cultivated cotton accounted for 40 percent of American exports. Remarked a Scottish traveler, "Niggers and cotton—cotton and niggers; these are the law and the prophets to the men of the South."

Politically, slavery infected the nation like a virus. All but two presidents, the Adamses, had owned slaves, while slave owners had continuously enjoyed outsized representation in every sector of government, including the cabinet, the Supreme Court, and both houses of Congress. In the so-called three-fifths clause, the first of the nation's long roster of compromises with slavery, the Constitution had bestowed disproportionate power on slave owners by allowing them to count three-fifths of their slaves for the purpose of congressional representation. The South had thus dominated the House of Representatives despite its smaller population of free citizens. That gradually began to change as European immigrants flowed almost exclusively to the free states, where they would not have to compete with slave labor. As southern power in the House waned, control of the Senate became all important. For decades, slave states and free states had been admitted to the Union more or less in pairs: Vermont with Kentucky, Mississippi with Indiana, Missouri with Maine, Florida with Iowa, and so on. At the end of the 1840s, fifteen free states were matched evenly against fifteen slave states, giving the South virtual veto power over any legislation that seemed to threaten slavery. If the territory conquered from Mexico were divided up into free states, as the South feared, its hegemony in Washington would end. As South Carolina's senior senator, John C. Calhoun, the architect of states' rights ideology, implacably put it, "The day that the balance between the two sections of the country—the slaveholding States and the non-slaveholding States—is destroyed, is a day that will not be far removed from political revolution, anarchy, civil war, and widespread disaster."

Despite slavery's sixty-year domination of the federal government, its defenders portrayed it as chronically endangered by radical fanatics and conniving Yankee politicians who, they charged, were always ready to betray the nation's founding principles—that is, the protection of slavery—in return for a few abolitionist votes. They found proof of the North's malign intent, as they saw it, in the Wilmot Proviso of 1846—"A vague, indefinite, erroneous, and most dangerous conception of private individual liberty," Calhoun called it—which sought to bar slavery from all the new territories that had been seized during the war. The proviso's sponsor, a shambling, overweight, and otherwise undistinguished Pennsylvania Democrat named David Wilmot, professed no "morbid sympathy for the slave," but believed as many northerners did that if slave labor seeped into the new territories, it would soon drive out free white labor. Wilmot's proviso repeatedly passed in the House, and was just as often thwarted in the Senate. To slavery's defenders, it represented "a perfect firebrand between the North and the South," a dire warning of what they would face if they ever lost Senate control.

At mid-century the United States stood poised uncertainly between the heroic age of its founders and the transformative capitalism that would become fully manifest after the Civil War. In 1849, the Union was just sixty years old, the span of a single lifetime. There were still Americans alive who had fought in the Revolution, and many who not only remembered but had even served in government with Washington, Jefferson, Adams, and Madison. But the America of the 1840s was no longer an infant. In the previous decade, its population had jumped by more than a third from seventeen million to 23 million. Isolated communities were being drawn together in new ways by the telegraph, steamboats, and railways. Where it once took three bone-jarring days by coach to reach Washington from Philadelphia, it now took three *hours* by train. Telegraphic messages sped halfway across the continent by "lightning post" in just hours, and politicians were even talking about a transcontinental railroad to link the East Coast with California. Americans increasingly embraced rapid, unruly, often chaotic change. Violence was endemic, and sometimes horrific—on the frontier, in urban slums, and on the plantations of the Deep South. Immigration was changing the face of northern cities, and industrial slavery was reaching its economic apogee. Everywhere, the fracture lines of class, race, ethnicity, religion, and region shuddered with seismic threat. Patriotic as Americans were, they also felt that the principles of union were still tentative, arguable, and open to renegotiation.

As the members of Congress gathered for the opening of the Thirty-first Congress in December of 1849, anxious Americans were tormented by profound and seemingly unanswerable questions: how were the new territories to be governed? Could they even *be* governed? How was the country to digest such a vast new region peopled with fierce and unfamiliar Indian tribes and Mexicans who didn't want to belong to the United States at all? Could the country expand and survive, or would it crack into a congeries of unfriendly states that would fall prey to the ambitions of foreign powers? How were southern demands for the westward expansion of slavery to be placated? Would the South secede if its demands were not met? If it did, would the federal government fight back? Could Northerners be made to stem the flood of fugitive slaves? These were not academic questions: they were the stuff of violent argument in taverns and churches, on Southern plantations and New England factory floors, in prairie hamlets, mills, and merchants' counting rooms, and they were tearing the country apart. Everywhere there was ominous talk of disunion and war.

The ten-month-long struggle that ensued displayed antebellum politics at its most brilliant, and its most desperate. The men charged with containing the crisis were an extraordinary assortment that included some of the most eloquent men to appear on the American political stage. Like politicians of every age, they were also flawed—sometimes deeply flawed—hobbled by conceit, jealousy, illness, alcohol, and a habitual tendency to bully and insult when conciliation was called for. Many despised each other's doctrines. Some hated each other. Among them were some who were as close to living gods as democracy can produce, who inspired gale-force passions among friends and enemies alike. Paramount among these were the four aged lions of the Senate: silver-tongued Henry Clay of Kentucky, repeatedly frustrated in his lifelong quest for the presidency; John C. Calhoun of South Carolina, a near-cadaver rousing himself to deliver his own valedictory on behalf of slavery and states' rights; Daniel Webster of Massachusetts, once the inspiration of the antislavery North, who would betray those who believed in him most; and blustering Thomas Hart Benton of Missouri, determined to thwart the solution that many believed was the Union's only salvation.

Others embodied the younger generation that stood poised to seize the nation's reins: Stephen A. Douglas of Illinois, the full-throated voice of the frontier West; Jefferson Davis of Mississippi, the war hero of Monterrey and Buena Vista, and Calhoun's heir apparent; William H. Seward of New York, whose abolitionist certitudes fed the South's worst fears. There were others, too, some of them forgotten today: the nation's paradoxical president, crusty Zachary Taylor, a slave owner who opposed the extension of slavery; John Munroe, a hard-drinking colonel of artillery who for a few months held the nation's fate in his hands; and a New York parson's son, John A. Quitman, the governor of Mississippi, who would appear in the year's most bizarre episode as the avatar of southern ambitions in the Caribbean.

Before the denouement, a president would die in office, as would one of the most powerful and fearsome men in the Senate. Weapons would be drawn on the floor of Congress. Careers would be made and reputations ruined. Discordant visions of the United States would come into menacingly sharp focus. Meanwhile, in the outer reaches of the American empire, events shaped by the statesmen's words would play out with bloody intensity. Civil war would threaten, not in Charleston harbor but in the mountains of New Mexico.

The near-collapse of the Union in 1850 has been overshadowed in our history by the civil war that began a decade later. In some way the events of 1850 may seem remote from the concerns of our day, the artifact of an era in which black-skinned Americans were property, Indians were hunted for sport, and politics was the nation's most popular entertainment. But as the legislative battles of recent years have shown us, the doctrine of states' rights, invented largely as a firewall in defense of slavery, is still with us, as is the struggle to enlarge the orbit of freedom for marginalized Americans. The great debate of 1850 also crystallized divisions over other issues alive in our own time, such as the implications of territorial overreach and the moral dimension of American power. Like the congressional gladiators of the antebellum era, we live in an era of intense political partisanship, when it seems close to impossible to bridge the nation's ideological divide. The quest for compromise amid the crisis of 1850 may offer lessons in how agreement may be achieved between the most unyielding adversaries, and also in the unintended consequences of compromise. Although the epicenter of crisis lay in the halls of Congress, the great debate of 1850 is also a story of the opening of the West, Americans wrestling for the first time with the burden of empire, and of the culminating contest between freedom and slavery. It is, in short, a story about the struggle for American identity.

CHAPTER I

"A FRENZY SEIZED MY SOUL"

———— •◆• ————

The Mexican War stoked the furnace of crisis: the spark that set it aflame was struck by an itinerant New Jersey carpenter in a fold of California's Sierra Nevada on a chill morning in January 1848. Morose, tall, and bearded, James Marshall had been drifting west for more than a decade, first to Illinois, then to Omaha where he took up fur trading, then to Missouri, where he tried farming. In 1844, he joined a wagon train bound for Oregon. After a few months he moved on to Mexican-ruled California, where his modest skills counted for something in a place where craftsmen were few and far between. Now thirty-seven, for the past three years, he had worked for John Sutter, the lordly Swiss owner of the largest *rancho* on the Sacramento River, crafting looms and spinning wheels, furniture and tools for Sutter's army of peons.

Sutter had dispatched Marshall to the mountains with a crew of Mormons and forty Mokelumne Indian laborers to build a sawmill to cut lumber, which was always in short supply in the largely treeless country to the west. The work of digging and drilling had been under way for several weeks when, on the morning of January 24, Marshall noticed an unusual pebble—a "pellicule" he later called it—gleaming at the bottom of the millrace, in about a foot of water.

Accounts of Marshall's first words vary. According to one, he announced "I have found it" to a Mormon named Bill Scott, who was en-grossed in shaping a paddle for the mill wheel.

"What is *it*?" Scott asked.

"Gold."

"Oh! No," Scott replied, perhaps reflecting the whiff of skepticism that seemed to hover around Marshall—"a notional man," the Mormons called him, a man given to fantasy. "That can't be!"

Nevertheless, over the next few days, Marshall and the Mormons collected several handfuls of nuggets, which turned out to be abundant in and around the millrace.

Had Marshall been a different sort of man, he might have seized opportunity and made his fortune by searching out the best lodes and staking claim to them. Unambitious and innocently loyal, however, after a few days of dithering he saddled up and rode to Sutter's Fort to see his patron. Sutter was also a drifter, whose long history of false starts and hustling opportunism lay mostly concealed beneath his veneer of continental panache. Passing himself off to the Mexican authorities as a former general in the Swiss army—he had served briefly as a lieutenant in the militia—he was granted a hundred-thousand-acre domain where, ensconced behind eighteen-foot walls guarded against the "wild" natives of the hinterland by cannons and his uniformed Indian militia, he ruled what was in effect a medieval manor, with hundreds of peons tilling his fields, tending herds of cattle and sheep, tanning leather, and making almost everything from hats to furniture in a sprawl of adobe workshops.

Marshall appeared at Sutter's office door mud-spattered and over-wrought, dripping rainwater from his soaked serape. He took a cotton rag from his pocket and extracted from it a small green jar containing his collection of "pellicules." Sutter went off to find scales and several silver coins. Marshall put the pebbles on one side of the scale, and a stack of coins on the other. Then he placed the scales in a bowl of water.

"By God, the gold went down and the silver up!" as Marshall put it.

Sutter immediately sent Marshall back to the American River, warning him to keep his head and get back to work. The land on which the mill sat lay outside Sutter's Mexican land grant. Eleven days after Marshall's visit, the two men invited leaders of the local Indian bands—the euphoniously named Pulpuli, Gesu, Colule, and Lole—to Coloma, the Indian name for the Valley where Sutter's mill was located. There they negotiated a lease granting the two Americans the right to build roads, "and likewise open such Mines and work the Same" along the banks of the river for twenty years. In return, they promised to grind corn for the tribe, and to pay the four chiefs $150 in clothing and farming tools annually.

It was impossible to keep the discovery secret. Word soon spread among the Mormons at Sutter's Fort. In spite of the wet and blustery weather, men began appearing at Coloma with pans, shovels, hoes, and picks. Marshall sent them off in all directions, telling them that they would find gold in one place or another, if they just looked for it. "It appeared that they would dig nowhere but in such places as I pointed, and I believe such was their confidence in me that they would have dug on the very top of yon mountain if I had told them to do so," he later wrote. He had just started the California Gold Rush.

Sutter was in a quandary. In an effort to protect his interests, he dispatched one of his workmen to Monterey, then the capital, to have his claim to the mill site officially certified by California's military governor, Colonel R. B. Mason of the 1st Dragoons. Apart from Mason and a handful of troopers who were responsible for keeping order over a region the size of New England, California was virtually without government. California was no longer Mexican nor yet American in anything more than name, more a *notion* of a territory than it was a real one, a place with only vague boundaries, inhabited by Indians and Spanish-speaking Californios, who were discovering that they had few rights that American newcomers felt bound to respect.

Here on the West Coast, the Mexican War had been a scattered affair of skirmishes involving tiny bands of armed men on both sides. The central figure in this parlor drama was one of the more flamboyant figures to tread the stage of American empire: John C. Frémont, who had trekked thrice across the continent, mapping and surveying as he went, and was romantically known far and wide as "The Pathfinder." Born to a runaway Virginia plantation girl and a vagabond French teacher, he managed to overcome his embarrassing origins to become a nationally respected topographical engineer, and to win the patronage of powerful political men, most significantly Senator Thomas Hart Benton of Missouri, whose beautiful daughter he had wed.

On his third overland expedition in 1846, Frémont had deliberately provoked the Mexicans by raising the American flag over his camp outside Monterey. He was soon in command of a thrown-together force of buckskin-clad backwoodsmen, Delaware Indians, and disgruntled American settlers who first proclaimed an independent nation, the so-called Bear Flag Republic, and then, after a few weeks of bluster and more or less uninhibited plunder, morphed into a movement for affiliation with the United States. Opportunely, a flotilla of American warships arrived off Monterey to punctuate with its guns the news that the United States had formally declared war against Mexico. The Americans occupied California as far south as San Diego with relative ease. In September, pro-Mexican rebels based in Los Angeles overwhelmed the puny occupation force there and arrested the American consul. Just as it looked as if southern California might be peeled away from American control, General Stephen Kearny unexpectedly arrived overland, seemingly from nowhere, culminating one of the boldest exploits in American military history.

Kearny, a former student of classics at Columbia University, looked the part of the celebrated soldier that he was: six feet tall, ramrod-straight, and famous for both his self-discipline and his finesse in negotiating with Indian tribes. (At one diplomatic gathering, he was known to have graciously shared a dinner of boiled dog, and drunk blood-tinged water from the paunch of a buffalo.) He had left St. Louis in June with 1,458 men, and trekked nine hundred miles across territory that had never before been traversed by an army, to capture the Mexican provincial capital of Santa Fe without bloodshed. Having pacified New Mexico, he set off westward with a hundred dragoons across eight hundred miles of mostly trackless desert, to emerge near Los Angeles where, in January 1847, emaciated, filthy, and shouting "New Orleans!" in honor of Andrew Jackson's victory over the British on that day thirty-two years before, he and his men defeated the last organized Mexican opposition in the province, bringing 150 years of Spanish and Mexican rule over California sputtering to an end.

A year later, when Sutter's agent arrived at the office of Colonel Mason in Monterey, California's status still was unclear. Technically, conquered though it was, California was still a Mexican province. Mexican law, on which Sutter's claim was based, was now meaningless, but U.S. law did not yet officially apply either. (Nine days after Marshall's discovery the United States and Mexico had signed a peace treaty, but none of the men inspecting the gold samples in Mason's office yet knew that.) The governor supposed, as did President Polk in faraway Washington, that Indian land would automatically become part of the public domain once American rule was made permanent, and that the Indians—no matter that they had lived and hunted there longer than any white man knew—had no legal right to sell or lease it. In short, Sutter was out of luck: there was no law that applied to his claim. Mason was sorry to disappoint him, and sent along a letter amiably reassuring the Swiss that since there were no settlements within many miles of Coloma, he was not likely to be bothered by trespassers in any case.

Meanwhile, men began turning up in towns all over California with nuggets in their pockets and firsthand reports of digging a hundred or even a thousand dollars of gold from the ground in a single day with nothing but a pickax and a tin pan. One of those who listened in amazement was James Carson, a resident of Monterey. "A frenzy seized my soul," he recalled. "Piles of gold rose up before me at every step. Thousands of slaves, bowing to my beck and call, myriads of fair virgins contending with each other for my fevered imagination. One hour after I became thus affected, I was mounted on an old mule, armed with a wash basin, fire shovel, a piece of iron pointed at one end, a blanket, rifle, a few yards of jerked beef, and going at high-pressure mule speed for the diggings." The news electrified San Francisco, then still known as Yerba Buena, whose port served the *rancheros* nearby. By summer, almost the entire male population—schoolmasters, blacksmiths, ministers, gamblers, mechanics—had decamped for the American River. "Male and female, infants and grandfathers, the cradle and the crutches have gone; hardly a soul remains," one San Franciscan wrote to family on the East Coast. The *Californian* ceased publication when all its staff ran off. Sailors abandoned their ships, and their captains followed. A whole platoon of soldiers fled the fort at Monterey, leaving only their flag behind. When others were sent to catch them, they never returned.

By June, news of the strike spread across the Pacific to Australia. It took longer to reach the East Coast, via Cape Horn, and it was not until August that the first reports reached Washington, in the person of the frontiersman Kit Carson, who had spent nearly three months on the road with dispatches from General Kearny. Then, in mid-September, a naval lieutenant arrived at the White House bearing the first actual samples of gold. Newspapers were soon filled with advertisements and enticements offering every kind of "necessity" for would-be travelers to the goldfields. "What will this general and overwhelming spirit of emigration lead to? Will it be the beginning of a new empire in the West—a revolution in the commercial highways of the world—a depopulation of the old States for the new republic on the shores of the Pacific?" the *New York Herald* wondered amazedly in January 1849. What was happening in California— this "new and wonderful commercial spirit" was utterly unprecedented, the *Herald* concluded, a phenomenon whose full meaning and impact could not yet be known, but was certain to be transformative and far-reaching.

Of course there were skeptics. One was the contrarian Senator Benton of Missouri, who hated all the fuss and declared on the floor of the Senate that, in his opinion, the sooner the goldfields were exhausted the better. "I am a friend to gold currency, but not to gold mining. That is a pursuit which the experience of nations shows to be both impoverishing and demoralizing to a nation," he harrumphed. "I regret that we have these mines in California, but they are there and I am for getting rid of them as soon as possible. I care not who digs it up. I want the fever to be over. I want the mining finished. Let all work that will. Let them ravage the earth—extirpate and exterminate the mines. Then sober industry will begin which enriches and ennobles a nation."

Tom Benton aside, all Washington was in ferment. Democrats, Whigs, Free Soilers, southern nationalists, and Yankee abolitionists alike—all were agog with talk of California. The capital was also on the cusp of seismic quadrenniel change. On James Polk's watch, the nation's stature had grown immeasurably on the world stage. Britain had been maneuvered out of the Oregon Territory. Mexico had been trampled by American armies. The Far West had been brought under U.S. control. Polk had sworn to serve only one term, and he kept his promise. In November 1848, Zachary Taylor, the hero of Buena Vista, the candidate of the Whig Party, defeated the Democratic Party's candidate, Senator Lewis Cass of Michigan—"a dull, phlegmatic, lymphatic, lazy man," whose brain "was so torpid that nothing but a powerful appeal to his selfishness or his vanity could arouse it into action," caustically remarked a journalist.

That the sixty-three-year-old Taylor was physically brave no one disputed. In Mexico, he had repeatedly exposed himself to enemy fire, and when warned by an aide that the enemy was marching against him in force, had replied, "Let them come; damned if they don't go back a good deal faster than they came." No previous president rose as rapidly from political obscurity to the White House, and there were those who feared the worst. "I pity those who have hopes resting upon the firmness, or sagacity, of Gen'l Taylor," Senator Sam Houston of Texas, a military hero himself, wrote to his wife. "Poor Gentleman, he will be in deep water, and I apprehend those who follow him will find themselves in the same Predicament that Pharaoh's boat did in the Red Sea. They will find two shores, but can reach neither." About the best that Houston could say of the new president was that, "He, on all occasions acknowledges his 'ignorance, and incompetency.' " Faint praise indeed.

Taylor was devoid of civilian accomplishments beyond the management of his Louisiana plantation, and its 145 slaves. He had rarely voted, and it was said by some that he knew no more of statesmanship than a Comanche. Clay growled that "Old Rough and Ready's" main qualification for office was apparently "sleeping forty years in the woods, and cultivating moss on the calves of his legs." But then Clay had a personal grudge. He had expected the Whig nomination as of right, and was deeply hurt when he failed to get it.

Taylor's enemies underrated him. He was neither the illiterate nor the bumpkin that some portrayed him to be. Although his punctuation was eccentric, and his sentences rushed on like cavalry at the charge, his thinking was crisp, clear, and to the point. His grasp of the nation's political landscape was surprisingly current for a soldier who had been on campaign in the far reaches of Mexico. As a military man, he was a consummate professional; however, he hated what he termed the "unnecessary and senseless" war that he was obliged to fight, and which, he scathingly commented to a friend, "has been carried on mainly to see how many of the enemy we could destroy, & the extent of the country we could overrun."

But what about slavery? Taylor's position on its expansion was ambiguous. All his life he had bought, sold, and hired out human property. And when the New York Whig Millard Fillmore was selected to run as his ticket-balancing vice president, Taylor wrote reassuringly to one of his southern supporters, "I am much satisfied to learn that, like yourself, he has always been sound on the subject of slavery." Yet—though he was careful not to broadcast this during the campaign—Taylor regarded the South's pressure to push slavery westward as tantamount to aggression against the Union. "It is now evident that we cannot without destroying the Constitution attach any territory to the U. States by treaty South of the Missouri Compromise; two thirds of it will not adhere to it without the Wilmot proviso; nor will two thirds do so with it; I should like to know what we are fighting for, unless it is to array in deadly hostility one portion of the country against the other."

When the admission of Missouri as a slave state sparked bitter section conflict in 1820, the Missouri Compromise—crafted mainly by Henry Clay, Daniel Webster, and John C. Calhoun—had pragmatically set a dividing line between future slave and free states, excepting Missouri itself, along the line of 36° 30′ latitude. The line had held for almost thirty years, but Taylor was not alone in his anxiety that if it were once breached, sectional crisis would resume with a vengeance.

Taylor agreed to accept the Whig nomination only on the condition that he was permitted to maintain a posture of independence with respect to party demands. In that era, it was considered poor form to campaign too publicly. But Taylor refused to campaign at all. He declined even to express views on perennial issues such as the establishment of a national bank and tariffs, not to mention the Wilmot Proviso. "My opinions, even if I were the president of the United States, are neither important nor necessary," he rather astonishingly wrote to one supporter. This hardly reassured Whigs, who were still smarting from the misfire of their only other victorious presidential candidate, William Henry Harrison, who had died after one month in office, in 1841. Taylor thus went into the election an empty vessel into which voters could pour their hopes, desires, and expectations, no matter how contradictory. This was a kind of strategy, and it worked. But what the country could expect from Taylor, no one could say.

The inauguration would not take place until March 5, 1849. Until then, Polk would remain the chief executive, and he had no intention of yielding his bully pulpit before he had to. On December 5, he for the first time officially addressed Congress and the nation on the subject of the California gold strike, and the organization of the West. In his message—it was read by a clerk, since presidents did not then address Congress in person—Polk predicted that the absorption of the newly acquired territories would add more to the strength and wealth of the nation than any territory since the adoption of the Constitution. He praised Texas first: "The salubrity of climate, the fertility of soil, peculiarly adapted to the production of some of our most valuable staple commodities"—he mostly meant cotton—"and her commercial advantages must soon make her one of our most populous states." He then extolled New Mexico, with its "rich mines of the precious metals." But California was the real star of Polk's message. "From its position it must command the rich commerce of China, of Asia, of the islands of the Pacific, of western Mexico, of Central America, the South American states, and of the Russian possessions bordering on the ocean," he soaringly declared, asserting that a "great emporium will doubtless speedily arise on the California coast"—a prediction that would be more speedily fulfilled than he imagined. But the gold, *the gold*: after more than a century and a half, one can almost feel the senators and representatives, wads of tobacco swirling in their cheeks, shifting impatiently in their seats, turn expectantly toward the rostrum. *When will he get to it?* "The accounts of the abundance of gold in that territory are of such an extraordinary character as would scarcely command belief were they not corroborated by the authentic reports to officers in the public service," Polk announced. The president thus turned the rumors into a new national destiny, telling Americans that not only was their country to be vaster than they had ever known, but also rich beyond imagining. Hard-boiled realist that he was, Polk then got down to the practical matter of what to do about all this gold, whose true extent no one could yet estimate. Polk proposed that the government undertake an immediate geological assessment of the mining districts. Nearly all the gold had so far been found on lands claimed by the United States, and so must be protected in the national interest. This was eminently reasonable: survey the lands, then release them slowly when their real value was known. But the plan was a dead letter even as he uttered it. Perched on the banks of the Potomac, months late in the news chain, Polk had already been superseded by events on the West Coast.

There was more. Polk was well aware that to make the conquests viable, to bind them firmly to the United States, it was urgent that California be brought under the aegis of organized government. If not, what soldiers had gallantly won on the battlefield could all too easily slip away in an irresponsible peace. "The existing condition of California, and of that part of New Mexico lying west of the Rio Grande, and without the limits of Texas"—what he was saying here, just in case anyone had missed the point, was that Texas extended all the way to the Rio Grande—"imperiously demands that Congress should, at its present session, organize territorial governments over . . . these rich and extensive possessions." Congress should have acted already; but it had failed inexcusably. Other nations must look with astonishment at elected leaders paralyzed by "the agitation of a domestic question" which was "trivial and insignificant" compared to the opening of the West. That "domestic question" was, of course, slavery, which like a beast chained in the basement of the nation's political psyche threatened to burst loose and wreck all it touched.

Polk asked rhetorically if any part of the newly acquired territory would really be developed for slavery? Then he dismissed his own question as a mere "abstraction." Given the climate of the new territories, slavery could never exist in the larger portion. Debate over such an artificial problem was therefore sterile and meaningless. The solution was obvious: simply extend the Missouri Compromise line westward from the boundary of Texas—wherever that was—all the way to the Pacific Ocean. All below it would be open to slavery; all above it closed. Polk was thus accepting Texas's violently disputed claim to all the land between that state's undefined western border and the town of Santa Fe, on the upper Rio Grande, a region over which Texas exerted no authority whatever, and whose inhabitants fiercely opposed the extension of Negro slavery. In practical terms, this would mean that the area comprising the future states of New Mexico and Arizona, and a presumed state in southern California, would all automatically become slave states.

Since the army of conquest had drawn its soldiers from North and South alike, surely a "spirit of harmony and concession" commanded that no section be excluded from the spoils. "If this be done, a large majority of the people of every section of the country would cheerfully and patriotically acquiesce in it, and peace and harmony would again fill our borders." It was a pretty vision, and it had the virtue of simplicity. But it was rooted in a stolid denial of political reality.

The Constitution charged Congress with the responsibility for establishing temporary governments in new lands, fixing their boundaries, appointing officials, supervising the formation of legislatures and the writing of constitutions, and eventually guiding territories to statehood. Crafting territories and states—the sculpting of political units from the raw clay of unbounded landscape—was essentially a creative process. It could be glacial: Michigan had remained a territory for thirty-eight years, and after forty-five years most of the Louisiana Purchase from the Missouri River to the far side of the Rockies still lacked even embryonic territorial government. The Mexican War had added almost half a continent of new national real estate. Organizing it could take decades. But the nation enjoyed no such luxury now. The discovery of gold had changed everything.

CHAPTER 2

ONE BOLD STROKE

———— .◆. ————

From every state in the Union, gold seekers swarmed west, an estimated 35,000 of them in the spring of 1849 alone. They traveled by steamboat, in covered wagons, on horseback, and on foot, dreaming of riches, and weighed down with every conceivable kind of baggage, from collapsible houses, to personal armories, to Buffum's don't-leave-home-without-it "wonder-working, gold-saving, triple-rapid separator"—just $2!—and buckets of "California Gold Grease," which the gold seeker was supposed to smear over him, then roll downhill and collect the gold dust as it stuck to his body—a bargain at $10 a container. Midwesterners jumped off from St. Joseph, Missouri, southerners from Fort Smith, Arkansas, or Brownsville, Texas. Thousands took ship for Panama, trekked through its malarial jungles, and embarked on northbound boats up the Pacific coast. Many others chugged around Cape Horn in a seemingly continuous seagoing caravan from every port on the Atlantic coast. Yankee promoters attuned to the standards of the carriage trade advertised seats in "express trains" of "comfortable, even elegant wagons" drawn by the "finest mules," while one enterprising enthusiast even proposed thousand-foot-long steam-driven dirigibles capable of carrying two hundred travelers to the goldfields in just three days, at a cost of $50 per head.

Those who survived dysentery, cholera, malaria, gunshots, accidents, heat prostration, and fever to reach San Francisco found not a city but tents and huts pitched helter-skelter, and merchandise of every imaginable sort scattered in all directions. Everywhere gongs clanged, hammers rang, gamblers cried, and a cacophony of accordions, fiddles, and banjos wheezed and shrilled from canvas saloons as furious winds hurled clouds of dust through the unpaved streets where a human gumbo of shaggy-bearded miners dressed in corduroy and red flannel jostled alongside sleek gamblers, pig-tailed Chinese, Hawaiians crowned with flowers, *vaqueros* chasing escaped bulls, half-naked Indians, Negroes both free and enslaved, runaway soldiers, and prostitutes of every description who were auctioned from the poop decks of their ships before they even set foot on shore. All of them, at least for this glorious, dazzling moment, seemed to be making money. In barely a year, California's white population had reached an estimated 100,000, and it showed no sign of slackening.

The day before Polk's message to Congress, Senator Stephen A. Douglas of Illinois dropped a bombshell. He announced that he intended to introduce a bill to deal with the situation in California in a single stroke. He told his fellow senators in his melodious baritone, "The discovery of vast mineral wealth and the completion of a line of steamers connecting that country with the United States" called for bold action. Douglas wanted to skip the whole lumbering process of territorial organization, and admit the *entire* Mexican cession as one gigantic state. Squat and barrel-chested—he stood just five feet four—with a tumble of brown hair swarming across his squarish head, and radiating a blustery good-fellowship, his furious energy was legendary. Although his bluff, boozy, tobacco-chewing style won the hearts of the farmers and laborers who repeatedly reelected him, there were some who found him immensely irritating. "His legs are too short, sir," Tom Benton, who regarded *himself* as the Senate's leading authority on the West, remarked churlishly. "That part of the body, sir, which men wish to kick, is too near the ground."

Douglas incarnated the bumptious spirit of the frontier, but he had been born in northern Vermont, that most Yankee of all states, near

Middlebury in the flat country near Lake Champlain. Apprenticed to a cabinetmaker, he might well have spent his life as a small-town craftsman had he not discovered in himself a driving lust for book learning, which he recognized as his ticket out of working-class oblivion. In 1830, Douglas moved to Canandaigua, in central New York, the epicenter of a region so overcharged by flaming waves of evangelical revival that contemporaries tagged it the "Burned Over District." However, he was remarkably impervious to both the lure of religion and the tide of faith-driven reform movements that surged in its wake: temperance, moral reform, and—this last would loom large in Douglas's later life—antislavery.

If education was the tool by which Douglas levered himself up to respectability, his passion was politics, and his idol Andrew Jackson. The victor of the Battle of New Orleans appealed powerfully to a backcountry dreamer already infatuated with tales of Caesar and Napoleon. Douglas also responded viscerally to the broader Jacksonian message of workers' rights, libertarian economics, and distaste for religious sanctimony. The Bible had not provided the United States with its Constitution or its government, he reminded his constituents in a paean to grassroots democracy that was unusually sharp for that pious age: men like themselves had. To the end of his days, he would emphasize that the fundamental principle of government was the democratic right of every people to regulate their "domestic institutions" in their own way.

In June 1833, Douglas left Canandaigua for the West. "Finding myself in straightened pecuniary circumstances"—he was broke—"I determined upon removing to the western country and relying upon my own efforts for a support henceforth." En route he received a plaintive letter from his mother, asking when he planned to come home to visit. "On my way to Congress," he flippantly (and presciently) predicted. Illinois was promising turf for an ambitious young lawyer: New Yorkers and New Englanders poured down from the lake ports, and southerners came up from Kentucky and Tennessee, giving the state's upper counties a distinctly Yankee cast and shaping the lower ones as a cultural extension of the South, where the forced servitude of black Americans was openly practiced long after slavery was outlawed in the state. Douglas planted himself in the politically ambiguous turf that lay in between.

Scrambling for money—he arrived with just $5 in his pocket—he first found work as an auctioneer's clerk, being apparently the only literate person to hand, and then as a teacher, before finally settling in Jacksonville, where he hung out his shingle, and hurtled around the countryside, making speeches on behalf of local Democrats. His rise was meteoric: state's attorney at twenty-one; legislator at twenty-three; named to the Illinois Supreme Court at twenty-seven; elected to Congress at thirty; and elevated to the U.S. Senate at thirty-three. The raw exuberance of the frontier energized him, opened him up, swept away whatever remained of his New England self-restraint. "The people of this country are more thoroughly Democratic than any people I have ever known," he enthused. "They are democratic in principle and in practice as well as in name. No man acknowledges another his superior unless his talents, his principles and his good conduct entitle him to that distinction."

As a boy, Douglas claimed, he had memorized every mountain and valley, plain and river from the Mississippi to the Pacific. Now his dreams of national grandeur encompassed not only the West, but the Caribbean, Mexico, and Canada. In 1845, as he steered the annexation of Texas through the House of Representatives, he sweepingly declared, "I would exert all legal and honorable means to drive Great Britain and the last vestiges of royal authority from the continent of North America, and extend the limits of the republic from ocean to ocean. I would make this an ocean-bound republic, and have no more disputes about boundaries or red lines upon the maps." So impressed were his peers with his performance as chairman of the House Committee on Territories that when he moved up to the Senate, in 1847, he was handed leadership of that body's new territorial committee—an extraordinary honor for a freshman—and immediately set about shaping it into the leading vehicle for the development of the West, and for his own presidential ambitions. His only route to the presidency, he knew, lay through the Democratic Party, which had dominated the government since the days of Thomas

Jefferson, apart from the brief interregnums of John Quincy Adams and William Henry Harrison. He also knew that only if he kept slavery off the national agenda could the strained alliance between southern and northern Democrats survive.

Douglas, like President Polk, would have preferred to extend the line of the Missouri Compromise to the Pacific Ocean, leaving the question of slavery for future settlers to decide for themselves. But he knew that such a bill would never pass the House, where a small but adamant band of Free Soilers who wanted slavery banned outright in the territories held the balance of power. Instead, the bill that Douglas proposed joined Oregon, California, and New Mexico into a single epic agglomeration, and prohibited any future territories carved from it from passing laws that either favored or disfavored slavery. This had an alluring but illusory simplicity, and a fine democratic ring. The settlers already in Oregon, however, had already made clear that they wanted slavery kept out. No one supposed that slavery would actually be established in Oregon, but neither southerners nor northerners wanted to set a precedent that would strengthen the armament of the opposing side in the battle—everyone could see it coming—that must soon begin over slavery in the lands newly seized from Mexico.

"We of the South have contributed our full share of funds, and shed our full share of blood for the acquisition of our territories," Calhoun, mentor to the growing ranks of southern nationalists, menacingly warned. "There is no power, under any aspect the subject can be viewed in, by which the citizens of the South can be excluded from emigrating with their property into any of them." To avert the complete defeat of his bill, Douglas agreed to strip out California and New Mexico, permitting Oregon to become a territory with its antislavery prohibition intact. The debate opened more questions than it answered: Americans agreed that citizens of a *state* could decide whatever they wished regarding slavery— but could the inhabitants of a territory? Did Congress have the power to regulate or prohibit slavery in the territories? The gap between South and North, proslavery and antislavery, yawned wider than ever.

The situation in California, meanwhile, was growing more dire by the month. What order had remained after the Mexican withdrawal had disintegrated into a Hobbesian free-for-all. San Francisco was in the grip of a brutal outfit known as the "Hounds," most of whose members were graduates of New York's notorious Bowery gangs, and openly held court in a tent they dubbed "Tammany Hall." In the mining camps, police power, such as it was, lay in the hands of exhausted, overwrought, often drunken mobs festooned with six-shooters and bowie knives. "Rarely a day passes when some are not killed," an emigrant doctor wrote to his friends in New York. "Murder and highway robbery are everyday occurrences. Many and many a poor fellow is waylaid, and his life is taken without it ever being known to the world." Lynchings were capricious and savage. In one grisly incident, an Irishman denounced as a thief was given a choice of three punishments: hanging, five hundred lashes, or the amputation of his ears. When he collapsed after just fifty lashes, his ears were hacked off anyway. Armed mobs attacked anyone who sounded like a foreigner. Violence against Indians became epidemic. Gold seekers overran John Sutter's land, ran off his livestock, trampled his crops, and tore down his fences for firewood. "It is as though the communion of men gathered together in California is a race damned by the Lord, condemned to wander the globe without God, without a country, without a government, without law, or religion," one terrified miner wrote in his diary.

Douglas was determined to bring order out of California's chaos. On December 11, he stumped through the damp, labyrinthine, underheated halls of the United States Capitol, a building that reminded some of a gloomy Bastille, and unveiled his new plan. Legally, American military authority over California had lapsed with the end of the war. The current federal proconsul in Monterey, General Bennett Riley, had no power to enforce his edicts, and virtually no troops to back them up. No one knew what the Californians might do in the absence of a civil government. Polk feared they would outlaw slavery, or even declare independence from the United States. "There was nothing to prevent them from establishing a monarchy, or from disposing of the public lands," he worried. His anxieties were not far-fetched. "It is a fact as certain as anything can be that if our wiseacres at Washington delay furnishing us with a government, and allow sectional prejudices as such things as the Wilmot proviso to interfere with their duty and our rights, that the prediction so often made in the United States, of a separation from the Union, will be realized," opined a transplanted New Yorker.

Douglas's strategy was a clever one. It would provide a state government for California while, so it seemed, sidestepping the problem of slavery. By bypassing the territorial stage entirely, the bill would leave that conundrum to the Californians themselves. But it soon became clear that enemies were massing to foil Douglas's muscular attack. The proposed state of California was too big. It didn't have enough people. It had no constitution. It was too wild. "The whole of it [is] the undisputed domain of savages," protested Missouri's Tom Benton. Douglas dismissed the objections as mere details. Too big? Pieces of it could be chopped off to form additional states anytime Congress wanted. No constitution? The first three states to be admitted after the original thirteen—Kentucky, Vermont, and Tennessee—had all lacked constitutions when they were admitted. Not enough people? Soon there would be enough for three states. This was not a time to get bogged down in side issues, Douglas declared. He barked, "I wish, sir, to put an end to the eternal agitation of this question upon this floor. I desire forthwith to give a government to the people of California that will yield them protection in their lives and in their property." That was up to Congress. "The only issue now presented is, whether you will admit California as a state, or whether you will leave it without government exposed to all the horrors of anarchy and violence."

CHAPTER 3

"ORDER! ORDER! ORDER!"

———— ·◆· ————

To become law, Douglas's bill of course had to pass both houses of Congress. In the House of Representatives, opposition was intense. Douglas's maneuver, declared Joshua Giddings of Ohio, the House's most outspoken abolitionist, was "one of the grossest frauds ever perpetrated upon a free people." He and other antislavery men refused to accept anything short of the "absolute, unconditional, and uncompromising [Wilmot] proviso." Douglas detested abolitionism as a sort of fringe phenomenon and abolitionists themselves as fanatics whose pity for slaves was an insidious pretext for subverting the constitutional equality of the states. He also seriously suspected that abolitionism's roots lay in a British plot to destroy the economy of the southern states, and drive North and South to war. (Abolitionists returned the sentiment: the editor of the antislavery *Chicago Western Citizen* derided Douglas as "the most servile tool that has crawled in the slime and scum of slavery at the foot of the slave power," that is, the slaveholding oligarchy's outsized influence over the national government.) Douglas told his fellow senators in January 1849, "Let the people of such states settle the question of slavery within their limits, as they would settle the question of banking, or any other domestic institution, according to their own will. If we of the North but mind our own business, and you of the South will be quiet and mind yours, and let California act for herself, I think we shall have very little to trouble us."

It was not slavery but rather too much talk about slavery that bothered Douglas. Slavery, as far as he was concerned, was simply a means of economic development. Where the majority rejected slavery, it should not exist; where the majority wanted slaves, they should have them. Beyond that, it was none of his business. Then again, quite literally, it *was* his business. Although Douglas was careful to obscure the fact in Illinois, he was himself for all intents and purposes a slave owner. Technically, the Douglases' three-thousand-acre plantation belonged to his wife, Martha, the daughter of a wealthy slave owner who had intended to bestow it on Douglas personally as a wedding present. Pleading ignorance of plantation management, Douglas graciously declined, but he was also well aware that it would not serve his long-term political interest to be publicly identified as a slave owner by voters in northern states whose support he would need for his presidential ambitions. Despite vague, unfulfilled promises to "remove all our property to Illinois as soon as possible," Douglas never did so, although he did erase his name from transactions relating to the estate.

Douglas could ignore the abolitionists. But he couldn't ignore the proslavery South; no solution to the problem of California could be wrought without its backing. His challenge was to convince southerners not only that he was personally sincere, but also that the solution he proposed reflected the South's real interests. His biggest obstacle was John C. Calhoun, one of the Senate's living (if just barely) legends, the leading spokesman for what was arguably the least loyal, and the most slavery-dependent, state in the Union.

Arrestingly handsome in his younger years, with near-violet eyes, and a lean build that set him apart from the flabbily rotund politicians of his time, by the late 1840s, anger, resentment, and illness had carved and hardened his chiseled features to forbidding crags. His personal austerity—he neither drank nor smoked—and his humorless reserve made him seem, to some, as Puritan as a Yankee. So condescendingly aristocratic was Calhoun that a stranger typically felt there was a barrier between him and the South Carolinian "which, though slight as gossamer, was as impenetrable as granite." In politics he was the ultimate inversion of a New Englander, devoted to slavery with a zealot's enthusiasm, and employing some eighty slaves on his nine-hundred-acre plantation in the red-clay foothills of upland South Carolina. Still, among his patrician planter allies, Calhoun was a bit of an anomaly. His origins were modest; he was born in 1790 to Scots-Irish farmers who had pioneered on the Cherokee frontier in the 1750s, and as a boy plowed their land by the force of his own muscle. After graduating from Yale University, he returned to South Carolina with a well-honed mind and a deepened faith in what he considered the birthright of white men to rule black. Rising quickly in South Carolina politics, he was elected to the House of Representatives in 1811, where he met the young Henry Clay and Daniel Webster, beginning a mostly rivalrous relationship with them that would last for the next forty years. After stints as secretary of war under James Monroe, he served as vice president under both John Quincy Adams and Andrew Jackson. By the 1830s, he was one of the most influential senators of his age.

Calhoun was a genuine intellectual, "the Marx of the Master Class," as historian Richard Hofstadter aptly termed him, who saw society in terms of capital and labor, class struggle, and pervasive exploitation of workers by the wealthy. In contrast to Marx, Calhoun believed that the world had always been and would ever be thus. He maintained that not only was slavery no evil, but rather the very foundation of American democracy, a divinely inspired institution that enabled the South's best men to engage in politics. More broadly, he saw the slaveholding South as a sort of conservative balance wheel that helped the free northern states damp down the threat of social revolution, in return for its support in preserving slavery. He ridiculed the idea that the Supreme Court had unlimited power to interpret the Constitution, and would have preferred to replace popular democracy with a form of government that assigned power to elite interest groups and geographical sections. When he resigned from the vice presidency during the Nullification Crisis, medals were struck in South Carolina, bearing his image and the words: "John C. Calhoun, First President of the Southern Confederacy." In 1832, South Carolina had claimed the right to reject, or nullify, any federal law of which it did not approve. Although the crisis focused on tariff policy, both southerners and northerners recognized nullification as a precedent for states determined to protect slavery from future federal interference.

A nominal Democrat through most of his political career, in 1847 Calhoun proposed the formation of a new southern party founded on four principles: that new territories clearly be declared the common property of all the states; that Congress be clearly denied the right to enact any law, or undertake any act, that would deprive a state of its "full and equal right" in any United States territory; that any law barring the citizens of any state from carrying their property into any territory was a violation of the Constitution; and "that people have the unconditional right to adopt the government which they may think best calculated to secure their liberty, prosperity, and happiness." This last was a virtual invitation to secession, an action that was nowhere granted by the Constitution. The protection of slavery was rarely far from his thoughts. Profit by the example of the abolitionists, he told a Charleston audience. "Small as they are, [they] have acquired so much influence by the course they have pursued. As they make the destruction of our domestic institution the paramount question, so let us make, on our part, its safety the paramount question."

If Calhoun did not actually hate the North, he came close. It was difficult, he said, "to see how two peoples so different and hostile can exist together in one common Union." He tended to conflate radical abolitionists—they actually came in many varying degrees of commitment to the cause—with all northerners into a monstrous, grasping, and seemingly all-powerful conspiracy that was mercilessly determined to monopolize the powers of the national government and to shut off the emigration of slave-owning settlers to the western territories. "Let us be done with compromises!" Calhoun cried. "I would rather meet any extremity upon earth than give up one inch of our equality—one inch of what belongs to us as members of this great republic! The surrender of life is nothing to sinking down into acknowledged inferiority!" By 1849, Calhoun had wholly slipped his moorings in the Democratic Party and drifted toward oracular isolation on the far shore of party politics. But his moral authority among younger southern nationalists was immense.

As Calhoun strove to keep the protection of slavery at the top of the South's agenda, Stephen Douglas strove just as mightily to push it out of political sight. Like a monstrous sponge, however, slavery absorbed into it everything it touched, finally swelling out of all proportion and driving the well-upholstered men of the Senate to the brink of violence. Simultaneous with Douglas's proposal, Congress received a petition from a convention held a few weeks earlier in Santa Fe, begging that New Mexico be organized under civilian authority as a territory. This would reduce by half the unwieldy size of Douglas's giant new state. The petition, read out by booming Tom Benton, also reflected the kind of grassroots self-determination that apostles of Jacksonian democracy such as Douglas normally adored. There was a problem, however; in fact, there were several problems, all of them sick-making for legislators who hoped for a tidy solution. First, the petitioners protested against the "dismemberment" of New Mexico in favor of Texas, whose desire to absorb that region was well known. Next, they declared their opposition to slavery, and asked Congress to prevent it from being introduced into New Mexico.

Then, on January 22, Senator John Adams Dix of New York attempted to read into the Congressional Record a petition from the New York state legislature. Senators read all sorts of stuff into the record: resolutions calling for the construction of new mints and customs houses, encomiums to assorted favorite sons, and the like. But this one was electrically charged. In it, New York declared its support for the petitioners from New Mexico. "Whereas," intoned Dix, "it would be unjust to the people of New Mexico and California, and revolting to the spirit of the age to permit domestic slavery—an institution from which they are now free—to be introduced among them . . ." Southerners snapped awake. *What was this! The language was . . . incendiary. Protection against domestic slavery!*

"These resolutions are upon their face an insult to fifteen sovereign States of the Union," roared David Yulee of Florida, who modeled his fulminating style on Calhoun's. How could an institution that legally existed in fifteen states be declared "revolting to the spirit of the age"? *Outrageous!*

The territories were the common property of all the states, roared James W. Mason of Virginia, another Calhoun acolyte. If the North persisted on this course, "there will be no alternative but submission or resistance."

Throughout the debate, the thrust of the southern attack was carried mainly by Yulee, who was one of the Senate's more unusual members. Yulee's father, Moses Levy, a native of Morocco, having prospered in the timber trade, later turned to religious socialism, developed a plan to settle European Jews on an agricultural plantation in Florida, and eventually embraced abolition. David, who shared none of his father's sentiments, became one of slavery's staunchest defenders and an early advocate of secession. (Elected to the Senate as David Levy, its first Jewish member, he changed his name to the ethnically vague Yulee, married the daughter of Kentucky's governor, and eventually became a Christian.)

The South had suffered a "gratuitous and wanton insult," Yulee protested. She had contributed more than her quota of men to conquer the new territories, while the North was contributing more than *her* quota to dig mines in California. That is, while southerners fought for national honor, Yankees grubbed for gold, and insulted patriots into the bargain. Slavery—"which has contributed largely to the growth, prosperity, and wealth of this Union"—was perfectly consistent with the "spirit of the age." Indeed, no matter what Yankee hypocrites said, they benefited from slavery just as much as the South. (Yulee was on solid ground here: Yankee banks lent planters money to buy slaves, Yankee companies insured them, Yankee ships transported them, Yankee factories made clothing for them, and Yankee warehouses stored the fruits of their labor until it could be shipped abroad.) He climaxed with the no longer hollow threat that in recent years had capped almost every one of Calhoun's diatribes on the subject of slavery. "I am prepared to say that I place liberty before union; and I value union, and the Constitution under which it exists, only so far as it sustains the liberties of the people with whom I am associated," Yulee warned. He was saying, in other words, take away our slaves, and there is no point to our belonging to the Union.

The unhinged debate flew violently off in every direction. Dix attempted to insert into the record another resolution from the New York legislature instructing its senators and congressmen to exert "strenuous efforts" to put an end to the slave trade in the District of Columbia. Southerners retorted that northerners were betraying the nation's founding documents by refusing to cooperate in recovering fugitive slaves. "The dangers to which persons in pursuit of their property are exposed from infuriated mobs and the obstacles from legislation, the obstacles from fanaticism, the dangers to limb and even life to which gentlemen have been exposed, have literally abrogated [the Constitution]," declared Solomon W. Downs of Louisiana. The Union's foundations were already shaken, he warned, "and they may probably fall, and I believe they certainly will fall if the people who have been dealing these blows so fast and so heavily do not cease the agitation of this subject."

Douglas saw the Senate devolving into a collective ideological tantrum. "I think it is foolish and mischievous to be quarreling about a question which has no practical results," he pleaded. Why make such an emotional issue of slavery in the territories? "It is not a practical question because every man believes that, so far as New Mexico and California are concerned, the people have made up their minds which way they will settle this question, and that is, that no action here will either restrain or extend the institution of slavery one foot." This was the simple logic of the principle that Douglas and his allies called Popular Sovereignty— essentially to leave the question of slavery up to the settlers in each of the new territories as it became ripe for statehood. Douglas believed that if he restated this principle often enough and loudly enough, it must eventually sink in. Meanwhile, he bobbed and weaved, struggling to craft a bill that would win majority support. Perhaps if he just tinkered with California's boundaries? How about lopping off southern California? How about ceding everything south of Monterey to Texas? "All I ask is action," Douglas pleaded. But none of this proved any more acceptable to southerners than his original proposal.

Polk was eager for a solution before he yielded the presidency to Zachary Taylor. But his waning term was measured in weeks, and then days. The Senate's rules were unforgiving: if it failed to act before Polk left office, Douglas's plan would die an ignominious death, and he would have to start all over again with the new administration. No one knew what Taylor intended for California and New Mexico, or anything else for that matter.

Hopeful proposals continued to percolate through the Senate. One, by John Bell of Tennessee, would assign to California all the territory west of the Rio Grande and a line running due north from its headwaters to the 42nd parallel. It went nowhere. Senator Isaac P. Walker of Wisconsin then proposed extending U.S. law over the entire Mexican Cession, thus abrogating Mexican law, including the bar against slavery. Southerners liked this proposal, since it would automatically open the Far West to their cherished institution. Walker's amendment passed the Senate, but failed in the House, where it was replaced by a substitute amendment, which southerners in the Senate hated, continuing the military government and Mexican laws in both California and New Mexico until mid-1850. On March 3, Douglas tried one more time, by tacking onto an appropriations bill a rider calling for bestowing *territorial* status onto California. This was his last chance to get a California bill passed if the whole ordeal was not to start over again from the beginning in the next session of Congress. He was prepared to settle for almost anything.

The session was supposed to terminate at midnight, when the terms of a third of the senators in the chamber would end. The atmosphere was electric with tension and nervous exhaustion, and accumulated distrust fueled by righteous, alcohol-lubricated rage. Differences between the House and Senate bills had finally narrowed, but a gap still remained: the Senate version continued the laws of Mexico in force, and left to the people the right to legislate on the subject of slavery, while the House version left Mexican law in force without any special enactment regarding slavery. Everyone was sick of California, New Mexico, and slavery, irritated with fellow senators, and felt, like Daniel Webster, "an intense desire that this debate shall be terminated." Webster was one of the chamber's Olympians, having been a senator since 1827, and a major player in most of its important decisions ever since. But now he just wanted to go home.

The logorrheic Mississippi Democrat Henry S. Foote, who coupled a bent for compromise with one of the most peculiar personalities in the Senate, reiterated for what seemed the umpteenth time that unless Congress provided government for the territories, the laws of Mexico would remain over them. "Are we, who possess the lights of science beyond all people of modern times, to receive from that semi-barbarous people the laws by which we are to be governed?" Were Americans actually expected to live under Mexican law?

Everyone was sick of talk. "Oh! Let us have the question," voices cried. "We cannot talk it out! Question! Question!"

Douglas summoned all his powers of persuasion. He pleaded that he had supported every bill that had attempted to give a government to California. "I cannot consent now to abandon the whole thing," he cried. "And for what shall the people of California be thrown off? For what shall they be exposed to all the horrors of anarchy and of bloodshed, of murder and of rapine? For what? Merely because there is a technical difference between the amendment of the House and that of the Senate."

It was past midnight. Calls for adjournment began to be raised.

"We are not here by legal authority," Hopkins L. Turney of Tennessee announced, pointing out that the terms of one-third of the members had just ended. "Our time is up. The session has expired."

"We have no right to proceed with legislation!" Yulee protested.

But the debate droned on.

At 2:20 A.M. word was received that President Polk had gone home. Even if the bill were passed, he would no longer be in his office to sign it. "Very well," groused Webster, "but then we shall have the pleasure of sending him a bill tomorrow morning."

By now, the prized formality of the Senate had utterly disintegrated. Shouts were heard on all sides.

When Simon Cameron of Pennsylvania started to complain about the unruly atmosphere, Foote cut him off abruptly, declaring, "The Senator from Pennsylvania has no right to talk here. His term of office has expired."

The *Congressional Globe* is vague at this point, stating delicately that "other words were uttered by both the Senators from Pennsylvania and Mississippi, and something approaching a personal collision occurred." In fact, Foote and Cameron began pummeling each other until they were pulled apart by their fellow senators. Some southern Democrats then allegedly threatened to carve the hearts out of their Yankee colleagues if they refused to vote for the amendment.

"We have no right to sit here!" Turney continued to complain, to no great effect.

Just before 4 A.M., a vote was finally taken, and Douglas's amendment was defeated.

"Order! Order! Order!" Foote protested. "No members whose term expires at midnight has a right to vote." Foote, like a bald, angry elf, hopped apoplectically around the chamber, arms windmilling, red-rimmed eyes popping from their sockets, ignoring the presiding officer's attempts to calm him down. "We have no right to sit here!" he cried. "We are no longer a Senate!"

Sam Houston of Texas now plunged into the debate for the first time. "Although I have waded through scenes of anarchy and turbulence," he drawled, "though I have seen people forming a disorganized mass, a chaotic community, I never entertained the same feelings that I have on this occasion. I have seen order resolved from this mass of chaos, but I have never seen order resolved into chaos before." Coming from Houston, who as everyone knew had fought and lived through the bloody Texas Revolution, his words carried weight.

Foote then moved that the Senate adjourn. The motion failed.

As the sun rose on the first day of the new administration, the senators passed the appropriations bill. The gavel finally fell at 7 A.M. Douglas had failed again to bring a California bill to a safe harbor. The gap between South and North seemed wider than ever.

"Never in my life . . . have I felt more sorely oppressed with doubt and despondency, or considered the Union more in danger," Foote gloomily reflected.

The senators had more or less recovered from their all-night melee by the morning of Monday, March 5. (The inauguration should have taken place on the 4th, but it was considered improper to hold such an event on a Sunday, so the country was technically without a president for a day.) Beneath a bleak and lowering sky that would later that day disgorge a late winter snowfall, Zachary Taylor was escorted to the Capitol from his hotel by twelve companies of volunteer militia, brass bands, a hundred young gentlemen on prancing horses, and a cavalcade of "Rough-and-Ready" clubs from the surrounding area waving banners. Taylor and Polk traveled together in an open carriage drawn by four gray horses. It was a chilly ride. There was no love lost between the men: Taylor was known to have exclaimed with pleasure a few years earlier when he received a false report that Polk had died.

Speaking from the steps of the Capitol's East Front, Taylor did not cut much of a figure—portly and short-legged, his thin gray hair unbrushed, his skin weatherbeaten and furrowed. One observer remarked that he looked "like a monument of Quincy granite." His speech was awkward and almost inaudible. He promised tritely that he would be guided by the Constitution and would "defer with reverence" for its interpretation to the illustrious patriots of the past, "especially to his example who was by so many titles 'the Father of his Country.'" Those who had hoped for substance—for a revelation of what he intended to do about the crises in California and New Mexico, the widening fissures between North and South, and the expansion of slavery—were sorely disappointed. On these subjects, Taylor said nothing. The closest he came was a vague declaration to look to the "enlightened patriotism" of Congress to adopt "such measures of conciliation as may harmonize conflicting interests." This was awfully bland stuff. Presumably it reflected the blank slate of the new president's political mind.

"I think the Administration would have been stronger by taking *either* side than it will be taking *neither*," wrote one dismayed North Carolinian. Another critic lamented that Taylor, Old Rough and Ready, "is not considered so rough as had been expected, —unluckily, too, he is not found to be half as ready."

CHAPTER 4

"THAT DEMON QUESTION"

—— .•. ——

John Sutter's irrelevance was obvious when forty-five delegates from the mining districts and towns of coastal California met at Monterey in September 1849 to decide the territory's future. Although he was treated with courtesy as the father of the Gold Rush, the newcomers who dominated the convention, many of whom had been in California no more than a few months, had little time for a man who was already marked as a loser. The gathering had been instigated by the military governor, General Bennett Riley, a forbidding man best known for his colorful swearing, who on his own initiative—or more likely at the instigation of President Taylor—had called for a convention to either write a state constitution or organize a territorial government.

During his campaign for the presidency, Taylor had thrown everyone into consternation when he offhandedly remarked that events taking place on the West Coast were probably irrelevant, because California and Oregon were destined to become a separate country. By 1849, Taylor had grown more careful. He now considered it imperative that California be secured. He also believed, with a stubbornness that would nearly bring about the undoing of his presidency, that since Mexico had abolished slavery in 1829 it could not legally be revived in the conquered territories. The best way to end controversy, he felt, was to engineer its statehood as quickly as possible, since no one challenged a state's right to legislate on the subject of slavery as it saw fit. Statehood, he declared, "ought to be regarded as the *great object* of the administration, and its accomplishment sought with all its policy and energy."

It was clear virtually from the moment that the delegates gathered in two-story, sandstone Colton Hall that immediate statehood was their goal. Monterey was still more Mexican than American, a small town where ox carts with high wooden wheels trundled among the few blocks of adobe dwellings, warehouses, wharfs, and barracks that nestled beneath low bluffs on the edge of the Pacific. It was nevertheless a lively place that was awhirl with balls and parties, where new arrivals from the East were charmed to speechlessness by the enticingly dressed local *señoritas*. The delegates were a microcosm of the nation, America in the raw, from almost every state of the Union, and in the six weeks that followed they would argue about race, power, and freedom in ways that would reveal with unsettling bluntness the unfiltered psyche of mid-century United States. Most were remarkably young, many still in their twenties and early thirties. Lawyers were heavily represented; there were also farmers and merchants, several members of the active military, two printers, two doctors, and twenty-nine-year-old B. F. Moore from Texas, who listed his occupation as "elegant leisure."

The delegates met in a large room that filled the hall's second story, sitting at four long tables, a dozen per table, beneath a portrait of George Washington looming over the rostrum. The first president's image was apt, for they all knew that they were inventing a new state from scratch as Washington had helped to do for the United States sixty years earlier. "We are laying the foundation for a great empire; let it be broad and deep," intoned Lieutenant Henry W. Halleck, General Riley's baby-faced secretary of state and the author of most of the proposed state constitution. (The twenty-seven-year-old Halleck's round-eyed look of perpetual surprise belied what was probably the best mind in the room, and a strategic intelligence that had already produced the most influential American military textbook of his era.) "We are not legislating merely for a single day or a single generation, but for ages and generations yet in the womb of time," Halleck went on. California was not merely a piece of land, but a phenomenon unprecedented in history. "No other portion of the globe will exercise a greater influence upon the civilization and commerce of the world. The people of California will penetrate the hitherto inaccessible portions of Asia, carrying with them not only the arts and sciences, but the refining and purifying influence of civilization and Christianity; they will unlock the vast resources of the East and, by reversing the commerce of the world, pour the riches of India into the metropolis of the new state."

More mundanely, much of the discussion focused on vital concerns such as projected state revenues, taxes and banking, the legalization of corporations, the establishment of a state legislature and its rules, public education, the ownership of unclaimed lands, and the image of the state seal. There was extravagant talk of creating as many as six new states along the Pacific coast, of annexing the Sandwich Islands to California, and (perhaps tongue-in-cheek—or perhaps not) of even annexing *China*. More contentious was the problem of the new state's boundaries, an issue of dizzying complexity since Mexican California had no fixed limits. But the fiercest debate centered on what Winfield S. Sherwood, a thirty-two-year-old lawyer from upstate New York, aptly called "that demon question"—slavery.

One of the convention's first acts was the adoption by unanimous consent of a prohibition against slavery. Abolitionists experienced paroxysms of joy when this news reached the East Coast. "Never did we pen a sentence more exultingly than that which embodies the great feature of the news from California yesterday," crowed the Washington-based *National Era*. "CALIFORNIA IS FREE, beyond cavil." Beneath the delegates' seemingly principled declaration on behalf of human freedom lay a Rorschach blot of American racism. Few Californians were abolitionists by conviction, but hostility to the use of slaves in the goldfields was intense. The antislavery measure had been proposed by one of the convention's few genuine abolitionists, William E. Shannon, another young New York lawyer who had come west as a soldier during the war, and now owned a general store at Coloma. But it was seconded, startlingly, by William McKendree Gwin, a Mississippi planter, former congressman, and protégé of John C. Calhoun, who owned two hundred slaves back east. Gwin's seeming "conversion" boiled down to simple politics: he wanted to become a U.S. senator more than he wanted to defend slavery. Over six feet tall and already equipped with a senatorial mane of gray hair, he had arrived in California four months earlier with sample state constitutions in hand and begun preaching statehood on San Francisco street corners. Canvassing for support in the goldfields, he had discovered that white miners were violently opposed to competing at physical labor with black slaves.

What worried the great majority of delegates was not just that slave owners would import teams to compete with free white miners, but that once they had gotten their gold they would dump their slaves on the public. The prospect of footloose black hordes prowling the goldfields fed a viral nexus of racism, economic anxiety, and class resentment. "We will find the whole cotton plantations of the South depopulated of their negroes; they will work a few months in the mines, and then be told they are free," warned John McDougal, a dapper, alcoholic military engineer, whom Gwin had tagged as his personal candidate for lieutenant governor. "Mark my words."

This was not an abstract discussion. Back east, pressure to open up California for slavery was strong. Many slave owners calculated that the risk of losing their human property in lawless California was far outweighed by the profits that a slave—not to mention a whole crew of them—might dig from the gulches of the Sierras in a year of hard labor. It was estimated that a slave who netted his owner about $6,800 over his entire working life could earn him $4,000 in a single year in the goldfields. "I feel a most solemn conviction that the South must arouse from its negative position and assume that of the lion or this necessary outlet to drain off our surplus slave population will be cut off from us & the doom of our children sealed," one planter, Levin Coe, wrote to John Calhoun from Memphis.

Slaves were already being sold for premium prices on the streets of San

Francisco. Hundreds were at work in the Sierras, and many more were on the way. Twenty-five slaves from Georgia and South Carolina had been seen on a steamship en route from Panama. A Tennessee expedition included slaves who had been contributed in lieu of a cash investment by one of its white members. (Poignant stories abounded: a slave encountered on a Sacramento riverboat, when asked to whom he belonged, replied that he would have to wait until the end of a poker game in order to answer since his original master had lost him to a ship's clerk, who in turn had lost him to another player in a game that was still going on.) In the goldfields, angry white miners took things into their own hands. When a party of Texans and their fifteen slaves appeared on the Yuba River, the miners already there voted to bar any slave or negro from staking his own claim or working in the mines, and threatened the Texans with violence unless they left: they were gone the next morning. The miners' warning applied not just to black slaves. Three months later, a Chilean *majordomo* arrived on the Yuba with a gang of indentured peons. When he ignored the miners' ultimatum, they hanged him.

Only isolated voices protested the racism that characterized the convention. "Free men of color have just as good a right, and ought to have, to emigrate here as white men," Shannon, the Coloma storekeeper, asserted. In New York, he noted, many blacks were among the most respectable citizens, who enjoyed the rights of citizenship there. Why should they be disenfranchised simply by moving to California? Another New Yorker, Kimball Dimmick, from upstate Chenango County, begged the delegates to see themselves through the magnifying lens of history. "What will be said of our constitution if we assert one thing in our bill of rights—extend the privileges of our free institutions to all classes, both from foreign countries and our own, and then in another exclude a class speaking our own language, born and brought up in the United States, acquainted with our customs, and calculated to make useful citizens?" He appealed to their patriotism as Americans. "Let it not be said that we, the first great republican state on the borders of the Pacific, who should set the example of an enlightened policy to the nations of the Pacific—let it not be said that we have attempted to arrest the progress of human freedom." They were stirring words, worthy of the great abolitionist orators of the day.

Then in an apparent effort to curry favor with the other delegates, he hastened to assure them that he personally found blacks just as repellent as they did. "I have the same personal antipathies which other gentlemen avow," he protested. But surely blacks were as intelligent as Sandwich Islanders, Chileans, and "the lower class of Mexicans." It was a sad conclusion, but Dimmick counted as one of the few friends blacks had in California.

The problem of race also haunted the delegates' straining efforts to define who was a "Californian." Just who would be entitled to vote? Would former citizens of Mexico? Would free blacks? Would Indians? What about the descendants of Indians? Mixed-bloods? If any Indians could vote, then logically "an Indian in the mountains" had as much right to do so as a white man. If all Indians were excluded, what about the many native Californians who had Indian blood in their veins, but were not considered Indians? There was no end to confusion and perplexity. "What is the true signification of the word 'white'?" asked one of the few Californios who participated in the debate, a man by the name of Noriego. "Many citizens of California have received from nature a very dark skin; nevertheless there are among them men who have heretofore been allowed to vote, and not only that, but to fill the highest public offices. It would be very unjust to deprive them of the privilege of citizens merely because nature had made them not white." Then he helpfully added, "But if, by the word 'white' it was intended to exclude the African race, then it was correct and satisfactory."

The race debate in turn bled into the problem of the proposed state's boundary. What exactly was "California"? What territory did it really encompass? How big could it be? Was it to be just one state, or several? Hardly anyone at the convention knew much about California's geography. Myron Norton, a twenty-seven-year-old Vermonter, warned that unless the boundary was clearly fixed southerners would drive their slaves into California no matter what the letter of the law said: "You may say to the owners, You have no right to bring slaves or free negroes here. They will ask you, Where is California? What are its limits? You can say nothing but that California is here, somewhere on the Pacific coast—no man knows where." Delegates who had come overland at least knew what lay east of the Sierras, but many—including Gwin and Halleck, who were among the staunchest advocates of a "greater California"—had traveled to California by steamboat, via Panama or around Cape Horn, and had no grasp of the enormous inland distances.

Generally, the delegates broke into two camps. Many of the antislavery men, the Californios, Halleck, and the Machiavellian Gwin, argued for a state that stretched from the Pacific across present-day Nevada to the Mormon colony around the Great Salt Lake. No one asked the Mormons if they were interested in being included in California; nor were the California delegates aware, as they blithely divvied up the West, that settlers in "Deseret"—centered on present-day Utah—were drawing boundaries for their own new territory, which included three-fourths of California and an outlet on the Pacific. Many argued that it would simply be foolish to yield all the land east of the Sierras before anyone knew what it was worth. Others pushed for a more compact, more governable state with its eastern border running along the crest of the Sierras. McDougal, for one—describing the Deity as a sort of master surveyor in the employ of Manifest Destiny or the army's topographical survey—asserted of the crest that "God has designated her limits, and we ought not to go beyond the line traced by the Omnipotent hand."

Although he wanted to exclude slavery from as large a region as possible, he grasped that only in a smaller California could the prohibition be made to stick. No one knew what Congress would do when the new state was finally presented to it as a *fait accompli*. Claiming an immense, undefined country to the east would only invite further meddling, and doom the entire statehood venture. It was imperative that the delegates deliver to Congress a California that had fixed and rational borders, said Shannon. He proposed drawing the state's eastern boundary just beyond the crest of the mountains, then southeast to the Colorado River, and finally down the river to the Mexican border. "This secures to us, in the first place, all that is valuable in the territory," he argued. The North would gain a new free state, and with it one or two representatives and two senators, while the South, he added, has "always maintained the doctrine of the right of the states to determine this question for themselves, and they will not be disposed to deny it now." This was what a later age would call a win-win solution. And it prevailed, giving California the border that it has today.

If the convention could claim to have a hero, surely it was William Shannon. A man of moral courage, warmth, and considerable personal charm, he piloted fractious delegates around the shoals of two seemingly intractable problems: the dicey question of slavery and the uncertainty of the state boundary. He was likable and lively—"frolicsome," in the words of one of his contemporaries—a natural politician in the best sense of the word, a man who got things done without calling undue attention to himself.

Shannon was well positioned to become a creative force in the new state's political landscape, which was so densely populated by sharp operators, moneymen, and thugs. Soon after the convention, he was elected mayor of Coloma; his future seemed bright. But he would die at Coloma of cholera in November of 1850, at the age of twenty-nine.

The convention concluded on October 13, 1849. On its last day, the delegates elected the ineffectual John Sutter the convention's president, a gentlemanly if empty gesture, and with him walked arm in arm to General Riley's office, where they formally presented him with the new constitution. The delegates had achieved something Congress had failed to do. They had written a constitution, designed a state government, crafted laws, and drawn California's borders. They had boldly barred slavery, legally if not in actual practice. The irritating question of admitting free black settlers had finally been voted down, though it would repeatedly surface on the state legislature's agenda for years to come. In the end, something close to common sense had prevailed. Popular Sovereignty had, it seemed, been vindicated. The convention had created a state, or at least the idea of a state. But would Congress accept it? Would the South? No one in Washington even knew that the convention had taken place, much less what it had created. What would happen when the next Congress convened? No one knew.

In November, Californians ratified the constitution by 12,061 to 811, out of a total pool of 107,000 potential voters.

On the face of it, the convention's outcome looked like a victory for President Taylor. He wanted a plan for statehood, and he had apparently gotten it. Ideally, this would forestall another congressional bloodletting over the Wilmot Proviso. But proslavery forces were furious at the president, nowhere more so than in Texas. "Now that he is elected, it is but too apparent that he is ready to sacrifice the rights of one-half of the Union, in an attempt to preserve a political popularity, whose foundation is as rotten as it has hitherto been concealed," the *Texas State Gazette* angrily declared. This was more than rant. A crisis that dwarfed California's was already developing on Texas's remote western frontier.

CHAPTER 5

"ULTIMA THULE"

———— ·•· ————

In 1849, New Mexico was America's back-of-beyond—"the Ultima
Thule, the outside boundary of speculation and enterprise," Senator
Tom Benton vividly termed it—a country barely known but to trappers,
outlaws, and traders on the Santa Fe Trail. Almost nothing about New
Mexico had been published in English. Maps were wildly inaccurate.
"What is New Mexico?" wondered Daniel Webster. "How is she limited
and bounded? Who is to say who her people are?" Some said it was a land
of endless potential, others so worthless that it took "ten acres to keep
alive one black-snake." Travelers described New Mexico's landscape as a
depressing desolation of deserts, mesquite, greasewood, and naked mas-
sifs looming like great derelict ships over a waterless sea of gravelly hills,
a land "scathed to barrenness, its streams dried up, the soil scorched to
powder by volcanic fires." It was also a ferociously dangerous country.
New Mexico's few thousand Spanish-speaking and Pueblo Indian inhabitants huddled for safety in a chain of scattered towns along the Rio
Grande Valley from El Paso to Taos, surrounded by native tribes whose
constant raiding left hillsides bare of sheep and cattle, swaths of once
settled land depopulated, and crumbling adobe ruins pocking the plains.
Navajos pressed in from the west, Mescalero and Jicarilla Apaches from
the south and north, and from the wastelands east of the Pecos the ter-

rifying Comanches, roaring in like human hurricanes, hunting for food, livestock, and slaves. Where farming survived, it barely rose above the subsistence level.

Anglo Americans were, with few exceptions, disdainful of the "semi-civilized" *Nuevo Mexicanos,* but they were fascinated by Santa Fe. Cradled in a fertile valley at the foot of the Sangre de Cristo Mountains, it seemed like an alien planet where anything and everything was possible. "I doubt whether the first sight of the walls of Jerusalem were beheld by the crusaders with much more tumultuous and soul-enrapturing joy," recalled one trader, arriving from the grueling eight-hundred-mile overland journey down the Santa Fe Trail from Missouri. Not every newcomer was so enthralled: "I can only compare it to a dilapidated brick kiln or a prairie dog town," remarked George Ruxton, a dyspeptic Briton, who found himself there just after the Mexican War. The town's dusty lanes were a phantasmagoria of tumbling half-naked children, black-robed priests, reeling drunks, alluring girls in low-necked chemises, tinkling guitars, barking dogs, wandering goats and pigs, strings of red peppers drying on old adobe walls, saloons, whorehouses, gambling hells, nightly fandangos, and open-air markets where vendors hawked mutton, wild plums, and carcasses of slaughtered bears. It was simultaneously repellent and magnetic, terrifying and charged with an erotic excitement.

After Kearny's capture of Santa Fe, the Americans assumed, with the irrational optimism that would often characterize the nation's foreign adventures, that they would be welcomed with open arms by the humiliated locals, who had never asked to be invaded. Hardly had Kearny left for California when rebellion broke out, in January 1847. All over northern New Mexico, Americans were murdered wherever they could be caught. By the time the army regained control, three hundred *Nuevo Mexicanos* and Pueblo Indians had been killed, and about thirty Americans. The facile democratic pretensions that had been used to justify the American invasion were stripped away as the rebellion's surviving leaders were charged with "treason" against a government of which they were not, in fact, citizens. Soldiers treated it as entertainment: a Missouri officer was heard to shout to a civilian traveler as they passed on the road to Santa Fe, "How are ye—would ye like to hang any more Mexicans?"

With relative stability established, New Mexico's English-speaking population rapidly swelled to more than a thousand and business soared, as wagons laden with trade goods and army supplies trundled down the Santa Fe Trail. Government, meanwhile, rested on the bayonets of the United States Army, a situation which irritated Anglophone newcomers who had been reared on the roisterous politics of the East, and now found themselves living under what many of them considered a military dictatorship.

On December 13, 1848, when Tom Benton rose from his desk in the last row of the Senate to read the petition he had received from Santa Fe, he was arguably the most intimidating member of the Senate, by turns crude and startlingly erudite, a man whose "egotism was as proper to him as its apex is to a pyramid," as well as the body's longest continuously serving member. Benton was, in the words of one biographer, "a unique, robustious, always interesting, controversial person." In the eyes of contemporaries, as in his own, he was a large man in every sense: large of body, large of voice, and large in his views on everything he considered. Born in 1782 in North Carolina, he was imbued with an almost religious awe for both the Union and popular democracy. He had served variously as a lawyer, soldier, and editor, and had represented Missouri in the Senate since it gained statehood in 1820. Until the arrival of Stephen Douglas, he was the nation's undisputed political advocate for the West, and had championed the concept of a grand national road from the Mississippi to the San Francisco Bay, a once laughably visionary notion that now seemed supremely practical, as settlers in their Conestoga wagons snaked by the tens of thousands across the deserts and mountains to California. He had also earned Henry Clay's undying enmity for leading the successful assault against the Kentuckian's most cherished project, the Bank of the United States.

White though Benton's hair now was, he seemed physically indestructible. In him, commented Oliver Dyer, a phrenology enthusiast who covered the Senate as a journalist, "All the animal propensities, especially those which give cunning and courage, were powerfully developed. His organs of observation were large and active, and his firmness and self-esteem were so prominently developed that his massive head ran up to a peak like the Island of Teneriffe." He was, said Dyer, who respected him, "cold, hard, ruthless," and impervious to criticism, with "the corrugated hide of a rhinoceros." (This last remark wasn't gratuitous. It was Benton's custom, in accordance with what he understood to be a custom of the Roman gladiators, to scrub down his body to his hips every morning, and from his hips to his feet every afternoon, with the roughest kind of horsehair brush. When a friend who saw the brush shook his head at it, Benton replied, "Why, sir, if I were to touch you with that brush, sir, you would cry murder.")

Benton's feelings about slavery, like Clay's, were an epitome of border state ambivalence. Though a slave owner all his life, as a young member of the Tennessee legislature Benton had fought for a bill giving slaves the right to trial by jury. And though never an abolitionist, he adamantly opposed the creation of any more slave states. Virtually alone among slave state senators, he believed that Congress had the power to prohibit slavery in the territories, and considered the Wilmot Proviso, although politically unhelpful, merely a restatement of the ban on slavery in the territories that had been articulated in the Northwest Ordinance of 1787. "If there was no slavery in Missouri today, I should oppose its coming in," he had declared. "If there was none in the United States, I should oppose its coming into the United States." He knew that New Mexico offered the only real avenue for slavery to advance westward, and he intended to place his considerable weight in its path.

The petition, it will be remembered, had been sent to Benton by a convention of New Mexicans who had met in October, and were begging for the replacement of the military regime there with a civil government. But that wasn't all: "We respectfully but firmly protest against the dismemberment of our territory in favor of Texas or from any cause," Benton read, knowing that this would hit southern expansionists like grapeshot,

and that what came next would agitate them even more: the petitioners declared themselves unalterably opposed to Negro slavery anywhere
in New Mexico. Although Benton implied that the petition had come
to him out of the blue, he may in fact have instigated it himself, to out-
maneuver Texan agents who were already at work in Santa Fe.

Texans and their southern supporters in Congress were furious. The
petition was preposterous, they objected: everything east of the Rio
Grande—the entire eastern half of New Mexico, including Santa Fe, that
is, not to mention a long arm of territory that extended far north into
present-day Wyoming—belonged to Texas. "Has Congress any power to
alter the boundaries of a State that are recognized by the people of that
State? I think not," stormed Senator Thomas Jefferson Rusk of Texas, a
South Carolina stonecutter's son who had risen to command Texan forces
during a decade of bloody conflict with the Indians. "We have an indisputable right to the territory, which we can never surrender!" Calhoun,
presuming as always to speak for the entire South, professed astonishment
at the "impudence" of the New Mexicans. The petitioners were a mere
"conquered people"—they had no business petitioning anyone, yet now
they wished to exclude the very men who had conquered them! "Our
right to go there with our property is unquestionable," he declared.

Through the winter, the fate of New Mexico lay half-submerged in
the cascading debate over California. But it would bob repeatedly to the
surface, exposing the menacing reefs that divided North and South, buf-
feted by the roiling currents of escalating demand and counterreaction, as
Yankee legislatures from New England to Wisconsin called for a federal
barrier to the extension of slavery, and slavery's proponents defended
Texan ambitions with seething appeals to southern honor, moral right,
history, and the law.

In truth, Texas's claim to New Mexico was little more than naked empire
building steeped in a mumbo jumbo of legalism. The upper Rio Grande
had never been part of Texas. There had barely even been contact between the regions, which lay separated by hundreds of miles of sunbaked

emptiness populated by hostile tribes. The claim's earliest, wispy rationale lay in the colonial adventurism of seventeenth-century France and Spain. Extrapolating from the perfunctory landing of Robert de la Salle on the western Gulf Coast in 1685, the French extravagantly claimed everything that lay inland as far as they could imagine as part of "La Louisiane," a highly elastic concept that supposedly extended all the way to the pueblos of the upper Rio Grande. The Spanish arrived on the scene a bit later but, unlike the French, they actually established settlements, though they rarely ventured far from their forts and missions on the coast.

The United States acquired France's lingering claim along with its purchase of Louisiana in 1803, and for almost twenty years reasserted it with what the diplomatic historian Richard Kluger termed "an Olympian display of territorial hubris." American diplomats—among them the usually phlegmatic Secretary of State John Quincy Adams, who asserted that the American right to Texas was "as much the law of nature as that the Mississippi should flow to the sea"—insisted that the international border lay on the Rio Grande rather than on the Sabine River, which had always been the de facto western limit of French Louisiana. (The Sabine forms the present-day border between Louisiana and Texas.) The Spanish dismissed such pretensions out of hand until, in 1819, the United States agreed to abandon its claim to Texas in return for Spain's relinquishing her equally dubious claim to Oregon. Jingoist assertions like Adams's nonetheless persisted like a virus in the nation's political bloodstream, assuring many Americans that their right to the Rio Grande was not only legally valid but a question of national honor.

The Mexican Revolution of 1821 delivered Texas to new masters who were not only determined to hold on to the province but also to people it with—this seemed a brilliant idea at the time—land-hungry Americans. Nearly thirty thousand Anglo Americans arrived in the 1820s, the vast majority of them from the South, lured to the fertile river valleys and rolling prairies by the offer of five thousand acres of free land, sweetened by the promise of fifty more acres for each slave brought in to work it. When Mexico abolished slavery in 1829, Texas's governor José Maria Viesca appealed for an exception, arguing that the Americans' slaves were essential to the province's development. "Texas *must be* a slave country," Stephen Austin, the leader of the American settlers wrote in 1833. "Circumstances and unavoidable necessity compels it."

The settlers had other grievances as well, and in March 1836, they declared independence. The war that ensued was characterized by gruesome savagery. Mexican threats to liberate the Americans' slaves shot terror into the hearts of slave owners. When slaves revolted in anticipation of their emancipation by the Mexicans, they were slaughtered. "Near 100 had been taken up many whipd nearly to death some hung," one Texan reported. The Mexicans were ruthless, too. An exposed force of 189 Texians was wiped out at the Alamo. Another contingent of 330 men commanded by the Georgia slave trader James Fannin was captured soon afterward, and massacred at Goliad. Settlers fled for their lives.

Through the tumult strode flamboyant, whiskey-swilling Sam Houston, who had ruined his life in Tennessee and had come to Texas hoping, like so many others, to reinvent himself at the edge of civilization. Large-boned and craggily handsome, he made a vivid impression: togged in buckskins, fur cap, and boots jangling with brass eagle spurs, physically fearless, depressive, and, it was said, as quick to spout Homer as to draw a gun. In command of Texan forces at San Jacinto, near the present-day city of Houston, he faced a Mexican army four times the size of his own, and in just eighteen minutes defeated it, killing, wounding, and capturing almost 1,500 Mexicans, and taking prisoner Mexican president Antonio López de Santa Anna. Although Santa Anna later repudiated the peace treaty he signed, the Texan Congress asserted that, treaty or no treaty, the Rio Grande to its source was the new republic's international border.

The rickety republic that emerged sported the trappings of a nation: a legislature, a statehouse, an army, a governor's residence—even if the governor had to bunk on the floor when he had visitors, since there was only one bed—a diplomatic corps, an army, even a minuscule navy. But the republic's real size was uncertain. On maps, Texas spread amoebalike, waxing and waning according to the biases of the cartographers, stretching sometimes deep into Mexico, sometimes extending a wiggly tentacle northwest into present-day Colorado, and metastasizing westward across the Southwest to the Pacific. Like "California," Texas was as much an idea, a bundle of imperial dreams, as it was an actual place. "Once its glorious march shall have commenced," the *Telegraph and Texas Register* crowed in September 1837, "no power of Mexico shall avail, but that glorious march shall be onward, till the roar of the Texan rifles shall mingle in unison with the thunders of the Pacific."

Texas was politically ramshackle, financially bankrupt, awash with grievance and ambition, proud to a fault, unstable, nationalistic, violent, and infested with a viral racism that shaped its relations with its neighbors. Rootless, gun-toting adventurers swarmed everywhere, looking for free land and the main chance. For most, acquiring land meant fighting and killing Indians. Native peoples still occupied the entire region: Tonkawas and Karankawas near the coast, and further inland Comanches, Apaches, Kiowas, Wichitas, mingled with fragments of dislocated tribes pushed from their lands in the East, perhaps thirty or forty thousand in all. To the tribes, the creation of the republic meant unending war. Rumors of Indian atrocities were ubiquitous. Typical reports formed a steady drumbeat of "fiendish murders and outrages" of hapless farmers "literally hacked to pieces," of women "inhumanly violated," of children carried away into "a captivity worse than death" by "red devils" and "wily savages" who descended upon defenseless settlements "like a cloud of vampires," with "demoniac yells." Although there was much exaggeration, some tribes practiced appalling acts of cruelty that confirmed settlers' worst fears. Women and children were scalped, tortured, and raped as a matter of course. Small children were casually murdered when they inconvenienced their captors. Male captives who were deemed cowardly were often castrated, and others killed if they failed to measure up to Comanche standards of bravery.

Indians watched train after train of behemoth ox-drawn wagons plod steadily onward up the valleys of the Brazos, the Trinity, and the Colorado, wiping out game and pushing entire peoples west in an epic slow-motion chain reaction, tribe colliding with tribe, across millions of square miles of prairie. Surveyors came first. ("The chain and compass have ever been regarded among [the tribes] as the emblems of fraud and usurpation," remarked a Texas official.) Behind them came the Texas Rangers with their Colt revolvers. Prisoners were rarely taken. Across the frontier, tribes collapsed under the strain of repeated attack, disrupted food supplies, and ravaging illnesses imported by settlers and their slaves.

Beyond the elimination of the "wild cannibals of the woods," the most pressing question facing Texas was its prospective annexation by the United States. The republic's second president, Mirabeau Buonaparte Lamar, a South Carolinian, who succeeded Sam Houston in 1838, spurned annexation as a "suicidal" surrender that would reduce Texas to the level of a mere "tributary vassal to remote and uncongenial communities who are known to be opposed to her peculiar and essential interests, including slavery." Instead, Lamar urged Texans to seize their own destiny as a continental power "from the Sabine to the Pacific and away to the South West as far as the enemy may render it necessary for the sword to mark the boundary." One day, he promised, she would become the "cornucopia of the world."

Lamar's dream would come to nothing unless Texas occupied the Rio Grande country, which lay athwart its path to the Pacific. There was also the unhappy matter of Texas's finances. The republic was chronically broke, and spiraling deeper into debt. New Mexico's trade with the United States along the Santa Fe Trail was estimated to be worth $20 million a year, money that by all rights, Lamar thought, ought to be channeled into Texas. His solution to this imperial and financial conundrum was worthy of his Napoleonic namesake: the invasion of New Mexico. In 1840, he dispatched a three-hundred-man military force toward Santa Fe. The result was an utter fiasco. Incompetent guides led the Texans astray, then fled. Oxen stampeded. Scouts were murdered by Indians. Forage and water ran out. "Snakes, lizards, tortoises, polecats—in short, almost every living and creeping thing upon the face of the prairie, were eaten with avidity," later wrote a New Orleans journalist who accompanied the expedition. When the Texans staggered, filthy and starving, into New Mexico four months later, they expected to be treated like heroes. Instead, they were arrested, and marched twelve hundred miles to prison in Mexico City.

In revenge for alleged Mexican "atrocities" against the expedition's survivors, Texan guerrillas staked out the Santa Fe Trail, where they looted the caravans of Mexican traders, nominally to collect "duties" on behalf of the Texas government, and descended on hapless villages, where they killed any feebly armed militiamen who stood up to them. In the winter of 1841, twelve hundred rebellious members of the Texas army launched another invasion of Mexican territory, first looting and raping their way through Laredo—a town that Texas claimed was inside its own borders—and then crossed the Rio Grande to sack the town of Mier. None of this did anything to endear Texans to the inhabitants of New Mexico, who could only imagine what was in store for them if the Texans ever managed to reach Santa Fe.

After nearly ten years amidst the whiplash politics of the republic, Sam Houston had matured into a pragmatic, astute, and increasingly sober master of statecraft. In contrast to rabid nationalists like Lamar, Houston had always hoped to pilot Texas into the safe harbor of union with the United States. Following his return to the Texas presidency in 1841, he advised his agents in Washington to play hard to get. Then, to whet the American appetite, he asked Andrew Jackson to communicate to his friends in Washington that if rejected by the United States, Texas would surely "seek some other friend." That "friend," they would assume, must be Britain. It was an effective ploy. Most Americans regarded Britain as a predator bent on insinuating itself into what they considered their own sacred sphere of influence. Jackson predicted that if the British were allowed to occupy Texas they would launch an army against Louisiana, and choke off New Orleans within days.

Meanwhile, "Texas mania" swept the South. Governor Benjamin

Fitzpatrick of Alabama, just one among many, declared, "The great importance of the annexation of Texas to the southern slaveholding States is, that by adding numbers and territory to the weaker section of the Union, it adds security to the institutions already assailed, which nothing but numbers and territory can give." Whigs who doubted the wisdom of the whole imperial enterprise, on the other hand, Henry Clay among them, saw Texas as a fatal wedge that southern extremists were heedlessly driving into the fissure that already existed between the sections. Annexation, Clay warned, "would introduce a new element of distraction and discord" into the body politic. The United States was big enough already! Ignore Texas, he pleaded, to no avail. In March 1845, Congress approved a treaty of annexation providing for the eventual subdivision of Texas into as many as four new states of "convenient" size. New Mexico now became not just Texas's problem but the nation's. It was in defense of Texas's hoary claim to the Rio Grande, with its ancient French origins dripping from it like Spanish moss, that Polk sent American troops forward to provoke Mexico to war in 1846. And it was in the name of that claim that General Stephen Kearny justified his invasion of New Mexico to its inhabitants in 1846.

Texans had expected that everything east of the Rio Grande would automatically be turned over to them after the war. By 1848, their patience was running out. That March, Governor George T. Wood asked President Polk to order the military authorities in Santa Fe to cooperate "to the end that the State of Texas may in no wise be embarrassed in the exercise of her rightful jurisdiction." Believing that New Mexicans would supinely acquiesce, Wood appointed a young lawyer from Nacogdoches, Spruce Baird, to personally carry his writ of jurisdiction to Santa Fe. The hustling, red-haired Baird was emblematic of the buccaneering spirit that drove Texan ambitions, but a poor choice for a mission that required diplomatic finesse. He spoke no Spanish, and was as interested (if not more so) in finagling business opportunities for himself as he was in carrying out his official duties. When New Mexicans learned that Texas meant to enforce its claims, they reacted with alarm. Anglos and Latinos alike took to the streets. The Santa Fe *Republican* thundered "New Mexico does not belong, nor has Texas even a right to claim her as a part of Texas," adding, "We would so advise Texas to send with her civil officers for this country, a large force, in order that they may have a sufficient bodyguard to escort them back safe."

When Baird arrived in Santa Fe he initiated a stumbling political ballet that was hobbled at every step by the sheer difficulty of communication between Santa Fe, Austin, and the national capital. For weeks, Baird, Colonel John Washington—New Mexico's military commander, and its de facto chief executive—and local civilian politicians struggled to grasp control of the situation, while guessing at what the federal authorities really wanted. Months passed waiting for letters, reports, and orders that traveled hundreds of miles at the pace of an ox. Meanwhile, Baird strutted around Santa Fe, appointing clerks and law officers to serve his imaginary Texan administration, and professing "astonishment" that the army still dared to exercise authority. Colonel Washington, a remote descendant of the first president, had served with distinction in the Indian wars and in Mexico, and was not about to yield to a jumped-up, speechifying hack from Nacogdoches. "I shall continue the existence of the Government of the Territory of New Mexico at my peril, and shall only desist when the Executive or the supreme legislative power of the United States shall so ordain," he informed Baird.

In Zachary Taylor, Texans faced a man who had no respect at all for their claims. Nor did he have much use for Texans. Freewheeling, trigger-happy Rangers had caused him more trouble than they were worth during the war, when like "packs of human bloodhounds" they had pillaged their way across northern Mexico, slaughtering civilians as they went. Taylor believed that everything acquired from Mexico was now federal land. And that was that. Hoping to head off the congressional collision that loomed, he resolved with a soldier's decisiveness to make both regions full-fledged states, and to do it without delay.

In a personal letter to the president, Governor Wood confessed that Texas was embarrassed—it desperately wanted to sell New Mexico land to pay off its creditors. But such crass concerns were beside the point: Texan *honor* was at stake. "To yield to a severance of any portion of her soul would be as humiliating to Texas as it would be unjust on the part of the United States," he wrote. Wood's restrained language veiled a threat: Texas would not surrender her claim, come what may.

In frustration, Baird issued a proclamation that had been burning a hole in his pocket for the past half-year. Santa Fe was now officially a part of Texas, he declared to all, and the town of Santa Fe was its county seat: "All proceedings not in accordance with the laws of [Texas] will be held as absolutely null and void." There was no going back now. The rest was in the hands of his compatriots. A few weeks later he left for home.

In Santa Fe, rival political factions staged dueling rallies. The so-called Territorial Party, led by Judge Joab Houghton, a transplanted New York merchant with a thrusting beard and commanding eye who staunchly opposed slavery, initially wanted Congress to declare New Mexico a territory, arguing that statehood was impractical until the boundary with Texas was defined. In September, Houghton and his allies, with the direct, if long-distance, encouragement of Tom Benton, organized the convention that begged Congress for the establishment of civil government and protection from the Indians, asserting that "industry and enterprise are paralyzed, and discontent and confusion prevail throughout the land." The delegates tiptoed through the minefield that had thwarted their earlier petition, hinting at a willingness to compromise on the problem of slavery, and fuzzily describing New Mexico's eastern boundary simply as the "State of Texas." But their hedging came too late. Texas was aroused.

It was now clear to Texans that Zachary Taylor was actively working to snatch the prize from their grasp. Protest meetings demanded action against the "greasers' rebellion" in Santa Fe, while the drum-beating *Texas State Gazette* editorialized, "Rather than surrender to the usurpation of the General Government one inch of our blood-won territory, let every human habitation in Santa Fe be leveled to the earth, and we, if the necessity of the case requires it, buried beneath the ruins."

The threat of a Texan invasion of New Mexico had become, as Henry

Clay memorably put it, the "crisis of the crisis," the single issue that had the capacity to tumble the country into a civil war overnight. In Washington, as the winter wore on, proposals flew like cannonballs across the Senate chamber, South to North, North to South, Democrat to Whig, and back again. *Turn over New Mexico to Texas, and be done with it! Divide New Mexico along the line of the Missouri Compromise! Give Texas an outlet to the Pacific!* Free Soilers appealed on behalf of the rights of white settlers. Texans countered with the "revolutionary right" to territory earned by their war of independence. Abolitionists appealed against the expansion of slavery, and southern nationalists appealed to their proclaimed right to carry their human property wherever they wished. In an effort to win over the southern radicals, Stephen Douglas proposed that if Texas would abandon its claim to lands lying north of the Missouri Compromise line—that is, 36° 30′ north latitude—it be rewarded with jurisdiction over *all* of New Mexico on *both* sides of the Rio Grande. For Texas, this was a spectacular offer. She would lose nothing of value, and gain even more of the Southwest than she hoped for. Douglas felt sure that the president would sign off on this, and thus swing the federal government firmly behind Texas's claim. Ironically, however, this time it was Calhoun who stood in the way.

Calhoun's dream, tirelessly articulated, was the creation of a solid southern front to protect slavery against northern "aggression," politically if possible, and if necessary by secession. He reasoned, pleaded, and bullied the South's senators and congressmen to put their names to a defiant ultimatum. "If you become united, and prove yourselves in earnest, the North will be brought to a pause," Calhoun wrote in January 1849, in an extended polemic that he hoped would rouse the South to action. "If it should not, nothing would remain for you but to stand up immovably in defense of rights, involving your all—your property, prosperity, equality, liberty, and safety." He assured his fellow southerners that as the "assailed" they "would stand justified by all laws, human and divine, in repelling a blow so dangerous, without looking to consequences." Forty-four southern members of Congress signed their names to this flaming document, which came to be known as the Southern Address. Others—significantly including Texas's senators, Sam Houston and Tom Rusk—considered Calhoun's language flagrantly subversive, and refused to sign. Calhoun was furious, declaring that they had "betrayed the South." Vengefully, he refused to support Douglas's compromise proposal, and like so many other such attempts that winter, it went down to defeat. By the end of the Thirtieth Congress, it was clear that Congress was no more capable of deciding the future of the vague, wild country west of the Pecos than it was California's. The ideological divisions were too deep, the geography too confusing, the passions too hot.

CHAPTER 6

OLD HARRY

————— ·◆· —————

There was only one man, many believed, who could staunch the cascade of crises that was threatening to overwhelm the nation: the tired and tubercular Kentuckian who only months before had been regarded as a political corpse. At seventy-two, Henry Clay was one of the oldest Americans still in public life, a living link with the nation's founders, having been born almost with the nation, in 1777, and still stirred by the boyhood memory of hearing in person the fiery Virginia patriot Patrick Henry. No American had enjoyed a longer or more eminent political career, and no one except Daniel Webster was so highly praised as an orator. He had served with distinction in both houses of Congress, and crafted much of the most important legislation of his era. He was a member of the diplomatic delegation that had brought an end to the War of 1812, and spent four years as John Quincy Adams's secretary of state. Five times he had sought the presidency, and thrice run as his party's nominee, most recently in 1844, when he was nudged out—just barely—by Polk.

Clay's popularity was phenomenal. "Old Harry can never be a greater man [than] he is at this time in the Estimation of every one whose opinion is worth having," wrote one typically adoring Whig. He was graced with a first-class personality that combined "high-toned chivalric dignity," natural aplomb, and a rare ability to project tenderness and warmth. "Whenever he saw a blacksmith forge, or a carpenter shop, or a mill, or a factory, or a stone quarry, or a steam engine, or a printing press, or a mart of commerce," the journalist Oliver Dyer remarked, "his heart thrilled with interest and went out in patriotic affection for the people who were at work in those places."

Even in old age, he stood a reedy and loose-limbed six-feet-plus. Recalled Dyer, "His limbs were long, his body was long, his neck was long, and his head was long from the base to the crown." Although he was not particularly handsome—small blue eyes peered from a bony face, beneath a huge forehead that phrenologists claimed was proof of Clay's intelligence—he had an almost erotic effect on the legions of devoted followers who besieged him wherever he went. Kissing him was a public obsession. "Tens of thousands of females, with a careful exclusion of the grosser sex, were presented, for each of whom he had a word of gallantry," former mayor Philip Hone, a Clay supporter, and a close observer of the national scene, noted with pardonable exaggeration during a visit by the great man to New York City. "They all pressed his hands; many kissed him; and one hand, 'more lucky than the rest,' prompted by a spirit of Amazonian hardiness and armed with 'the glittering forfex,' did actually commit a new 'Rape of the Lock' "—in other words, she whipped out a pair of scissors and cut herself a piece of Clay's hair. (Annoyed by a tiresome local belle who couldn't stop announcing that Clay had kissed her three times, a Jersey City pol advised her not to wash her face again in a month, "and Informed her Rouge and Cologne had fell in price 30 per cent during his short stay here in consequence of the ladies not washing their hands and sweet faces.")

Clay also had an unfortunate knack for making enemies, including both the most popular political man of the age, Andrew Jackson, whom Clay repeatedly slandered as an ignorant tyrant, and the supercilious John Calhoun, who, when he claimed that he had "overmastered" Clay in debate, prompted the Kentuckian to snidely retort: "He, my master! I would not have him for a slave!" No insult could have been more calculated to offend Calhoun and the two men did not speak to each other for four years. Although Clay was matchless at political maneuver, "his imagination frequently ran away with his understanding, while his imperious temper and ardent combativeness hurried him and his party into disadvantageous positions," observed his early biographer Carl Schurz. Clay's speeches, Schurz added, while ingenious, ardent, packed with data, and filigreed with entertaining sarcasm, were sometimes weakened by a failure to follow a proposition to its logical conclusion. Put another way, too often Clay resorted to flash over substance. Enemies damned him as everything from a rake to a "Sabbath-breaker," but none surpassed John Randolph, whom Clay had humiliated in the House of Representatives and who in return famously scorned him as a "being so brilliant yet so corrupt, which like a rotten mackerel by moonlight, shined and stunk."

Clay claimed humbler origins than he had actually had, frequently asserting that he had grown up "an orphan boy; who had never recognized a father's smile, nor felt his warm caresses; poor, penniless, without the favor of the great, with an imperfect and neglected education." His father was in fact a prosperous Virginia tobacco planter who owned twenty-one slaves, two of whom the four-year-old Henry inherited at his father's death. Nor was Clay's education scanted: he studied law at the College of William and Mary, where he trained under Thomas Jefferson's mentor, George Wythe. In 1797, he opened a practice in the frontier town of Lexington, Kentucky, where he acquired a reputation for dazzling and persuasive oratory that translated into courtroom victories, and soon enough into considerable wealth, which would in time include real estate, a salt mine, a hemp factory, and a steadily growing workforce of slaves to tend the six-hundred-acre estate where he raised prize-winning hogs and racehorses. Two years after his arrival in Lexington, he joined the local elite by marrying Lucretia Hart, who would bear him eleven children, more than half of whom died prematurely, a lifelong source of heartache to a man whose affections, for both family and country, were always close to the surface.

Clay's political rise was swift. He was first elected to the United States Senate in 1806 to finish out the remaining months of a departing senator's term—he was actually below the constitutionally mandated minimum age of thirty, though no one seemed to care at the time—and went on to serve in either the Senate or the House with ten presidents. In 1811, he began his career in the House, where he was elected speaker on his first day, and on the first ballot, an event still unique for a freshman, and vivid proof that his reputation for parliamentary art had preceded him. During the ten years that he held the chair, he created the speaker's role as the political leader of the chamber and one of the most powerful offices in the government. Like most westerners at the time (the term then applied to anyone living west of the original states), Clay was a roaring jingo who believed that Americans had the right to seize any part of North America they desired. As early as 1810, he had pressed the conquest of Canada as an inspirational national cause, and predicted that the Kentucky militia could seize Montreal on its own, memorably proclaiming, "I prefer the troubled ocean of war . . . to the tranquil, putrescent pool of ignominious peace." As speaker, in 1812, he goaded the United States into one of the most ill-advised wars in its history. Largely untrained and incompetently led American forces, including the Kentucky militia, were repeatedly hurled back from Canada, and further humiliated when, in 1814, the British captured Washington, burned the White House and the Capitol, and sent President James Madison fleeing for safety. Clay, fortunately, was far from their torches and bayonets, serving in Europe with the team of American negotiators hoping to conclude a peace treaty with the English.

After the war, Clay became known principally as an economic nationalist, supporting a national bank to stabilize the currency, pushing for federal support for public works—roads, canals, and later railroads—that would facilitate communications, and advocating the protection of American manufacturing against foreign competition. The sight of smoking chimneys and clattering machinery inspired him. "Who has not been delighted with contemplating the clock-work regularity of a large cotton manufactory," he poetized, where young women "with ruddy complexions and happy countenances watch the work before them, mend the broken threads, and replace the exhausted balls or broaches" then go off to their meals "and return with light and cheerful step." Clay believed that such policies—the "American System," he dubbed it—strengthened the country as a whole by making the sections more economically inter-dependent, deriding states' rights conservatives for treating everything they gained from the federal government "as something snatched from a foreign power," and defending the creative possibilities of big govern-ment: "I consider it as a government coordinate with them, and the true construction, I think, is to give to it all that vigor and vitality which rightfully belong to it."

Clay was forced to confront the national implications of slavery for the first time in 1819. At the end of the previous year, in his capacity as speaker, he had submitted a petition from the inhabitants of the Missouri Territory for admission into the Union. Missouri met all the criteria for statehood. Its population had grown rapidly. St. Louis was a booming entrepôt that linked the Ohio Valley and the territories of the upper Mis-sissippi with the Gulf of Mexico. Emigrants were already pushing far up the Missouri River to found new frontier settlements that were destined to be gateways to the vast unexplored regions beyond. No one doubted that Missouri should be admitted. The problem was, Missourians had elected to come in as a slave state, threatening—as California's demand for admission would a generation later—to upset the sectional balance of power. The eleven free states' overall population of 5,152,000 already surpassed the eleven slave states' 4,485,000, of which 1,500,000 were slaves. However, thanks to the Constitution's three-fifths clause, the South enjoyed seventy-six seats in Congress rather than the fifty-nine that its free population alone warranted. Missouri's admission also had wider implications: slave or free, it would likely set a precedent for all the other territories that were part of the 1803 Louisiana Purchase and soon would be clamoring for admission.

In February 1819, as Congress debated Missouri's admission, James Tallmadge, an independent-minded Republican from Poughkeepsie,

New York, proposed an amendment providing that the introduction of slaves into Missouri be banned, and that all enslaved people in the new state be automatically freed at the age of twenty-five. Tallmadge based his proposal on the peaceful process of emancipation that had already taken place in the northern states. If slavery's westward march was to be halted, Missouri—which had only about ten thousand slaves, about the same number as New York when it embarked on gradual emancipation in 1799—was the place to begin. In the words of Tallmadge's home state ally John W. Taylor, the amendment, if adopted, would "set in motion the machine of free government beyond the Mississippi," and "decide the destiny of millions." During the debate that ensued, northerners generally held that Congress had a right to set any conditions it wished for the admission of new states, and that the nation's founders had always intended to bar slavery from all new territories, based on the evidence of their exclusion of it from the Northwest Territory in the 1780s. Southerners contended that Congress had no right at all to prescribe the "details" of government for any state, and maintained that slavery, once established, could never be removed from any state or territory without the inhabitants' consent.

Clay initially threw his support to the South. (Compared to Calhoun and his ilk, Clay could sound like a liberal on race, evoking images of "fellow human beings deprived of all the rights which make life desirable, transferred like cattle from the possession of one to another," but he was harassed by abolitionists for failing to free his own slaves, whom he unsentimentally bought and sold as if they were pieces of farm equipment.) Clay at first dismissed Tallmadge's amendment on constitutional grounds. Only states, he believed, had the authority to legislate on slavery; moreover, the Constitution guaranteed the citizens of each state all the privileges and immunities enjoyed by every other state, thus to take away a man's slaves was obviously unconstitutional. Why argue the point further? But months of debate eroded his complacency. He was horrified when Georgia congressman Thomas W. Cobb accused Tallmadge of "kindl[ing] a fire which all the waters of the ocean cannot put out, which seas of blood can only extinguish." Tallmadge's retort scared Clay even more: "If a dissolution of the Union must take place, let it be so! If civil war, which gentlemen so much threaten, must come, I can only say, let it come! If blood is necessary to extinguish any fire which I have assisted to kindle, I can assure gentlemen, while I regret the necessity, I shall not forbear to contribute my mite." Although Tallmadge's amendment failed in the Senate, it passed the House. It was an early warning sign to slavery's defenders that the North's growing population was chipping away at its once unchallengeable power in that chamber.

Clay didn't single-handedly engineer the compromise that seemed to untie slavery's Gordian knot. But he did convert it from a speculative concept into a political reality. As it happened, Massachusetts's northern district of Maine was also seeking admission to the Union as a separate state. It had already been suggested that the two statehood applications be combined into a single bill. Then, in January of 1820, Senator Jesse Thomas of Illinois proposed what became the linchpin of the compromise. Missouri would be admitted as a slave state; however, all the territory north of 36 degrees, 30 minutes north latitude would forever be free from slavery, while the territory south of that line would remain open to it. (The line was a tortured one, running along Missouri's *southern* boundary, making the new state a sort of sore thumb of slavery, surrounded on three sides by the free state of Illinois, and the so far unorganized but presumed-to-be-free territories that would eventually become Iowa, Nebraska, and Kansas.) Though he continued to believe that Congress had no business legislating on slavery at all, Clay now pragmatically reversed himself, and backed Thomas's amendment. Using every parliamentary maneuver at his command, Clay cajoled and bullied the House into narrowly striking out Tallmadge's restrictions, and then into decisively enacting what came to be known as the Missouri Compromise.

One of Clay's many clever maneuvers shows him at his most skillful. When Virginia's John Randolph, a steadfast defender of southern privileges, moved for a reconsideration of the Missouri bill, which had just been passed, Clay ruled him out of order until all the rest of the day's business had been dispensed with, repeatedly gaveling him down over the course of a long afternoon session. Clay meanwhile surreptitiously directed the clerk of the House to personally take the bill down the hall to the Senate chamber for action. At the end of the day, Randolph once again moved for reconsideration. Clay abruptly ruled his motion out of order on the grounds that it could no longer be acted on—because the bill was already on its way to the Senate. John Quincy Adams, who cared little for Clay, later described it as an "outrage . . . an unprincipled artifice." Carl Schurz, who rather liked Clay, commented, "The history of the House probably records no sharper trick."

Clay had barely congratulated himself on the bill's passage when the Missourians themselves suddenly upended all his painstaking work. Their new state constitution not only (as expected) legalized slavery, but also explicitly prohibited free Negroes and mulattos from even entering the state. Proslavery ideologues predictably supported Missouri. What rights did Negroes and mulattos have that anyone was bound to honor, asked John Floyd of Virginia. But Clay recognized that the provision was blatantly unconstitutional, since it curtailed the right to free movement of individuals who, though black, were full citizens in several northern states. Although the Senate voted to accept Missouri's constitution, the House voted it down, effectively turning its hard-won statehood into a dead letter overnight.

The situation was further complicated by the counting of ballots for the presidential election that had just taken place in November. Missouri considered itself a state, and demanded that its votes be counted. Antislavery northerners demanded the opposite. Violent rhetoric flared anew in Congress. "The words civil war and disunion are uttered almost without emotion," Clay lamented to a friend. Once again he stepped into the fray. His solution was simple but brilliant: he proposed that votes would be tallied twice in the Electoral College, over which Clay himself, as it happened, would preside: once with Missouri's ballots, and then a second time without them. The outcome was never in doubt, since incumbent James Monroe was running unopposed. Southern radicals attempted several times to protest, but Clay ruled them out of order.

With the election out of the way, Clay now led the fight for a second Missouri compromise. Using all his personal powers of persuasion, supplemented by superhuman patience, he went from congressman to congressman, to friends, enemies, and fence-sitters alike, begging them to "have mercy" on Missouri, while simultaneously hammering them with his argument that no matter how one felt about free blacks, Missouri's restrictions were simply and intolerably unconstitutional. Using his power as speaker, he appointed thirteen reliable men to a Committee on Compromise, and enjoined them to unanimously support the committee's findings. In February 1821, the committee returned with a proposal that not surprisingly reflected Clay's own desires: that Missouri be admitted on condition that the irritating clause should never be construed so as to exclude any American citizen from the enjoyment of his rights—a condition the Missouri legislature would have to agree to "by a solemn public act." The House narrowly enacted this second compromise. Four months later, Missouri's legislature "solemnly" voted to accept Clay's compromise, though it objected that Congress had no actual right to impose any restrictions on the state. Clay's hocus-pocus had worked. The compromise was thin, but it would hold for the next thirty years. Clay entered the Missouri crisis a clever if conventional border state politician. He came out of it a statesman. Across the country, he was hailed as "the Great Pacificator."

The debates of 1819 and 1820 made it all too clear that the nation could shatter over the problem of slavery. The aged Thomas Jefferson was distraught. In April 1820, he famously wrote, "This momentous question, like a fire bell in the night, awakened and filled me with terror. I considered it at once as the knell of the union." He saw the compromise as a mere reprieve. "A geographical line, coinciding with a marked principle, moral and political, once conceived and held up to the angry passions of men, will never be obliterated," he opined, his once proud radicalism having withered into a resigned embrace of the southern status quo. Of slavery he despaired, wishing that somehow the nation could be magically relieved of "that kind of property," deploying a delicate circumlocution that southerners favored. "But as it is, we have the wolf by the ears, and we can neither hold him, nor safely let him go. Justice is in one scale, and self-preservation in the other."

The battle over Missouri had changed the political landscape in fundamental ways. Slavery would now be permitted to cross the Mississippi River into the lands of the Louisiana Purchase. However, slavery's protectors had apparently granted Congress the right to exclude bondage from at least some territories—a concession fraught with implications. The compromise also invented a new guiding principle: that states would now be admitted to the Union in balanced pairs, one free, one slave. Although by simply looking at a map anyone could see that more free states were likely to be formed north of the compromise line than slave states from the territory south of it, in practice new slave states would often be admitted before they had reached the legally required population, to ensure that parity was maintained. (On average, southern territories had only 63,000 inhabitants when they were admitted to statehood, compared to an average of 160,000 in northern ones.)

The debate had delivered some hard lessons. The North now understood that proslavery forces would fight ferociously to defend their prerogatives. The South had learned to its distress that slavery's enemies could muster enough votes to dominate the House of Representatives, in spite of the bonus seats that the South enjoyed thanks to the three-fifths clause. Slaveholders had also learned something else that would prove to be of great political value: that enough northerners were sufficiently frightened of the nation's collapse that they could be bullied into surrendering their principles when it came to slavery. "The slave power learned the weak spot in the anti-slavery armor," as Schurz put it. From now on, the Senate would become slavery's bastion, where its defenders believed that they were permanently guaranteed equal representation.

Henry Clay, too, was transformed by the Missouri debates. From a lockstep defender of southern prerogatives, he had been won over not by northern views but by the imperatives of compromise to the conviction that if the nation was to survive the wrestling match over sectional power, it would require creative politics of a new order, a willingness to reconcile the seemingly irreconcilable. He had come to understand that effective government had nothing to do with ideology or fixed doctrines and everything to do with creative parliamentary strategy coupled to the dynamic force of human persuasion.

Clay's reputation for compromise was enhanced in 1833 when he again walked the country back from the brink of crisis. Five years earlier, with his vigorous support, Congress had enacted a protectionist 50 percent tax on imports that was intended to benefit native manufacturers. The tariff was opposed most vigorously by heavily indebted southern elites, who, egged on by Calhoun, now the vice president, decried it as a "Tariff of Abominations." Essentially, Calhoun argued that the federal government lacked the constitutional power to protect industry through taxation. Speaking of his fellow planters, Calhoun complained, "We are the serfs of the system—out of whose labor is raised, not only the money paid into the treasury, but the funds out of which are drawn the rich rewards of the manufacturer and his associates in interest." No nation based on the "naked principle" of majority rule—Calhoun regarded democracy as a "disease"—could preserve its liberty for more than a generation. It was thus South Carolina's sacred duty, he pompously declared, "to herself—to the Union—to the future and present generations—and to the cause of liberty over the world, to arrest the progress of a usurpation which, if not arrested, must, in its consequences, corrupt the public morals and destroy the liberty of the country." The nullification of an unpalatable federal law was every state's best, and perhaps its only, defense short of secession, he maintained. By this time, Calhoun had so closely allied himself with the "Nullifiers"—those who refused to obey federal law—that his position became untenable. In 1832, he became the first vice president to resign from the office. (The only other would be Spiro Agnew, in 1973.)

Clay considered Nullification a beastly idea. He passionately believed that the laws of the nation were supreme over those of any state and that no state had a right to enact laws that failed to conform with those of the national government. "It is not possible that a state should move a single inch in the line of secession," he declared, "much less could it nullify a law of the United States. To attempt either would be a rebellion, and a revolution." Although South Carolina claimed to be acting for itself alone, it would in effect be legislating for the whole Union, he argued, for if one state negated federal law, surely others would do the same, or else Congress would have to repeal the law for all. The logic of Nullification, it was perfectly obvious, could be applied to any future attempt by a majority to limit or abolish slavery.

As a conciliatory gesture, President Jackson reduced the tariff by one-half. However, the Nullifiers swept South Carolina's elections that fall, and in mid-November a raucous convention filled with men sporting the blue-and-orange cockades of the State Rights and Free Trade Party declared the tariffs of both 1828 and 1832 unconstitutional. If the federal government used force against their state, the Nullifiers swore, they would "forthwith proceed to organize a separate government"—that is, secede. Throughout 1833, the crisis deepened. "Disunion by armed force is *treason*," Jackson furiously declared. He threatened to personally lead fifty thousand troops into South Carolina to enforce federal law, and Congress supplied him with an enforcement bill to back up his words.

By mid-December, war seemed imminent. Into the widening breach Henry Clay stepped once again, brandishing the banner of compromise. Clay had been one of the tariff's most ardent promoters. Now he prepared to let it sink. He thus faced opposition not only from secessionist Carolinians, but also from irate New Englanders, whose manufacturing benefited most from the tariff. Clay refused to compromise on the constitutionality of the tariff, but he proposed to gradually reduce it over the course of the following decade until it reached a floor of 20 percent in 1842. Both sides could claim victory: South Carolina could assert that it had "defeated" the tariff, while the manufacturers could profitably enjoy "some years of repose and tranquillity," before its demise. In his final speech on the compromise, on February 25, Clay further declared: "The difference between the friends and the foes of the compromise is that they would, in the enforcement act, send forth alone a flaming sword. We would send out that also, but along with it the olive branch, as a messenger of peace. They cry out, the Law! The law! The law! Power! power! power! We too reverence the law, and bow to the supremacy of its obligation; but we are in favor of the law executed in mildness, and of power tempered with mercy." It was Clay at his superb best. The Great Pacificator had now become the "Great Compromiser."

CHAPTER 7

"WE HAVE ANOTHER EPIDEMIC"

———— •◆• ————

Henry Clay *knew* that he was destined for the presidency. A great many Americans agreed. No man of his generation strove more relentlessly for that office. He habitually claimed that he was never motivated by anything more than a humble desire to serve God and man. "Ambition! I have been accused of ambition! I have no desire for office, not even the highest," he announced with seeming astonishment at one point during the Nullification debate. "Yes, I have ambition; but it is the ambition of being the humble instrument, in the hands of Providence, to reconcile a divided people, once more to revive concord and harmony in a distracted land." He was ready, he swore, to renounce public service forever and return to Ashland. But no one was fooled. Americans could smell ambition on him like the barnyard aroma of his prize hogs.

Clay made his first run for the presidency in 1824. Candidates then were nominated by caucuses of their supporters in Congress, and were expected to modestly refrain from self-promotion. Four candidates were in serious contention. Clay fancied himself the one true voice of the West. However, the twanging Tennessee accent of his nemesis, Andrew Jackson, rang louder. Jackson trounced his opponents in the popular vote: 43 percent to 31 percent for John Quincy Adams, and 13 percent each for Clay and the fourth candidate, William Crawford. Since none received a majority of electoral votes, the election went to the House of Representatives. Clay realized that he could not win, but was determined to do anything to deny victory to Jackson, whom he considered a mere "military chieftain." He threw his support to Adams, who then appointed Clay secretary of state, traditionally the stepping-stone to the presidency. It was a smart move for both men. But for the rest of Clay's life his enemies would accuse him of having made a "corrupt bargain"—trading support for office—a deal that, if it ever occurred (scholars are divided), seems today like elementary political horse-trading, but which piqued the high-toned sensibilities of that era.

Clay waged his second battle for the presidency in 1832. This time, Jackson was his only serious opponent. Clay, attractive as he was to many, rather like Adlai Stevenson and Al Gore in later ages, lacked the common touch that could translate admiration into mass appeal. Jackson, by contrast, though worrisomely authoritarian—some called him "King Andrew"—was wildly popular among both western yeomen and newly enfranchised urban voters. A decade older than Clay, he galloped around the country, pressing flesh at party gatherings and pig roasts, while Clay immured himself in a fortress of lofty reserve, issuing finely polished policy statements that he posted from his estate at Ashland. Jackson's Democrats issued no coherent platform beyond celebration of Jackson himself and demonization of the Bank of the United States, the centerpiece of Clay's American System, damning it as a "monster" that served only the interests of "aristocracy." When the votes were tallied, "Old Hickory" had crushed the Great Pacificator by 219 electoral votes to Clay's 49.

From the ruins of defeat, Clay and his allies constructed a new political party that would eventually become known as the Whigs. (The party's self-consciously populist name was meant to link it in voters' minds with the eighteenth-century opponents of strong monarchy in England, and to the American rebels who revolted against King George III, connections that likely eluded all but the well educated.) It drew together Yankee bankers and manufacturers, the promoters of expensive railroads and canals, and the western farmers who would benefit from them, along with a smattering of Democrats, temperance advocates, evangelicals, anti-Masons, and abolitionists in a shaky alliance that included men as diverse as the conservative Daniel Webster, the antislavery radical William Seward of New York, and a substantial number of wealthy southern planters. In contrast to the Democrats' more southern orientation and suspicion of strong federal government, the Whigs embraced a fundamentally more modern vision of a dynamic industrial society, and in opposition to the Democrats' demand for unlimited democracy—they supported the direct election of senators and members of the Supreme Court, abolition of the Electoral College, and presidential term limits—the more elitist Whigs leaned toward government by "the better sort." It was said by them, self-approvingly, that "Whigs knew each other by the instinct of gentlemen."

In 1836, Jackson's handpicked successor, Martin Van Buren, easily won election against scattered regional challengers. In 1840, a year when almost anyone could have beaten Van Buren, who had failed to stem the catastrophic depression that dominated his entire term in office, the Whigs passed over Clay to nominate their own war hero, the aged Indian fighter and frontier governor William Henry Harrison. His ego battered, declaring "I had rather be right than be President," Clay disdained the vice presidential nomination, but loyally supported Harrison, gambling that by remaining in the Senate he would be positioned to exert a dominating influence in both Congress and the new administration. When Harrison suddenly died after just one month in office, his successor, the ticket-balancing vice president John Tyler, who was essentially a disgruntled Democrat, abandoned both the Whigs and Clay. In spite of the Whigs' nominal majority in Congress, Clay found himself isolated and frustrated as Tyler's supporters repeatedly derailed his efforts to enact traditional Whig measures on banking and tariffs. Furious, Clay talked about impeaching Tyler. He proposed amendments to the Constitution that would have allowed Congress to override a presidential veto by a simple majority, and have given Congress the power to appoint the secretary of the treasury and the treasurer of the United States. When possible,

Clay pleaded, and when that didn't work, he ranted. But he lost vote after vote to Tyler's men, backed by the Democrats, who accused the Kentuckian of attempting to foment revolution. As Thomas Hart Benton cruelly but aptly put it, "by a singular process of political filtration Clay's influence was dissipated until he found himself a dreg in the party of which for years he had been the conspicuous leader."

Early in 1842, Clay finally gave up. After eleven continuous years in the Senate, he resigned. In a tear-filled valedictory, he declared that he was retiring forever. Sometimes choking with emotion, he delivered an extended apology for behavior that had hurt or offended. "That my nature is warm, my temper ardent, my disposition, especially in relation to the public service, enthusiastic, I am ready to own; and those who suppose that I have been assuming the dictatorship, have only mistaken for arrogance or assumption that ardor and devotion which are natural to my constitution, and which I may have displayed with too little regard to cold, calculating, and cautious prudence, in sustaining and zealously supporting important national measures of policy." Yes, he admitted, in the heat of debate, he had sometimes used offensive language, he had wounded the feelings of "brother senators," he had departed from the rules of parliamentary decorum. "I go from this place under the hope that we shall, mutually, consign to perpetual oblivion whatever personal collisions may at any time unfortunately have occurred between us." He concluded, "I bid you all a long, a lasting, and a friendly farewell." Senators wept openly. Clay had played such an Olympian role in the chamber that fellow senators could scarcely believe that he was gone. Lamented his Kentucky successor, John J. Crittenden, it was like "the soul quitting the body."

When Clay had first arrived in Lexington, the town consisted of little more than a sprawl of log cabins where shaggy frontiersmen and visiting Indians were more common than patricians from east of the mountains. By the 1840s, Lexington fancied itself the "Athens of the West," sporting academies for both boys and girls, a university, theaters, and bookstores, hemp, livestock, and horse-breeding industries, and a thriving slave market. Ashland's centerpiece was Clay's handsome two-story Federal-style home, with its splendid skylighted octagonal library designed by Benjamin Latrobe, the former architect of the U.S. Capitol, with its books on, among other favorite subjects, phrenology, agriculture, racing, the classics, and the poetry of Robert Burns. Serpentine paths and carriageways wound among exotic trees, many of them imported from abroad: broad-boughed walnut, slender birch, European larch, Asian gingkos with their delicate fan-shaped leaves, tulip poplars, maples, black cherry. Prize-winning Arabian horses and Maltese asses filled his stables, gigantic hogs rooted in slave-tended pens, while sheep and cattle wandered at will around the grounds, creating an Arcadian idyll that soothed Clay's eye and warmed his bruised heart.

Certainly Clay was happy to return home, but was far from done with politics: he intended to run for the presidency in 1844. He was this time blessed, so it seemed, with a weak and little known opponent, James K. Polk, "Young Hickory," as he was familiarly called by his Jacksonian supporters. Once again, Clay's smug self-confidence was his worst enemy. He managed to alienate voters both South and North: southerners already distrusted him for his equivocation over the annexation of Texas and his wobbly views about slavery. Now he annoyed northern supporters as well. Antislavery voters recalled a widely publicized incident that had occurred in 1842 at a Clay rally in Indiana, at which Clay had been approached by a Quaker named Hiram Mendenhall, who presented him with a petition with two thousand signatures calling upon him to emancipate his own slaves. After sarcastically dismissing its signers with a racist joke—he alleged with a laugh that the petition had probably been concocted by "Democrats and those of a shade darker"—he then went on to claim that he had never bought or sold a slave, a flat lie, and that half his slaves were so old and infirm that it would be an act of cruelty to emancipate them. Then, in a clever rhetorical turn, he challenged Mendenhall and his friends to purchase his slaves' freedom for $15,000. "If the abolitionists will raise and give them the same amount, I will liberate them," he proposed, to the crowd's amusement. "You have put abolition back fifty

years," he sneered. "Go home, Mr. Mendenhall and mind your own business." At the time, Clay was credited with brushing off the annoying
Quaker with panache, but his cavalier dismissal of the petition cost him
antislavery votes where it mattered in 1844.

As always, Clay expected to win the election. "There is no doubt of a
triumphant result," he buoyantly predicted a week before the election. He
almost made it. But the abolitionist Liberty Party drew just enough votes
in the key state of New York to deny him a victory there, thereby hand-
ing the state to Polk, and with it the presidency. Equally catastrophic for
the Whigs, the Democrats also won control of the Senate, and two-thirds
of the seats in the House of Representatives. It was a debacle. "Bad news
needs no herald," William Seward wrote to Clay. "All is lost."

It was arguably one of the most pivotal elections in American history. Had he won, Clay himself later wrote, "there would have been no
annexation, no war, no imputation against us by the united voice of all
the nations of the world of a spirit of aggression and inordinate Territorial aggrandizement." Indeed, the map of the United States might have
been very different from the one we know today. In an intriguing 2003
counterfactual essay titled "Rethinking the Coming of the Civil War,"
Gary J. Kornblith speculated that Clay would probably have preferred
the independence of Texas and California to annexation. The Republic
of Texas would likely have extended north into Kansas, but would be
only about half as wide from east to west as the present-day state. A gold-
rich Republic of California would include Nevada and part of present-
day Oregon. Most of New Mexico and Arizona, Nevada and Colorado
would have remained part of Mexico. By avoiding war, Clay would have
freed himself to focus on the issues that he really cared about, especially,
fostering American industry, the development of infrastructure, and the
strengthening of a national banking system. "Without the Mexican War,"
wrote Kornblith, "there would have been no Wilmot Proviso. Without
the Wilmot Proviso, there would have been no debate in the late 1840s
over the status of slavery in federal territories." He added, "Under a Clay
presidency, the debate over slavery would have persisted and probably
intensified, but without territorial expansion, it would not have been

framed in terms of irreconcilable constitutional interpretations, each with passionate popular support."

Clay tried again for the Whig nomination in 1848. He was the most eminent member of the party, certainly. But he was seventy-one years old in an age when comparatively few people lived beyond sixty, and he now had about him the whiff of a perennial loser. "We should not be defeated by the dimming ambitions of one old man, and his idolators," one Kentucky defector wrote to another. Worse yet, in the eyes of Whig power brokers, Clay's principled stand against the Mexican War and territorial aggrandizement had ruined him as a candidate.

In November 1847, when Mexico City was in the hands of General Winfield Scott, and Mexico prostrate, Clay had delivered one of the strongest antiwar speeches ever by a leading American politician. Although he never mentioned his beloved son Henry, who had died bravely under Zachary Taylor's command at Buena Vista, Henry couldn't have been far from Clay's mind. "War unhinges society, disturbs its peaceful and regular industry, and scatters poisonous seeds of disease and immorality, which continue to germinate and diffuse their baneful influences long after it has ceased," he declared, in a speech near his home at Lexington, to an audience that included one of his admirers who had just been elected to Congress from Illinois, Abraham Lincoln. "Of all the dangers and misfortunes which could befall this nation, I should regard that of its becoming a warlike and conquering power, the most direful and fatal." The United States, he cried, was on the path that had led Rome and empires of Europe to ruin. This was a different Clay from the man who, thirty-five years earlier, had whipped the nation to war against England, and sworn that the Kentucky militia could conquer Canada by itself. But it was not what war-fevered Americans wanted to hear. They had tried Clay thrice before. Now they wanted another war hero, and they had him in Taylor.

Once again, Clay declared that his political life was at an end. But his announcement of his demise was premature. When one of Kentucky's U.S. Senate seats became vacant after the election, Clay's friends in the state legislature elected him to fill it. "I shall hardly feel myself at liberty to decline," Clay allowed in a spirit of weary resignation. "A sense of duty, and the possibility of my being able to do some good, overcome my repugnance." He was not in a hurry to uproot himself from Ashland. His crops of hemp and corn were "uncommonly fine" that year, and the races at Lexington were, as always, powerfully seductive. Age and illness were also taking a toll. In spite of repeated visits to spas and mineral springs, he lived in almost constant discomfort from painful respiratory ailments, flus, and "bilious cholick." He was also afraid to leave home for another reason. Cholera was stalking along the rivers and canals, coursing through urban slums, insinuating itself into the smallest towns, swallowing entire families. The epidemic was particularly savage in the Ohio River Valley, where Clay's friends and neighbors dropped around him. Travelers, it was said, took their lives in their hands.

Politics nonetheless was at a heightened pitch. "In Kentucky, we have another epidemic, the Emancipation question, which rages with as much violence as the Cholera," Clay wrote to a friend in Washington. Candidates were vying for seats at a long-awaited convention to reform the state's constitution. Professed enemies of slavery, Clay among them, were urging that the new constitution include a plan for gradual emancipation similar to those that had ended slavery painlessly in the northern states at the turn of the century. Torn between their unease about slavery and their affinity with the South, Kentuckians liked to think that their 211,111 slaves enjoyed a gentler bondage than elsewhere. Kentucky slaves were of course subject to the same workaday brutality, sexual abuse, and control of their movements, and had no more right to protest their treatment than did slaves in South Carolina or Mississippi. However, in contrast to states where laws barred any challenge to slavery, white Kentuckians fiercely debated it in their newspapers, on their street corners, in barbershops, and front parlors. Henry Clay's own radical nephew, Cassius M. Clay, who published his opinions widely in the state, provocatively likened the expansionist ambitions of proslavery to the propagation of Islam by fire and sword, and predicted that poor whites would one day rise in revolution against the wealthy owners of slaves. (He was also a slave owner, but, well, that was Kentucky.)

Clay's ambivalence was to a large degree Kentucky's. As the master of about fifty slaves at any given time, he was one of the larger slave owners in the state. Although he declined to challenge the legality of slavery where it already existed, he had never defended slavery as an institution. "I should rejoice if not a single slave breathed the air or was within the limits of our country," he told a Lexington audience. "But here they are, to be dealt with as we can." His ambivalence was reflected in quite personal terms during a curious episode that unfolded that summer. Clay eventually sallied forth to travel to Newport, Rhode Island, for sea bathing, his favorite form of therapy. In August, his manservant Levi suddenly abandoned him there, "inveigled away, I suppose, by some of his color or some of the abolitionists," Clay wrote his son James, yet he would not attempt to recover him. Then, surprisingly, Levi returned hours before Clay was to leave Newport, claiming that abolitionists had paid him $300 to run away, and that he had wanted to con them out of the full amount before he returned; however, he had become "distrustful" of them, and left them in Boston. Just what Clay thought of this tale, he did not record. But off he and Levi went to Buffalo. Ten days later, Levi disappeared again. Clay's reaction was revealing: "If [he has left] voluntarily, I will take no trouble about him, as it is probable that in a reversal of our positions I would have done the same thing." But Levi turned up yet again a few weeks later to reclaim his job, offering Clay no explanation for his wanderings, or at least none that Clay revealed.

In February, Clay offered a summation of his thinking on slavery in a letter to Richard Pindell, a Whig stalwart he invited to make the letter public. Clay began by trashing the theory, vigorously promoted by Calhoun and his followers, that slavery was actually a "positive good" for all concerned. If slavery was really so essential to "civilized" society, Clay retorted, then logically half the human race ought to be enslaved to serve the other half, since there weren't enough blacks to go around. "If the principle of subjugation founded upon intellectual superiority be true and applicable to races and to nations, what is to prevent its being applied to individuals?" he asked. "And then the wisest man in the world would have a right to make slaves of all the rest of mankind!" Indeed, wouldn't it impose a duty on the intellectually superior to make slaves of their fellow men, in order to "improve" them? This was of course sophistry, he admitted. Most men regarded slavery as a great evil to both races. But immediate emancipation was no remedy at all, and if it were ever attempted would only lead to "frightful disorders" and "fatal consequences."

There *was* a solution, however, one that Clay had tirelessly advocated for more than thirty years: deportation under the auspices of the American Colonization Society. Founded in 1816, partly with Clay's assistance and with James Madison as its leader, the society maintained that freed slaves must be returned to their ancestral home, Christianized, and prepared to redeem Africa from barbarism and idolatry. In his Pindell letter, Clay proposed that about five thousand emancipated Kentucky slaves be shipped to Africa each year; he estimated the cost at about $50 "per head." All slaves born before 1855 or 1860 would remain slaves for life, while those born after the selected year would be freed at a specified age, say twenty-five, but then be liable to be hired out by the state for a period of three years in order to raise a sum to pay the cost of their transportation. The offspring of those who were free at twenty-five would be free from birth, but would be apprenticed, essentially as indentured servants, until the age of twenty-one. In the meantime, slave owners would retain all their usual rights. None of them would actually be required to free any slave; Clay, in idealist mode, simply expected them to do the right thing.

Opposed to slavery though he was in principle, he was still deeply racist in his sentiments. His colonization plan was predicated on his ironbound conviction that peaceful "amalgamation and equality" between whites and free blacks was inconceivable. The beauty of the scheme (in Clay's view) was that it would cost taxpayers nothing, since it would be paid for by its beneficiaries, the slaves themselves, who would be hired out by the authorities until they had paid off the cost of their passage. Free white laborers would then soon replace the departed slaves. For Clay, the vision was a glorious one: "We shall remove from among us the contaminating influence of a servile and degraded race of different color; we shall enjoy the proud and conscious satisfaction of placing that race where they can enjoy the great blessings of liberty, and civil, political, and social equality; we shall acquire the advantage of the diligence, the fidelity, and the constancy of free labor, instead of the carelessness, the infidelity and the unsteadiness of slave labor; we shall elevate the character of white labor . . . improve the agriculture of the state, attract capital from abroad . . . and redress, as far and as fast as we safely and prudently could, any wrongs which the descendants have suffered at our hands, and we should demonstrate the sincerity with which we pay indiscriminate homage to the great cause of liberty of the human race."

It seemed a winning formula. Not only was "colonization" visionary, it was practical, Clay insisted. Abolitionism—the dream of men like the wild-eyed William Lloyd Garrison of Boston and the new senator from New York, William Seward—wasn't policy, it was fanaticism, Clay felt. There was a problem, however. Or rather two problems. Hardly any slave owners had any desire to relinquish their human property. And very few black Americans, slave or free, wanted to go to Africa: in the American Colonization Society's best year, 1832, only 632 departed for Africa from the entire United States. True abolitionists damned colonization as an intellectually dishonest scam to dispose of free blacks, who provided a dangerous model of independence for the many who remained enslaved, while enabling slave owners—such as Clay himself, abolitionists pointed out—to loftily profess their opposition to slavery without actually freeing any slaves. Others pointed out the obvious: that the natural increase of the slave population was likely to overwhelm the trickle of deportations. It would "be like baling [sic] the ocean with a ladle," one Kentuckian remarked.

Even so, as flawed as the theory of colonization was, it took political courage for Clay to attack slavery as forcefully as he did. Proslavery ideologues waved the Pindell letter as proof that Clay was a race traitor. "Henry Clay's true character now stands revealed," the *Richmond Inquirer* claimed. "The man is an abolitionist." This was far from the truth, but it conveyed the deep distrust of Clay that percolated through the South. In Kentucky, his enemies in the legislature, who now included even fellow Whigs, demanded that Clay either resign his appointment to the Senate or vote a straight proslavery line. Clay ignored them. He was old, frail, and beleaguered, but he was beyond intimidation.

In the autumn of 1849, Kentucky became a microcosm of the larger national crisis as candidates for the convention to reform that state's constitution campaigned across the state, sometimes in the face of mob violence. There were other issues: the proposed elimination of life tenure for public officials, reduction in the number of appointive offices, speedy repayment of the public debt. But it was slavery that was on everyone's lips. Emancipationists argued, quite correctly, that slavery depressed free workers' wages, pointing out that when Louisville carpenters and painters had recently struck for a ten-hour workday, employers broke the strike by hiring slaves to replace them. Slavery's defenders attacked in kind. Oliver Anderson, a self-proclaimed "thorough pro-slavery man" campaigning in Fayette County, declared, "So far from admitting [slavery] to be a necessary evil, I believe it tends to exalt the free population, and would be unwilling to give it up, even if by a word I could remove the negro population to Africa."

As cholera continued to stalk the state, slaying hundreds, including a number of candidates for the convention, violence erupted. In Louisville's First Ward, a gun battle broke out between proslavery and antislavery election observers. In Paducah, an antislavery man campaigning as a delegate to the convention was shot and killed by his opponent in the midst of a debate. In Madison County, Cassius Clay was attacked by an armed mob. "They quarreled about *negrismo*—drew pistols—both snapped and they closed with bowie knives," reported an eyewitness.

The emancipationists went into the convention with high hopes for reform. They were bitterly disappointed. Not only did the convention fail to adopt a plan for gradual emancipation but, even worse, it approved an aggressively proslavery constitution which included a Bill of Rights that

proclaimed: "The right of property is before and higher than any constitutional sanction; and the right of the owner of a slave to such slave, and
its increase, is the same, and as inviolable as the right of the owner, of
any property whatever." Henry Clay was "mortified." Always disposed to
see the emotional dimension of things, he blamed the failure on interference by "violent abolitionists" from other states, who had inflamed local
feelings. As he prepared to leave for Washington, he wrote gloomily to a
friend, "I confess that I have not much hope that slavery will be extinguished in any of the States, by legal enactment, at least for a long time
to come."

The reformers' defeat also profoundly influenced a Clay admirer, by
then *ex*-Congressman Abraham Lincoln, who in 1855 would remark:
"There is no peaceful extinction of slavery in prospect for us. The signal
failure of Henry Clay, and other good and great men, in 1849, to effect
any thing in favor of gradual emancipation in Kentucky, together with a
thousand other signs, extinguishes that hope utterly."

CHAPTER 8

THE CITY OF
MAGNIFICENT INTENTIONS

———— •◆• ————

Clay disclaimed any desire to return to Washington, saying, "[I] shall go back with something like the feelings which the day laborer may be supposed to have, who having worked hard all day by sunshine, is sent again at night into the field to work by moonlight." He somewhat disingenuously told friends that he intended to play only a passive role in the Senate, "to be a calm and quiet looker on, or occasionally offering a word of advice or pouring a little oil on the tempestuous billows." But for Clay modesty was merely a flag of convenience. His agile mind was already working at a solution, "some capital scheme," in the words of one supporter, to cut the knot that was choking Congress.

Clay was nonetheless "buoyant and elastic of spirit" when he set off from Lexington for New York and Washington in early November. His wife, Lucretia, who hated Washington, as usual remained behind. Even with improvements in steamship travel, and the westward extension of railway lines, the journey was still an exhausting one, especially for a man of Clay's age and precarious health. ("For seven days I never had my clothes off me and only lay down just one time and that for the space of four hours," groaned Sam Houston of the trip across the Alleghenies.) Clay traveled by steamboat from Cincinnati to the upper Ohio, then switched to a stagecoach, which tipped over near Uniontown, Pennsylvania, leaving him bruised but intact. He reached Philadelphia on November 8, where he attended a wedding, and from there went on to New York, where his journey became a royal progress. Everywhere, his arrival excited the usual tumultuous throngs of supporters. The New York crowds "pester him to death, haunt him by day, serenade him by night, follow him in his walks, shouting, hurrahing, Henry Claying him wherever he goes," Clay's aristocratic friend Philip Hone noted in his diary. "They insist upon a speech for every hurrah which proceeds from their vulgar throats, and compel him to return the unmerciful squeeze of every dirty hand." Arriving in Baltimore on November 27, Clay begged to be spared any public ceremonies. A huge mob nonetheless gathered to meet him at the railway station and trailed him to Barnum's City Hotel, where they kept cheering and begging him to address the "threatening and alarming questions" of the moment, until he at last appeared at his window. "I stand pledged under all circumstances and in all storms TO STAND BY THE UNION," he assured them.

Physically drained, Clay finally came to rest in Washington on December 1. He gratefully took up residence in a suite of comfortably appointed rooms at his favorite hotel, the National, on Pennsylvania Avenue at Sixth Street, where streams of well-wishers pushed into his rooms, importuning him to save the country, to save the Whig Party, and sometimes just to save them a political appointment in the administration. At a White House levee, he was pleased to find himself as much a focus of attention as the president. Taylor treated Clay with politeness, but there was no warmth between the two men. The old general never invited the Kentuckian into his inner circle, and had not helped matters during his own journey to Washington, when he miffed Kentuckians by turning up his nose at a banquet in his honor at Frankfort. Clay, meanwhile, sniped at the mediocre caliber of Taylor's cabinet, and complained that his followers had been shortchanged in the distribution of patronage appointments. In an effort to spread oil on the roiled waters, Taylor obligingly named Clay's son James to be ambassador to Portugal, a plum post. But Clay never forgave Taylor for edging him out of the Whig nomination and going on to win the office that he believed by right should have been his.

Despite his disclaimers, Clay was thrilled to be back in the great game of congressional combat. The political landscape had dramatically altered since Clay's departure from the Senate in 1842, but the physical appearance of the capital was comfortably, raggedly familiar. Although it continued to swell in size—its population of forty thousand included some 29,000 whites and more than ten thousand free blacks and slaves— it still seemed like little more than a half-built village crisscrossed by pretentious boulevards trickling away into cow pastures that turned into swamps when it rained. Hunters shot rabbits and snipe in the vicinity of present-day DuPont Circle. Hogs and goats sunned themselves even in the busiest streets. The reek of slaughterhouses perfumed the air. Pennsylvania Avenue, little more than an overblown country road when Clay first came to Washington in 1806, now teemed with activity: on its north side, foreign legations jostled alongside luxurious hotels and gambling emporiums where tourists could rub elbows with congressmen and senators, including the high-rolling Clay. The seedier south side of the avenue was another world entirely, where shabby boardinghouses, taverns, and whorehouses served less posh clientele; only the bold and the foolhardy ventured into the warren of dark and filthy lanes nearby, known not without reason as Murder Bay. From his window, Clay could see the stump of the new Washington Monument gazing reproachfully over the malodorous canal that oozed along the Mall toward Capitol Hill, where the Capitol's squat wooden dome suggested the half-built state of American democracy. Charles Dickens, who had visited a few years earlier, hated the place, scornfully dismissing it as a city of "magnificent intentions" and the "headquarters of tobacco-tinctured saliva," a pompous podunk of "spacious avenues that begin in nothing, and lead nowhere; streets, mile-long, that only want houses, roads, and inhabitants; public buildings that need but a public to be complete."

Still, when Congress was in session social life accelerated from a somnolent trudge to a frenetic whirl of balls, teas, and levees, where guests savored sherry cobblers and mint juleps, French wines, and the best Kentucky bourbon. Phrenology and mesmerism were all the fashion that winter. Even the rough-hewn Sam Houston was hooked on mesmerism, though he was careful to assure Margaret, his exceptionally pious wife back in Texas, that it in no way contradicted Christianity. To the contrary, "It increases the wonders of the power of an Almighty God," he enthused. "It is indeed wonderful, and its curative powers great."

Tawdry and foul as much of the city was, the Capitol was a unique repository of meaning and passions for Americans from all parts of the country. In an age when the fever of patriotism ran high, Congress was the nation's most popular public theater. Antebellum Americans would be shocked by the cynicism and apathy that present-day Americans display toward politics. Nor did they complain of mudslinging and "negative campaigning": voters expected the men they elected to fight passionately and hard for what they believed in. "As we got out of the depot, behold, there it stood, a most magnificent edifice upon a rise of ground not more than 40 rods from the depot," a dazzled young visitor from Maine, George Bryant, wrote home to his grandfather. "Without further ceremony and with hurried step we all rushed up the avenue which led to its entrance; and after ascending many stone steps, more noble than I ever before imagined, we came to the long anticipated spot. And here we beheld architecture approximating as near to perfection, seemingly, as art or science ever can produce. But with this we were not satisfied; we longed to see the great men and renowned patriots of the ages."

The Capitol was in a very literal sense the "people's house." Although a fence surrounded the building, it was there to keep out cows, not people. Only one or two security guards were on duty at any given time, and they made no attempt to check the identity of visitors. Ordinary citizens rambled in and out at will, milled in the vestibules and stairwells, perused the shelves of the Library of Congress—then on the second floor of the Capitol—and wandered onto the floors of both houses, where they felt free to chat with their elected representatives, and to install themselves at their desks if they happened to be unoccupied. The atmosphere in both chambers was usually smelly and musty, and anything but refined. Congressmen spat, snuffed, ate sandwiches, and puffed pungent cigars without inhibition, or slipped off to gobble oysters and guzzle wine at an eatery called the Hole-in-the-Wall that was lodged in a chamber just off the Senate floor. From time to time, auctions were even held in the Rotunda. Nonetheless, tourists were still awestruck in the presence of democracy at work. "You can scarcely imagine our feelings of sublimity as we mused upon the scene," reported young Bryant.

Splendid though it appeared to outsiders, the Capitol was effectively obsolete, having been designed in the 1790s, and rebuilt after the British sacking in the War of 1812 when the nation was just a fraction of its current size, with a government whose employees then numbered only in the hundreds. The building was now painfully overcrowded. Between its two branches, Congress now had fifty-seven standing committees, but only forty rooms available for their use. Senators and congressmen had no private offices or staff, and conducted all their work on the floor of their respective chambers, at desks crammed with speeches, notes, books, petitions, correspondence, and everything else that couldn't fit into the plain black wooden boxes that they carried back and forth between the Capitol and their often overcrowded lodgings. The Library of Congress desperately needed more space, while the Supreme Court, lodged in a cramped basement chamber, also craved a better situation. Closets spilled their contents out into the corridors, and rooms that had once been high and airy were now squashed with "temporary" mezzanines. The House chamber, in particular, was a monster of bad acoustics, plagued by echoes so severe that congressmen often could not hear each other across the floor. Sanitation was equally unsatisfactory: members of Congress were obliged to relieve themselves in a row of privies on the western slope of Capitol Hill.

Washington was the nation's only truly national city, where sleek Yankee businessmen, slave-driving southerners, swaggering bravos from New York's immigrant ghettos, sombrero-wearing Texans, sober Quakers, delegations of feathered Indians, backwoodsmen from the far reaches of Tennessee and Missouri, impassioned abolitionists, African Americans both enslaved and free, and assorted sharpers and hustlers of every conceivable kind mingled in its lobbies and smoky back rooms. (One species of American was noticeably thin on the ground, however: there were no more than twenty journalists assigned to the Capitol, many of whom also worked part-time for the government, in an era when the concept of conflict of interest was virtually unknown.)

That said, the city was indelibly southern in one key respect: slavery was woven into almost every aspect of its life. Slaves performed most of the manual work in the Capitol. They served guests at the city's soirees, drove many of its carriages, opened its doors, cooked its food, tended its children, and shared the beds of ordinary citizens and politicians alike. It was an open secret that any number of prominent men lived in concubinage with enslaved mistresses. "One could neither go out nor stay in without meeting indisputable testimony of the truth of Thomas Jefferson's statement: 'The best blood of Virginia runs in the veins of her slaves,'" caustically remarked the journalist Jane Swisshelm, correspondent for Horace Greeley's *New York Tribune* and the first female reporter assigned to Congress. Even Godlike Daniel Webster, Swisshelm claimed, supported a family of eight mulattos "bearing the image and superscription of the great New England statesman, who paid the rent and grocery bills of their mother as regularly as he did those of his wife." Swisshelm despised Webster for his temporizing on slavery, and never proved her assertion to most people's satisfaction. However, back in the 1830s a mulatto boy had apparently appeared at the door of the Senate chamber one day asking for his father, "Mister Webster."

At the same time, even many southerners considered the flourishing slave trade in the District of Columbia a national embarrassment. By the 1830s, the capital had become the regional center of slave trading, where consignments of slaves from as far away as Baltimore and Maryland's Eastern Shore were mustered for sale in bulk lots for shipment to the expanding markets of the Deep South. Men handcuffed in pairs and chained together, trailed by boys and girls, and women with infants in wagons, guarded by traders, "like a butcher's drove of hobbled cattle," trudged along the avenues that fed into the city, often passing by the Capitol itself, and visible from its windows. "Cash! Cash! Cash! Negroes Wanted," newspaper ads blared. Shoppers for human flesh could find every sort of slave for sale at Gadsby's auction house, conveniently located just off Lafayette Park, or browse in a more leisurely fashion at any one of several large holding pens, such as Gannon's on the present site of the National Archives, or Robey's—"that infernal hell," abolitionist congressman Joshua Giddings called it—surrounded by high wooden palings at the corner of Seventh Street and Maryland Avenue. The capital's largest slave dealer, Franklin & Armfield of Alexandria, shipped as many as two thousand slaves to the Deep South annually, in its own ships, before the portion of the District that lay on the south bank of the Potomac voted to "retrocede" itself to Virginia in 1846.

Although slavery was firmly embedded in the capital, the Federal District also incorporated a substantial population of free blacks, which had grown from virtually none at the turn of the century to 1,700 in 1820, and to more than eight thousand in 1849. The law, as it did in most parts of the South, barred blacks from voting, testifying against whites, and owning firearms; it also presumed that all black people were slaves unless they could prove otherwise, a technicality that all too often facilitated the kidnapping and sale of free blacks back into slavery. Free blacks, who outnumbered slaves in the District by about four to one, worked not only as servants but also in a multitude of independent professions, as shopkeepers, restaurateurs, tradesmen and skilled workers, washerwomen and nurses, draymen, oyster fishers, teachers, and the ministers of independent black churches. Many were literate, some wealthy, and a few deeply involved in clandestine efforts to facilitate the escape of slaves by means of the Underground Railroad, which by the 1840s annually spirited scores of fugitive slaves from Virginia, Maryland, and the District north toward Pennsylvania and beyond. Still festering in the memory of slavery's defenders was the dramatic capture of the schooner *Pearl*, which in April 1848 had slipped out of Washington in the dead of night with more than seventy fugitive slaves on board, including two belonging to the aged Dolley Madison, in one of the largest attempted mass escapes of slaves on record. After their recapture at the mouth of the Potomac, a mob had nearly lynched the *Pearl*'s New Jersey captain, Daniel Drayton, as he was being marched at gunpoint to the city jail.

As a federal property, the District of Columbia had a unique constitutional status: it was the only slaveholding jurisdiction in the United States where, since it was not a state, the national government had the clear right to regulate slavery. Since the early years of the century, antislavery societies and northern state legislatures had repeatedly petitioned Congress to abolish slavery, or at least the slave trade, within the District. Southern-dominated Congresses had always dismissed such petitions out of hand. When, in the mid-1830s, slavery in the District became the focus of a massive national petition campaign by the newly organized American Anti-Slavery Society—34,000 Americans signed such petitions in 1836, and 87,000 in 1838—the House of Representatives suppressed the issue completely by voting to impose a gag rule on discussion of any subject relating to slavery. Although slavery continued to decline in the District, as it did generally in the surrounding counties of Maryland, proslavery politicians remained dogmatically committed to protecting it for fear of setting a potent precedent for emancipation elsewhere.

Undeterred, abolitionists continued submitting petition after petition throughout the 1840s. Indeed, few issues inflamed the growing northern antislavery community more than visions of the capital city, a supposed beacon of freedom to the world, stained with the sin of slavery. Widely distributed broadsides contemptuously proclaimed: "The Land of the Free, The Home of the Oppressed," alongside engravings of slave auctions and trudging coffles. In January 1849, Congressman Abraham Lincoln, declaring that he had the support of fifteen of the most eminent residents of the capital, introduced a bill calling for the automatic emancipation of all children born to slaves in the District as of January 1, 1850, and for the compensated emancipation of adult slaves thereafter, with the agreement of their masters, who, he felt sure, would acquiesce when they realized that the death of slavery in the capital was at hand. Lincoln may have been motivated in part by having witnessed a few weeks earlier the seizure at gunpoint of a slave who worked in his boardinghouse, and who had saved for years to buy his freedom, only to be shackled and dragged away to be resold before he could make the final payment. Like every other attempt before it, Lincoln's bill was buried by his own party's leadership for fear of alienating the Whigs' southern wing.

In December, as the Thirty-first Congress began to assemble—without Lincoln, who had lost his seat—the atmosphere of crisis was as inescapable as the rank odor of the city's sewage. In salons and saloons, on street corners and the steps of the Capitol, everyone seemed to be arguing about New Mexico and California, fugitive slaves, the outrages of the abolitionists, and disunion. What would Clay do, they asked each other. The wild-eyed Calhoun? Bullying Tom Benton? That redheaded demon from New York, Seward? The slavery question seemed to have "unhinged" both political parties, worried one Kentucky Whig. The South was aboil with revolutionary talk. In state after southern state, conventions passed resolutions declaring unconstitutional any federal law barring slavery from the territories, and threatening to nullify any such law if Congress dared pass one. In October, delegates from several of the states meeting in Natchez, Mississippi, openly threatened secession if their demands were ignored. Southern members of Congress were geared for political war. Clay was frightened for the nation. "The feeling for disunion, among some intemperate southern politicians, is stronger than I supposed it could be," he confessed to a friend in Kentucky. "The masses generally, even at the South, are I believe, yet sound; but they become inflamed and perverted."

On December 3, Clay made his entrance into the Senate. Waves of applause cannonaded from the chamber's galleries and echoed from its coffered ceiling. Female visitors smothered him with kisses. Senators clutched his hands, and wished him well. They all seemed to expect miracles. Clay asked the Senate to spare him from committee work, so that he could concentrate on the national crisis without distraction.

"I fear for the Country," he wrote to his friend Mary Bayard a few days later. "From both parties, or rather from individuals of both parties, strong expressions are made to me of hopes that I may be able to calm the raging elements. I wish I could, but fear I cannot, realize their hopes."

Clay would have plenty of time to think, since Congress was about to come to a complete standstill. The election of the speaker of the house was normally just institutional housekeeping, a pro forma exercise in which the dominant party elected one of its members to organize the chamber—assigning members to committees, and presiding over the body during debates. During the previous session, with the Whigs in the majority, the speaker had been Robert C. Winthrop, a bespectacled Massachusetts patrician and protégé of Daniel Webster. Winthrop was once more the candidate of the Whig establishment. But in the Thirty-first Congress, Democrats now had a majority of 112 to 105 Whigs, and had selected as their candidate affable, corpulent thirty-four-year-old Howell Cobb, one of the largest slave owners in Georgia, but nonetheless still a strong Unionist. Thanks to the Constitution's three-fifths clause, the South enjoyed about twenty additional House seats in 1850, including both Democrats and Whigs. The balance of power, however, was held by thirteen members belonging to the Free Soil Party, some of them former Whigs and the others former Democrats, all of them committed above all else to opposing extension of slavery into the western territories.

Since the Whigs as a whole were more tolerant of antislavery views than the Democrats, Winthrop should have been able to win election easily with the support of the Free Soilers. However, as the next three weeks of tortuous debate would amply prove, Free Soilers were fed up with the Whigs' temporizing on slavery in general, and in particular with Winthrop, both for failing to press the Wilmot Proviso, and for banishing antislavery men to insignificant committees where they would have no influence on legislation. Deep fissures had opened in both parties as the wedge of slavery drove ever deeper into the body politic. Both the major parties were divided into southern and northern wings, and by largely but not entirely overlapping proslavery and antislavery factions.

The Free Soilers themselves were divided between advocates of immediate abolition, such as their nominal leader, shambling Joshua Giddings of Ohio, and—this was a distinction that eluded proslavery ideologues, who pretty much considered anyone who supported constraints on slavery to be a traitor—men who were prepared to accept the continued existence of slavery where it already existed, but were adamant about barring it from new territories where it would compete with white labor.

Voting began on December 3. One hundred and eleven votes were needed for election. (This number would change over the coming weeks as more congressmen arrived to take their seats.) On the first ballot, Cobb received 103 votes to Winthrop's 95, with most of the rest scattered among minor candidates. Most of the Free Soilers voted in a bloc for Wilmot, the father of the eponymous proviso. Three more votes were taken that day, and six more the next. The numbers barely changed, though Cobb's total dropped to 99, while Winthrop's rose to 97. A sense of vertigo began to creep through members of both houses of Congress. Not only was the House unable to function without a speaker, but the Senate was also stymied since so much of Congress's work required joint action by the two houses. Henry Clay, who had virtually created the office of speaker back in the 1810s, watched appalled from his perch in the Senate. It was impossible to get any joint work done with a body that, technically at least, did not yet exist. "There is no organization in the House, which is in a very curious state," Clay wrote to his son James on December 4. That was an understatement. The House was about to descend into chaos.

The next day, Zachary Taylor dispatched his first State of the Union message to Capitol Hill, where, in the tradition of the time, it was probably read to each chamber by a clerk. Taylor's presidency had begun auspiciously enough. Voters had opted for the safe center, it seemed, leaving the extremists of both the North and the South marginalized. But optimism soon faded. In part, Taylor personally lacked the gravitas that the political class expected in a chief executive. He liked to ramble the streets in battered old clothes, gawking at the markets and shop windows like a rube. Sophisticates snickered that his wife smoked a corncob pipe on the front porch of the White House. And his conversation was so excruciatingly awkward that visitors cringed. The man was *embarrassing*. Newly arrived Free Soil congressman George Julian of Indiana found to his surprise that he liked the president's "kindly, honest, farmer-like face, and his old fashioned simplicity of dress and manners." But he frequently mispronounced words, stammered, and sometimes simply broke down in the middle of a sentence, telling the nonplussed Julian after one particularly long silence, "I would like to visit Indiana, and see your plows and hoes." More to the point, he was an outsider with no personal base in Congress, or for that matter in the Whig Party, and no skill at the creative play of political negotiation. And he had already stunned the country by declaring unambiguously in a speech at Mercer, Pennsylvania, "The people of the North need have no further apprehension of the extension of slavery."

Taylor's address reviewed recent altercations with Britain over its navigation acts, relations with France, Mexico, and the German empire, the revolution in the Papal States, efforts to resolve lingering American claims against Portugal, the signing of several commercial treaties with Latin American states, proposals for a canal across Nicaragua to speed travel to the goldfields. The Sandwich Islands—Hawaii—should be supported in their efforts to remain independent, he declared. Tariff rates should be revised. Postage should be reduced to 5 cents per letter. Embedded in this litany was a subject that resonated more deeply with members of Congress, and had far wider implications for the territorial debate, than Taylor's terse words suggested. "Having been apprised that a considerable number of adventurers were engaged in fitting out a military expedition within the United States against a foreign country," he announced, "and believing from the best information I could obtain that it was destined to invade the island of Cuba . . ." *Cuba!* With this, the president signaled the beginning of what was to prove a long, extraordinarily tortured entanglement with the large and alluring island that lay tantalizingly off the tip of Florida. Taylor's rather fleeting reference to what had happened the previous summer hardly did justice to a gathering movement that was opening another front in the expansionist dreams of the slaveholding South, one that every senator and congressman knew had the potential not just to expand slavery's economic reach, but also to add one or more new states to slavery's power in Congress.

Cuba, to be sure, topped the to-do lists of most American imperialists, both North and South. As the *New York Herald* proclaimed in January 1849, Cuba "cannot resist the contagious spirit of the age." Southerners, however, had a special interest in the island. Cuba was the world's largest sugar producer, its international commerce was worth almost $50 million annually, its plantation agriculture was highly developed—and it was already full of slaves. Once Cuba was occupied by the United States, trade with the Mississippi Valley alone, it was predicted, would increase by a factor of ten and turn New Orleans into the Constantinople of the South. It was almost universally believed in the United States that Cuba was ripe for revolution, and that the Creoles, that is island-born whites of Spanish descent, would eagerly embrace annexation as the best way both to preserve their slaves, and to counter by force of American arms the dreaded prospect of a slave rising. Britain and France were known to be pressuring Spain to emancipate its Cuban slaves: if they succeeded, American defenders of slavery feared, it would set yet another subversive model of black emancipation in the Caribbean, added to Haiti and the British Caribbean islands. James Polk had tried to purchase Cuba outright, without success. If it couldn't be bought, expansionists proclaimed the shortest route to annexation lay by invasion, either by an American army or by proxy.

As if on schedule, history delivered the debonair, mustachioed, and histrionic Narciso López, a Venezuela-born soldier who had settled in Cuba, where he made and lost a fortune in farming and mining. His admirers, and many Americans were among them, found him magnetic, with dark eyes that fairly burned with greatness. In 1849, with financing from wealthy planters and Cuban émigrés, and the imprimatur of the apostle of Manifest Destiny, John L. O'Sullivan, López arrived in the United States, where he began cultivating support for a pro-annexationist revolution. In Washington, López met with Calhoun, who assured him that Cuba would "eventually drop into the lap of the Union," and introduced him to Jefferson Davis and Stephen Douglas, who in his capacity as chairman of the Committee on Territories, would have the job of pushing annexation through the Senate. A revolution would take place that summer, López told his new friends.

López first offered the command of his invasion force to Davis, promising him $100,000 immediately, and another $100,000 (or a coffee plantation) after the invasion succeeded. Davis, newly elected to the Senate, politely declined, but suggested that López approach a certain promising captain of engineers who had performed brilliantly during the Mexican War, Robert E. Lee, who was sufficiently interested to meet with López but deemed the project incompatible with his status as a serving officer of the U.S. Army. In the end, López decided to lead the expedition himself. By midsummer, eight hundred "reckless adventurers," as one naval officer called them, had arrived at Round Island, a scrubby patch of sand and marsh off Pascagoula, Mississippi, having been promised $7 a month pay, a $1,000 bonus after a year's service, and "plenty of plunder, drink, women, and tobacco."

This was too much for President Taylor, who had no fondness for freelancing warriors—he had seen plenty of the type on the Texas frontier—and no desire for a war with Spain in order to extend slavery. Although he didn't say so in so many words to Congress, he saw no great difference between slaveholders' ambitions in the deserts of New Mexico and in the Caribbean. On August 11, Taylor denounced the expedition as a violation of the Neutrality Act, and ordered a naval blockade of Round Island. Any American citizen participating in the expedition would be liable to a $3,000 fine and three years in prison. The president's forceful measures had the desired effect. By the end of September, nearly all of López's hungry, thirsty, mosquito-bitten, and bored army had melted away. "The expedition has been suppressed," Taylor told Congress in his State of the Union. This was not the last that Americans would hear of López, however.

Finally Taylor came to the question of the western territories. "No civil government having been provided by Congress for California, the people of that Territory," he said, "impelled by the necessities of their political condition"—that is, virtual anarchy—were about to apply for admission into the Union. "Should such be the case, and should their constitution be conformable to the requisitions of the Constitution of the United States, I recommend their application to the favorable consideration of Congress." Taylor then said that he expected the people of New Mexico to soon apply for statehood, too, and that he would look favorably on their application. "By awaiting their action all causes of uneasiness may be avoided and confidence and kind feeling preserved," he promised. Taylor went on to discuss administrative matters—the dispatch of an officer to collect customs duties at San Francisco, the establishment of a federal mint there, the rationalization of Indian land titles in both California and New Mexico—but that was like picking through the fragments of an exploded bomb. Taylor was committed to statehood for both California and New Mexico, and he wanted as little debate about it as possible. There was to be no compromise. In essence, he intended to give the North the substance of the Wilmot Proviso—which sought to ban slavery from the new territories taken from Mexico—without making the South swallow it as an established principle.

"For more than half a century, during which kingdoms and empires have fallen, this Union has stood unshaken," Taylor concluded. "Upon its preservation must depend our own happiness and that of countless generations to come. Whatever dangers may threaten it, I shall stand by it and maintain it in its integrity to the full extent of the obligations imposed and the powers conferred on me by the Constitution." Although his words had the ring of boilerplate, he was a simple man whose belief in the transcendental spirit of the Union trumped everything else, including sectional interest and slavery, and he meant what he said. At a time when some of the nation's leading men were threatening disunion, he was making it clear that he would not surrender to the bullying—or treason—of the South's slave owners, and would defend the Union at all costs. He stood as he had on the battlefield of Buena Vista, fairly daring the enemy to attack.

CHAPTER 9

DEADLOCK

———— •◆• ————

Balloting for the speaker of the house resumed on December 5, and continued throughout the day. By the fourteenth ballot, it was clear that Cobb was in trouble when he received only 89 votes to Winthrop's 99. The roll was called again and again. Winthrop's numbers inched upward to 100, then 101, as Cobb's dropped to 66 and then to 63. By December 8, on the twenty-fifth ballot, Winthrop had reached 102, while Cobb had plummeted to just 9, as southerners seemed to recognize that as much as they wanted the Georgian, he would never attract enough crossover votes to be elected.

The Free Soilers could easily have pushed Winthrop over the top. They made it clear to the Whig leadership that they would throw their weight behind him if he would support Wilmot's proviso. But he wouldn't, and the Free Soilers stubbornly continued to cast their votes for Wilmot. In essence, they were playing chicken, trying to force the reluctant Whig mainstream to embrace more radical antislavery positions, predicated on their belief that the South's blustering talk of disunion was just "mock thunder" that, Giddings gibed, "has ceased to frighten [even] the nervous misses at our boarding schools," and had "become the jest of our schoolboys." But Giddings was wrong. The South was in earnest.

Nerves were fraying. An atmosphere of unease and menace pervaded the Capitol. Just before the opening of Congress, a slave who worked in the Capitol's restaurant learned that he was to be sold into the Deep South and had attempted unsuccessfully to escape; before his captors realized what he was doing, he pulled a knife from his pocket and cut his own throat. Then, on the 6th, a madman named Robinson was arrested for threatening to kill Henry Clay on the floor of the Senate. Clay was unhurt. But it left legislators jumpy and worried.

Frustration and disgust percolated through the House. The situation was "ridiculous," declared Isaac Morse, a Louisiana Democrat. Why not just put Winthrop's and Cobb's names in a hat, and let the clerk be blindfolded and just pick one of them? he proposed. Couldn't the House do better than select its leader by means of a virtual lottery? scoffed Free Soiler Joseph Root of Ohio. More practical suggestions were made—that the candidate with a plurality of votes become speaker, or that the last session's speaker (that is, Winthrop) be invited to preside temporarily, until a new speaker was elected—but these were dismissed as unprecedented and unhelpful. Members knew that too much was at stake to acquiesce in a stopgap measure.

If a wealthy plantation owner like Cobb could not be elected, some southerners now reasoned, their best strategy was to promote a "dough-face," that is, a "northern man with southern principles," a free state Democrat who would protect the interests of the South and deflect the antislavery legislation that everyone expected to be introduced into Congress. That candidate was William J. Brown, an amiable party stalwart from Indiana who had served without distinction as a second assistant postmaster general under Polk, and was best known for his fund of anecdotes and friendliness toward slavery. On December 11, Brown started out with a solid 80 votes on the thirty-third ballot. By the thirty-seventh, he had leapt past Winthrop—now stuck at 101—to win 109 votes on the thirty-ninth ballot. Winthrop, realizing that he was in as hopeless a position as Cobb had been in a few days before, abruptly withdrew his name from consideration. It was the Whigs who were now thrown into consternation. They began thrashing about for a new candidate. On the fortieth ballot, Brown received 112 votes, just 2 short of election. (More members having arrived, it now required 114 votes to win.)

Curiously, a number of congressmen noted, five of the firmest Free Soilers, including both Wilmot and Giddings, had voted for Brown, who represented precisely the sort of craven acquiescence to the South that they claimed to despise. What was going on?

No one had mentioned slavery up to now, but the shadow play was over. All that had been held back now would be said. The catalyst was the rumor—it was quite accurate—that the Free Soilers had been dickering behind the scenes with the Democrats, their worst enemies. Who could believe it?

In fact, intensive deal making had taken place. There had been letters exchanged, assurances given. Brown had apparently agreed to appoint Free Soilers to important committees, where they would gain a national platform for their incendiary views in return for their votes. He had even conferred with Wilmot himself.

Big-bellied and ill-kempt, Wilmot was a man of modest demeanor and modest accomplishments, who sometimes seemed startled that his proviso had become the pivot on which the fate of the Union turned. "All that I, and those associated with me, asked or desired was to give expression to the great public sentiment of the people of the country," the Free Soiler now explained. Brown had merely assured him that he would appoint "men who would not give their aid to stifle the expression of the sentiments of the people of the North."

"What public 'sentiment' was that?" Edward Stanly, a North Carolina Whig, asked.

"It is that slavery shall go no further," Wilmot blandly replied.

The cat was out of the bag. Brown, the reliable doughface, had committed himself to Wilmot's proviso.

"Minorities, however small, deserved to be represented," Wilmot added.

In a country that proclaimed so loudly and incessantly the perfection of its democracy, there should have been nothing exceptional in this. Except that for decades the South had worked, with considerable success, to suppress discussion of slavery in any form, and in every public forum that it could control. The notion that Free Soilers (forget outright abolitionists) deserved to be represented on committees where they might actually affect legislation or influence the public bordered on subversion.

Brown attempted to protest his fairness to all sections, but Democrats rose to express their shame and indignation. *Betrayal! Deception! Fraud!* Even in ordinary times, the acoustics in the chamber made it difficult for members to hear each other in the normal course of debate. Now, with hoots, shouts, threats, and catcalls flying in every direction, it was impossible. Brown was finished as a candidate, and withdrew his name from consideration, joining the growing scrap heap of other failed contenders.

What would it mean if, for the first time in its history, the House failed to elect a speaker? What would Americans think? What would foreigners think? "The country is alarmed," worried James Thompson, a Pennsylvania Democrat. "It will go forth to the world that dangers exist in organizing the Congress of the United States. It will be felt everywhere." The world would see weakness and division, a failed government, a failed state, a nation no longer capable of governing itself.

Virginian Richard K. Meade, a forty-six-year-old Democratic lawyer from Petersburg, now rose to say what most southerners had been thinking all along. For many days now the House had been enduring a "farce" that was becoming less and less entertaining. The root of the problem was fear of the introduction of bills that would produce "agitation on a question which threatens the peace and integrity of the country—bills which, if passed, will either destroy this Confederacy, or enslave a large portion if it." When Meade, a disciple of John C. Calhoun, spoke of "slavery" he was of course not objecting to the enslavement of African Americans, but asserting that any restriction on the expansion of slavery amounted to the "enslavement" of the South by northern tyranny. "Let a proposition be made and supported by those who are desirous of crushing this demon of discord," he went on. It was time for the conservatives of both parties to come together to block any measure that led to the abolition of slavery in the District of Columbia, or a prohibition of it in the western territories. The passage of any such bills, he warned, would sound the death knell of the Union. In words that would ring in the air for months to come, he stated: "If these outrages are to be committed upon my people, I trust in God, sir, that my eyes have rested upon the last Speaker of the House of Representatives." The menace in his voice was inescapable. "If these measures be passed," he said, "there will be but one determination at the South—one solemn resolve to defend their homes and maintain their honor. Let the issue come when it may, and you will find every southern sinew converted into a spring of steel." If there were any southern men who would refuse to stand by their "country" in such an emergency . . .

"There are none!" shouted a chorus of southern voices.

". . . he would not merely be execrated by his own people, but his own children would heap curses upon his grave," Meade concluded.

Events were slipping out of control. Why not vote by secret ballot, someone suggested. Party leaders scotched that idea: it was already hard enough to keep their members in line on open ballots. Someone else suggested electing a speaker but depriving him of the power to appoint the members of controversial committees. This, mocked a disgusted Ohioan, would be like staging *Hamlet* with the part of Hamlet himself omitted.

At this point one of the House's most patrician members, William Duer, an antislavery Whig, scion of an old New York banking family, and grandson of one of Alexander Hamilton's closest associates, rose to speak. The exasperation in his voice was palpable. He declared that after nine fruitless days he was prepared to organize in any way at all, and give his vote to a Whig, a Democrat, a Free Soiler, or anyone else except a "disunionist."

"There are no disunionists in this House," Thomas Bayly of Virginia pompously piped up.

"I wish I could think so," Duer tartly replied.

"Who are they? Point them out!" Bayly challenged.

"I think I see one of them now," Duer replied, pointing directly to Meade.

"It is false!" retorted Meade, who had of course just completed a speech explicitly threatening secession.

"You are a liar, sir!" Duer exclaimed.

Meade thereupon rushed at Duer, and was only with difficulty dragged back by his friends, as was Duer by his, before they could come to blows. "Shoot him! Shoot him!" Meade's friends urged. "Where is your bowie knife?" Bedlam erupted, with voices on every side uttering threats, demanding order, calling for immediate adjournment. Visitors from the gallery swarmed onto the floor and joined the melee. "The House was like a heaving billow," the *Congressional Globe* reported. "The clerk called to order, but there were none to heed him." Finally the sergeant-at-arms of the previous session, a man with the quaintly coincidental name of Nathan Sergeant, plunged into the fray brandishing over his head the chamber's huge ceremonial mace, a hoary artifact based on the ancient Roman fasces, a bundle of rods surmounted by an eagle with its wings outstretched.

"Take away the mace, it has no authority here!" voices cried.

But it had some effect. The sergeant-at-arms stood by Duer's side, as if to protect him, and gradually the tumult began to subside. The visitors were pushed out of the chamber, and a fragile sense of order was restored. Duer, regaining the floor, declared that his party—the Whigs—would not make an "unconditional surrender," and abruptly sat down, disheveled and unnerved. In the eyes of many, the scene they had just witnessed presaged a total national disintegration.

In the aftermath of this traumatic event, one of the South's leading men rose to speak. Robert Toombs of Georgia had made a fortune in slaves and real estate, but had campaigned as a Unionist against the radical southern nationalism of Calhoun and his followers. The large, hollow-eyed Toombs and his close ally and fellow Georgia Whig, the wizened and intellectual Alexander Stephens, had for years assured the people of their state and the wider South that their interests would be better protected in a unified country than in an independent but weak southern one, that their allies in the North would remain steadfast in the South's defense. Both Toombs and Stephens commanded respect on both sides of the aisle. As Whig support eroded in the South, their loyalty was also increasingly crucial to the party.

Stephens and Toombs had enthusiastically supported Zachary Taylor's candidacy, and had been instrumental in shaping Taylor's campaign persona as a political blank slate acceptable to all segments of the electorate. They were shocked when, in the summer of 1849, Taylor had remarked that he considered slavery a moral and political evil, and vowed that he had no intention of permitting slavery to move west. The Whigs were subsequently crushed in the autumn's state elections, a grim harbinger of their fate across the South if they failed to stop the administration's worrisome antislavery drift. By the time Congress met in December, the Georgians had come to believe that Taylor was determined to betray the slaveholders who had sent him to the White House. They had pleaded within the Whig caucus for a resolution that explicitly committed the party to oppose any law against limiting the movement of slavery into the western territories or abolishing slavery in the national capital. When the caucus failed to act as they demanded, Toombs, Stephens, and four other southern Whigs walked out, and pretty much out of the Whig Party as well.

Toombs's black, uncombed hair stood out from his massive head as if charged with electricity, "his eyes glowing like coals of fire, and his sentences rattling forth like volleys of musketry," in the words of one eyewitness, as he addressed the (in his view) intransigent men of the North. "I do not hesitate to avow before this House and the country, and in the presence of the living God, that if by your legislation you seek to drive us from the territories of California and New Mexico, purchased by the common blood and treasure of the whole people, and abolish slavery in this District, thereby attempting to fix a national degradation upon half the States of this Confederacy, *I am for disunion*"—he virtually shouted the words—"and if my physical courage be equal to the maintenance of my convictions of right and duty, I will devote all I am and all I have on earth to its consummation." Since 1787, he said, the South had asked nothing but justice. But the "great constitutional right" to reclaim fugitive slaves had been repeatedly violated. The District of Columbia had been a gift of the slave state of Maryland, which had trusted the nation's founders to protect the rights of its slave owners. "Your fathers accepted the trust," he said. "[I]t was left to their degenerate sons to break their faith with us." Now the opponents of slavery were attempting to appropriate the entire West for themselves. Provide guarantees for the protection of slavery, and he would cooperate with his party. "Refuse them and, as far as I am concerned, let discord reign forever."

Wild bursts of applause rang through the chamber, and one after another a procession of southerners recited the now familiar litany of perceived wrongs and abuse that their section had suffered at the hands of the tyrannical North.

The balloting went on and on, with no end in sight. On December 13, the forty-first ballot recorded 59 for Winthrop and 40 for Cobb, both of whom had formally withdrawn from the contest. The rest were scattered among twenty-eight different candidates. David Wilmot rarely received more than 8 or 9 votes. On the forty-second ballot, Linn Boyd of Kentucky, a potential compromise candidate, jumped to 51, Winthrop dropped to 36, and Cobb to just 18. On the forty-fourth ballot, Boyd climbed to 82, and Winthrop slipped further to 27. And so it went. Nearly three weeks had now passed. The solution, such as it was, was both unprecedented and desperate, as befitted the posture of men gazing into an abyss. It was proposed that if no candidate received an outright majority in the course of three ballots, then on the next ballot whoever received a plurality would be declared the next speaker of the house. No candidate received a majority on the next three ballots, so, in accordance with the resolution, the winner of the next ballot needed only a plurality to become speaker. The sixty-third roll call began, and when it was done, Cobb had received 102 votes and was declared the new speaker of the house. The slaveholding South had once again prevailed. And the anti-slavery movement had shown that it had the power to cripple moderate Whigs, in a foretaste of countless political contests that would take place in the northern states in the years to come.

Henry Clay, for one, was relieved at Cobb's election. "It was so much more important that the House should be organized than whether a Whig or Democrat should be chosen," Clay wrote to his son James. At last Congress could get down to business, and leave the field clear for the all-encompassing assault on the nation's intractable dilemma that was forming in Clay's capacious mind. Not all Americans were so sanguine. From Maine to Louisiana, Americans were dismayed, frightened, and angry by what was happening in Washington. "Madness rules the hour," wrote the New York diarist Philip Hone. "Faction, personal recrimination, and denunciation prevail, and men for the first time in our history do not hesitate openly to threaten a dissolution of the Union. Well, be it so; if faction is to prevail, and the South can get along without us, the sooner the issue comes the better."

CHAPTER 10

THE GODLIKE DANIEL

———•◆•———

On New Year's Day 1850 a huge crowd gathered at the White House for the president's open house, a tradition stretching back to the early years of the republic. No one was turned away. Senators and congressmen, Democrats, Whigs, Free Soilers, southern nationalists and abolitionists mingled in democratic and vulnerable abandon—it was reported that "several gentlemen lost their pocketbooks, containing small sums of money; and a valuable gold watch was taken from the belt of a lady." Meanwhile, Henry Clay, shunning the gaiety a few blocks away, brooded gloomily in his suite at the National Hotel. Every letter from home seemed to announce a new problem. His wife, Lucretia, was ill and depressed. His son Thomas's debts were an ongoing embarrassment. The weather was rotten. Mules had to be sent to Georgia for sale. Cholera had swept off several of the slaves, and the overseer was having trouble finding replacements. "If there be no better alternative, I suppose that I shall be obliged to purchase one or two young men, if good ones can be bought," Clay irritatedly wrote back. Above all, however, he brooded on the fate of the Union. "No certain developments are yet made of what Congress may do on the vexed subject of slavery," he wrote on January 2 to his son James. "I have been thinking much of proposing some comprehensive scheme of settling amicably the whole question, in all its bearings but

I have not yet positively determined to do so. Meantime some of the Hotspurs of the South are openly declaring themselves for a dissolution of the Union, if the Wilmot Proviso be adopted." He woke every morning wracked by apprehension. There must be a solution: there always had been. He would probably never be president, he supposed, but he could still save the Union.

The House's acrimonious wrangling over its speaker—Clay knew this, everyone knew it—was only the prelude to what would happen in the Senate. That body was also split, with thirty-four Democrats, twenty-four Whigs, and two Free Soilers. However, these official divisions included both proslavery and antislavery Whigs and Democrats, whose passions and polar ideologies trumped party loyalty, making it impossible for anyone to predict, much less control, the outcome of debate. The Senate's semicircular chamber did not suffer from acoustical problems, although the hubbub of visitors in the lobby sometimes reached the floor. Mottled gray Ionic columns rose behind the vice president's tall chair, which stood on an elevated dais beneath a crimson canopy adorned with a bronze eagle, and above it, on the wall, a portrait of George Washington. The senators' mahogany desks formed concentric arcs on carpeted platforms, one long-armed chair and a cuspidor for each senator. The admission of new states had more than doubled the size of the Senate since the Capitol's construction, which meant that sixty men had been shoehorned into a space designed for half that number. So tightly were the desks jammed together that during debates, particularly when visitors spilled over from the gallery onto the floor, senators who preferred to move around when they spoke, as Clay did, had a hard time maneuvering, and when they turned to address the body from the well in front of the vice president's throne they stood nearly on the boots of their colleagues in the first row.

The opening days of the session were deceptively, lullingly businesslike. Then the demon issue intruded. David Atchison, a proslavery Democrat from Missouri, read into the record a series of resolutions that had just been passed by his state legislature. Atchison was merely reporting these to the Senate, as members often did with legislation from their home states. But it was the opening salvo—like artillery testing the enemy's range. He matter-of-factly announced that Missouri wished to remind Congress that it had no authority to legislate on the subject of slavery . . . that the territories conquered from Mexico were the common property of all the states . . . that the North's "conduct" with respect to slavery had released slaveholding states from any further obligation to compromise with them . . . Like an answering barrage, Senator William Upham of Vermont then read a set of resolutions that had just been passed by *his* state urging Vermont's senators and House members to resist the extension of slavery, to ban it from the District of Columbia, and to work for the establishment of free governments in the western territories. "Resolved," Upham read stentorously, "Slavery is a crime against humanity, and a sore evil in the body politic . . ."

David Yulee of Florida, with the slaveholders' customary resort to double standards, demanded that the Vermont resolutions be suppressed immediately, fuming that "the language with which these resolutions open is more violent, offensive, opprobrious, and reprehensible, than any ever before presented to this body." Following him, one after another proslavery senators stormed that in the face of such "insults" the time for conciliation and compromise was past. "Argument has been exhausted," declared Solon Borland of Arkansas. "I cannot argue with the robber, who meets me upon the highway and demands my purse; I cannot argue with the assassin, who seeks to stab me in the dark; I cannot argue with the midnight incendiary, who stands ready to apply the torch to my dwelling, and to consume my wife and children." Jeremiah Clemens of Alabama went even further. The value of slave property in the South exceeded $900 million, he asserted—a fantastic sum in 1850. What people would ever agree to the "destruction" of such vast wealth without a long and desperate struggle? "We do not intend to stand still and have our throats cut because the butcher chooses to soothe us under the operation with honeyed words," he raged. "I now proclaim that you"—he was speaking to all the North—"have reached the utmost limit to which you can go. There is a line beyond which you must not pass. You have marched up to it, and now cross it if you dare."

Jefferson Davis was even more blunt. With respect to slavery, the

forty-one-year-old lord of a rich cotton-growing plantation near Vicksburg was a true believer. Human bondage, he maintained, was fully
justified by the Bible, validated by the U.S. Constitution, and a blessing
for the slaves themselves, since they had been delivered from human "sacrifice" by the barbarians of their African homeland. Although a lusterless
orator, his aggressiveness in the Mexican War and his tireless campaigning for his fellow Mississippi Democrats had won him many friends.
"Davis is one of those brilliant meteors that shoots along and illuminates
the military horizon of the world, at intervals, long and far between,"
one swooning Mississippi editorialist purred. Though a newcomer to the
Senate, he had been named chairman of the powerful Military Affairs
Committee immediately upon his arrival. Dogmatic, humorless, and stoically tight-lipped—the lingering result, perhaps, of a Mexican bullet that
had driven pieces of his spur into his ankle, leaving a wound that never
properly healed—more admired than loved, Davis was expected by many
southerners to storm forward with the banner of southern nationalism
that was falling from Calhoun's enfeebled hand. (Not all southerners:
there was no love lost between him and his Mississippi colleague Henry
Foote.) No power known in the world could dictate "to my little state,"
Davis declared to the Senate, adding menacingly, "If this is to be the hotbed of civil war, if from this as a center the evil is to radiate throughout
our country, here let the first battle be fought!"

Calhoun's South Carolina colleague Andrew P. Butler, indicating
that the South did not intend to pursue a passive strategy, introduced a
bill to radically toughen the Fugitive Slave Law of 1793. His target was
the Underground Railroad. Respect for the existing law had deteriorated
shockingly, Butler complained. Barely twenty years ago a southern man
could go to New York and seize a runaway slave almost as easily as in
Charleston. Since then, northern states had enacted intolerable laws
declaring that fugitives could not be arrested without a warrant, and
imposing unconscionable penalties on honest masters who were simply
attempting to recover their property. (Known in the North as "personal
liberty laws," these statutes generally guaranteed to alleged fugitives the

rights of habeas corpus, legal representation, and trial by jury; in 1842, the Supreme Court had declared such laws unconstitutional, but the federal government lacked the personnel to enforce the Fugitive Slave Law in communities that refused to cooperate.) Butler's bill would empower any master or his hired agent to arrest an alleged fugitive, and to bring him (or her) before any federal official—including local postmasters—who on the basis of "oral testimony" would be required to remand the fugitive back to the state from which he had escaped; anyone who obstructed the recapture of a fugitive, or assisted in his escape, would be fined $1,000.

To these provisions, James Mason of Virginia proposed adding two even more draconian amendments: first, that half the fine should be paid to any informer who brought such "miscarriage of justice"—that is, assistance lent to a fugitive—to the attention of the authorities; and, second, that in no hearing under the act should the testimony of any fugitive be admitted as evidence. Hundreds of millions of dollars' worth of property was subject to "wanton depredation" by the people of the free states, Mason alleged. Speaking of Pennsylvania and Ohio, he asserted, "It is just as impossible to recover a fugitive slave now in either of those states as it would be to bring him up from the depths of the sea." If a stricter law was not enough, he urged that "reprisals" be taken against the property of the citizens of the offending state. He further proposed creation of what was essentially a national police state, including a system of ubiquitous surveillance, and an ongoing dragnet to catch escaping slaves, carried out by a permanent force "to be located at every point, in every county of the non-slaveholding states."

Throughout January, an atmosphere of violence insinuated itself, sometimes subtly, sometimes stridently, into debate, ratcheting pragmatic disagreement into threat and confrontation. Benton initiated the first of many collisions with the prickly, chronically overheated Henry Foote when he proposed cutting troublemaking Texas in half. "She is too large, either for her own convenience or for the proper equality and well-being of the other States," he charged. The western lands that she claimed would become federal property, the border crisis with New Mexico would evaporate and, as the reward for acquiescence, the South would gain two more senators from the new state. A few days earlier, Foote himself had introduced a somewhat similar bill, which would have provided territorial governments for California, New Mexico, and Mormon "Deseret," and also have created a new state from western Texas, which Foote dubbed "Jacinto."

Even on good days, Foote's natural posture was one of rhetorical apoplexy. And he absolutely hated Benton: he hated his politics, he hated his vacillation on slavery, and he probably hated his towering, bullying bulk. Now he accused Benton of stealing his bill, and then of carrying out a sort of sneak attack on slavery. During an almost unbelievably vicious ad hominem harangue, he as good as called Benton a coward, a liar, an abolitionist, a fraud, and a boor given to language "of the coarsest scurrility and most envenomed abuse." He even accused Benton, a slaveowner himself, of using such inflammatory Free Soil rhetoric that it inspired scores of Missouri slaves to drop their hoes and run away to Illinois. Benton, a practiced duelist, usually did not take this sort of thing lying down. (In 1813, he had almost killed Andrew Jackson in a barroom fracas.) On this day, however, he got up from his seat and, with uncharacteristic restraint, stalked silently out of the chamber. Foote was left holding the field, for the moment.

President Taylor, meanwhile, was under almost continuous attack from southern senators who demanded to know if he was responsible for those provocative and suspect pleas for statehood that were coming out of California and New Mexico. How had those delegates to the California convention been elected anyway? *Were they even elected?* What authority did they have? Was the president himself behind the recent events in Santa Fe? Had that so-called convention there been held at his prompting? Taylor was no diplomat, and he was tough. He treated his congressional assailants as if they were oncoming Mexican columns. On January 21, in a letter sent to both houses of Congress, he admitted that, yes, he had communicated to "the people" of California and New Mexico that each territory should adopt a state constitution and submit it to Congress with a request for admission to the Union. But he denied authorizing the establishment of any new governments without the consent of Congress. And he had not ordered either the Californians or the New Mexicans to bar slavery. (This was a bit disingenuous; Taylor had, in fact, dispatched agents to both California and New Mexico who had indicated that the administration would approve free soil constitutions.)

Under the Constitution, Taylor went on, every state had the right to alter its "domestic institutions" however it wished. If it made slavery illegal, so be it. Moreover, he added, had New Mexico already been admitted to the Union, its border dispute with Texas would be moot, a matter for the courts to calmly resolve rather than a reason for war. Even if Congress forced slavery on a territory, once admitted to the Union it could rewrite its laws and ban it again, if it so wished. (It seems to have eluded Taylor that the reverse of this was also true.) The inhabitants of the rest of the territory that had been ceded by Mexico—that is, "Deseret"—would likewise decide for themselves what they wanted to do about slavery. If Congress left well enough alone, the situation "which now excites such painful sensations in the country" would sort itself out. Had Taylor enjoyed control of Congress, this might have been the end of the matter. *It was clear what California and New Mexico wanted, and by God, they would have it!* But he had few friends there at all, and none who were willing to stick their necks out for him.

Bundled against the damp chill, Henry Clay left the National Hotel, turned north on Fifth Street, and walked one block up the slight hill to the three-story brick building at 503 D Street, the home of Daniel Webster. Clay and the senior senator from Massachusetts had known each other for thirty-six years, since Webster's arrival in the House of Representatives during Clay's reign as speaker. Like Clay, Webster had long aspired to the presidency, and for that matter still did, and like the Kentuckian had repeatedly been frustrated. (Webster had come close, too, having been offered the vice presidency by William Henry Harrison, but disdained it as second-best.) There was no warmth between them—they were too outsized, too self-centered, too rivalrous for that—but Webster was the closest to a peer that Clay had in the Whig Party. Clay needed his help if the grand plan of compromise congealing in his weary mind was to work.

Webster was, in the eyes of those who admired him, and of many who didn't, a figure of Olympian proportions, magnetic, seductive, terrifying when aroused. Often called the Godlike Daniel, it was a name many felt fitted him as perfectly as the fine black broadcloth that he favored. Webster, alone among the sixty senators, was permitted to keep a private hideaway in the Capitol, his "wine room," where he could tipple at leisure with his friends. Physically, he was a massive man, broad-shouldered, deep-chested, with a head, wrote Oliver Dyer, who covered Congress for the *National Intelligencer*, that was "phenomenal in size, and beauty of outline, and grandeur of appearance." His sunken eyes seemed to burn like great lamps set deep in the mouths of caves, it was said, and during the heat of argument, he seemed to glow like the burnished surface of ancient statuary. When he appeared in the Senate voices dropped and heads turned, as he moved across the floor with majestic tread.

His speeches were major public events, erudite, artfully crafted, thrillingly theatrical, a seamless tapestry of minute detail and grand principle. "His voice," recalled Dyer, like deep bass notes on an organ, simultaneously was "resonant, mellow, sweet, with a thunder roll in it which, when let out to its full power, was awe inspiring." For dramatic effect, he had a way of magnifying a word with such prodigious volume and force that it would drop from his lips "as a great boulder might drop through the ceiling, and jar the Senate chamber like a clap of thunder." His ringing refutation of Nullification in 1830 was still widely cited as the best speech ever delivered in the Senate. "When my eyes shall be turned to behold for the last time the sun in heaven!" he had cried on that occasion, "but everywhere, spread all over in characters of living light, blazing on all its ample folds, as they float over the sea and over the land, and in every wind under the whole heavens, that other sentiment, dear to every true American heart,—Liberty and Union, now and forever, one and inseparable!"

Webster was deeply conservative, and advocated forcefully on behalf of New England manufacturers and shipping interests, which paid him generous "retainers" beyond his Senate salary. In his younger years, he had also enjoyed a reputation as an eloquent antislavery man. In 1820, on the bicentennial of the Pilgrims' landing, he had stood upon the sacred altar of Plymouth Rock and invoked the spirit of his Puritan forefathers in a famous denunciation of New England's entanglement in the "odious and abominable" slave trade, through its investment in shipping and in the manufacturing of products that were of use to slave traders and slave masters. "It is not fit that the land of the Pilgrims should bear the shame longer," he memorably declared. "I hear the sound of the hammer, I see the smoke of the furnaces where the manacles and fetters are still forged for human limbs." It was one of the gems of antislavery oratory.

But time and history were passing Webster by. His antislavery speeches belonged to an era characterized by ringing moral pronouncements that required little action on the part of those who espoused them. Although he considered slavery unjust, he maintained, as Clay did, that it was the exclusive responsibility of the states. He loathed "agitation," and advised Americans both white and black to be patient, and wait for the "mild influences of Christianity" to remove the problem in accordance with God's inscrutable plan. All this was perfectly acceptable to the Yankee businessmen among whom he nestled, as well as to most southerners, but it was profoundly out of touch with the flood tide of radical abolitionism that was sweeping New England, much of it emanating from his own city of Boston. Legendary though he might still be, Webster's best days were behind him. At sixty-seven, five years younger than Clay, he was chronically depressed, deeply in debt, and bloated by drink.

Clay was also ill, and coughed almost continuously during the hour he spent at Webster's home. Step by step, he laid out the components of his plan. He accounted for everything: California, New Mexico, the Texas border, the slave trade in Washington, southerners' concerns over fugitive slaves. Webster was probably the first person to hear Clay's strategy in full. The two men found themselves in close agreement. Like Clay, Webster opposed extending slavery westward, but considered it stupid to gratuitously irritate the South by banning slavery where it was unlikely to go naturally. At least some Democrats and most Whigs—excepting a few "violent" radicals from both North and South—would back the plan, Webster ventured. He promised Clay his complete support. Clay went back out into the night with a surge of hope.

Preoccupied with his grand strategy, Clay rarely intervened in the debates that month. However, three days after his tête-à-tête with Webster, he asked for the floor. Given the inflammatory atmosphere, his tone was almost startlingly emotional. He had just that morning learned, he said, that a manuscript copy of George Washington's Farewell Address had become available for purchase, and he urged Congress to buy it for its library. It was one thing to celebrate the nation's great men in story, "yet some physical memorial of them, some tangible, palpable object, always addresses itself to our hearts and to our feelings," he told his fellow senators. This was an atypical view at a time when relatively few Americans regarded the artifacts of the past as worth preserving. At Ashland, he said, in his own "humble parlor" he cherished a broken goblet that Washington had used throughout the Revolutionary War. Yes, these were mere objects. But they had the power to inspire and, though he didn't say this in so many words, also to heal. Clay reminded his audience of Washington's solemn warning "to beware of sectional divisions, to beware of demagogues, to beware of the consequences of the indulgence of a spirit of disunion." Although no one would yet admit to such sentiments, there were among Clay's listeners men who, perhaps, were already envisioning themselves as the founding fathers of a new southern nation that would supersede Washington's.

Congress would approve the purchase, but not before Jefferson Davis pointedly complained that, in his opinion, Congress had enough Washington memorabilia already—there was nothing more to be gained from the proferred manuscript than from some walking stick that Washington might have used. "No benefit can result to the country, or the people generally, from the ownership of these sheets of manuscript," Davis drawled. "We are utilitarians, and it is not in keeping with that character to be led away by sentiment." He might just as well have been describing his views on slavery.

If Clay imagined that his gentle prodding toward conciliation would have much effect on the fire-eaters, he was mistaken. That very afternoon, the deceptively avuncular-looking Andrew Butler, whose unruly white hair was surpassed for dramatic effect only by Calhoun's, made it clear that he considered the South done with compromise. "Oh! That word compromise, it has ruined a confiding people!" Butler exclaimed, in tones of intertwined grievance and militancy that often imbued southern rhetoric. Compromise, he said, "has been proposed by craft and adopted by generosity; it has subserved the ends of one party, and has been used, not as a shield, but as a sword or a serpent, to strike or bite the party that submitted to it in confiding honesty." Repeatedly, he charged, the South had foolishly trusted in northern honor, only to be victimized by the "insolent" northern majority—a majority that was destined only to grow as Minnesota, Nebraska, California, New Mexico, and "Deseret" all became states. Turning to his fellow southern senators, he demanded, how long would they permit the South to remain a victim? "They will never be stronger than they are now; they will certainly be weaker. Is it to be supposed that we are to stand by while, I may say, the sections are in battle array, and see battalion after battalion marching over to the enemy without firing upon them?" In conclusion, he cried, "Equality or Independence!"

Clay knew that he had his work cut out for him.

CHAPTER 11

"A GREAT SOUL ON FIRE"

———— ·◆· ————

On January 29, Clay was at last ready to deliver the grand plan that he had been working on. The cathedral-like compromise that he had constructed in his mind had room enough in it, he was convinced, for the interests of both North and South. But whether he had the physical strength to fight the battle through to the end he could not be sure. He felt so depleted that when he arrived at the Capitol he had to pause to rest several times as he climbed its steps, and then again as he made his way through the crowds that pressed around him outside the Senate chamber. Clay's speeches were great oratorical events. His language was simple, his eloquence translucent, and his voice full, rich, clear, sweet, musical, and as inspiring as a trumpet. "He spoke to an audience very much as an ardent lover speaks to his sweetheart when pleading for her hand," recalled Oliver Dyer. "As he set forth proposition after proposition with increasing energy and fire, his tall form would seem to grow taller and taller with each new statement, until it reached a supernatural height; his eyes flashed and his hair waved wildly about his head; his long arms swept through the air; every lineament of his countenance spoke and glowed, until the beholder might imagine that he saw a great soul on fire." All eyes turned to watch as he rose from his desk in the last row of the chamber, where he sat with unintended but appropriate sectional symbolism between William H. Seward of New York, and William C. Dawson of Georgia, and loped to the front of the chamber.

He intended, Clay said, to "propose an amicable arrangement of all questions between the free and slave States, growing out of the subject of slavery." He then methodically unfurled eight resolutions that, taken together, formed "a great national scheme of compromise and harmony."

It was one of the great moments in Senate history, when one of the finest orators to grace the chamber spread before that august if often bellicose body one of the most complex, far-reaching, and politically fraught pieces of legislation that it had ever confronted. The chamber fell uncharacteristically silent. Not a soul doubted that he, or she—there were all those swooning admirers in the visitors' gallery—was witnessing history in the making. And they weren't wrong. If ever a speech could change the course of the country, to deflect it from its careening slide toward a collision of epic proportions, this, they hoped, would be it.

First, Clay proposed that California be admitted to the Union with no restriction on slavery imposed upon it by Congress. What that meant—it was what the opponents of slavery's expansion had been demanding, and what the South feared—was that Congress should accept California with whatever laws it had enacted for itself. California would thus come in as a free state. Unless Congress acted quickly, Clay underscored, "scenes of disorder, confusion, and anarchy" would soon take over. (In fact, they already nearly had.)

He then moved on to the other western territories. Since slavery did not exist and was unlikely to be introduced into either New Mexico or "Deseret," Clay asserted in his twanging drawl, it was "inexpedient"— a weasly but useful word that!—for Congress to either exclude or introduce it there. "Not within one foot of the territory acquired by us from Mexico will slavery ever be planted," he declared, "and I believe it could not be done even by the force and power of public authority." Congress should immediately form territorial governments for both regions, with no mention of slavery. This would only defer the slavery question until the time when those territories applied for statehood, but since—in Clay's opinion—slavery would never be established there, the territories would likely come in as free states. This must have made certain southern senators squirm in their seats, but they kept their silence.

His third resolution was complicated. The western boundary of Texas was to follow the course of the Rio Grande as far north as "the southern line of New Mexico," then turn sharply eastward again along that same line to the border that had been agreed to by the United States and Mexico in 1819, and—these were Clay's words—"excluding any portion of New Mexico." If senators with a hazy grasp of geography felt confused, they had a right to be. New Mexico's southern boundary was far from certain, and Texans had never accepted the line of 1819 as their western border. What was clear, however, was that Clay intended to give the Texans no part of New Mexico. Anticipating their reaction, and that of their proslavery supporters, Clay asserted that Texas would still be left with enough land "to form two or three states," which ought to satisfy the "highest ambition" of Texas's "greatest men." Clay's fourth resolution offered a further sop. If "by some solemn and authentic act" Texas relinquished its claim to New Mexico, the United States would pay off the state's public debt.

Having riled the Texans, Clay now offered something to the South. In his fifth resolution, he declared that it was "inexpedient" to abolish slavery in the District of Columbia without the consent of Maryland and the residents of the District itself, neither of which was likely to be forthcoming. In short, Congress would guarantee that slavery continued in the nation's capital. This naturally would inflame slavery's opponents. But he had something to give them, too. In his sixth resolution, Clay declared "that it IS expedient to prohibit" the slave *trade* within the District. That meant that the pens and auction houses would be closed, or at least pushed across the river to Virginia, and those appalling lines of shackled slaves passing down Pennsylvania Avenue would no longer offend the eyes of congressmen. "I am sure I speak the sentiments of every Southern man, and every man coming from the slave States, when I say let it terminate, and that it is an abomination," Clay passionately cried.

If the Senate's antislavery men were reassured by this, they were jolted by Clay's seventh resolution: "That the most effectual provision ought to be made by law, according to the requirement of the Constitution, for the restitution and delivery of persons bounded to servitude or labor in any State who may escape into any other State or territory in the Union." Clay's neutral, lawyerly language echoed the South's demand for a far tougher Fugitive Slave Law, which would affect not only the thousands of runaway slaves who sought safe haven in the North, but also the many white men and women, and free African Americans who helped them to freedom.

Clay's eighth resolution was meant to give the South one final guarantee. It stated simply: "That Congress has no power to prohibit or obstruct the trade in slaves between the slaveholding States." Congress, Clay was saying, would explicitly recognize the right of slaveowners to buy and sell the human beings they owned, and to enjoy the fruits of their labor evermore.

So far, Clay had been matter-of-fact. Now he rose to his full oratorical power. He believed, he said, that he had asked for roughly equal forbearance and concession from both sides. However, he went on, formally addressing the Senate's presiding officer, Vice President Millard Fillmore, although he was actually appealing to his fellow senators, and beyond them to the citizens of the thirty far-flung states. His long arms rose and fell, sweeping, at least for a time, even skeptics and enemies into his oratorical embrace. "Sir, I might, I think . . . have asked from the free States of the North a more liberal and extensive concession than should be asked from the slave States. And why?" he asked. What was antislavery to the North? A mere "abstraction, a sentiment," if a noble one, "when directed rightly." Extend to the South some brotherliness, some "Christian charity," he asked. "You are in point of numbers greater, and greatness and magnanimity should ever be allied together. On your side is a sentiment without sacrifice, a sentiment without danger, a sentiment without hazard, without peril, without loss." In the North, it cost nothing to profess a desire to emancipate slaves. But what was at stake for the South? In the first place, a vast and incalculable amount of property to be sacrificed. And not your property, by the way, he pointed out. "The social intercourse, habit, safety, property, life, everything, is at hazard to a greater or lesser degree, in the slave States."

Clay now approached his dramatic climax: his voice rose and his arms flew, conjuring up a whirlwind nightmare of servile revolution that fed the deepest fears of every southerner. "Sir, look at that storm which is now raging before you, beating in all its rage pitilessly on your family. They are in the South. But where are your families, where are your people, Senators from the free States? They are safely housed, enjoying all the blessings of domestic comfort, peace, and quiet in the bosom of their own families. Behold, Mr. President, their dwelling house now wrapped in flames. Listen, sir, to the rafters and beams which fall in succession, amid the crash; and the flames ascending higher and higher as they tumble down. Behold those women and children who are flying from the calamitous scene, and with their shrieks and lamentations imploring the aid of high Heaven. Whose house is that? Whose wives and children are they? Yours in the free States? No. You are looking on in safety, whilst the conflagration which I have described is raging in the slave States, and produced, not intentionally by you, but produced from the inevitable tendency of the measures which you have adopted, and which others have carried far beyond what you have wished. In the one scale, then, we behold sentiment, sentiment, sentiment alone; in the other property, the social fabric, life, and all that makes life desirable and happy."

In closing, Clay resorted to a clever piece of theater. He said that a man had come by his hotel that morning, while he was working on the speech that he had just delivered, and had unexpectedly presented him with a "precious relic." Clay paused for effect, then brandished aloft a piece of wood so that all could see.

"It is a fragment of the coffin of Washington," he announced.

Was this splintered plank a sad omen of what might happen to the Union, to the fabric of the nation which the sainted Washington's virtue and patriotism had established? "No, sir, no!" he cried, his aged eyes flashing. It was a warning direct from the grave, telling Congress "to beware, to pause, to reflect before they lend themselves to any purposes which shall destroy that Union which was cemented by his exertions and example."

With that, Clay was done.

There were scattered protests. Tom Rusk of Texas protested that Congress had no power whatever to set Texas's western borders. Henry Foote, asserting that he intended to make only "a few remarks," then, long-winded as always, declared that in his opinion slavery was "a prohibited subject" upon which Congress had no right to legislate for any conceivable cause. Jefferson Davis worried aloud that the Senate—"this conservative branch of government"—seemed to be infected by the spirit of antislavery "fanaticism" which he claimed was spreading across the United States. A few more senators lent their voices in similar protests. But all of this was mere skirmishing. Clay declined to answer any questions. In a week's time, he promised, he would explain his thinking in greater detail, and the battle would begin.

On February 5, the Senate assembled again like the audience of the world's grandest theater, poised to witness another bravura performance of the Jenny Lind of American politics. When Clay rose he again emphasized the urgency of "mutual forbearance." To the South, he said— doubtless looking directly, as he spoke, at the hunched figure of Calhoun, the soldierly Jefferson Davis, Butler, Yulee, Mason, and their friends—if Congress dared to attack slavery in the states where it was protected by the Constitution, "My voice would be for war." But to fight a civil war in order to carry slavery into lands where it did not exist? "What a spectacle we should present to the astonishment of mankind, in an effort not to propagate rights, but a war to propagate wrongs. It would be a war in which we should have no sympathies, no good wishes; in which all mankind would be against us; in which our own history would be against us." Here was Clay the father pleading with his errant children to pull back from a decision that would ruin their lives.

That said, he suddenly became the angry parent, admonishing and impatient, calling upon antislavery men to simply *calm down*. He demanded, his voice rising, "What do you want?—What do you want?— you who reside in the free States? Do you want that there shall be no slavery introduced into the territories acquired by the war with Mexico? Have you not your desire in California? And in all human probability you will have it in New Mexico also. What more do you want? You have got what is worth more than a thousand Wilmot provisos. You have nature on your side—facts upon your side—and this truth staring you in the face, that there is no slavery in those territories."

Of the problems facing Congress, Clay admitted, none was so difficult of solution as that of the Texas boundary. The North sought to confine Texas to its narrowest possible limits; the South to enlarge those limits in order to obtain "an additional theater for slavery." New Mexico infinitely complicated matters. When Texas was annexed, Congress had specified that slavery was barred north of the old Missouri Compromise line. But one-third of New Mexico lay above that line, so that when the Texas claim was taken into account "free and slave territory, slavery and non-slavery" were mixed together. The boundaries of New Mexico remained undefined, it was true. But it was the responsibility of the entire nation, not just Texas, to define them. His proposal, as he had outlined it the week before, provided Texas with enough western land to carve out two or three new states. "Is that not," he asked, "concession, liberality, and justice?"

When he resumed the following day, February 6, Clay moved on to the question of slavery in the District of Columbia. He reiterated his belief that Congress had the clear constitutional authority to regulate slavery in the District. Abolition was "inexpedient," however, since, in his opinion, it required the consent of Maryland and the residents of the District itself. Clay was on thin ice here; this was nowhere in the Constitution. He was inventing reasons for nonaction, since even if outright abolition was legally possible, it remained politically unthinkable. But the slave trade was another matter. Terminating it would salve the delicate sensibilities of Americans who were more disturbed by the sight of slave sales than by slavery itself. "Why should the feelings of those who are outraged by the scenes that are exhibited by the *corteges* which pass along our avenues of manacled human beings," brought from distant areas to be sold here, no less—as if this made the crime somehow worse—"why should the feelings of those who are outraged by such a scene—who are unable to contemplate such a spectacle without horror—why should they be thus outraged by the continuance of a trade so exceptionable, so repugnant, as this?" Clay's eely ability to wriggle onto every side of an issue, or even several sides simultaneously, was breathtaking: having belittled the sentimentality of the abolitionists, here he was making a purely sentimental argument for ending the slave trade in Washington.

Clay then took up the problem of fugitive slaves. For them, there was no room for sentimentality at all. The Constitution already required that every state cooperate in the recapture of "persons bound to service," as Clay delicately called them. "I go one step further," he declared. The Senate had seen Clay as a loving parent, then as an admonishing one. Now he was Jehovah himself, flaming with righteous fury at the political sinners of the North. How those mesmerizing eyes must have flashed! The recapture of fugitives was not just a legal duty, but a *moral* one. "It extends to every man in the Union and to the officers of every State in the Union, and devolves upon him the obligation to assist in the recovery of a fugitive slave from labor, who takes refuge in or escapes into one of the free States." The states of the Upper South were hemorrhaging slaves, Kentucky most of all. Indeed, Kentuckians were taking their life in their hands to cross the Ohio River to attempt to recapture their runaway property. In Cincinnati, a "negro mob" had even attacked a man attempting to bring a fugitive back home, while the local police stood by and did nothing. On this score, the free states had indeed failed to meet their obligations. "It is a mark of no good brotherhood, of no kindness, of no courtesy, that a man from a slave State cannot now, in any degree of safety, travel in a free State with his servant. It is but the right of good neighborhood, and kind and friendly feeling, to allow the owner of the slave to pass with his property unmolested." (Clay had his own ax to grind on this score, remembering how Levi had been lured away by Boston abolitionists just months earlier.) But for poor, deluded slaves, Clay's Jehovah felt only paternal mercy. Such poor souls, he asserted, typically wound up "wretched and unhappy," and begging their masters to take them back. Clay's listeners might well feel that they would be doing fugitives a favor to expedite their return to their owners.

With respect to the eighth resolution, Clay said: "I hope it will forever put an end to the question whether Congress has or has not the power to regulate the slave trade beyond the different States."

Clay then confronted the South's most popular solution to the territorial problem: the extension of the Missouri Compromise line for another two thousand miles across the continent to the Pacific Ocean. On the face of it, this was a neat and politically logical solution, ignoring those irritating old Mexican borders, the confusing courses of half-known rivers, and tangles of barely explored mountains. Jefferson Davis, for one, repeatedly said that he would settle for nothing less. But in hardheaded political terms, Clay flatly declared this notion impossible. In practical economic terms, slavery would *never* be viable south of that line in the West. It would serve the South's interests far better to take no action either for or against slavery in the West. Why? Because allowing Congress to bar slavery north of the Missouri Compromise line would set a precedent for federal legislation on slavery, which was just what the South most resisted. Moreover, to give the South what it really wanted, a western outlet for slavery, Congress would have to vote to explicitly guarantee the legality of slavery south of the line. This Clay flatly refused to do: "I never can, and never will vote, and no earthly power will ever make me vote, to spread slavery over territory where it does not exist."

He then posed to the South the hovering question that no one really wanted to ask: What if the slave states seceded? Did it make sense? Would it remedy the ills of which the South complained? The emotional Clay and Clay-as-Jehovah were now gone. In their place was Clay the lawyer logically pleading his case in a country courtroom to a jury of men who, he seemed to trust, must respond to pure reason. "Are you safer in the recovery of your fugitive slaves in a state of dissolution or of severance of the Union, than you are in the Union itself?" he asked. He begged southerners to think hard. If the Union were broken into pieces, "slaves taken from the one into the other would be like slaves now escaping from the United States into Canada. There would be no right of extradition—no right to demand your slaves—no right to appeal to the courts of justice. Where one slave escapes now, by running away from his owner, hundreds and thousands would escape if the Union were severed in parts."

Secession would also, inescapably, mean war. Even if there were mutual agreement on the South's right to secede, he predicted, "in less than sixty days, I believe, our slaves from Kentucky would be fleeing over in numbers to the other side of the river, would be pursued by their owners, and the excitable and ardent spirits who would engage in the pursuit would be restrained by no sense of the rights of those on the opposite side." Having reasoned with his fellow senators, he now scared them. The dissolution of the Union wouldn't end with just two "confederacies." Once begun, fragmentation could prove unstoppable. As "dissatisfaction and discontent were disseminated over the country," the South and North themselves might crumble into confederacies of New England and the Middle Atlantic states, the Great Lakes region, and the Mississippi Valley, not to mention the Far West. How long would it be before a military dictator—"some Philip or Alexander, some Caesar or Napoleon"—rose to crush once and for all the liberties of all the parts of the shattered Union?

Here perhaps—the dry record of the *Congressional Globe* rarely reports such details—one might imagine the exhausted old man wiping his brow and gazing around the chamber as if awakening from a bad dream, then turning to face the vice president. "But, sir, the veil which covers these sad and disastrous events that lie beyond a possible rupture of this Union is too thick to be penetrated or lifted by any mortal eye or hand. Mr. President,"—Clay was here addressing Vice President Fillmore—"I am directly opposed to any purpose of secession, of separation. I am for staying within the Union, and for defying any portion of this Union to expel or drive me out of the Union. I am for staying within the Union, and fighting for my rights—if necessary with the sword—within the bounds and under the safeguard of the Union. Here I am within it, and here I mean to stand and die."

Clay had now spoken for five hours over two days. He was spent. He came to an end with a plea whose desperation resonates across the generations: "I conjure gentlemen—whether from the South or the North, by all they hold dear in this world—by all their love of liberty—by all their veneration for their ancestors—by all their regard for posterity—by all their gratitude to Him who has bestowed upon them such unnumbered blessings—by all the duties which they owe to mankind, and all the duties they owe to themselves—by all these considerations I implore them to pause—solemnly to pause—at the edge of the precipice, before the fearful and disastrous leap is taken in the yawning abyss below."

There was one last grim note. "And finally," Clay said, "Mr. President, I implore, as the best blessing which Heaven can bestow upon me upon earth, that if the direful and sad event of the dissolution of the Union shall happen, I may not survive to behold the sad and heart-rending spectacle." If compromise failed, he said, he would rather die than witness the result.

In the North and in the shrinking Whig strongholds of the South, the salient public reaction to Clay's speech was a collective sigh of relief. Unionists praised it as a "noble," "magnanimous" speech, "a spectacle of sublimity that ought to shame all the politicians at Washington, and the miserable drivelers of both parties, and all parties, there and elsewhere." At a giant pro-Clay rally in New York City, speaker after speaker proclaimed in Clay's proposals "the basis of a harmonious and brotherly" adjustment of the nation's perils. Others were not so sure. New York's former mayor Philip Hone was deeply depressed. Clay's charm could not avert catastrophe, he brooded in his diary: "The fever of party spirit is beyond reach of palliatives. Where will all this end? I see no remedy!" Troubling rumors continued to multiply: that southern radicals would abandon Congress if California were admitted, that the House of Representatives was to be seized by a force of armed southerners, that blood-shed was imminent in the Capitol . . . "The fanatics of the North and the disunionists of the South have made a gulf so deep that no friendly foot can pass it," Hone wrote. "Compromise is at an end."

Clay's soothing words had failed to win over either abolitionists or southern nationalists. Frederick Douglass decried Clay as a "moral monster" for his willingness to support a new Fugitive Slave Law, declaring, "In no man living is there more completely combined, nor more strikingly exhibited, the dignity of the human intellect with the savage brutality of a beast of prey, than is to be found in the character of this distinguished senatorial kidnapper." Moderates could dismiss Douglass as a trouble-making abolitionist and a *black man* to boot. But the southern radicals were another matter: they wielded real political power. *"Compromise?"* roared South Carolina's massive Andrew Butler, who with his streaming silvery hair and flaming certitudes attempted to fill the vacuum left by his ailing—some said half-dead—colleague, John C. Calhoun. "Its name is frailty—its consequences treachery—giving the stronger party the power to use it as an instrument, and throw away at its pleasure."

Just months earlier it had seemed treasonous even to suggest the dis-solution of the Union. Now it was the subject of daily harangues in both houses of Congress. Increasingly, southern radicals sounded as if secession had already taken place, and talk of compromise were mere playacting. Solomon Downs of Louisiana, a lawyer and planter, whose imperious, clean-shaven face still projects frosty disdain through the scratched surface of a 150-year-old daguerreotype, predicted that not only would the South flourish after its secession, but that it would draw to it all the so-called free states of the Mississippi Valley, and even Pennsylvania, since "she derives ninety-nine of the hundred dollars made in her extensive fac-tories in Pittsburgh" from markets on the Mississippi. Besides, he added, the ever "cost-counting" North would never fight to defend the Union anyway. "They will find that there is not much inducement to fight—not much money to be made by fighting."

The Senate's proslavery forces were on the march.

CHAPTER 12

"WOUNDED EAGLE"

———— ·◆· ————

If anyone doubted that the South's threats of secession were in earnest, their doubts were dispelled on February 13, when Jefferson Davis
delivered the most defiant speech yet. He wasted no time on niceties.
As befitted a professional soldier, he launched a frontal attack on Clay,
the North in general, and abolitionists in particular. He had hoped for
a "serious" compromise from Clay, he said, but he had been grievously
disappointed. Instead, Clay had thrown his weight behind the "aggressive
majority" and its campaign of subversion against the vital interests of the
South. Northern opposition to slavery had nothing to do with morality:
it was all about power, "the cold, calculating purpose of those who seek
for sectional domination." Why should the South continue to support
a government that, he asserted, was committed to slavery's overthrow?
"Fanaticism and ignorance—political rivalry—sectional hate—strife
for sectional dominion, have accumulated into a mighty flood, and pour
their turgid waters through the broken Constitution," Davis floridly
declaimed. He was alluding to the tidal wave of abolitionism that he supposed was washing over the North. Davis regarded abolitionists as political vermin, and in December had urged that they and their sympathizers
be excluded from the Senate floor. Now Clay—*a southern man!*—refused
to lend his hand to arrest the flood and, worse yet, was abetting the abolitionists' rapacious schemes.

Having left Clay prostrate on the field, Davis hoped, he launched into a defense of slavery itself. Black Africans were destined for bondage, which was immutable and eternal: to challenge it was mad. "Is it well to denounce an evil for which there is no cure?" he asked. "Why not denounce criminal laws, declaim against disease, pain, or poverty, as wrong?" The enslavement of Africans had been "established by decree of Almighty God," sanctioned by the Bible from Genesis to Revelation, and since the dawn of time had flourished "in nations of the highest proficiency in the arts." In short, it was one of the defining marks of civilization. "Whenever the hieroglyphics of Egypt have been deciphered, and have told the story of ages not otherwise recorded, they show that the Ethiopian, so far as he has been traced, has been found in the condition of bondage."

Not only was slavery sanctioned by religion and history, but the modern slave trade—condemned by ignorant abolitionists—was actually a blessing to the slave. "It brought him from abject slavery into a Christian land, where civilization would elevate and dignify his nature," Davis went on. "It is a fact which history fully establishes, that through the portal of slavery alone, has the descendant of the graceless son of Noah ever entered the temple of civilization." If there *was* anything "horrible" about the slave trade, as abolitionists alleged, it was the abolitionists' own fault, thanks to their misguided efforts to suppress it. He charged that the British and American naval patrols that were intended to interdict the transatlantic trade caused long delays for shippers, which resulted in famine and disease among slaves awaiting export, and compelled slavers to resort to smaller and faster ships, which in turn fostered overcrowding, and increased the suffering of the slaves in transit. (The U.S. Constitution had banned the importation of slaves into the United States after 1808. Although American cruisers joined the Royal Navy in patrolling the West African coast, American enforcement of the blockade was lackadaisical, reflecting the nation's ambivalence toward slavery in general. By contrast, the British regularly impounded slave ships, and set the victims free in the crown colony of Sierra Leone.)

Davis urged slavery's enemies to look south of the nation's border to see the woe that emancipation would bring. After the abolition of slavery, the economies of Mexico and the rest of Central America collapsed, while Jamaica and Haiti sank into barbarism; Cuba and Puerto Rico, on the other hand, where slavery continued to flourish, fairly glowed with prosperity. Meanwhile, slaves in the United States were "advancing in intelligence," they enjoyed the kindest relations with their masters, they were usefully employed, and they were "restrained from the vicious indulgences to which their inferior nature inclines them." Yet northerners insisted that an institution that brought only good to the black race should be abolished, and replaced by a freedom that could only be a curse for the race they claimed to want to help.

If abolitionists sincerely cared about the slaves, they should *open*, not close, the West to them, Davis said. The diffusion of slavery would benefit the slave as much as it did the white man, if not more. If there was any cruelty to be charged against slavery, it resulted from the crowding of slaves onto large plantations, where the kindly patriarchal relationship between the master and his human property was more likely to break down. The more slaves were spread out among whites, the more "domestic" the practice of slavery. This was, Davis maintained, a "fact" known to everyone. A little later in the debate, Davis would slyly suggest that general emancipation—an outcome he certainly did not approve—would become possible only if "a door opened, by which they may go out, and that door must be toward the equator." By damming slaves up in the small territory they now occupied, increasing in number year by year, emancipation would remain an utter impossibility, unless Americans were prepared "to see the slave become the master, to convert a portion of the states of the Union into Negro possessions, or to witness the more probable result of their extermination by a servile war."

Clay had claimed that slavery was somehow automatically excluded from the West by some mysterious climatic or topographical barrier. This Davis considered so preposterous that he hardly bothered to argue the point, scoffing "that the will of the conglomerated mass of gold-hunters, foreign and native, is to be taken as the 'decree of nature.'" In fact, he declared, there was a great future for slavery in the West. "I hold that the pursuit of gold-washing and mining is better adapted to slave labor than to any other species of labor recognized among us, and is likely to be found in that new country for many years to come," he told his colleagues. Not only that: since "only the African race are adapted to work in the sun," slave labor was also uniquely adapted to the irrigation-based agriculture that, he claimed, characterized the arid West. Some senators, he patronizingly observed, claimed that Mexican law barred slavery from the new conquests. Well, Mexican laws had also excluded cotton, salt, tobacco, grains, and leather: were all those now to be barred from the new territories as well? "What is there in the character of that property"—slaves, that is—"which excludes it from the general benefit of the principles applied to all other property?" There was, in Davis's mind, no difference at all.

To Davis, slavery was an essential part of the American dream. It was not only blameless, but charitable; not only moral, but sacred; not only practical, but patriotic, since it formed the foundation of true American democracy by ennobling even the least privileged white man. ("He who seeks for that portion of our country where, in fact, as in theory, political equality does exist, must be pointed to the slaveholding states," he told the Senate a few days later, adding that the same could not be said about the nonslaveholding states, where "white men are sunk to menial occupations.") Concessions to the North would inescapably lead to slave revolution and economic ruin. Framed thus against this specter, Davis saw himself and his allies as courageous racial heroes standing against the onrushing tide of anarchy. In this Manichaean battle between Light and Darkness, compromise smacked of treason.

At a minimum, Davis reiterated, he would accept no less than the continuation of the Missouri Compromise line to the Pacific Ocean. More ominously, he demanded a restructuring of political power to ensure lasting protection of the South's interests. Since population growth in the North meant that the House of Representatives doubtless would be dominated by ever larger Yankee majorities, the South must be guar-

anteed control of the Senate, regardless of the number of states that were
admitted to the Union.

The North was already "waging war" on the South, he declared.
There was no difference between circulating "incendiary documents"—
abolitionist literature, that is—and promoting the escape of fugitives, or
the mounting of an armed invasion. If such assaults had been delivered
by a foreign country, they would be a cause for war. Beware of bringing it
on, he warned: it was the North that would suffer most. "Grass will grow
on the pavements now worn by the constant tread of the human throng
which waits on commerce, and the shipping will abandon your ports for
those which now furnish the staples of trade," he prophesied. "Wake before it is too late from the dream that the South will tamely submit."

The day after Davis's speech, his hyperactive Mississippi colleague
Henry Foote suddenly moved to seize control of the debate. What seemed
on its face to be a mere procedural formulation was actually Foote's first
gambit in a strategic maneuver that would shape the debate's course. He
called for the creation of a special committee to consider all the items that
Clay had proposed, claiming that only his plan could fend off catastrophe
by embedding the problem of California in a single bill that definitively
settled every aspect of the "unhappy controversy" that threatened the
Union.

At forty-six, slight of build and delicately featured, Foote suggested a
balding and extremely irritating elf. He was the very incarnation of contradiction. Though capable of eloquence, he could be so stupefyingly pro-
lix that his fellow senators sometimes literally begged him to stop. Told
that Foote had a remarkable command of language, one fellow senator
replied, "On the contrary, I think *language* has a remarkable command of
him." Though a tireless defender of slavery and a slave owner, he was also
one of the staunchest Unionists in the Deep South. He often proclaimed
his conciliatory intentions, but had a nearly uncontrollable temper—an
Alabama newspaper compared him to "a high pressure steamboat on
fire"—and a knack for picking nasty fights even with those who agreed

with him. He had fought four duels and been wounded in three of them, and on Christmas Day 1847, during an altercation over Popular Sovereignty, he assaulted Jefferson Davis in a Mississippi tavern; before the current month was out he would provoke a street corner brawl with Senator Solon Borland of Arkansas. Enemies dismissed him as "a pestiferous demagogue," while the abolitionist Boston *Daily Atlas* sneered: "Clad in the panoply of his own disgusting conceit and impudence, he is ever ready to encounter"—that is, duel—"whomever his buzzing body may buzz against." Few took him seriously. But no senator would work harder than he to square the circle of the South's self-interest with the nation's survival.

Clay didn't care at all for Foote's plan to incorporate all his proposals in a single Omnibus Bill—so called because a bill packed with disparate elements resembled a horse-drawn omnibus, which made room for passengers of every sort. Clay wanted the proposals kept separate, fearing with reason that it would prove impossible to pass them all in a single bill. The enemies of each different measure—the admission of California, for instance, or the Fugitive Slave Law—might be tempted to unite the way southern radicals and northern abolitionists had a year earlier, in the chaotic last hours of the Thirtieth Congress. A comprehensive defeat could destroy the opportunity for any compromise at all. Clay wanted his proposals to be sent individually to the appropriate committees for consideration, a process he optimistically expected to take just two or three weeks.

Foote, who could be counted on to cast his simplest thoughts in overwrought hyperbole, was "mortified" by Clay's disapproval. Why, it was Clay himself who had called for a "general scheme of pacification." Foote protested that if California's admission were to be taken up in isolation it would surely pass—he could count the votes as well as anyone—but it would be seen by the "persecuted South" as an insulting attempt to trample their most vital interests underfoot. Without concessions to the South—Foote now floated one of the lush metaphors for which he was famous—"the vessel of state will certainly be found to have sprung a new leak, and she will suddenly go down amid the roaring billows that surround her, never more to be seen majestically riding the surface of ocean, and bearing onward and aloft that sacred banner of freedom which has for so many years been seen streaming from her masthead."

Foote's strategy was to outflank the secessionists by co-opting their intransigent tone, while advancing the cause of compromise on the best terms that he could get for the South. To accomplish that, he had to take on both Clay and Benton, who, though nominally a Democrat, was emerging as the administration's strongest ally in the Senate. Like the southern radicals, Foote tended to see his opponents as part of a vast, sinister conspiracy that included pretty much everyone who expressed resistance to slavery's westward expansion, from Zachary Taylor to William Lloyd Garrison. Clay, Foote suspiciously charged, was "throwing into the hands of his adversaries all the trump cards in the pack."

Clay was miffed. "I know of no South, no North, no East, no West to which I owe any allegiance," Clay dramatically replied. "My allegiance is to this Union and to my state; but if gentlemen suppose they can exact from me an acknowledgment of allegiance to any ideal or future contemplated confederacy of the South, I here declare that I owe no allegiance to it; nor will I, for one, come under any such allegiance if I can avoid it."

Foote then turned viciously on Benton, who so far had barely participated in the debate. Benton, he charged, in the aghast tone of someone reporting a particularly lurid crime, had been spotted conferring with none other than Senator Seward of New York, the incarnation of all the evil that slave owners attributed to abolitionists. "Rest assured there is some scheme afoot for the betrayal of the South," Foote warned. He then went on to mock Benton's Missouri accent—his "imposing nasality"—his alleged hypocrisy, his supposed connivance with England to subvert the peace treaty with Mexico, his contempt for parliamentary procedure, and his venal self-interest in promoting California statehood, because his son-in-law, John C. Frémont, was one of the newly elected California senators. Back in December, Benton had stalked out of the chamber rather than respond to Foote's insults. Now Foote taunted him, wondering aloud if he would manage to stay put in his seat, or would again flee the chamber. Finally, he threatened Benton directly: "*Public justice is certain,* and the time of vengeance has already arrived."

On February 20, Foote went after Benton again, accusing him of revealing by a "peculiar significance of tone, look and gesture" that he was in secret collusion with the Taylor administration to sneak California into the Union. Benton, he blared, was motivated only by "an intense self-love" that "was eminently calculated to sow discord among the state of this confederacy." Put bluntly, he was calling Benton a monster and a subversive bent on wrecking the nation for his own selfish ends. And no, Foote added, he would not remain silent "from feelings of morbid delicacy," or from a "silly regard for certain unmeaning and antiquated, or indeed, as I think, mere imaginary rules of parliamentary decorum." He would denounce "vice" wherever he saw it. Through all this, Benton remained impassive. But his patience was wearing thin.

Clay gently chided Foote as "a gentleman of imagination and of great fancy." But he also refused to be drawn into a shouting match. He melo-dramatically declared that death was closing in on him. He felt himself standing "as it were, upon the brink of eternity," already almost beyond earthly concerns. He would go to the grave convinced that slavery was evil, and he would not apologize for what he believed. The South pro-tested that his proposals were all concession to the North, and the North cried that they were a capitulation to the South. "I assure you," he said, "it has reconciled me very much to my poor efforts, to find that the ultraists on the one hand and the other equally traduce the scheme I propose."

Brushing Clay aside once again, Foote renewed his calls for the Kentuckian's proposals to be bundled together and rolled forward in an omnibus. The Senate must seize the initiative—it must not be left to the White House, or to the House of Representatives, with its overwhelming northern majority. "Would it not be better to have some definite plan be-fore us," he pleaded, "especially when we consider that all we have before us at present are abstract resolutions, leading to wild, stormy, and almost unlimited debate?"

• • •

Every senator was waiting to hear from John C. Calhoun. That he would not seize the South's standard and carry it forth into the enemy's ranks was inconceivable. He had but rarely appeared in the Senate since the opening of the session. Yet the debate itself was a tribute to the towering influence he had exerted for more than a generation. He had fathered, nurtured, disciplined, and inspired the reactionary idealism which for the proslavery fire-eaters defined the rhetorical battlefield on which they were now engaged. He had stripped away the South's defensiveness about slavery, and bestowed upon it an ideology that lent dignity to an institution that virtually everyone outside the South deemed despicable. To his followers, he was, in the words of the early-twentieth-century historian Vernon Parrington, a figure without parallel, "commanding every highway of the Southern mind." But a generation ago, there was only one John C. Calhoun: now there were many.

A friend, Maria Dallas Campbell, who visited him in his rooms a block east of the Capitol, found Calhoun but a shadow of himself, feeble and cadaverous, with his iron-gray hair hanging upon his shoulders in massive folds. His fiery, restless eyes flashed from his emaciated face as he slumped in a large armchair, his head lolling against its back for support.

"Mr. Calhoun, I fear you allow yourself to become too much excited by public affairs," Campbell gently advised him.

"Oh, no, not excited, only intense," he told her.

"Can nothing be done to save the Union?" she asked.

At this, a pall spread over his ravaged face, and his features became rigid. His eyes took on a distant gaze, as if he were looking into the future. He replied that nothing could be stronger than his sentiment for the Union except the South's necessity to preserve itself from the menace to her "social institutions."

Calhoun had privately confessed to other friends that the admission of California as a free state probably could not be prevented, an outcome that he believed would "utterly emasculate" the power of the slave states. He also believed that, once admitted, California would be subdivided into five or six new free states, effectively overwhelming the slave state bloc in the Senate. Only one course remained open. "There is an increasing disposition to resist all compromises & concessions and to agree to nothing," Calhoun wrote approvingly to former South Carolina governor James Hammond. "There is, I think, little prospect that the North will come to our terms, or that any settlement of the questions at issue will be agreed on. The impression is now very general, & is on the increase, that disunion is the only alternative, that is left to us."

Though his political outlook remained grim, by mid-month Calhoun felt that he was at last physically on the mend. "I have for the last week been completely free from disease," he optimistically wrote to his son-in-law, Thomas Clemson. More than his body's hesitant recovery, however, it was Jefferson Davis's defiant speech that had heartened him. It was proof to Calhoun that his protégés were coming of age.

But his recovery was an illusion. His daughter Anna Maria feared for his life, and urged him to resign from the Senate. "You have spent a long life in the service of your country, & it is now time to take care of yourself for our sakes," she begged. "Go home then, my dearest father, live quietly, & generously, & be a good deal in the open air." If such a thought crossed Calhoun's mind, he never confessed to it. He was eager to resume his seat in the Senate. At the end of the month, he felt feverish again, but he was determined to join the debate that was raging virtually within sight of his sickbed: he wrote to Anna Maria, "I am exceedingly anxious to be heard."

On February 20, Lewis Cass, the Democratic Party's standard-bearer in the 1848 contest for the presidency, eager to stave off the defection of his angry southern friends, tried to assure them that the seeming crisis was really no crisis at all. At sixty-three, Cass was typically referred to by his fellow senators as "General," in remembrance of his long-ago service in the War of 1812, though it was now hard for anyone to imagine this collapsed mountain of a man leading anyone into battle. Cass had served for eighteen years as the governor of the Michigan Territory, as ambassador to France, and as secretary of war had presided over Andrew Jackson's remorseless removal of native tribes from the Southeast, in what came to be known as the Trail of Tears. Antislavery agitation, he now soothed, was just one more silly fad propagated by the woolly-minded spirit of the times, and not to be taken so seriously. Slavery was a fact all men ought to accept, "an existing institution for which no living man is responsible." Its so-called evils were much exaggerated. If slavery posed any kind of problem, it was the South's business alone—they would doubtless deal with it "justly and wisely." Outside interference only made things worse. However, he warned, the South's inflammatory rhetoric also was making things worse—"and may go far towards converting a just cause into an unjust one."

Cass's warning was fulfilled when, on March 4, supported by friends, Calhoun shuffled and wheezed into the Capitol and up the narrow stairwell to the packed Senate chamber a little after noon. He was immediately surrounded by senators, who crowded around him as he hobbled to his desk near that of his acolyte James Mason of Virginia. "It seemed generally understood that Mr. Calhoun will never again be seen, certainly not heard, in that Chamber," a reporter wrote. "Physically he seemed barely alive. Yet, his nervous, restless and brilliant eye glared and loomed around him more remarkably than ever before." To Andrew Butler, who adored him, he seemed like a "wounded eagle." Too feeble to read the speech that he had written, Calhoun handed it to Mason to read, and hunkered beneath a heavy cloak to listen.

The speech was vintage Calhoun, cold and unyielding. These were, everyone in the chamber felt, the last words of an oracle who, shrunken and haggard, like the denizen of an ancient shrine, was summoning a political doomsday for his mesmerized audience. "What is it that has endangered the Union?" Mason read, in a haughty and defiant voice that matched the tone of Calhoun's remarks. There could be only one answer: "the almost universal discontent which pervades all the States composing the southern section of the Union." This discontent was the inevitable fruit of a long-standing pattern of systematic aggression against southern rights that had destroyed the "equilibrium between the two sections in the government" that had existed when the nation was founded. This "disequilibrium" would only grow worse as the territories of Oregon and Minnesota, and—if admitted—California, New Mexico, and "Deseret" delivered at least ten more senators hostile to southern interests. California would be the test question. "If you admit her under all the difficulties that oppose her admission, you compel us to infer that you intend to exclude us from the whole of the acquired territories," Mason intoned.

Belief in this principle of "equilibrium" had, thanks to Calhoun, become an article of faith among southern nationalists. In fact, it was the South that had enjoyed a preponderance of power far out of proportion to its size. Even though the North's population was larger than the South's—in 1850, it was more than twice as great—men from the slave states had held the presidency for fifty, and served as chief justice of the Supreme Court for fifty-two, of the nation's sixty-two years. Of fourteen secretaries of state, all but five had been from the slave states. Twelve of twenty speakers of the house had come from the slave states, giving them control over the appointment of committees, and thus over the business of the House. Thanks to the three-fifths rule prescribed in the Constitution, the slave states had benefited from thirteen extra congressmen in the First Congress, in 1790, and had an extra twenty-one in the current Congress. The process of statehood had also been manipulated to the North's disadvantage, with new slave states often being admitted with less than the legally required number of inhabitants. The free state of Ohio, Senator Salmon P. Chase pointed out during the debate, in 1840 had more than a million and a half inhabitants, 328,000 of them voters, while seven slave states occupying an area twelve times larger than Ohio had a total population that was a quarter-million less, and had ninety thousand fewer voters. Yet, because those states also included 456,000 slaves, they enjoyed three more seats in the House than Ohio, on top of their twelve additional votes in the Senate, for a total of fifteen votes more than Ohio in the Electoral College. Facts of this sort, Calhoun, Davis, and the rest of the radicals studiously ignored.

Calhoun acknowledged that at the root of the nation's crisis lay "the relation between the two races in the Southern section." Some northerners, he knew, regarded that "relation" as a sin, a crime, or at the least a stain on the nation. Well, that was too bad. Slavery was indissoluble. Without decisive action to protect the South's interests, disunion would inexorably follow. "It is only through a long process, and successively, that the cords can be snapped until the whole fabric falls asunder," Mason read. "Already, the agitation of the slavery question has snapped some of the most important, and has greatly weakened all the others. If the agitation goes on, the same force, acting with increased intensity, will finally snap every cord, when nothing will be left to hold the States together except force." The only way to guarantee the South's security was to affirm the right of slavery in the conquered territories, enforce the Fugitive Slave Law, and end abolitionist agitation. Then Calhoun dropped a bombshell: he called for the Constitution to be amended to "restore to the South, in substance, the power she possessed of protecting herself before the equilibrium between the sections was destroyed by the action of this government." Just what Calhoun had in mind was never clear. He may have wanted congressional districts to be redrawn according to a new formula favoring the South, to ensure that slaveholding areas were guaranteed still more congressional seats and northern urban areas fewer, regardless of the disparity in their populations. Or he may have been thinking of a sort of co-presidency based on the model of consulship in the Roman Republic, in which power would be shared by two executives—one elected by the South, the other by the North—who would hold veto power over all government decisions.

The burden of concession was on the North, Mason intoned, still reading Calhoun's words. It was entirely up to the North to decide if the "great questions" could be settled or not—on southern terms. "If you who represent the stronger portion cannot agree to settle them on the broad principle of justice and duty, say so; and let the States we both represent agree to separate and part in peace. If you are unwilling we should part in peace, tell us so; and we shall know what to do when you reduce the question to submission or resistance."

CHAPTER 13

"SECESSION! PEACEABLE SECESSION!"

———— •◆• ————

As slavery increasingly cleaved the Senate into warring factions, a few members were left stranded in the widening space between. One of the loneliest was Sam Houston, who took the floor, as he quaintly put it, "to cast in my mite." At fifty-seven, Houston was, in the words of journalist Oliver Dyer, "a magnificent barbarian, somewhat tempered by civilization," a large-framed man, stately of bearing, with "a lion-like countenance capable of expressing fiercest passions," who often strode the streets of the city garbed in "a vast and picturesque sombrero and a Mexican blanket." He was also unstable, depressive, and wrestling with the alcoholism that had plagued him most of his life, avoiding parties and taverns, and occasionally recounting his struggles at a "Temperance blowout." His contribution to the debate was not particularly substantive, but it irritated the southern radicals no end. He called upon senators from all sections "to come forward like men," and find common ground for compromise. He declared his opposition to any federal legislation on slavery south of the Missouri Compromise line from Texas to the Pacific Ocean, and expressed no more than "regret" that Clay had questioned Texas's right to her western boundary. For a nominal southern man, this was weak tea compared to the firewater of the radicals.

Among the southern senators, Houston stood out for his stubborn refusal to pay even lip service to the radicals' culture of grievance. In October, he had refused to sign Calhoun's Southern Address, for which he was savaged as "soft" on slavery and disloyal to the South. This would have been politically fatal for anyone else, and it would eventually prove to be so for Houston, too. But he was not just a senator, he was as close to the father of his country as Texas had. Houston was contemptuous of abolitionists: "They are bastards, they are aliens to their fathers' principles," he declared. But he had no respect at all for southern nationalists, whom he regarded as little short of traitors. His hatred for Calhoun was intense. "Calhoun is mad and, and vicious, on the subject [of slavery]," he wrote to his wife during the 1848 debate. "I will watch him as I would an *adder*! He is a bad man, and all his views are selfish. I trust there will be enough, of good men, and true, to save the Union!" The South Carolinian, he wrote again to her, looked upon the entire South "as so many political plantations, belonging to him, and its Representatives as so many slaves to his silly abstractions."

Those abstractions were now pushing southern Unionists one by one toward the radical edge, or out of politics entirely. Houston was a stoic, but the attacks had wounded him, and his real theme now was his own defense. "I have been charged with being a *deserter* from the interests of the South," he exclaimed to his fellow senators. "What? Forget the South? If I am of the South, can I not recollect the North? What is our country? It is an entirety. There are no fractions in it. It is a unit, and I trust it will so remain. But I have been charged with being an alien—an alien—a 'deserter.' Am I to be questioned of having a southern heart, when that heart is large enough, I trust, to embrace the whole Union, if not the whole world? A nation divided against itself cannot stand," he ringingly declared—eight years before Abraham Lincoln would make the phrase famous for all time. "I wish, if this Union must be dissolved, that its ruins may be the monument of my own grave, and the graves of my family. I wish no epitaph to be written to tell that I survived the ruin of this glorious Union." It was a brave speech. But Houston stood almost alone.

• • •

Although Henry Foote was one of the least likable men in the Senate, he was, in his badgering way, as committed to the Union as was Houston, and was desperate to engineer a workable compromise that would obtain for the South what it wanted. Calhoun had not helped at all. Indeed, Foote felt, he had virtually erased all that the Mississippian had done to attempt to convince the Senate that proslavery men were loyal and flexible enough to cut a deal.

"To speak plainly, I almost felt that a noose was put around my neck, while asleep, and without having antecedently obtained my consent," Foote complained, in his inimitably wordy Latinate fashion. Calhoun, he said, had denounced the very name of compromise. In June, delegates appointed by several Southern states were planning to convene in Nashville, where it was widely feared—and anticipated by others—that they would proclaim a Southern confederacy. If Congress accomplished nothing before then, momentum would surely pass to the delegates there. Foote did not have to say, because everyone already knew, that many of the delegates nominated by their states to attend the convention were going there with immediate secession in mind. Calhoun's speech had only created mischief. Foote had just received a message from Missouri reporting that a St. Louis rally had called for the reelection of Tom Benton as an antidote to the disunionism that Calhoun had been preaching—an outcome, Foote groaned, "that could not deplore me more."

"Was it a telegraphic report?" Calhoun queried.

"I believe it was," Foote replied.

"I distrust all telegraphic reports," Calhoun rasped. He then accused Foote of pretending to know the opinions of everyone in the Senate, and claiming that they all agreed with him.

"I am on good terms with everyone," Foote protested.

"I am not—I will not be on good terms with those who want to cut my throat," Calhoun replied, referring to William Seward in terms that no one could mistake. "The honorable senator from New York justifies the North in treachery. I am not the man to hold social intercourse with such as these."

No, there was to be no flexibility, no compromise, from the dying John C. Calhoun.

In spite of the deepening anxiety that Clay had expressed to him a few weeks earlier, well into February Daniel Webster remained unmoved by the South's talk of disunion. To be sure, he was distracted by poor health, debts, and the demands of his legal clients. But still, he sounded surprisingly blasé when he wrote to a friend of the turmoil in the Senate, "Things will cool off. No bones will be broken—& in a month all this will be apparent." Before the month was out, however, the dire state of things had finally penetrated.

On February 13, President Taylor formally submitted California's constitution to Congress. Five days later, Representative James Doty of Wisconsin introduced a resolution that instructed the Committee on Territories to frame a bill for California's admission to the Union. Had Doty's proposal come to a vote, it would easily have passed. However, Democrats and southern Whigs led by diminutive Alexander Stephens and hollow-eyed Robert Toombs thwarted every attempt to debate it by means of a clever and galling parliamentary maneuver: they instructed their foot soldiers to run out the clock with an endless succession of stalling motions and roll call votes. If they could fend off debate until midnight, the resolution would no longer be considered under the definition of the day's business, and—in accordance with the rules that governed the House—could not be brought up again until the next date that was specifically allotted for the introduction of "new" resolutions, two weeks hence. Morning dragged into afternoon, and afternoon into evening, when pieces of a chandelier dramatically crashed to the floor. The *Congressional Globe*'s bored reporter, left with time on his hands during the numbing parade of votes, revealed an unexpected literary bent that had lain hidden behind his usual arid rendering of procedural minutiae.

"The evening was closing in apace, and darkness became somewhat visible in the Hall," he wrote. "In the far-off dome above, some gleams of light, emitted from the massive chandelier (now in the process of ignition), fell dimly on the shadows below. The chandelier gave a sort of exulting rattle (as if in triumph at the resplendent glories which were bursting from its confines) and a few scattered pieces of glass fell in chorus upon the floor of the Hall. There was an ominous looking up, as if in expectation that the smashing feat which its predecessor had performed several years ago was about to be repeated; and some few changes of seats might be observed."

To general laughter, Robert W. Johnson of Arkansas asked the speaker if the rules of order permitted the lamp to be removed, as if it were a disorderly intruder.

"The chandelier," wrote the *Globe*'s reporter, "as if conscious of the rebuke, remained mute as marble—content, as it seemed, to cast its burning rays in silence upon the councils of the nation."

This amusing hiatus past, the southerners resumed their dreary procedural ballet. Finally, David K. Cartter of Ohio, frustrated as were many other northerners, demanded of Speaker Howell Cobb, the Georgians' friend and ally, who was presiding, "Is it in order to multiply one question upon another, in the way of calling the yeas and nays, without disposing of any of the questions before the House?"

"The gentleman from Ohio is transcending the rules of order," Cobb declared.

"I wish to make another point of order, then," Cartter persisted. "That is, that no question is in order that has the manifest purpose of arresting the legislation of the House."

This was common sense. But Cobb ruled, predictably, that Cartter was out of order.

The grinding comedy of procedural votes continued until midnight, when Cobb ruled—to northerners' chagrin, and southerners' relief—that the legislative day was at last at an end.

The defenders of slavery had proved once again that they had the power to bring the House to a standstill.

A few days after this show of force, the triumphant Stephens and

Toombs showed up at the White House. Having demonstrated their power, they apparently expected the president to abandon California statehood. Both Georgians had campaigned for Taylor, and they anticipated a friendly reception. They didn't get one. The president practically kicked them out of his office. Just what was said between them was never precisely recorded. However, Senator Hannibal Hamlin of Maine, who was waiting to see Taylor on other business, found him prowling around his office, firing off a fusillade of profanity, and swearing "that if they attempted to carry out their schemes while he was president they should be dealt with by law as they deserved and executed." Another visitor that day reported that Taylor declared that if the Georgians made good on their threats of secession he would put himself at the head of an army, and hang them less reluctantly than he had hanged deserters and spies in Mexico. The Zachary Taylor who during the 1848 presidential campaign had promised Jefferson Davis that he would decisively defend the rights of the South was now politically dead.

The same day as the Georgians' unfortunate visit to the White House, the *New York Herald* warned that war was about to break out: "We are on the very eve of bloodshed in the capital. There is no telling when its crimson streaks may deluge the halls of Congress. Without a moment's warning, civil war and massacre may commence." Even members of Congress went armed to the Capitol. Meanwhile, events far from Washington were causing growing alarm. Nine Southern states had named delegates to the region-wide convention in Nashville. South Carolina had appropriated $350,000 for arming the state, and Virginia, $200,000. Georgia had sanctioned a state convention to consider national dissolution. Mississippi's rabidly proslavery governor, John A. Quitman, declared that in the absence of remedies for the state's grievances, he would henceforth "look to secession." Across the North, meanwhile, state legislatures and public rallies demanded the immediate admission of California. Some radical abolitionists were even calling for the *North* to secede, to separate itself from the contamination of slavery. With talk of war and national collapse filling taverns, parlors, churches, and legislative chambers alike, financial markets began to shake, as investors feared the collapse of the cotton trade and southern real estate. Reflected Alexander Stephens, "A dismemberment of this republic I now consider inevitable."

Webster finally grasped, as did Foote, that if Congress failed to act, political momentum would pass irrevocably to the most extreme southern nationalists. Exhausted though he was, Webster knew that he had to act soon if he was to have any effect. "I am nearly broken down with labor and anxiety," he wrote to his son Fletcher. "I know not how to meet the present emergency, or with what weapons to beat down the Northern and Southern follies, now raging in equal extremes." Expectations for Webster were high. Americans who had admired him as the country's leading statesman for more than a generation expected a tour de force. "Your speech this week may be a turning point in the life of this nation," one Whig politician predicted.

Webster took the floor at noon on March 7. Rapt crowds jammed the chamber, overflowing the visitors' gallery, and pouring onto the floor, so closely packed that they clung for stability to the iron columns that supported the gallery. The heat was intense, the congestion almost unbearable. The atmosphere fairly vibrated with anticipation. Dressed in his customary blue coat with metal buttons, with one hand thrust into his buff vest, the "golden-throated Daniel" rose from his seat near the center of the chamber, as impassive as a statue. "I wish to speak today not as a Massachusetts man, nor as a Northern man, but as an American," he sonorously intoned. "It is not to be denied that we live in the midst of strong agitations. The imprisoned winds are let loose. The East, the North, and the stormy South combine to throw the whole sea into commotion, to toss its billows to the skies, and disclose its profoundest depths."

Webster had scarcely begun when a very real tumult erupted in the halls outside the chamber, where frustrated latecomers were angrily trying to push their way in, interrupting the proceedings. "The Sergeant-at-Arms must display more energy in suppressing this disorder!" cried Lewis Cass. Belatedly, reflecting his usual aversion to confrontation, Vice

President Fillmore, who was presiding, finally ordered that no one else be admitted to the floor.

When he resumed, Webster launched into a review of the history of slavery in language that was reminiscent of that used by Jefferson Davis, a verbal strategy that was presumably intended to prick the ears of the South. "We all know, sir, that slavery existed in the world from time immemorial," he said. "At the time of Christ, the Roman world was full of slaves. But the teachings of Christ were intended to touch the heart, purify the soul, and improve the lives of men. Based on their understanding of the Gospels, many Northerners have come to believe that slavery was morally wrong." It seemed that Webster was on the brink of accusing the South of failing to follow the teachings of Christ. But no, he made an abrupt right-angle turn and flattered slave owners with a friendly allusion to their humanity, they "having been taught in general to treat the subjects of this bondage with care and kindness."

Tacking again, he reiterated his long-standing opposition to the acquisition of new slave states or territories. That said, the corrosive debate over slavery's migration westward into the new territories was, in his opinion, purely academic. There was no practical point to enacting laws to bar slavery from California or New Mexico. Both regions were, he oddly asserted, "Asiatic, in their formation and scenery," being composed of vast ranges of enormous barren mountains capped by perennial snow. "This country is fixed for freedom by as irrepealable and a more irrepealable law"—a law of topography, apparently—"than the law that attaches to the right of holding slaves in Texas." Legislating a bar against slavery there would needlessly "wound the pride" of the South. He meaningfully added, "If a proposition were now here for a government for New Mexico and it was moved to insert a provision for a prohibition of slavery, I would vote against it." No matter how splendidly he phrased this, no matter how caressingly mellifluous the voice that delivered it, Webster had just effectively repudiated the last thirty years of his opposition to slavery's expansion. It was up to nature to stop the westward migration of slavery, not Daniel Webster.

He steadily grew more animated as he talked, his voice swelling with emotion, pausing theatrically for effect, sometimes turning his famously piercing gaze upon the shriveled figure of Calhoun, who had once again trekked to the Capitol from his sickbed to listen. So far, Webster had said much to hearten the South. Now he turned to the dogmatism about slavery that he felt was warping and crippling the national discourse and the functioning of government itself. "In all such disputes, there will sometimes be found men with whom everything is absolute; absolutely right, or absolutely wrong. They deal with morals as with mathematics; and they think what is right may be distinguished from what is wrong with the precision of an algebraic equation. They have, therefore, none too much charity towards others who differ from them. They are apt, too, to think that nothing is good but what is perfect, and that there are no compromises or modifications to be made in consideration of difference of opinion or in deference to other men's judgment. If their perspicacious judgment enables them to detect a spot on the face of the sun, they think that a good reason why the sun should be struck down from heaven. They prefer the chance of running into utter darkness to living in heavenly light, if that heavenly light be not absolutely without any imperfection." No American, including Clay, had ever deployed a more majestic metaphor on behalf of political compromise.

Webster went on to rebut Calhoun's and Davis's assertions that the national government had been dominated by the North since the early days of the republic. "If that be true," boomed Webster, "the North has acted either very liberally and kindly, or very weakly," for if they had such a majority, they never exercised it. Indeed, it should be obvious that it was the South that had really driven the politics of the nation for three-fourths of its history. At last, it seemed, Webster was hitting the southern radicals where it might hurt. He had given a great deal of ground, but now, perhaps, he was finally going to turn his artillery on slavery's defenders. Then he swerved once more.

The South had complained that in the North both individuals and entire state legislatures refused to perform their "constitutional duties" with respect to the return of fugitive slaves to their masters. "In that respect," he declared, "the South, in my judgment, is right, and the North is wrong." Every member of every northern legislature was bound by oath to uphold the Constitution, and the Constitution explicitly declared that the responsibility to deliver up fugitives was binding. "I put it to all the sober and sound minds at the North as a question of morals and a question of conscience," he plowed on. "What right have they, in their legislative capacity or any other capacity, to endeavor to get round this Constitution, or to embarrass the free exercise of the rights secured by the Constitution to the persons whose slaves escape from them? None at all; none at all." Such men obviously failed to understand their duty. In case anyone still remained uncertain where he stood, Webster bluntly declared his firm support for an enhanced Fugitive Slave Law. Abolition societies, he disdainfully added, were nothing but "interfering mischief-makers." From now on, he would refuse to even receive abolitionist petitions of any kind from his own constituents in Massachusetts.

The antislavery men were reeling. Webster had not only defended the South, he had embraced the most hated of all the South's laws—hated because it turned northerners into slave catchers whether they liked it or not—and had virtually spat on the right of petition, which was explicitly guaranteed by the Constitution itself. Almost parenthetically, Webster did concede that the North also had reason for complaint. In 1787, the North had agreed to extra representation for slave states in the belief that slavery would naturally disappear. Instead, the South continually pressed for more territory for its ever-growing slave population. Northerners also felt offended by the harsh polemics of the southern press, which blurred the distinctions between ordinary citizens who were content to mind their own business and the rabble-rousing abolitionists. In addition, free black sailors were continually arrested and imprisoned while their ships were berthed in Southern ports. "This is not only irritating, but exceedingly inconvenient in practice," noted Webster, who for decades had espoused the interests of New England shipowners. Balanced against Webster's defense of southern interests, however, this was pallid stuff.

Having made it abundantly clear that he was not afraid to offend Yankee sensibilities, he finally went after the southern nationalists. "I hear with distress and anguish the word 'secession,'" he cried. "Secession! Peaceable secession! Who is so foolish, I beg everyone's pardon, as to expect to see any such thing? Who sees these states, now revolving in harmony around a common centre, and expects to see them quit their places and fly off without convulsion, may look the next hour to see heavenly bodies rush from their spheres, and jostle against each other in the realms of space, without causing the wreck of the universe. Peaceable secession is an utter impossibility. Is the great Constitution under which we live, covering the whole country, is it to be thawed and melted away by secession, as the snows on the mountain melt under the influence of a vernal sun, disappear almost unobserved, and run off? No, sir! No, sir! I will not state what might produce the disruption of the Union; but, sir, I see as plainly as I see the sun in heaven what that disruption itself must produce; I see that it must produce war.

"Peaceable secession! Where is the line to be drawn? What states are to secede? What is to remain American? What am I to be? An American no longer? Am I to become a sectional man, a local man, a separatist, with no country in common with the gentlemen who sit around me here, or who fill the other house of Congress? Heaven forbid! Where is the flag of the republic to remain? Where is the eagle still to tower? Or is he to cower, and shrink, and fall to the ground? What is to become of the army? What is to become of the Navy? What is to become of the public lands? How is each of the thirty states to defend itself? To break up this great government! To dismember this glorious country! To astonish Europe with an act of folly such as Europe for two centuries has never beheld in any government or any people! No, sir! No, sir! There will be no secession!"

By now Webster was bathed in sweat, his depthless eyes radiant with passion. Instead of dwelling in these "caverns of darkness," he rumbled, "let us come out into the light of day. Let us not be pigmies in a case that calls for men. Let us make our generation one of the strongest and brightest links in that golden chain which is destined, I fondly believe, to grapple the people of all the states to this Constitution for ages to come."

He was done. The chamber rang with shouts of approval.

It was peak Webster. He had spoken for just under four hours. Speeded on its way by the telegraph, and almost instantaneously made available to the public in printed pamphlet form, the speech was soon the talk of the nation. No other orator could deploy such splendid imagery, such resonant turns of phrase, such sheer *poetry*. Clay was immensely pleased. Webster's tongue had established a rhetorical beachhead upon which moderate northerners could now land with relative safety. But what did it all boil down to? What was missing—utterly missing—was even a hint of feeling for enslaved people, or for those who against all odds had managed to make their way to the North, and who lived in constant fear of discovery and repatriation to slavery. He had proposed no solution to the smoldering problem of slavery. And only as an apparent afterthought had he suggested that he would support a scheme to dispose of free blacks by deporting them "to any colony or any place in the world," always a comfortable stance for a northern man who wished to cast himself as an opponent of slavery but feared to offend the slaveholding South. Still, in some respects, it was a courageous speech. Webster had risked, if not wholly wrecked, his reputation in the North. He could also have thrown his heft behind the president's policy, and would surely have been rewarded with a voice in Taylor's inner councils, and perhaps with a cabinet post. Instead, he had made himself an obstacle in the president's path.

Establishment figures—"discreet, reflecting men," as Philip Hone put it in his diary—largely approved of the speech. An estimated ten thousand people packed into New York's Castle Garden to praise Webster and to decry secession as a "gigantic crime against the Peace, Prosperity, and Freedom of our country and of mankind." Eight hundred prominent Bostonians signed a petition expressing their support for conciliation. Isaac Hill, a New Hampshire politician who had long opposed Webster, praised his "kindly answer" to Calhoun, declaring that "its tranquilizing effect upon public opinion has been wonderful." Stock prices rose as Yankee businessmen gloated that with Webster's backing there might be a solution to the crisis after all. Among conservative Whigs, there was even talk of him as the party's presidential candidate in 1852.

Southerners were openly exultant. "Webster Against the Proviso!" trumpeted headlines across the South. The most famous Yankee of all had trashed the abolitionists, and come out for the Fugitive Slave Law. "This speech is Mr. Webster's apotheosis . . . an historical event; a monumental column on which his name will be transmitted to the latest posterity," claimed the *Baltimore Sun*. "The South prefer it to any speech that has been made 'on the other side' of the question,' " the *Alabama Daily Journal* gushed, declaring that the entire country now owed a debt of gratitude to the "great Massachusetts statesman." Even the *Charleston Mercury*, the most extreme paper in the most radical state in the South, pronounced it "emphatically a great speech; noble in language, generous and conciliating in tone."

Less conservative Whigs were worried, however. Many openly denounced Webster, including members of the Massachusetts congressional delegation, most of whom publicly repudiated his views. Robert Winthrop, who had been defeated by Robert Toombs for the House speakership, worried that Webster's concessions to the South would "overturn every Whig state north of the Potomac" in the November elections. To countless admirers, who for a generation had looked to him for inspiration, he had become in the course of four hours a fallen angel, a ruin of former greatness.

In Rochester, New York, a public rally—one of many held across the North to condemn Webster's course—protested his speech as "perfidious and heartless," and a disgrace to Massachusetts. "O, Daniel Webster, Daniel Webster! The proud, the obsequious, the magnificent, the shriveled," lamented a former supporter in Maine. Theodore Parker, one of Boston's leading abolitionists, compared him to Benedict Arnold. There was worse. In Boston, Ralph Waldo Emerson scrawled in his diary, " 'Liberty! Liberty!' Pho! The word *liberty* in the mouth of Mr. Webster sounds like the word *love* in the mouth of a courtesan." The poet John Greenleaf Whittier mournfully wrote of Webster's "dim, dishonored brow":

> *All else is gone; from those great eyes*
> *The soul has fled:*
> *When faith is lost, when honor dies,*
> *The man is dead!*

One of the most eloquent responses of all came in an open letter to Webster from Henry Clay's heartbroken abolitionist nephew, Cassius Clay of Kentucky, who just a few months before had been stabbed nearly to death by a proslavery mob for daring to call publicly for the inclusion of an emancipation clause in the state's new constitution. "As much as the Union is to be loved, it is not to be loved more than a national conscience," Clay wrote. "I cannot but regret that you did not feel it your duty as a Northern Senator, as Daniel Webster, as a MAN, to say a word in favor of freedom, which would encourage its friends, and carry terror into the hearts of its enemies."

CHAPTER 14

"A HIGHER LAW"

———— •◆• ————

With Webster having surrendered to the South, as abolitionists saw it, their hopes focused on William Seward. Among the Senate's brotherhood of outsize personalities and swollen egos, the urbane Seward stood out for his ordinariness and lack of affectation. At forty-eight, he was naturally gregarious and cheerful, devoted to his intellectual wife, Frances, and fond of cigars, flowers, and pets. (Their home in Auburn, New York, was a virtual menagerie of dogs, cats, and birds.) His life was one "of surpassing industry," as his ally Charles Sumner of Massachusetts put it, which was perhaps an elliptical way of saying that he was a workaholic. He rose early, usually at five or six in the summer, and took great pleasure in early morning walks to the botanical garden at the foot of Capitol Hill. Physically, he was short and hawk-nosed, and graced with red hair that was fading to a less dramatic shade of brown. As a public speaker, he was no match for the outsize personages who had preceded him. His style lacked, in the diplomatic words of historian Frederic Bancroft, "the amplitude, the weightiness, the laboriousness, the sense, the high flight" suited to the vital questions of the day. In other words, he was full of conviction, but rather dull. He spurned oratorical theatrics, spoke in a voice that was sometimes grating or shrill, and often seemed to be talking to himself rather than his audience. When he concluded, he typically reached for his snuffbox, and loudly blew his nose on a huge yellow handkerchief.

Seward was, however, one of the most gifted statesmen of the rising generation, and certainly the most intellectually astute of the Senate's handful of abolitionists. He had been born into the world of slavery, in the farming town of Florida, New York, north of New York City. Although his father owned three slaves—emancipation was not completed in New York until 1827—he grew up devoid of color prejudice, rare even among fellow antislavery men, the vast majority of whom, though willing to sacrifice themselves in the fight against slavery, were personally uncomfortable around blacks. Seward warmly remembered his family's slaves as affectionate, "vivacious and loquacious" women, whose lively conversation was a relief from the "severe decorum" that prevailed in the family's quarters. Before he was out of boyhood, Seward decided that he would be an abolitionist.

Following in his father's footsteps, he was elected to the State Senate, where he became a protégé of the brilliant political boss Thurlow Weed, who launched him into the governor's office in 1838. As governor, Seward embraced the gamut of the era's progressive causes, including temperance and public education, prison reform, Indian rights, the plight of immigrants, and, most significantly, civil rights for African Americans. Despite the South's often hysterical attacks on him, he did not advocate immediate abolition, but rather a national commitment to compensated emancipation. He advocated (unsuccessfully) for granting the right to vote to black New Yorkers, and he successfully pushed the state legislature to enact a landmark law providing a jury trial for fugitive slaves, which became a model for similar laws in other northern states. As governor, he repeatedly refused to surrender fugitive slaves to their southern masters, or to prosecute those who had assisted in their escape, asserting in several high-profile cases that since no New York law recognized slavery, it was impossible for either fugitives or their benefactors to be guilty of a crime. He also turned the South's states' rights argument on its head by declaring that slavery's defenders had no authority to interfere with state sovereignty in the North, and urged New Yorkers to "extend a cordial welcome to the fugitive who lays his weary limbs at your door, and defend him as you would your paternal gods."

Seward's boldness made southerners' blood boil. Just days before Seward's speech, Andrew Butler of South Carolina had alleged that $30,000 of slave property was stolen—he actually said "abstracted from"—every year from Kentucky alone by insidious persons who "inveigled" the slaves away from their homes. Another senator exclaimed that masters who had tracked runaways to Michigan had been set upon by a mob there and seized as if *they* were the criminals. A third complained that an honest slave catcher who had found his quarry in New York City had been ordered by a judge to produce statutory proof that Maryland was a slave state—and when the Marylander failed to do so in a timely fashion, the judge outrageously freed the recaptured slave. Seward, the most prominent abolitionist in elected office, received rafts of scurrilous letters from the South, including death threats, such as this from an anonymous correspondent in Savannah: "If we ever find you in Georgia, you will forfeit your odious neck, you scamp. How dare you meddle with the South?" Tough as Seward was, he confessed to his friend Alfred Conkling, a federal judge in upstate New York, "I am alone, in the Senate, and in Congress, and about in the United States, alone. I must stand in that solitude, and maintain it, or fall altogether."

Seward understood, as many Whig politicians of the older generation did not, that slavery could not be eradicated through half-measures or complacent patriotic declarations. He also knew something about fugitive slaves. Central New York teemed with them, and his hometown of Auburn was one of the busiest junctions of the Underground Railroad in the state. Several lines converged there, receiving fugitives from Pennsylvania and points south, and redirecting them west toward Buffalo or north toward Lake Ontario, whence they crossed easily to Canada. Several of the Sewards' friends and neighbors, including the philanthropist Gerrit Smith, a leading patron of the abolitionist movement, provided new arrivals with food, shelter, support, and directions—and often with work and a safe permanent home in Auburn or its vicinity. Although the Sewards probably did not host fugitives in their own home before 1850, it is very likely that they had met some as they passed through town, and heard their riveting stories of brutal mistreatment, ruptured families, and hectic flight.

Seward's defiance of federal fugitive slave legislation was inseparable from the evangelical idealism that he shared with many other abolitionists. Characteristically, in the course of his impassioned defense of an Ohio farmer who had been arrested for transporting fugitives—this was in 1847, after he had left the governor's office—he declared, in words that would never be forgotten or forgiven by the South, "Congress has no power to inhibit any duty commanded by God on Mount Sinai, or by his Son on the Mount of Olives." In contrast to confrontational activists such as William Lloyd Garrison, however, who denounced the Constitution as "a covenant with death" and the ballot box as a device "of Satanic origin, and inherently wicked and murderous," Seward was firmly committed to mainstream politics, and to the Whig Party, which he sensibly regarded as the most practical vehicle for the advancement of antislavery, as well as his career. In 1844, when the Liberty Party, the nation's first to advocate immediate emancipation, tried to recruit him as its presidential candidate, he turned them down. And in 1848 he offended many of his abolitionist supporters by campaigning vigorously for Zachary Taylor, and urging them not to throw their votes away on the Free Soil Party, which he argued would split the antislavery vote, thereby electing proslavery Democrats.

In 1849, as he prepared to take up his seat in the Senate, Seward wrote to his wife: "The world seems almost divided into two classes, both of which are moving in the same direction; those who are going to California in search of gold, and those going to Washington in search of offices." He settled into an unpretentious ten-room red-brick house on F Street, a stone's throw from the huge new classically inspired Post Office Building, and not much further than that from Clay's digs at the National Hotel. To Seward's dismay, many of his fellow Yankees seemed cowed by the

South's bullying, and he was determined to show them and the southern-ers alike that he was "of different metal." He barely knew Zachary Taylor, and initially found the president frank but naive. "It remains to be seen how far honesty and the very purest and most exalted patriotism will cover the defect of political sagacity," Seward ruminated.

The unlikely pair came together with Seward's longtime New York rival, Vice President Millard Fillmore, in a complex pas de trois over the allocation of federal jobs in New York. Charmed by Seward, and intui-tively grasping the value of a direct connection to political boss Thurlow Weed, Taylor handed Seward control over the distribution of virtually all the New York patronage, leaving Fillmore out in the cold. Seward could write to Weed—one can almost hear him chuckling—that for poor old Fillmore "there is as yet no ascertained way upstairs through the kitchen of the White House." Crowed one Seward ally, "We could put a cow up against a Fillmore nominee and defeat him." Rumors abounded that Tay-lor had become "a perfect Automaton" in the hands of the Senate's most notorious abolitionist. Taylor, for his part, was nothing if not stubbornly independent and, remarkably for a man of the South, he liked Seward, and never held his abolitionist ideas against him. Seward's enemies credited him with more influence than he probably possessed. Although southerners considered Seward the éminence gris behind Taylor's about-face on slavery in the West, it was more likely that Seward acquired what influence he had by supporting policies that had already been embraced by Taylor. Whatever the source of their chemistry, when Seward ad-dressed the Senate on March 11, he was seen by virtually all his colleagues as a member of the president's inner circle.

If tradition can be trusted, a shudder ran through the Senate when Seward rose from his seat. A few friends from the House gathered in a small knot near his desk to lend moral support. Of the speech that he was about to deliver, Philip Hone would write, "It was able, of course, but wild on the subject which agitates the country," warlike and un-compromising, "honey to the abolitionists, wormwood to the Southern factions." In protest, or perhaps reflecting Seward's reputation for uninspired oratory, most of the visitors' gallery and many of the senators' desks emptied within minutes. But Clay, Calhoun, and Webster all remained, listening carefully to what they all knew was the voice of a rising new generation that had to be reckoned with.

"No wonder if we are bewildered by the ever-augmenting magnitude and rapidity of national vicissitudes?" Seward declaimed. Rhetorically, this was not an auspicious beginning. Rather clumsily, he moved on to the Far West, declaring, "Let California come in!" Every new state was welcome into the Union, of course. But "California, the youthful Queen of the Pacific, in her robes of freedom, gorgeously inlaid with gold—is doubly welcome." He then lavished praise on the president, effusing that "Rome would have been standing to this day, if she had had such generals and such tribunes."

Twirling his glasses in his left hand, and gesturing stiffly with his right, he sketched a sort of benign Yankee version of Manifest Destiny. The New World, he said, seemed to have been appointed (presumably by God) as the nursery of future civilization, to develop self-government inspired by reason and judgment. While the Atlantic states dispatched the blessings of democracy to Europe and Africa, the West Coast would perform the same "sublime function" for the Asiatic lands that lay beyond the Pacific. In time, "a new and more perfect civilization will arise to bless the earth, under the sway of our own cherished and beneficent democratic institutions." Now this sublime destiny hung in the balance. If California was not immediately embraced by the nation, she would in all likelihood seize her independence, along with the rest of the Pacific coast.

There were those—Seward meant Clay, of course, and Webster—who insisted that California's admission be part of a general compromise. "I am opposed to any compromise, in any and all forms in which it has been proposed!" Seward fairly shouted these words—they were printed in capital letters in the published version of his speech—adding ferociously, "I think all legislative compromises radically wrong and essentially vicious. They involve the surrender of the exercise of judgment and conscience on distinct and separate questions." What was the North to get from this compromise anyway, in return for abandoning its effort to bar slavery from the western territories, surrendering to harsh new fugitive slave laws, and agreeing to tolerate slavery forever in the nation's capital? Its reward was apparently to be the exchange of human rights in one region for a mixture of liberty, gold, and power on the Pacific coast. Seward had it just about right, but he found such a deal repugnant.

He then denounced the Fugitive Slave Bill for depriving *"the alleged refugee"*—his choice of words was significant—of the most basic legal protections. He pointed out that although many Americans might have little sympathy for the fugitive slave himself, the punishment of anyone who failed to collaborate in the capture of fugitives subverted the fundamental rights of all Americans. This was precisely the kind of worrying connection that Webster had failed to make four days earlier. "You will say that these convictions of ours are disloyal," he suggested. "They are, nevertheless, honest; and the law is to be executed among *us*, not among *you*; not by us, but by the federal authority." He added provocatively, "Your Constitution and laws convert hospitality to the refugee from the most degrading oppression on earth into a crime, but all mankind except you esteem that hospitality a virtue." Having staked out his political turf, Seward now pushed his argument toward its moral climax. "We cannot, in our judgment, be either true Christians or real freemen, if we impose on another a chain that we defy all human power to fasten on ourselves. He alone who ordained the conscience of man and its laws of action can judge us." If you want this kind of law, be your own police, Seward told the South.

What Seward said next became one of the most famous political declarations of the antebellum era. Yes, the Constitution provided for the recapture of fugitive slaves. "But there is a higher law than the Constitution," he proclaimed. God's law not only allowed but *commanded* Christians to disobey laws that they deemed unjust—specifically those that upheld slavery. Although "higher law theory," as it was called, was gaining intellectual respectability in northern radical circles—Henry David Thoreau had made the same case when he refused to pay taxes during the Mexican War—never before had it been propounded on the floor of Congress. No state and no Christian nation, given the choice, would now choose to establish slavery, he said. It should be obvious that slavery by its very nature subverted democracy. "I confess," said Seward, "that the most alarming evidence of our degeneracy which has yet been given is found in the fact that we even *debate* such a question."

Was the Union really in danger of collapse? Could it be saved only by Clay's compromise? Such scaremongering was self-serving. Talk of secession was mere bombast. Alluding to Clay's memorable likening of agitated states to burning blast furnaces dangerously inflaming popular passions, Seward retorted, well then, they were doing exactly what they were supposed to in a democracy. "Let none of these fires be extinguished!" he cried. "Forever let them burn and blaze."

If the South did declare war, what would hinder the North from immediately decreeing the end of slavery in the national capital? Nothing. As for the territories—would the South carry slavery into them at sword point? Would war put an end to the debate over slavery? "No, that discussion will not cease; war will only inflame it to greater height," he prophesied. Slavery was doomed, he charged. "It is part of the eternal conflict between truth and error—between mind and physical force. It will go on until you shall terminate it in the only way in which any state or nation has ever terminated it—by yielding to it—yielding in your own time, and in your own manner, but nevertheless yielding to the progress of emancipation. You will do this sooner or later, whatever may be your opinion now." He conjured a vision of countless generations "rising up and passing in dim and shadowy review before us." From amongst the multitude, came forth a voice, saying: "Waste your treasures and your armies, if you will; raze your fortifications to the ground; sink your navies into the sea; transmit to us even a dishonored name, if you must; but the soil you hold in trust for us—give it to us free. Whatever choice you have made for yourselves, let us have no partial freedom; let us all be free."

Of all the speakers thus far, only the mocked and despised Seward saw the American future as it actually would be. Second-rate though his language may have sounded to ears measuring it against the fashionable oratory of Webster and Clay, he had scored a moral triumph, if an essentially empty one. Rarely if ever had such an unapologetically abolitionist speech been delivered on the floor of the Senate.

Somewhat to Seward's surprise, reactions to his speech focused mainly on his proclamation of a "higher law" that he said bound moral men to ignore unjust human laws. In the next century, civil disobedience in the name of moral principle would become a familiar principle, but in 1850 it shocked most Americans across the political spectrum, who regarded such a thing as a recipe for anarchy. "These principles destroy the foundations of all law and justice," asserted Senator George Badger of North Carolina, a Whig who was hoping to find some basis for compromise. "They give us a fanatical and wild notion, that every man in civilized society has a right, as a citizen, to make his own judgment a rule of conduct paramount to, and overruling, the law of his country." The Washington *Union*, a Democratic Party organ, accused Seward of setting himself up as the legislative agent of God himself. Taken on its own terms, however, the speech was not without shortcomings. Seward had focused effectively on the moral dimension of slavery and compromise. But politically he had provided scant help to the embattled president, who desperately needed the few friends he had. Instead, he seemed to justify the fears of conservative Whigs that Taylor had fallen into the hands of a madman.

Seward made no apologies for his words. "The thing is to go on, near a revolution," he wrote to Weed, four days after the speech. "While it is going on, could I, with consistency, or safety, be less bold, or firm? After it shall be over, could I endure that slightest evidence of irresolution should have been given on my part?" He had spoken not only for the oppressed black men, but for all mankind. "I am content that God has given me the place and the occasion."

CHAPTER 15

"GOD DELIVER ME FROM SUCH FRIENDS"

———— •◆• ————

Henry Clay was not happy with the way things were going. Initially, he had hoped to quickly push through the pieces of his great compromise. That seemed increasingly unlikely as the Senate he loved continued to disgorge the bile of disunion, and every day seemed to sharpen the confrontational tone of debate.

Congressman John Wentworth of Illinois, who also lived at the National Hotel and often strolled the city with Clay that winter, found him wound up with anxiety and frustration. He seemed lonely and embattled. When a committee of prominent Boston manufacturers met him in the parlor of the hotel to ask his support for some piece of favorable tariff legislation, Clay snapped at them in front of a large crowd: "Don't talk to me about the tariff when it is doubtful whether we have any country. Save your country, and then talk about your tariff." He left the businessmen mumbling to each other with astonishment. This was no longer the ever gracious Henry Clay they thought they knew.

One evening Clay took his seat at the hotel's communal dinner table in uncharacteristic silence, saying not a word to anyone.

"Mr. Clay, why don't you speak?" Senator John Berrien of Georgia asked. "Are you angry at everybody?"

"That is just it," replied Clay gloomily. "I cannot say that I am angry at anyone in particular. I think I am angry at everyone. Here is our country upon the very verge of a civil war, which everyone pretends to be anxious to avoid, yet everyone wants his own way, irrespective of the interests and wishes of others."

Two days after Seward's speech, in a surprise move, Clay offered his support to Henry Foote's plea for a special committee to be created to consider and bundle together all of Clay's proposals. An "amicable adjustment" of all the questions that divided the country was of such paramount importance, Clay told his fellow senators, that "I will vote for any proposition, coming from any quarter, which looks to, or proposes such an adjustment." He was not optimistic about its success, he confessed. "Still, I would make the experiment, and I would make experiments day after day, and night after night, if necessary."

The same day, Stephen Douglas took the floor for the first time in the debate. Anyone who cared to make such a wager would surely have bet that Seward was destined for oblivion and Douglas for the presidency. Coldly pragmatic, impatient with sentiment and moralism, Douglas soaked up power wherever he could find it. He had already positioned himself, at thirty-seven the youngest man in the Senate, as the voice of the frontier, impatient to fling aside the wearisome burdens of the polarized East. "There is a power in this nation greater than either the North or the South—a growing, increasing, swelling power, that will be able to speak the law in this nation, and to execute the law as spoke," he ringingly proclaimed. "That power is the country known as the great West."

If ever the nation had needed some creative political thinking it was now. Douglas was sure that he had the answer. The route of escape from the tangled thickets of slavery, he was certain, lay through the West. "There, sir," he boomed, "is the hope of this nation—the resting place of the power that is not only to control, but to save, the Union." Congress had once regarded its power over territories as absolute. Increasingly, however, settlers were demanding a role in decision making that affected them. Although Douglas, unlike many Democrats, believed that the federal government still had the constitutional authority to prohibit slavery in the territories, he thought that to insist on it was counterproductive, because it would only add to the rat's nest of sectional hostility that was already confounding Congress. (Although the southern radicals denied the federal government any right to legislate on slavery in the territories, there was a long series of well-established precedents for federal action. In 1787, the Northwest Ordinance had barred slavery from the Ohio Country. In 1798, Congress prohibited the importation of slaves from abroad into the Mississippi Territory, and it had done the same for the Louisiana Purchase in 1803. Later, Congress had reaffirmed the exclusion of slavery from the territories of Michigan and Illinois, and in 1820 it had explicitly banned slavery north of the Missouri Compromise line—a measure that even Calhoun had supported at the time.)

In Douglas's view, the best solution was, in a sense, no solution at all; that is, to keep Congress out of the problem and leave slavery up to the people who actually lived in the territories in question. "Popular Sovereignty": the slogan sounded simple, efficient, and above all democratic. Although it sidestepped the troubling question of slavery's morality, it had the virtue of simplicity, and appealed deeply to Americans' abiding faith in the majority vote as the ultimate solution to all problems. Lewis Cass had campaigned for president on essentially that platform in 1848. But Cass was a tired, uninspiring man of the old generation. From Douglas, the same ideas sounded fresh and innovative. *All power to the people!* Who but plutocrats and the corrupt could argue with that? Wasn't it the principle that had sent Massachusetts farmers into battle at Lexington, Concord, and Bunker Hill? Douglas's unbounded confidence in Popular Sovereignty was rooted in the town meetings of his Vermont youth, and sharpened by the rowdy Jacksonian democracy of the Illinois frontier to which he had moved. But there was more to it than nostalgia and political philosophy. Douglas's future also hung in the balance.

His route to the presidency lay through the Democratic Party. But southern radicalism threatened to tar the entire party with the taint of disloyalty, a trend that threatened Douglas's appeal to northern voters. Whigs and Free Soilers had already made hay with charges that he was nothing but a compliant lap dog to southern interests: a few days earlier, he had complained that Illinois newspapers were so "obsessed" with slavery that they engaged in "a studied suppression of all I say and do upon the slavery questions and the constant publication of what I have neither said nor done." In January, in an effort to advertise his independence, he had declined the South's offer of support to make him chairman of the prestigious Foreign Relations Committee, to replace Benton, who had been summarily removed, as payback for his objection to the extension of slavery. This day, Douglas spoke as ardently of free soil as many an abolitionist, but this represented political calculation rather than any spiritual conversion. The morality of slavery didn't interest him in the least. He was an unapologetic white supremacist, who believed that blacks were irrevocably inferior and had no claim to civil rights. ("This government was established on the white basis," he would state eight years later, in his famous debates with Abraham Lincoln. "It was made by white men, for the benefit of white men and their posterity forever, and never should be administered by any but white men.") He was perfectly willing to help force the North to "do its duty" by strengthening the Fugitive Slave Law. However, he knew that only by moving slavery off the national agenda could he rescue the splintering alliance between southern and northern Democrats, and his own ambitions.

Douglas now intended to lay out more clearly and forcefully than he had before the principles on which he would campaign for the rest of his career. First—no Douglas speech was complete without a windmilling attack on his enemies—he savaged the Whigs in general as expedient hypocrites who had "rendered themselves odious to the people, by taking sides with the public enemy in a state of war," that is Mexico, and then run a war hero for president to sneak back into power. Seward, in particular, he claimed had perpetrated political fraud on the voters of New York, and was now "enjoying the substantial results of that system of double-dealing and deception" with his seat in the Senate. (Which lay nine desks to Douglas's right, to be precise.) This partisan duty accomplished, he launched his main line of attack against the South's claim that the North was systematically depriving the South of its "due share" of the conquered lands. "What share had the South in the territories? Or the North?" Douglas demanded. "I answer, none—none at all. The territories belong to the United States as one people, one nation and are to be disposed of for the common benefit of all. It is no violation of southern rights to prohibit slavery, nor of northern rights to leave the people to decide the question for themselves." From a northern Democrat who had often made common cause with the South, this was strong stuff.

Leave each community to regulate its own affairs without outside interference, he urged. He illustrated his point with a clever and surprising reference to Illinois. Though Illinois was a free state, its territorial legislature had in fact legalized de facto black slavery in the form of virtually lifelong "indentures"; then, in 1818, under public pressure, the legislature confirmed slaves as property, but ordered that no more be allowed into Illinois, and provided for a process of gradual emancipation. That process was still peacefully taking place: according to the last census, in 1840, there were still some three hundred slaves in Illinois, about half the number there had been a decade earlier. Here was a perfect example of Popular Sovereignty in action: slavery was disappearing through the machinery of democracy. Southern radicals were claiming that "northern aggression" had excluded slavery from Oregon. But the North had nothing to do with it, Douglas asserted. It was the deliberate act of the people of Oregon themselves. Now the inhabitants of California wanted to make the same choice. Let them do it!

The South, he said, incessantly accused the North of attempting to prevent slave owners from emigrating there with their human property. "We propose no such thing!" he said. Southerners had a perfect right to take their slaves there if they wanted—but they had to abide by whatever laws they found there. Deploying a clever analogy, he said that any banker was free to emigrate to the territories of Minnesota, Oregon, or California—but not with his bank. Similarly, whiskey, brandy, and other alcoholic drinks were recognized and protected as property in most of the states, but no citizen could take this "species of property"—a favorite locution of slave owners—with him to sell in Oregon, where alcohol was barred by laws enacted by the popularly elected legislature. "Nor," he underscored, "can a man go there and take his slave, for the same reason."

Federal attempts to legislate on slavery were a waste of time. "I have no confidence in your unalterable provisions in favor of freedom, to be fastened upon a people in opposition to their wishes," he declared. Government had no business forcing people to do what they didn't want to do. Carried away by his enthusiasm for Popular Sovereignty, he predicted extravagantly that Delaware, Maryland, Virginia, Kentucky, Missouri, and even North Carolina and Tennessee, would eventually declare themselves free. He was on firmer ground in the West where, he pointed out, northern emigrants would make every new territory into a free state, regardless of what Congress did. He predicted that seventeen new states would eventually be formed from the unsettled West, all of them free, apart from a single new slave state that he was willing to carve out of Texas. The old principle of balance between slave and free states was dead, and the permanent "equilibrium" that Calhoun demanded was hopelessly unrealistic. "Where is the territory adapted to slave labor, out of which new slave states can possibly be formed?" he demanded. "There is none—none at all."

Why, he asked, was it proving so difficult to settle the slavery question? The root of the problem, he believed, was simply personal ego—"pride of opinion," as he put it. Douglas was intellectually shallow, but he was not a bad political psychologist. "It requires but little moral courage to act firmly and resolutely in the support of previously expressed opinions," he observed. "Pride of character, self-love, the strongest passions of the human heart, all impel a man forward and onward. But when he is called upon to review his former opinions, to confess and abandon his errors, to sacrifice his pride to his conscience, it requires the exercise of the highest qualities of our nature—the exertion of a moral courage which elevates a man almost above humanity itself." He urged senators to rise above partisan loyalties and hidebound positions. Webster had already provided a "brilliant example" of the kind of political self-sacrifice that he was calling for. As for himself, a year earlier, he had tried and failed to convince Congress to admit the entire Mexican Cession as a single state. (Had they followed his advice, he didn't fail to point out, they wouldn't be in the fix they were in today.) He now felt that California should be divided into three states, "with a view of increasing the political power of the great Pacific slope in the Senate of the United States." However, his own preferences mattered less than a solution based on the bedrock of Popular Sovereignty. He was willing to accept California into the Union as she was, he said. The South, he pointedly added, ought to be happy with this, since it would mean the admission of just one new free state instead of three.

It was a powerful performance. For the next decade, Popular Sovereignty—and the booming, barrel-chested figure of Stephen Arnold Douglas, the "Little Giant" as he was known to many—would loom over every debate that concerned slavery and westward expansion. Not surprisingly, the radicals were irritated. Many echoed Alabama senator Jeremiah Clemens's sour exclamation: "God deliver me from such friends as the northern Democrats!" As far as California was concerned, even the Wilmot Proviso would be preferable to "the will of the conglomerated mass of goldhunters, foreign and native," grumbled Jefferson Davis. Simply by entering it, however, Douglas had enlarged what had seemed the pitifully small arena where compromise was still possible. Significantly, for such a partisan Democrat, he had lavished praise on the two aged lions of the Whig opposition, citing Webster as a model of the compromising spirit, and fairly gushing over Henry Clay as "the pioneer in the glorious cause." Two conclusions now seemed apparent. That Clay had the strategic support of the most dynamic northern Democrat in the Senate. And that Douglas, a first-rate architect of the political deal, was determined to put his talents to work.

In a significant coda to Douglas's speech, and doubtless in coordination with him, Lewis Cass threw his ponderous heft against the South's demands for political "equilibrium." Was every section of the country—North, South, East, and West—to have a veto? Was every interest—manufacturing, agricultural, commercial, and mechanical, to be weighed each against the other? "Is each to hold the government in a state of 'equipoise'?" Cass asked. "Who ever heard or dreamed of such a government?" What Calhoun's and Davis's "equilibrium" really meant was a plan by which a sectional minority—the South alone—could cripple the government at will. There were such governments, he dryly observed. There was the czar's in Saint Petersburg, the sultan's in Constantinople, and the emperor's in Vienna. They didn't care much for the rights of the majority, but they took very good care of the rights of the minority. The logical result of the South's plan was in essence a monarchy. "That, I suppose, is the perfection of a minority government," Cass bitingly concluded. Coming from the Democratic Party's last presidential candidate, who everyone knew was eager to conciliate the South, Cass's remarks underscored the fissure that was widening between the party's northern and southern wings.

If anyone still wondered how much slavery really had to do with the South's aggressive posture, the debates of March 1850 erased any lingering doubts. Never, perhaps, had slavery been defended so explicitly and with such sheer gusto in a national forum. George Badger of North Carolina, a relative moderate, declared that slavery could never be a sin since it had been expressly approved by Moses, and charged that it was not slave masters but abolitionists whose posture on slavery was immoral, exclaiming, "Immoral for a man to do what the associates of John, and James, and Paul did! Immoral for a man to do what the wisest and best men that ever lived upon the earth have done!" Solomon Downs of Louisiana embraced the utilitarian approach. A rational age should laugh at the "fanaticism and absurdities" of the past, and judge slavery by its results. It was such an efficient and beneficial institution that, so he had read, it had been seriously suggested in the North that *white* poor be sold into it to raise enough money for the support of themselves and their family—

an idea that Downs found praiseworthy and enlightened. Hopkins Turney of Tennessee declared the protection of slavery to be a national security issue, since abolitionism was sustained only by "the interference of foreign governments," which had turned gullible Yankees into mere pawns "for the purpose of effecting that which they themselves could not accomplish—the overthrow and dissolution of this Union."

Robert Hunter of Virginia, the black-maned chairman of the Committee on Finance, outdid them all by startlingly linking abolitionism to the specter of socialism. Slavery, he maintained, was simply another word for "involuntary servitude," which in turn was fundamental to the human condition. There was no such thing as "voluntary" servitude, since all wage labor was inherently *involuntary*, and therefore a form of slavery. "To destroy that, we must destroy all inequality in property," Hunter said. "Your socialist is the true abolitionist, and only he fully understands his mission." It should thus be obvious to all that abolition doctrines would eventually subvert the security of all forms of property. "There are schoolmasters already abroad in the North, who understand their mission, and know how to estimate the force of the machinery by which the institutions of property are to be shaken and disturbed," he warned. Take heed, and unite behind those who saw clearly what the future held—that is, the enlightened slave owners of the South. Civilization as *all* Americans knew it depended on slavery's survival.

CHAPTER 16

"HE IS NOT DEAD, SIR"

——— ·◆· ———

On March 26, after weeks of near-silence, Tom Benton finally waded into the debate. "I wish to give notice to the Senate, that the friends of California now mean to go into this question," he announced. "California, sir, is entitled to consideration. She is not to be postponed in this manner. As a friend to the State of California, I now come into the action, and from this time forth I will struggle for the admission of the state."

Predictably, the first senator on his feet was Foote. "I am glad that the honorable senator from Missouri has come into the war," he cackled, then ridiculed Benton as "the Caesar, the Napoleon of the Senate" swaggering at long last onto the field "with sword and buckler." Well, he wouldn't frighten anyone. "I am delighted that he has at last taken up the glove which, as a humble champion of the constitutional rights of the South, I have long ago thrown down to him."

"I believe, by the laws of this Senate that personalities and attacks upon motives are forbidden," Benton correctly protested. "I also believe they are forbidden by the rules of decorum."

Foote stuck his goad deeper. "This gentleman"—Foote's voice dripped with scorn—like a "regular ale-house disputant . . . now whiningly complains that personalities have been resorted to for his annoyment. Did he not commence this contest by parading himself as the peculiar friend and champion of California? Did he not thus most clearly insinuate that those of us whom he was combating so justly were enemies to California?" Now, referring clearly and scandalously to Benton's daughter Jessie's elopement with John C. Frémont, Foote sneered that Benton wanted "to drag California into the Union before her wedding garment had been cast about her person."

Foote then challenged Benton to a duel. "If he feels in the least degree aggrieved at anything which has fallen from me," Foote purred, "he shall, on demanding it, have full redress accorded him, according to the laws of honor. I do not denounce him as a coward"—though of course that was exactly what Foote was doing—"but if he wishes to patch up his reputation for courage, now greatly on the wane, he will certainly have an opportunity of doing so whenever he makes known his desire in the premises." But perhaps Benton was too old—"shielded by his age"—to defend himself like a man. Even for Foote, this was the apotheosis of insult.

Benton, who had maintained a nearly superhuman restraint, finally exploded. "I pronounce it cowardly to give insults where they cannot be chastised," the old lion roared. "Can I take a cudgel to him here?"

Cries for order were heard from every side of the chamber.

"I have done with the subject here," Foote contemptuously remarked, one of the rare moments when he managed to express himself in just a single sentence.

"Is a senator to be blackguarded here in the discharge of his duty, and the culprit go unpunished?" Benton demanded.

Vice President Fillmore, roused temporarily from torpor, declared Benton out of order.

The Missourian roared on as Fillmore's gavel pounded, and more voices pleaded for calm. "I know the rules of the Senate, sir," Benton at last rumbled, as he subsided into his seat.

"Mr. President, may I be permitted to make a single remark?" Foote now piped up.

"No! No!" a chorus of senators cried, as others yelled, "Proceed! Proceed!"

Foote, apparently satisfied that he had achieved his goal of humiliating Benton once again, left the chamber, leaving behind his victim like a wounded boar.

Senators asked themselves, where would all this end?

Through the first months of the debate, California had been a monstrous political conundrum to be sure, but something of an abstraction. One southerner had blithely dismissed the inhabitants of the aspiring state as a gang of "Indians, Mexicans, and a wild band of adventurers from every quarter of the globe," while Clay, striving to drum up support for its admission, characterized it as a pitiful orphan: "You abandoned your child," he admonished senators, "and now, when that child comes to you, having shifted for itself as well as it could in the absence of your parental authority, you reproach it with usurpation, with impudence, and are ready to repel her from your doors." (It was an evocative vision in an era when orphans were tragically numerous, and the image of a helpless girl hinted at a future of unspeakable degradation.) The reality of California suddenly snapped into focus in mid-February, however, when its newly elected congressional delegation appeared in Washington in the flesh, after an arduous six-week journey via the Isthmus of Panama.

John C. Frémont, the wilderness-striding Pathfinder, had been almost everyone's first choice for one of California's two seats in the U.S. Senate. There was considerable competition for the second seat, which ultimately went, after several ballots, to William McKendree Gwin, a slave-owning Mississippian who had campaigned aggressively in the mining camps, and enjoyed the ardent support of southern emigrants. Frémont had every reason to expect to be the leading man of the new Pacific state. (He and his wife, Jessie, may already have set their eyes on the White House.) However, when straws were drawn to determine which man would get the six-year term and which the two-year—the full six-year term for this second seat would begin in 1852—Frémont drew the short straw, instantly making him the junior of the two.

Although southern radicals fulminated against California's ban against slavery, many of its officials had, like Gwin, come from slave states, among them Governor-elect Peter H. Burnett, a violent racist from Tennessee, who as a politician in Oregon urged that blacks found in the territory be flogged every six months until they left, and had declared, with respect to California natives, "that a war of extermination will continue to be waged between the two races until the Indian race becomes extinct." Frémont, though born in South Carolina, had wholeheartedly gone over to the free state camp. The two congressmen-elect were also free staters. George Washington Wright was a Boston businessman who ran as an independent; Edward Gilbert, a printer from upstate New York, was now editor of the *Daily Alta California*, California's only newspaper, and had the backing of the northern wing of the Democratic Party. However, it was Gwin who metamorphosed from a dark horse into the effective leader of the delegation.

Gwin was a swashbuckler in the southern frontier mold. Tall, broad, hatchet-faced, and crowned with a stiff brush of hair that looked as if it had been charged with electricity, he had served as secretary to Andrew Jackson, made a fortune in land speculation and then lost it, trolled for adventure on the Texas frontier, and served a term in Congress from Mississippi. He had arrived in San Francisco only in June 1849 with the express ambition of running for the Senate. (On his arrival, he made a splash, and plenty of friends, when he opened a sack of silver dollars in his room, and invited anyone who needed money to take a handful.) Though a protégé of Calhoun, and an old friend of both Jefferson Davis and Henry Foote, he was canny enough to have lent his name to the constitutional convention's unanimous rejection of slavery: as much as he believed in human bondage, he believed in his own political destiny more.

Frémont's bad luck dogged him from the West Coast to the East. First, Jessie contracted tropical fever crossing Panama. Then he fell ill as well, and they were forced to interrupt their journey in New Orleans to recuperate, while the rest of the party continued on to Washington. When Frémont finally arrived some weeks later, hardly anyone noticed. While Foote ranted and Benton roared, Gwin squired the Californians around the capital, introducing them to Fillmore, the members of the Supreme Court, and the luminaries of the House and Senate. Only the dying Calhoun declined their visit, though he later met with Gwin alone, to express his dismay that a slavery man should have so surrendered to the free staters as to approve California's antislavery constitution. Gwin pleaded political realism: there was no support at all in California for slavery. But that was not enough to satisfy Calhoun or his acolytes, most of whom gave the Californians the coldest of southern shoulders.

The Californians had left San Francisco complacently anticipating that their self-invented state would be admitted to the Union in short order. This, they speedily learned, was not to be as they grasped that California's fate, and theirs with it, was but one strand of the great political knot that was choking Congress. Despite Clay's support and Douglas's encouragement, and the praise lavished personally on Gwin by Foote, who recalled on the floor of the Senate how Gwin had once nursed him back to health in Texas, the Californians realized that their arrival on the East Coast was only adding tinder to the fire in the Senate. Led by Gwin, they retired as a group to New York to impatiently await the outcome of the debate.

Clay's compromise package was not the only one before the Senate. Both Stephen Douglas and John Bell of Tennessee—like Clay, a Whig and compromiser by nature—had proposed broad, though less comprehensive plans. Both of these ignored the fugitive slave problem, and the controversy over the slave trade in Washington, and focused exclusively on the western territories. Bell, who supported President Taylor, proposed that California, present-day Arizona, Nevada, and Utah be combined in a single giant state and admitted immediately to the Union. This was the plan that Douglas had advocated a year earlier, but had since abandoned. Douglas and Bell also differed on the intractable problem of Texas and its claims on New Mexico. Douglas wanted to carve the existing state of Texas in two, to balance the admission of a free California with a new slave state. Bell's plan would carve Texas into three parts, creating two new states, the westernmost of which would include El Paso and all of southern New Mexico. A fourth state would incorporate the rump of northern New Mexico and the present-day Texas panhandle. Bell expected the two easterly states to be slave; the two westerly ones he *hoped* might be free.

There were still more plans. Benton—declaring that "Texas is too large for her own convenience or for the well-being of the other states"— proposed to divide Texas vertically in two, and assign all its western lands, including El Paso, to an enlarged New Mexico. Henry Foote had proposed redefining Texas as all the territory west of the Brazos, which flows roughly from north to south just west of Fort Worth and Houston, and peeling off that part of Texas east of the Brazos for a new state of "Jacinto." Only Clay's plan left the existing state of Texas intact. However, he proposed drawing a diagonal border from El Paso northeast to the Red River, and assigning to New Mexico everything that Texas claimed north and west of the line. Of this last idea, Benton had colorfully remarked that it would "cut New Mexico in two just below the hips, and give the lower half to Texas, leaving New Mexico to stump it about as she can, without feet or legs."

To all but a handful of the senators, the New Mexico borderlands they were debating were basically blanks on the map, and as remote as the far side of the moon. To Texans, however, New Mexico was a real physical landscape of arable valleys, pasturelands, and mountains laced with perhaps fabulously rich deposits of ore—and they wanted it. They wanted not a smaller Texas sliced up by their enemies in Washington, but one twice its present size that would dominate the Southwest. All this talk of dismembering Texas by Kentuckians, Tennesseans, and Illinoisans infuriated them. While Sam Houston whittled morosely at his desk, as was increasingly his habit, his colleague, Tom Rusk, told the Senate that as far as Texas was concerned, there was nothing to compromise. The state's border, he declared, "is fixed and settled, and this government cannot unsettle it." Texas had established it by right of revolution, and she had never granted the federal government the authority to redraw it. Besides—he didn't mince words—slavery needed room to grow, and it was going to grow in Texas. If the North was so eager to help the unfortunate Negroes, why did it keep demanding that slavery be confined to the narrowest and most cruelly crowded limits? "If you wish to get clear of them," he said sarcastically, "take them out and shoot them, I beseech you, because they will die immediately; but do not punish them with a living death, which is to last for generations."

While the contending armies marched their verbal troops back and forth beneath the coffered ceilings of Congress, the destiny of New Mexico rested, for the moment, with a leathery frontiersman to whom it had fallen to serve as the bayonet point of the South's drive west. A photograph of Robert Simpson Neighbors in the Texas State Historical Museum at Austin suggests (it shows only his face and shoulders) a man of considerable size: a broad, round face illuminated by surprisingly sensitive eyes, chin rimmed with a fringe of beard, thick hair growing low on the forehead, bestowing a vaguely, not unpleasantly ursine look. As an officer in the republic's army, he took part in the ethnic cleansing of East Texas, and in the ill-fated Texan raid against Mier, Mexico, in the winter of 1842. But there was more to Neighbors than the typical freebooter. In a land of easy cruelty and moral absolutes, Neighbors was an anomaly. He was a devout Methodist, a temperance man, and spoke five languages, including several Indian dialects. So respected was he by the tribes that Comanche friends invited him on at least one occasion to join them on a horse-stealing expedition to Mexico. (Reportedly, he declined.) Neighbors was also one of the few men who had already made the overland journey to El Paso.

Neighbors was the perfect choice to carry the imperial dreams of

Texans and their militant new governor, Peter Hansborough Bell, across the desert to New Mexico. Bell, a former Texas Ranger, had promised immediate action against the recalcitrant New Mexicans. "We have trusted too much and too long," he declared in his first message to the Texas legislature, on December 26, 1849. Declaring that further inaction would only embolden those who were already ignoring Texan rights, he asked for the authority to raise an army to enforce Texan claims at Santa Fe, "without reference to any anticipated action of the Federal Government." What those elliptical words meant was that Bell intended to fight for New Mexico, and that he would accept nothing less than a complete surrender of federal authority. There could be no question, in the minds of his listeners, that Bell was prepared to go to war with the United States.

Neighbors was given copies of the Texas constitution, sets of state ordinances, decrees, and laws that had passed the most recent sessions of the legislature, in both English and Spanish, and eighty copies of Bell's address to the people of New Mexico. In this ingratiating screed, the governor reassured his new subjects that Texas, having learned of New Mexicans' "friendly disposition towards us, and your expressed desire that such facilities should be extended to your people"—this was utter hogwash— Texas was now extending its "paternal guardianship" over them by fulfilling "the design which she has long entertained of extending wholesome and salutary laws over every portion of her territory." Bell promised them freedom of religion, peace, and liberty, and all the "advantages" of the Texas constitution, presumably including slavery. *Rejoice, New Mexicans!* "How many of our fellow beings, while groaning under the iron rod of despotism, would be made thrice happy could they embrace the golden opportunities which we are permitted to enjoy!"

Neighbors jumped off from San Antonio in mid-January with eight men, including five Texas Rangers, two black slaves, and a former doorkeeper of the Texas House of Representatives. It would have been a difficult journey at any time of the year, across a country that daunted even the toughest travelers, killed many of them, and drove some of them mad, such as the unfortunate and amazingly named Dr. Wham, a member of one recent expedition, who "rode off in a fury" one night, and was never heard from again. In the dead of winter, such a journey bordered on lunacy. Leaving behind the easy life of San Antonio, Neighbors and his men plunged into five hundred miles of stupefying emptiness, across a wind-stripped landscape of yellow dust, gravel, thorny chaparral, creosote bush, and naked tablelands that shimmered like heaps of metal scrap on the horizon.

Near the Pecos River—by eastern standards, the brackish and boggy Pecos was hardly a river at all, but a mockery of one—the two slaves took horses and sneaked away in the night, in a break for freedom. Their experience of it was brief. At Ben Leaton's Fort, a trading post, the two men were captured by white scalp hunters, who traded professionally in that profitable commodity with the Mexican authorities in Chihuahua. (The going rate, in 1849, was about $100 for an Apache man's scalp, $50 for a woman's, and $25 for a child's.) Leaton's men, as a respite from scalp hunting, tortured the two fugitive slaves for entertainment. One was killed quickly. The other was found by Neighbors half-flayed, and died three days later.

The Texans next ran into snowstorms that obscured the trail and made it sometimes nearly impossible to pick their way across the broken landscape. One by one, the mules began to break down. To ease the load of those that survived, Neighbors began jettisoning the copies of the Texas constitution and its laws along the trail, a mordantly apt metaphor for the unconstitutional enterprise in which he was engaged. On February 17, 1850, thirty-two days after their departure from San Antonio, the exhausted Texans finally emerged from the desert and rode into the brawling settlement of El Paso, where he informed the exuberant Anglo settlers, and considerably less enthusiastic Mexicans and Indians, that whether they liked it or not they were now citizens of Texas.

El Paso, with its cottonwood trees, gardens, and vineyards, was an oasis for California-bound Forty-niners and merchant adventurers. Politically, the outpost was a microcosm of the entire problem posed by New

Mexico. Mexican authority, such as it was, had disappeared with the Treaty of Guadalupe Hidalgo. As more and more freebooting Americans arrived, the climate became steadily more chaotic. Travelers and outlying ranchos were at the mercy of marauding Indians and outlaws from both sides of the border. Federal authority existed only in the brave but overwhelmed person of Major Thomas Jefferson Van Horne, and six far-flung companies of U.S. troops. Van Horne was in an impossible position. His post was actually located in Mexico, several miles below the ill-defined border with New Mexico, where he had no legitimate authority at all, beyond force of arms. Now here was Neighbors waving what was left of his tattered copies of the Texas constitution, and dispatching surveyors to block out Texan counties. In the absence of clear orders to the contrary, Van Horne let Neighbors do whatever he wanted.

Neighbors got briskly to work, appointing constables, clerks, and election officers. "I have no doubt you will be pleased to learn that I have been successful in organizing this county," he proudly wrote to Texas governor Bell. "The election went off in fine style [and] we had splendid balls in honor of the extension of civil law." Bringing the surrounding anarchy under control was another matter: Neighbors had no budget with which to actually administer the new counties. But he had planted the Texas flag in El Paso's sand, and his masters in Austin were ecstatic. Within the space of only a few weeks, Bell declared, Neighbors had "inspired" a people "imbued with prejudices against us as a race" with a desire to become good Texas citizens. This was, of course, what Texans wanted to hear. In fact, land-hungry Texans now felt free to expropriate the property of resident Mexicans with little fear of punishment. Neighbors's most fervent supporter was Major Enoch Steen, who commanded a company of U.S. dragoons, and to whom one of Neighbors's companions sold a headright to 640 acres of Mexican land, including the entire town of Doña Ana. The greedy Steen, Neighbors blithely assured Bell, "is a perfect Texan in principle. He declares openly that he would resign his commission and take up arms to defend the Texas claim to this territory."

When word of Neighbors's activities reached Santa Fe, it threw the opponents of annexation into a frenzy. The territory's leading civilian official, the hirsute Yankee Judge Joab Houghton, whose fragile writ was pretty much limited to the vicinity of Santa Fe, threatened to jail anyone attempting to extend Texan authority over the region. Local petitioners, probably encouraged by Houghton, demanded that the new commander of U.S. forces in New Mexico, Colonel John Munroe, stop the Texans from gaining control, warning that if he did not, "We shall then by all means and at all hazards vindicate the integrity of our soil & just rights." By late March, pro- and anti-Texas men were clashing in the streets, while rumors of another revolt among the Mexicans kept the garrison on alert. The Indians, meanwhile, had renewed their attacks on outlying settlements, and were murdering travelers almost within sight of the city.

Neighbors was not the only new arrival in New Mexico. In November, Secretary of War George W. Crawford had called to his office Lieutenant Colonel George A. McCall of the Third Infantry, a veteran of the Seminole and Mexican wars, who was about to depart for New Mexico to rejoin his regiment. Probably at the express direction of President Taylor, Crawford handed McCall a secret letter that he was to deliver personally to Colonel Munroe. It made the president's policy crystal clear: Texas was not to have New Mexico. "Should the people of New Mexico wish to take any steps toward [statehood], it will be your duty, and the duty of others with whom you are associated, not to thwart but advance their wishes," the letter advised. "It is their right to appear before Congress and ask admission to the Union." To remove any remaining obstacles in the path of statehood "may, in some degree, be part of the duty of officers of the Army." Taylor wanted statehood pushed through, and he wanted it done quickly. Munroe could not miss the unstated implication: if necessary, he was to use the army to forestall a Texan coup.

"I found politics the rage, engrossing the attention of all classes of people," McCall wrote back to Washington after his arrival in Santa Fe, on March 20th. Quickly taking stock of the situation, he concluded that the party that had thus far been agitating for statehood was actually the more likely to cut some kind of deal with Texas in return for its support. The so-called Territorial Party, on the other hand, led by the antislavery Houghton, was solidly pro-Union, and thus the president's natural ally. McCall convinced Houghton that Taylor was committed to statehood in order to settle the problem of the Texas border. Thus, with the army as a fulcrum, the fragile political machinery of New Mexico rotated 180 degrees, until Houghton's group became the leading advocate for statehood, while the former State Party in effect became the new Territorial Party, under the leadership of an ambitious former army officer with Southern connections, Richard Weightman, who McCall suspected was in secret league with Texas.

As March came to an end, Neighbors was preparing to saddle up for the three-hundred-mile trek from El Paso to Santa Fe. Much of the territory he had been deputed to organize for Texas, Neighbors explained in a letter to Governor Bell, was still "impassable on account of the Indians." Nearly all the troops on hand were infantry, and helpless at the pursuit of Apaches, who seemed to be everywhere at the same time. Just hiring an armed escort was difficult, since nearly all the available white men were in the pay of Ben Leaton, who was suspected of having collaborated in the murder of Neighbors's two escaped slaves and other hapless travelers. But Neighbors did not intend to be diverted from his purpose by Indians, bandits, the desolate ninety-mile *Jornada de Muerto* that began just north of El Paso—or a handful of Yankee politicians. He was well aware that Houghton—"a bitter, unprincipled, and vindictive Whig," he had been told—was likely to prove a problem once he reached Santa Fe. But he also knew that it was the army that held the real power. So far, the military authorities—the compliant Van Horne, and the enthusiastic Steen—had proved extremely cooperative. He was further encouraged when Major William Henry, another Texas sympathizer, offered to escort him with a troop of his soldiers to Santa Fe where, Neighbors had every reason to hope, Munroe would hand the territory over to him, and to Texas.

• • •

On March 31, Calhoun died. He was sixty-eight years old. Even in his last days, as his lungs began to fail, he continued dictating to his friend Joseph Scoville a series of militant resolutions that would guarantee power to slaveholders in the new territories, and declare void the effort to form a state in California—"a name without any reality whatever." Calhoun's prognosis for the Union was as hopeless as his own. "The Union is doomed to dissolution," he told James Mason, who came to visit him in his sickbed. "Even were the questions which now agitate Congress settled to the satisfaction and with the concurrence of the Southern States, it would not avert, or materially delay, the catastrophe. I fix its probable occurrence within twelve years or three Presidential terms," he predicted. "You, and others of your age, will probably live to see it; I shall not. The mode by which it shall be done is not so clear; it may be brought about in a manner that none now foresee. But the probability is, it will explode in a Presidential election." He was precisely, eerily correct.

The next day, after his death, the Senate suspended regular business to allow members to pay tribute to Calhoun. "He is gone!" cried Henry Clay. "No more shall we witness from yonder seat the flashes of that keen and penetrating eye of his, darting through the chamber. No more shall we behold that torrent of clear, concise, compact logic, poured out from his lips, which, if it did not always carry conviction to our judgment, commanded our great admiration. Those eyes and lips are closed forever!" Webster praised Calhoun's "undaunted genius," and finely tuned mind. No man, he said, had more resembled a senator of ancient Rome.

Senate tradition obliged Tom Benton, the chamber's senior member, to arrange Calhoun's funeral. He did what was required of him, but he refused to offer a eulogy. He had never made a secret of his hatred for Calhoun's treasonous disunionism. "He is not dead, sir—he is not dead," Benton growled. "There may be no vitality in his body but there is in his doctrines. Calhoun died with treason in his heart and on his lips. Whilst I am discharging my duty here, his disciples are disseminating his poison all over my state."

Clay, Webster, and Benton were all old men by the standard of their times. Clay was seventy-two, Webster sixty-eight, Benton seventy. They were the last great voices of the generation for whom the Founding Fathers were not just marble busts but living, breathing men. All three knew that they, too, would soon depart from the political stage. Like them, Calhoun had come to seem eternal, almost a natural force that defied age and ill health, just as he had repeatedly defied the national government. Calhoun had never fulfilled his dream of becoming president. Nor had he succeeded in remaking the structure of government to suit southern slaveholders. However, in the course of one of the longest political careers of any American of his generation, Calhoun had made slavery sound—at least to willing southern ears—not just respectable, but like a kind of idealism that ennobled masters and slaves alike. Amid the outpouring of public statements upon Calhoun's death was one from his former friend and instructor at Yale, the noted chemist Benjamin Silliman. He praised, as everyone did, the force of Calhoun's intellect, but blamed him for presenting the world with "the disgraceful spectacle of a great republic—and the only real republic in the world—standing forth in vindication of slavery; without prospect of, or wish for its extinction."

No man of his era did more than Calhoun to justify racism, to fuel slaveholders' most self-destructive instincts, to sow suspicion of the federal government, or to rationalize totalitarian tendencies in the United States. Had he gotten his way, the most reactionary class in the country would have maintained permanent control of the federal government, while the South's system of police powers would have been extended over the rest of the country to protect the interests of slave owners, and censorship of the press and restrictions on free speech would almost certainly have been imposed to silence slavery's enemies. It is possible that no political man in American history worked harder and longer to undermine the foundation of American democracy; it is certain that none did more to make the Civil War inevitable.

Calhoun's funeral took place on April 2. Admirers packed the Capitol for the ceremony in the Senate chamber, from which the desks had been removed to make room for the mourners. Afterward, Calhoun's casket was driven to the Congressional Cemetery overlooking the then bucolic banks of the Anacostia River, a mile east of the Capitol, where it was temporarily interred until it could be carried south to a permanent resting place in South Carolina. The vice president named six senators to accompany the casket on its journey south, among them Daniel Webster. For Webster, this was more courtesy than he cared to extend to his old antagonist. Deeming that he had already given the South enough of himself, he declined.

Congress had now been in session for four months, minus the last month of December, when muscle-flexing southerners led by the disaffected Georgia Whigs Alexander Stephens and Robert Toombs had paralyzed the House of Representatives until they elected a speaker who was to their liking. Frustration and impatience had only deepened. "What have we done? Nothing," complained Lewis Cass. "We have not passed a single law of the least national importance." Clay's hope for a swift compromise had faded. Foote's pleas for a special committee had gone nowhere. Every strand of the nation's political knot had led to a separate debate in itself: California, New Mexico, Texas, slavery in Washington, the fugitive slave problem . . . Crisis piled on crisis, with no end in sight. Meanwhile, the census bill, the financial bill, the appropriations bill, ordinary reports from committees—everything else twisted in the wind.

There was one uncertain glimmer of hope. In mid-February, as everyone remembered, Stephens and Toombs had again brought the House to a halt for a day and a night to prevent a vote on the admission of California from coming to the floor. Where most observers had seen yet another defeat for the northern majority, Stephen Douglas smelled an opportunity. He quietly sent out feelers—in the person of his House allies William Richardson and John McClernand, both of Illinois—to the Georgians, to find out if there was any common ground on which they could meet. Stephens intimated that at least some southerners might agree to California's admission if all the other territorial issues could be resolved to their satisfaction. This wasn't much, but Douglas sensed that it might form the delicate basis of an agreement. But where all this might go, if it went anywhere, no one could yet tell.

"We are just getting into the agitation," the *New York Herald* gloomily told its readers, "and God only knows when, or how, or by what process we are to get out."

CHAPTER 17

"LET THE ASSASSIN FIRE!"

————·◆·————

The spring brought no respite for Clay's declining health. The damp, cold weather tortured his rotting lungs. One cold bled into another, then another, then another. Although confident that he would achieve the "amicable adjustment" that he sought, he was growing increasingly irritable as the debate ground on. To his son James he wrote, "We are still in the woods here, on the Slavery questions, and I don't know when we shall get out of them. Bad feelings have diminished, without our seeing however Land. All other business is superseded or suspended." He blamed the abolitionists for subverting his efforts at compromise but he blamed the White House more, for failing to recognize that his plan (in his view) was the only one that could save the Union. Clay's relations with the president were civil but chilly. Personal feelings aside—he still felt that Taylor had poached from him an election that he ought to have won—Clay considered the administration incompetent in its dealings with Congress. "There is very little cooperation or concord between the two ends of the avenue," he groused.

Taylor had made it clear where he stood: for the immediate admission of California, in favor of New Mexico's and Utah's aspirations to statehood, and against any attempt to couple the territorial crisis to other issues. He had also made it clear that he was prepared to use force to defend New Mexico against Texan aggression, and that he would brook no talk of disunion whatever. The virtues of a soldier were, unfortunately, not those of a politician. He had proved incapable of translating what he wanted into actual political power. He faced a large, united, and defiant opposition, and a political climate that deserved, if any ever did, to be called the "Era of Bad Feelings." Taylor had a close relationship with no one in Congress except Seward, who had become virtually ineffectual since his "higher law" speech in February when, in Clay's opinion, he had "eradicated the respect of almost all men for him." Nor could Taylor appeal directly to the public. In the mid-nineteenth century, the chief executive was a far less public figure than he is today. There was no press corps assigned to the White House; there were no press conferences, no presidential interviews published in popular magazines. Like the brave, if uncreative, soldier that he was, Taylor was convinced that firm resolution must eventually triumph. But in the gloomy and rancorous spring of 1850, there was no evidence that it would.

From the first day of his return to the Senate, Clay had declared that his only goal was to see national harmony restored. His position had initially been close to the president's, but Henry Foote had convinced him that the admission of California without major concessions would drive the slave states to secession. Foote now offered him an alliance. This compromising incarnation of Foote was new. Perhaps, as he claimed, he had genuinely been persuaded by Webster's speech of March 7 that there were still in the North men who were prepared to meet the South halfway. Though he described himself as an "ultraist" when it came to slavery, he saw Clay's compromise as the best deal that the South was likely to get. To their budding alliance, Clay brought prestige, intellectual heft, and forty years of political experience; Foote promised to bring the support of southern Democrats, and as a down payment he delivered the backing of the Democratic Party's leading newspaper, the *Daily Union*, which flipped its editorial policy literally overnight from scathing attacks on Clay to lavish praise for his farsighted statesmanship. (There were outlandish rumors that Clay had bought the paper's support for a bribe of

$100,000.) Foote had reconciled himself to the admission of a free California. He intended in return to extract the highest price he could with amendments favorable to Texas, and the strongest possible Fugitive Slave Act. Foote also calculated that if the Omnibus Bill passed, it would be hailed throughout the nation as a breakthrough of historic proportions. When that happened, he—one of its architects—would doubtless be rocketed to fame as one of the great compromisers of American history, alongside Clay and Webster. It was a heady dream.

There were hurdles, of course: the southern radicals and the abolitionists. The main obstacle, however, was "Old Missouri," Tom Benton, who was both dead set against the compromise, and one of the body's most formidable debaters. His speeches were monsters of detailed, not to say sometimes mind-numbing, research, packed with facts, figures, minutiae of geography and history, and the arcana of British, European, and American law. Once when Benton charged his enemies with trying to drive him from his seat in the Senate, remarked Clay, who intensely disliked him, "There is no man whom we could not better spare—our arithmetic, our grammar, our geography, our dictionary, our page, our date, our ever-present library, our grand labor-saving machine." Clay then drolly added, "There is but one thing that posterity will more wonder at, and that will be how a man who had acquired so much knowledge could put it to such terribly bad use." In debate, Benton generally made up for what he lacked in refinement with sheer forcefulness, carefully enunciating every word so as to make it audible, and then when he wanted to flay an adversary, raising his voice to a sort of rasping, maddening squeal as his mighty arm swept through the air with majestic gesticulation. "It was easy to detect the whir of the tomahawk and the gleam of the scalping knife in his acrid sentences," wrote the New York journalist Oliver Dyer, adding that when he scented his prey, Benton would "deal blows at every head he could find."

Ironically, Benton, a lifelong Jacksonian Democrat, now found himself defending the policy of a Whig president, while Democrat Stephen Douglas—with whom Benton agreed on almost every major issue—

gradually emerged as the pivotal behind-the-scenes manager for the Senate's quintessential Whig, Henry Clay. Benton became the tacit rallying point for northern moderates who loathed the abolitionists but could not bring themselves to support a bill that seemed to open the door for slavery to travel west. Benton regarded the compromise as a scandalous concession to those who traitorously threatened secession. His own plan was to settle each measure by itself, "leaving the consequences to God and the country." The majority of senators were with him, he suspected, "but there are always men of easy or timid temperaments in every public body that delight in temporizations, and dread the effects of any firm and straightforward course." Benton, everyone knew, was incapable of any course but the most direct one.

Benton's bull-like strategy was to demolish the compromise by blunt force. He correctly estimated that Clay did not yet command a firm majority for his "comprehensive adjustment." Calhoun was not yet in his grave when the Missourian laid out his battle plan in a series of long, erudite, and fulminating speeches. Clay's scheme, he said, was "quack medicine" that would produce worse diseases than the one it hoped to cure: "I object to it on principle. I object to it on account of the nature of the subjects to be coupled. I object to it because California herself has objected to it. I object to the process." California deserved to be admitted on her own merits. The Texas controversy and the fate of New Mexico had nothing to do with California. The termination of the slave trade in Washington was "a subject of low degree, and not fit to be put into the balance against the admission of a state." It was a further disgrace to throw her admission "into *hotch-potch* with a fugacious bill for the capture of runaway negroes." Admit California immediately, he demanded, and be done with it.

He attacked the South's complaints of northern aggressions as overwrought and baseless. Indeed, he provocatively asserted, the North for decades had not only tolerated but collaborated in the enlargement of the area allocated to slavery, by lending its votes for the annexation of the Platte country to Missouri, the annexation of Texas, and the admission

The discovery of gold at Sutter's Mill, in 1848, prompted tens of thousands of Americans to race to California. Two years later, California's application to enter the Union as a free state threatened to tear the nation apart.

Sam Houston had led the Texan army in its war of independence and served as president of the Republic of Texas. He outraged fellow southerners when he refused to align himself with Calhoun and his radical supporters.

Texan threats to occupy the vast New Mexico territory reached a crescendo in 1850. Had civil war broken out, it would have begun at Santa Fe.

Colonel John Monroe commanded U.S. troops in New Mexico. If the Texans invaded, he had orders to fight. *(Courtesy of West Point Museum Art Collection, United States Military Academy, West Point, NY.)*

Popular enthusiasm for Manifest Destiny combined naked imperialism with an idealistic vision of settlement sweeping across the continent. For northerners it meant Popular Sovereignty and Free Soil; for southerners, it meant the unrestrained spread of slavery.

In 1848, the Whig Party picked politically untried General Zachary Taylor, a Louisiana plantation owner, as its candidate for president. He defied expectations by opposing the extension of slavery.

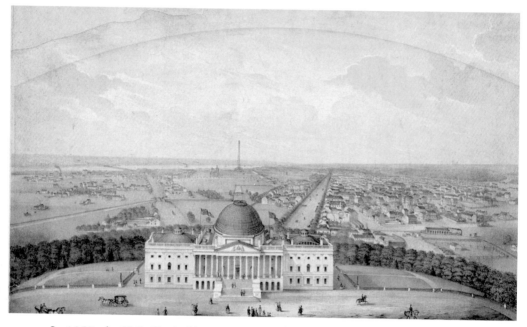

In 1850, the U.S. Capitol loomed over a straggling sprawl of one-story structures, frowsy patches of waste ground, muddy streams, and spacious avenues that seemed to lead nowhere. The visiting Charles Dickens disparaged Washington as a "city of magnificent distances."

Slavery was seamlessly woven into the life of the capital. Washington's slave pens embarrassed many legislators, however. They preferred that the slave trade be kept out of sight. After 1850, traders would move across the Potomac to Alexandria, Virginia.

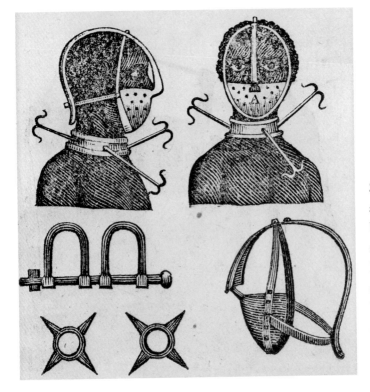

Slavery's defenders argued that it was as beneficial to the slave as it was to the master. But cruel punishments and other forms of brutalization were commonplace.

At the age of seventy-two and suffering from tuberculosis, Henry Clay left his retirement in Kentucky to attempt a grand compromise that he hoped would save the Union from collapse.

Daniel Webster had long been a leading voice of the antislavery North, as well as the Senate's finest orator. He shocked many of his longtime allies by lending his support to the Fugitive Slave Law.

The arc of John C. Calhoun's forty-year career in government had carried him from ardent unionism to a dogmatic commitment to states' rights. In 1850, he was a dying man, but he burned with a fierce certainty that the South's future lay in secession.

Following Calhoun's death, leadership of the Senate's southern radicals fell to Jefferson Davis, a wealthy Mississippi planter, Mexican War hero, and passionate defender of slavery.

David Yulee's father, a Moroccan Jewish immigrant, made a fortune in plantation agriculture. Spurning his father's conversion to antislavery, Yulee became Jefferson Davis's staunchest lieutenant during the 1850 debate.

Former New York governor William H. Seward proclaimed that a divine "higher law" superseded human laws that protected slavery. Although he was shunned as an extremist by many senators, his friendship with President Taylor enhanced his influence.

Henry Foote's Omnibus Bill won Henry Clay's support as a formula for comprehensive compromise. But Foote's biting sarcasm and combative style alienated many of his colleagues.

Thomas Hart Benton, the Senate's longest-serving member, considered himself the body's leading expert on the West. He was determined to destroy the Omnibus Bill.

Millard Fillmore, Seward's rival in New York politics, regarded abolitionists as troublemaking agitators. His ascent to the presidency after Zachary Taylor's death proved essential to a comprehensive compromise.

Stephen A. Douglas, a brilliant political strategist and the most dynamic member of the Senate's rising generation, seemed destined for the presidency. He drove the compromise forward after the wreck of the Omnibus.

Americans desperately hoped that the Compromise of 1850 would restore permanent peace between the sections. Idealized portrayals of the men who wrought the compromise portrayed them as god-like saviors of the nation. (This image generously added John Calhoun, who opposed the compromise; James Buchanan, who was not present for the debate; and General Winfield Scott, the commander of the army.)

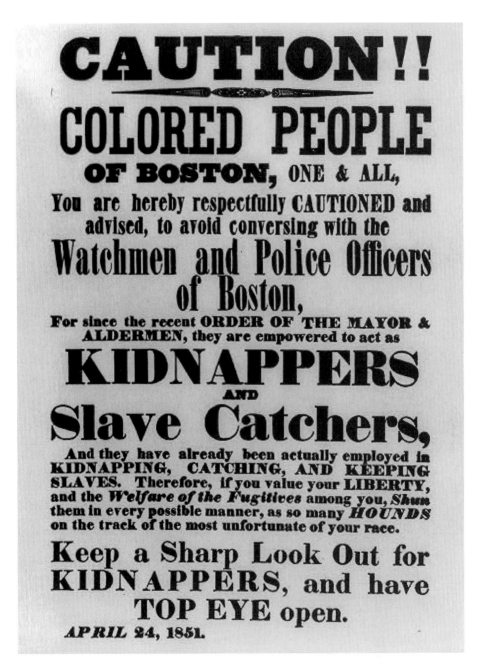

The Fugitive Slave Law prompted thousands of former slaves to flee to Canada. The law also radicalized white northerners by providing for the severe punishment of anyone who dared to obstruct the recapture of runaways.

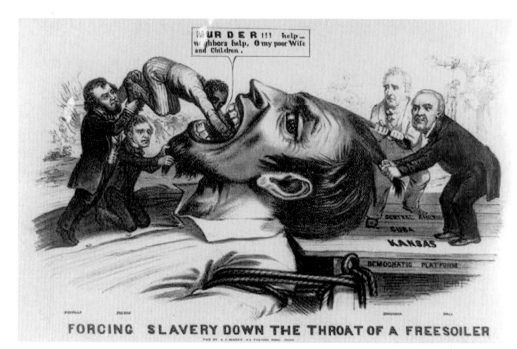

Free Soilers felt betrayed when Stephen Douglas's Kansas-Nebraska Act of 1854 effectively opened new territory to slavery. Sectional tensions would explode into violence in Kansas soon afterward.

of slaveholding Tennessee, Mississippi, Alabama, Missouri, and Arkansas. Then, limb by limb, he dismembered the South's argument against the admission of California. Congress hadn't authorized Californians to write a constitution? Well, no fewer than eight states had been admitted to the Union without approved constitutions. Aliens were said to have voted at California's constitutional convention? "The framers of the Texas constitution were all aliens." California was too large? Texas was three times the size of California. California lacked enough people to become a state? There were probably 600,000 there already—"It rains men upon California!"

Benton hoped to sway senators with his reasoning. If that failed, he aimed to wear out the Senate with a campaign of gruelingly repetitive speeches and hostile amendments designed to distort Clay's proposals beyond recognition, followed up by prolonged debate on every provision of each amendment, and then with demands for time-consuming roll call votes. Benton had, in short, begun a filibuster, though the term had not yet come into common political use. (It was then usually applied to soldiers of fortune, and derived from the Dutch *vrijbuiter*, or "freebooter," via the Spanish *filibustero*, meaning "buccaneer"; later it would be adopted to describe senators who seized and held the floor "like pirates.") In 1850, in accordance with the rules then in operation, every senator who desired to speak had to be recognized by the presiding officer; the Senate could not vote on a pending question as long as any senator wanted to debate it; once a senator had the floor, he couldn't be interrupted without his consent; and he was free to keep the floor as long as he was physically capable of doing so. Moreover, once recognized, a senator was free to speak on any subject at all, regardless of its relevance to the subject at hand. Taken together, the rules maximized free speech, but made it easy for a handful of senators, or a single determined senator such as Benton, to impede legislation indefinitely. In the absence of any means of cutting off debate—the cloture rule wouldn't be enacted until 1917—the Senate was obliged to depend on the flaccid constraints of personal courtesy and a sense of collegial responsibility to limit abuse of the body's patience.

In short, there was no way to make Benton stop talking. And as far as he was concerned, he was at war: "I cannot surrender. I cannot capitulate. No garrison, not even the weakest, will surrender until it sees the force of the enemy. Some will not surrender at all." Time, Benton believed, was on his side. He knew that Clay was in a hurry to enact his compromise, fearing that if the debate dragged on through the spring, Washington's torpid heat would sap his allies' endurance, and that they would abandon him and flee town before the cholera season arrived.

For months, all the rest of the Senate's pent-up business—the allocation of public lands, veterans' pensions, railroad rights of way, new patents, western roads, and numerous other concerns—had been shunted to the side with only perfunctory discussion, repeatedly postponed, or just plain forgotten. One of the most pressing matters, one that could not be indefinitely postponed, was the national census, which by law had to be taken before the year was out. The Senate had spent almost no time on this subject, and those responsible for it were frantic with impatience. On April 9, Clay's fellow Kentuckian, Joseph R. Underwood, chairman of the Census Committee, made his report. From it flowed a remarkable discussion that exposed not just southerners' tangled anxieties about race, slavery, and miscegenation, but also their fear of free scientific inquiry when it threatened to penetrate the closed world of the plantation. In the defenses of slavery that had studded the debate on the territories, southern senators had repeatedly emphasized slavery's "Christianizing" virtues and the warm personal bonds between the master and his slaves. Those speeches, the men who delivered them knew, would be reprinted in newspapers around the country. However, no journalist was interested in what senators said about the census. Now they said what they really thought.

The discussion began with a practical problem: just how were slaves to be enumerated? That they must be counted was a matter of considerable importance for the South. Under the Constitution's three-fifths rule, slave states were granted bonus representation in the House of Representatives for 60 percent of their enslaved slave population. The equation was simple: more slaves, more seats. Up to now, masters had simply reported to census takers the number of slaves they owned. Underwood and his committee were proposing that, for the first time, all the residents in a household—white and black—be listed by name and age.

But how exactly should they be listed? It was more than a technical question. To list slaves' names, to enshrine them in government records moreover, was to imply—however technically—that they stood on a par with their owners, and to humanize them to a degree that made the slave owners in the Senate deeply uncomfortable.

"On a plantation where there are one, two, or three hundred slaves, there are perhaps several of the same name, and who are known simply by some familiar designation on the plantation," complained Andrew Butler. "It can make no useful information, and will make a great deal of labor."

"What do you want of such names as Big Cuff and Little Cuff?" laughed George Badger of North Carolina.

"Or of Little Jonah and Big Jonah?" threw in Butler.

Many senators found this exchange uproariously funny.

Underwood ventured to say that it would simplify and speed up the whole process if census takers could list the slaves' names rather than classifying them only by number and subsets of age groups, which would require a great deal of tedious calculation.

"What public advantage can there be in having on the files of the department the names of all the inhabitants of the United States, white or black, without distinction?" challenged David Yulee, who like most of his slave state colleagues appeared to find the whole enterprise of detailed census taking pointless.

"There is not a man in the South owning a hundred negroes who knows scarcely any more of the names of the slave children than I do," threw in Jeremiah Clemens. "He would be obliged to send the census taker to the negro quarters himself, to ascertain the information." This, he suggested, was far too much to ask.

Underwood pointed out that if the slave owner didn't know the names of the children he owned, he probably wouldn't know their ages either. The information had to be gathered somehow.

Every slave owner knew how *many* children there were on his plantation, Clemens replied. "Say that he has a negro woman of the name of Eliza with four children—he can state about the time each was born. As to their names, he would not know anything about that until the children had reached the age of twelve or fourteen."

"I cannot see the use of taking the names," grumbled Butler. "In fact, I am surprised that the idea is even entertained."

William R. King of Alabama remarked that slave mothers often didn't even know the number of children they had. It was therefore simply a waste of the census takers' effort to ask slaves for such information. Even white women in many settlements wouldn't know the answer. Only the slaves' owners could be trusted to provide reliable information.

At this, William Seward, who so far had listened in silence, rose to exclaim incredulously that there was no woman on earth who could forget the number of children she had given birth to.

King bridled at this. "Does the honorable senator mean to say that all the women of his own state are so highly intellectual, so bright in their perceptions, so acute in their understanding, that they could give similar information if it were required of them?" he demanded, evidently in all seriousness.

Replied Seward, "I have only to say that, in regard to the women of New York, that they are able to read the question of the senator, and they will read it, and he will not find one, white or black, in the State of New York, that has forgotten the number of her children."

Would Seward be willing, Butler demanded—certain that he was throwing the New Yorker onto the defensive—for one of these "inquisitorial census takers" to go into New Yorkers' homes and ask every woman how many children she had, "and ask other questions which may very well be conjectured, but which my regard for decency, and other consideration, induce me to forbear mentioning?"

This was an elliptical way of hinting that census takers might learn too much. No slave owner wanted strangers poking their noses into the nature of sexual unions that took place on plantations, which might reveal the parentage of slaves who had been fathered by masters upon their female slaves, a common practice, though not one southern senators wished to discuss openly on the august floor of the United States Senate. (At no time during this discussion did any senator suggest that census takers collect data on children from the children's fathers.) Butler knew as well as every other elite South Carolinian, for example, the open secret that the state's former governor James Hammond had for years kept an enslaved mother and daughter as sex slaves on his plantation. (Hammond had also been caught molesting—the precise details were never made public—all three daughters of the aristocratic Wade Hampton, one of the largest plantation owners in South Carolina, but none of this would put much of a crimp in Hammond's political career: a few years later, the South Carolina legislature would elect him U.S. senator.)

"I have not the least objection in the world to have every woman in America asked how many children she has borne," Seward blithely replied.

King said that, as he understood it, one of the rationales for such a precise enumeration of slaves was to acquire scientific data that "would enable us to determine whether the really black race or the intermediate colors are the longest lived and the most prolific." He personally suspected that blacks lived longer and increased faster. But the collection of such information seemed to him totally "impractical."

William L. Dayton of New Jersey disagreed with this. Citing the research of Professor Louis Agassiz of Harvard University—the founding father of anthropology, and the most eminent man in that embryonic field—who argued that blacks and other nonwhite peoples were actually different species from white people, he said that he had also heard that mulattos lacked the "beneficial assets" of both races. For instance, it was widely believed, he understood, that the power of endurance for plantation labor decreased steadily with the admixture of white blood. (No senator ventured to comment on where this "admixture" was coming from.) Such questions were of profound intellectual interest, said Dayton.

If scientific discovery subverted the teachings of the Bible, no good could come from it, interjected Badger. "If it be to furnish an argument against the Mosaic account of the creation of man, it is idle, and in every point of view it is utterly useless," he said.

At one point Butler said that it was widely believed in the South that the mulatto was shorter lived than the black, but had more intelligence. Perhaps it would be possible to develop an instrument, a "phrenometer" of some kind, "to measure the line of difference between the minds of the black and the white." Indeed, if the government was to publish the results of its inquiries it would be worthwhile to "inquire who has the most sense, a black man or a mulatto."

The discussion trickled on in this vein for a while longer until, in exasperation, Solon Borland of Arkansas brought it to a halt, declaring that if they didn't move speedily on the census bill in the little time they had, "my state will still remain without her due representation at the other end of the Capitol."

In the end, it would be decided in June, slaves would be enumerated along with everyone else, but the counting would be left to unobjectionable local officials.

Day after day, as Henry Foote tirelessly pressed for the establishment of a special committee to turn Clay's proposals into a bill, Benton fired off caustic salvos of rhetoric. "I am against any concoction of a committee," he trumpeted, in full-throated populist mode. The struggle for the Union must not take place behind closed doors, in "the contrivances of politicians, or the incubations of committees," but in the hearts of its people. (There was nothing remarkable about hammering out agreements in committee, of course; Benton just didn't like *this* committee.) And if there was to be a committee, he demanded that in the Senate's instructions to it nothing should be construed as authorizing it to consider the abolition of slavery within the states, to consider the suppression of the slave trade between states, the abolition of slavery at federal properties such as forts, arsenals, and navy yards, or any question relating to domestic slavery in the United States. Clay was livid with frustration. "Nothing but a great and useless waste of time will result from this unprofitable struggle to avoid the committee," he groaned. That, of course, was exactly Benton's aim.

Benton then opened his floodgates still wider. "I have nine amendments, sir, now drawn up, and how many more I shall have occasion to prepare, this deponent saith not, for he doth not know," he mischievously warned. These new amendments, like the previous ones, were designed to cripple the debate, if not to kill the committee outright. The committee was to be instructed not to connect the admission of California with any other proposed legislation, with any measure "connected with a question of boundary," with any measure of unfitting "dignity," with any compact relating to slavery, or with any compact other than those already embedded in the Constitution. The committee was not to alter California's boundaries, not to connect California's admission to any compact that had not been required of Ohio, Indiana, Illinois, Florida, Iowa, and seven other named states. Finally, it was not to connect California's admission "with any matter foreign to the admission of that state on a precisely equal footing with the original states." If these amendments passed, the committee, the Omnibus, and Clay's hope of a grand game-changing compromise would be left a gutted hulk.

After the violent exchanges in March, Millard Fillmore, leaning down from his scarlet throne above the Senate floor, had cautioned senators to pay greater attention to the rules of order, in particular the admonition against unseemly "insinuations of a personal nature," which militated against dignified deliberation. For a few weeks, the vice presidential finger wagging seemed to have had some effect. Since then, the debate had stumbled along in a climate of sometimes strained but rarely broken mutual respect, apart from the slurs endlessly hurled at the two most outspoken antislavery men, William Seward and John Hale of New Hampshire, for whom the rules of courtesy were rarely applied.

April 17 began quietly enough. A number of committee assignments were made. William King delivered some words on the need for a customs house to be established at Mobile, Alabama. Then around midday the

Senate proceeded to the consideration of Benton's irritating amendments. Hostile amendments were proposed to Benton's amendments, abrasively argued, rebutted. Time crept past in procedural skirmishing. Everyone was soon on edge.

"He wants California admitted. So do I," said Clay, speaking of Benton. Clay was so visibly aroused that he fairly quivered with emotion. "He regrets the lapse of time before her admission can take place. So do I. But it is a little singular that the honorable senator himself—I must say it, in all deference and respect—is one of the causes which prolong the admission of California into the Union."

All he was doing, Benton mildly protested, was resisting a motion to send a "question"—that is, Clay's package of proposals—to a committee. He compared Clay's measures to dead babies in their cradles, then to the compromises of lovers—"made one evening to be broken the next morning"—then to a racehorse. "I never heard it supposed that a horse ran faster for having a load upon his back," he said. "But when I come to look at what is proposed to California, we shall find she has not only three hundred pounds upon her back, but we shall have a hundred pounds to tie to each leg, and still a pretty considerable weight to tie to the tail." He snapped, "I resist where I have a right to resist. It will be lost labor to undertake to scare me off the track by saying that I am obstructing legislation on the subject."

Stephen Douglas announced that, like Benton, he, too, personally preferred to bring California into the Union immediately. "But if I cannot have my own way, I will not delay the Senate by preventing the majority from having theirs." It was clear enough that most senators wanted to appoint Foote's committee, Douglas said, and as far as he was concerned, the majority was always right, in the territories and in the Senate alike. He intended to vote with Clay to cut off all amendments.

One after another, Benton's amendments were voted down. But the Missourian was unfazed. He simply introduced more amendments, or reintroduced his original ones with just enough of a twist in their language to claim they were new ones. He intended, he said, to call the South's bluff. "There has been a cry of 'wolf' when there is no wolf," he roared, making it clear that his broader target was the entire Calhounite agenda of threatening secession if the South was not given veto power over national policy in the territories. "I intend by these amendments to cut at the root of all that agitation, and to cut up the whole address of the southern members"—this was Calhoun's Southern Address of the previous year—"by which the country was thrown into a flame." Southern radicals swore they would secede if California was admitted as a free state: Benton dared them to do it.

Henry Foote repeatedly tried to gain the floor. When he finally did, he began calmly, with a plea for "all true patriots to unite in the pure spirit of fraternal conciliation." He went on to defend the Southern Address as a "holy work," and then—he just couldn't help himself—he went after Benton yet again for calling the defenders of southern rights "agitators," a term the South reserved for abolitionists. Foote promised to be "perfectly decorous" in his remarks, then demanded, "By whom is this extraordinary denunciation hurled against all those individuals who subscribed this address? By a gentleman long denominated the oldest member of the Senate—the father of the Senate. By a gentleman who, on a late occasion . . ."

Benton had earlier accused Clay of circulating a letter that suggested that he had once taken bribes, a charge that was probably true. Foote now rather slavishly jumped to Clay's defense and repeated the charge against Benton.

Benton snapped. The superhuman self-control that he had exerted over his temper for the past four and a half months finally burst. He was suddenly on his feet and striding toward Foote, who sat twenty feet away. The panicked Mississippian backed fearfully down the aisle toward the vice president's dais. As Benton closed on him, Foote pulled a long-barreled horse pistol from his coat. Fillmore cried uselessly for order. Senators rushed to their friends' defense. At last several of them managed to drag Benton back to his seat. But he broke away, and with an expression of frigid rage on his face again stalked toward Foote, who was now crouching and waving his pistol in front of the discombobulated vice president, and apparently ready to fire as the towering Missourian bore down on him. In the gallery, screaming visitors hurled curses at both men, while others rushed for the exits.

"Let him fire!" Benton cried, dragging along several senators who clung bodily to him in an effort to hold him back. He tore open his shirt-front and bared his chest. "Stand out of the way!" he roared. "I have no pistols! Let the assassin fire!"

Finally Daniel Dickinson of New York, the South's closest ally among the northern senators, pried Foote's pistol from his fingers, and locked it inside his own desk.

"We are not going to get off in this way!" Benton yelled, as his friends wrestled him back to his desk. "A pistol has been brought here to assassinate me. The scoundrel had no reason to think I was armed, for I carry nothing of the kind, sir."

"I brought it here to defend myself!" Foote protested.

"No assassin has a right to draw a pistol on me," Benton shouted.

Voices from every side called for order.

"Will the Senate take note of it," Benton cried, "or shall I be forced to take notice of it by going and getting a weapon myself?"

Fillmore begged the senators to sit down, but they could barely hear him or themselves over the tumult.

Even after all this, Foote kept attempting to regain the floor, to suggest that his retreat had really been an "advance," that Benton had threatened *his* life, and was probably carrying arms himself—which he was not—and admitting no responsibility at all for having provoked the confrontation by his months of insults and insinuations. "My life has been a defensive one from my boyhood," he preposterously whined. "I have never threatened any personal attacks, never." He declared that he had not "generally" worn arms in the Senate until a few days earlier, when he was allegedly menaced in the cloakroom by an unnamed senator with a cudgel.

Few observers were won over by Foote's protestations of innocence.

"I have never seen a well-whipped rooster run from his foe, without thinking of Foote's advance," journalist Jane Swisshelm, who was spending her first day in the press gallery, later recalled.

More than any other single event during the session, the fracas seemed to epitomize the razor-edge instability that infected Congress and the country. It was widely seen as a symbol of the larger national crisis, particularly in the North, where Foote's gunplay added to a deepening perception of southerners as rash, violent, and dangerous. "Pistols in the Senate!" the New York patrician Philip Hone lamented in his diary. "This Foote should be amputated from the body of which it is a disgraced member."

(In July, a committee to investigate the incident absolved Foote of attempting to murder Benton, suggesting—in line with Foote's interpretation of events—that he had drawn his gun in self-defense. The report granted that Foote had "indulged in personalities toward Mr. Benton of the most offensive character, such as were calculated to rouse the fiercest resentment in the human bosom," but recommended no punishment. Benton protested this verdict at characteristic length, to no avail.)

The donnybrook left the entire Senate embarrassed. Even Benton was momentarily chastened. The day after the confrontation, he was uncharacteristically subdued as the rest of his amendments were voted down. On April 19, the Senate finally sent Clay's proposals to Foote's long-delayed committee of six southern and six northern members, most of them supporters of the compromise, with Clay himself as its chairman and thirteenth member. Benton soon made clear, however, that although he had suffered a defeat—fourteen of them, actually—he was not beaten. Three days after the establishment of the Committee of Thirteen, as it would now be called, he returned to the attack, this time with an attempt to ban the committee from "tacking together" bills on what he said were unrelated subjects—in effect, to blow up the committee's mandate by means of a parliamentary technicality. Had any other senator attempted such a maneuver it would have been laughable. But Benton, as Calhoun once said of him, "could make more out of nothing than any other man in the world."

In his attack against cobbling together disparate measures—he meant grafting bills pertaining to Texas, New Mexico, fugitive slaves, or anything else onto the admission of California—Benton cited British parliamentary rulings stretching back to 1676, Blackstone's *Commentaries*, the Articles of Union between England and Scotland, Jonathan Swift, John Dryden, and a long litany of abstruse precedents, analogies, and mostly extraneous allusions to the meaning of the word "tacking." As he concluded, he informed his fellow senators—those who were still awake, at any rate—that all that he had thus far said was a mere overture to what he *really* intended to say when the "amalgamation bill" actually reached the floor. "And to that period I adjourn my speech," he concluded. "Then the war will begin." (One can only imagine the glances that senators must have exchanged at hearing this news.)

Against Benton's blunderbuss, Clay responded with a rhetorical rapier. "When the senator comes on with his war of words, which is terrible enough, I shall come on for peace," he loftily replied. "And if the senator's object is war against any proposition to connect together subjects which I shall show to be perfectly coherent, it is directly the reverse of mine, which shall be peace."

The odds against Benton seemed long indeed. Through the remainder of April and into May, the Committee of Thirteen—gathering somewhere in the cramped hive of ill-lit committee rooms on the Capitol's first floor—pruned, trimmed, hammered, and molded Clay's proposals, and those of other senators, into the Omnibus Bill that the fulminating Missourian so fiercely opposed. For all his roaring, Benton seemed like a relic of a lost cause, alone on the battlefield, unable to admit defeat, a blustering but ultimately ineffective obstacle on the road to peace and national revival. Clay, meanwhile, looked like a man at the peak of his powers.

CHAPTER 18

FILIBUSTERS

———— •◆• ————

Early in May, with the warmth of spring at last in the air, Clay delivered the long-awaited report of the Committee of Thirteen. This was the bulwark upon which the battle for the compromise would be fought. "The North, the glorious North has come to the rescue of this Union of ours," he sang. "She has displayed a disposition to abate in her demands. The South, the glorious South—not less glorious than her neighbor section of the Union—has also come to the rescue. The minds of men have moderated; passion has given place to reason everywhere." All the sources of the nation's "excitement and agitation" would now be removed, he promised. The plan he outlined was close to the one that he had proposed in January. The committee recommended that despite the "irregularity" with which California had been organized as a state, it ought to be admitted to the Union with the borders that its statehood convention had drawn. The bill omitted the Wilmot Proviso, but it also made no provision for the introduction of slavery into the territories. It recommended the establishment of territorial rather than state governments for New Mexico and Utah: given the regions' remoteness, dispersed population, vulnerability to Indian attack, and the inhabitants' "ignorance of our laws, language, and habits," Clay argued, neither was likely to qualify for statehood for a long time to come. He begged senators who might support one or another of the provisions but opposed the other to overcome their prejudices: "We must be reconciled to secure as much as we can of what we wish, and be consoled by the reflection that what we do not exactly like is a friendly concession."

Utah was as usual the debate's stepchild. In April, a delegation of Mormons had arrived in Washington, asking for admission to the Union as the state of "Deseret," a coinage from the prophetic Book of Mormon, which was said to mean "honeybee." To most senators, the region was still little more than the "certain somewhere," as one senator put it, that filled the vast, vague space east of California and north of New Mexico. Congress had already begun calling the place, wherever it was, Utah, after the Ute Indians who inhabited parts of the region. With respect to the Mormons who lived there, Clay said, "I care not whether they are as bad as they are represented by their enemies, or as good as they are represented by their friends; they are a portion of the people whom we are bound by treaty as well as by other high obligations to govern. Is it right to say we shall leave them to themselves?" (Not every senator felt quite so generous: "Unless their morals and manners have improved, so far from their needing protection against the Indians the Indians may soon have better cause to demand protection against them," grumbled William Dayton of New Jersey.) Since Utah lay north of the Missouri Compromise line, no one agonized unduly over its size, the complexion of its inhabitants, or who would actually govern the place. The committee contented itself with recommending that the new territory be bounded by California and Oregon on the west and north, and on the east and south, somewhat hazily, by the "dividing ridge which separates the waters flowing into the Great Basin from those flowing into the Colorado river and the Gulf of California."

On the most volatile issue of all, the committee declined even to attempt to express an opinion: Texas's "true and legitimate" border. Instead, Clay said, "We propose to buy our peace with Texas." Catastrophe was imminent unless Congress acted immediately. If the boundary was left unsettled, he predicted that before the year was out blood would be spilled between New Mexico and Texas. The committee recommended that the boundary run from the Rio Grande twenty miles north of El Paso to the Red River, where it crossed the 100th degree of longitude, giving it a chunk of New Mexico the size of Maryland, but leaving New Mexico its cities and towns; Texas was expected to relinquish its claims west of that line, in return for an unspecified payment from the federal treasury.

Clay then announced two more committee recommendations that were not formally part of the Omnibus Bill, but were nonetheless treated as essential to it throughout the debate. The committee had considered, and rejected, proposals for the complete abolition of slavery in the District of Columbia, which "could not be done without exciting great apprehension and alarm in the slave states," Clay said. But it had agreed to recommend termination of the slave trade there. The only inconvenience this posed, Clay reassured southerners, was that a District resident would have to travel a few miles to buy his slaves in Virginia, "a distance of five miles," nothing more.

Finally, the committee recommended the passage of the new Fugitive Slave Law that the South demanded. On this, the Constitution allowed no room for argument: it should be obvious to all that if some states felt free to ignore one part of the Constitution, other states would feel free to override other parts of it, leaving the document itself "inoperative and invalid." Clay noted that the Senate had received many petitions begging that alleged fugitive slaves be granted the right to trial by jury in the free states where they were captured. This, he said, would make a mockery of justice, by compelling slave owners to undertake long, expensive journeys from their homes, and endure frustrating postponements, and all other manner of unreasonable obstacles that might be placed in their path by free state courts. Instead, as a compromise gesture to the North, the committee recommended that fugitives be tried in the county from which they had escaped, where, he maintained, they could still be assured of "fairness and impartiality." This was absurd, but it was the bare minimum that even the moderate southern senators on the committee would consider.

If masters were thwarted by free state laws from recovering their property they should be reimbursed for the value of their lost slaves by the U.S. Treasury, Clay urged. "Ought we not to make this concession? It is but very little inconvenience. Our rights are to be maintained. But they ought to be asserted and maintained in a manner not to wound unnecessarily the sensibilities of others." Here, at least rhetorically, was Clay again at his best, pleading—in an era that had never heard of therapy—for sensitivity to feelings, explaining that people who feel wounded and not respected will naturally react defensively, and will be far less likely to cooperate in the future. The feelings of slaves never entered Clay's thinking. But he recognized that the fate of the Union, and the lives of the hundreds of thousands of Americans who would fight and die in a civil war, hinged upon the feelings of both slave owners and the antislavery men of the North.

In these bills, Clay said, "I have enlisted myself in the cause of my country; I have enlisted myself in the great cause of this Union, and of harmony among its distracted parts; and I stand here, and here I mean to stand, to vindicate what has been done, and to vindicate this report, too, if necessary, from beginning to end." What he was saying was that he had put his career, his word, his character, the weight of his entire political career, on the line.

Clay begged senators not to "pounce" on the report before they had even read it. This was rather too much to ask, however. James Mason, a member of the committee, announced that he disagreed with every measure that it had proposed. David Yulee declared that he would never consent to any settlement "which excludes the South from a face upon the Pacific Ocean." Solon Borland pronounced the revamped fugitive slave bill to "be worse than nothing"—imposing "gross personal indignity" on masters who were merely seeking to recover their rightful property. The abolitionist John Hale, no longer able to contain himself, complained that the bill turned the whole of the territories into "a slave pasture": "It seems to me that the South takes the whole thing." Using almost identical language, Pierre Soulé of Louisiana dramatically lamented, "I wish it was a *compromise*—a real *compromise*—containing *mutual* concessions." But it was a fraud. "The South *gives*, the North *takes*."

The bill's weakest link was its embrace of the principle of federal "noninterference," which made it all but impossible to tell whether slavery would ultimately go into a territory or not. "The mystery is the only thing which recommends the bill," one Yankee senator sarcastically remarked. For those who supported Popular Sovereignty, such as Stephen Douglas, the bill's creative ambiguity meant that the people of each territory would decide the question of slavery for themselves. Southerners, however, generally understood federal "nonintervention"—or "nonaction," as they sometimes said—to mean that the government would not protect slavery in the territories. To Free Soilers, it meant that the government would not forestall the advance of slavery there. Clay's hair-splitting did not clarify much, when he said, in a rather unconvincing attempt to explain his position, "I am in favor of actions as respects governments for the territories, but I am in favor of non-action as respects the question of slavery." As usual, when confronted with this irreconcilable contradiction, Clay retreated into his dreamworld certainty that no one would ever carry slaves west anyway. "Is it worthwhile for us to be disputing about—what? The right to carry slaves where no man on earth would ever think of carrying them—where they would not be held as a gift."

To the southern "Ultras," however, the Omnibus was an unabashed assault on southern rights. Voters in almost every southern state were in the process of choosing delegates to the region-wide convention planned for June in Nashville, where it was widely expected that they would declare outright secession. "It is necessary to begin an organization of the South, the want of which has left us a divided people, when union and co-intelligence was necessary for our safety," Jefferson Davis wrote to Franklin H. Elmore, who was about to be named to Calhoun's seat in the Senate. "Many will rue the day when they oppose us, and our strength will increase thenceforward." Davis had spent part of April and early May in South Carolina attending to John Calhoun's funeral arrangements. There in the seedbed of Nullification, he was doubtless heartened by the atmosphere of feverish hostility to the Omnibus. When a few Charleston Whigs dared to express support for it, the Spartanburg *Spartan* denounced them for being "willing to swallow that villainous concoction of Northern depravity and scoundrelism called a compromise."

On his return to Washington, Davis assailed the compromise with renewed vigor. Although he could not compete with Clay or Benton in oratorical skill or folksiness, he more than matched their single-mindedness in his quest to carve space for slavery in the West. He repeatedly rejected the argument that the West was unfit for slavery. Indeed, he reiterated, the climate of New Mexico and southern California was perfect for the crops that favored slavery, such as cotton, maize, olive, sugarcane, and the grape. "Wherever water is found in sufficient abundance, our enterprising people will develop the capabilities of the country," he predicted. "Why, then, may not this country become great in its agricultural resources, if permitted to introduce that species of labor which can bear the scorching of a tropical sun?" (Davis also made the amazing and disingenuous argument that only slavery could protect the sedentary Indians of the region from predatory white settlers: "Shall we abandon these men, peaceful and prone to servility, or warlike and with fixed habitations, to the laws of California and the aggression of reckless men?") Day after day, week after week, he stubbornly restated what he treated as a self-evident position: "I claim only our constitutional rights, and that, if it is our constitutional right to take slaves into the territories, Congress is bound to protect that as much as other constitutional rights."

Throughout the spring, Davis's speeches to Congress were a steady drumbeat of warnings and threats delivered in tones of superlative condescension. Criticized for intransigence by what he termed "degraded letter writers" in the press, he loftily informed the Senate, "Proud in the consciousness of my own rectitude, I have looked upon it with the indifference which belongs to the assurance that I am right." The South's defense of slavery, he said, was akin to the patriotism of the Minutemen at Lexington and Concord who faced but two stark alternatives: "submission or resistance." Politically, the North might prevail over the South by force of numbers, but "every breeze will bring to the marauding destroyers of [southern] rights the warning, Woe, woe to the riders who trample them down!" In a succession of amendments, Davis proposed the extension of the Missouri Compromise line to the Pacific Ocean, forcing territorial governments to recognize slaves as property under the Constitution, and the extension of southern slave laws into the territories: "This is the most delicate species of property that is held: it is property that is ambulative; property which must be held under special laws and police regulations to render it useful and profitable to the owner," he told the Senate. He also propounded one of the most extreme states' rights arguments ever advanced: that the United States didn't even have the constitutional right to purchase the western lands that Texas claimed, as if the states—many of which were but a few years old—once established, were immutable and eternal, and not subject to even the most mundane territorial transactions.

No northern man could effectively counter arguments like this. That was what Clay needed Henry Foote for. An Ultra by anyone's measure when it came to the defense of southern interests, he could defend both slavery and the compromise in ways that were closed to Clay and Webster. His counterattack against Davis was piercing. Until now, Foote reminded wavering senators, the South had staunchly insisted that Congress had no authority to legislate on slavery—that it was constitutionally permitted everywhere, except where it was explicitly barred by state law. He charged that Davis was seeking to "hatch into existence a sort of southern Wilmot proviso" by calling for federal legislation to protect slavery in the territories. This was effectively to surrender to precisely what the abolitionists had been saying all along: that slave owners had no constitutional right to take slaves into the territories. If Davis got his way, the inevitable result, he warned, would doubtless be "a sweeping congressional enactment, which will utterly exterminate our favorite domestic institution, and plunge the whole South in hopeless and remediless ruin." How could "strict constructionists" permit such a thing, much less advocate for it? The Omnibus was not a defeat but a great victory for the South, Foote declared, and its passage would "mark the year 1850 as the most happy and most glorious in our national annals."

To this retorted Jeremiah Clemens of Alabama, an ardent secessionist and one of Davis's firmest allies, that the bill constituted "little short of treason" to the South's interests. (The shaggy, broad-faced Clemens was a restless spirit, who though barely thirty-five years old had led a company of volunteers in the Texas revolution, served in the Mexican War, and was now one of the Senate's youngest members.) Clemens shouted, "I am told to take this bill because it is the best I can get. Good God, sir! Has it come to this, that an American senator is to ask himself not whether a measure is unjust, iniquitous, and oppressive, but whether *it is the best he can do?*—not whether he will consent to wear chains at all, but whether the links will be round or square?—not whether he will bare his shoulders to the lash, but what is to be the color of the cowhide with which they are inflicted? Sir, when I consent to ask myself such questions, I hope the walls of this Capitol will fall upon me and crush me."

Foote, who never admitted to error, denied that he had been inconsistent. He had always opposed the admission of California as a separate measure but now it was just one part of a comprehensive compromise. He beseeched Clemens and the other radicals to desist in their attacks on the compromise before it was too late. If the Omnibus failed, California would come into the Union with no concessions to the South, the territories would be left without government, the Texas and New Mexico boundary would be left unsettled, and the Fugitive Slave Bill—"the only truly efficient bill of the kind ever yet devised"—would go down to defeat. Foote asked: "Are they willing to mingle their energies with those of the worst enemies of the South in bringing about this state of things?"

During a lull in the debate, Davis's ally David Yulee begged urgently to be recognized. He spoke for only a minute or two, to offer a seemingly cryptic resolution: "That the President of the United States be requested to inform the Senate whether any and what information has been received by the Executive Departments respecting an alleged revolutionary movement in the island of Cuba." He had read in the morning papers, he said, that American warships had been dispatched to Cuba for "what seems to me to be a war without the authority of the Congress of the United States." What was this all about? To the casual spectator, the tourist from Maine or Missouri, say, perched in the gallery to savor the repartee of Webster and Clay, or the fulminations of Benton and Clemens, Yulee's interjection may have seemed peculiarly inapposite, if a bit unsettling. However, what had just happened—was still happening—in the Gulf of Mexico was in fact another battle in the complex political war that encompassed not only the western territories that were the subject of the Senate's grinding debate, but also the entire Caribbean Basin.

A dark game was afoot. In March, a short man with a swarthy complexion, large liquid eyes, and a crisply military bearing was admitted to the pillared Greek Revival home of Mississippi's ambitious Governor John Quitman. After exchanging Masonic handshakes, the two men got down to business. The exotic-looking visitor, the rebellious Narciso López, now married to the daughter of a South Carolina plantation owner, had put the previous year's Round Island fiasco behind him, and was preparing for a new invasion. López offered Quitman command of the "liberation army" of American filibusters, which he said was to sail from New Orleans in May, and appointment as the first ruler of an independent Cuban state, in a prelude to outright annexation. Once the American force had landed, failure was impossible, López told Quitman: tens of thousands of Cuban patriots were waiting to flock to his banner.

It didn't take much to hook Quitman. An extraordinarily handsome man, with a surge of silvery locks, penetrating eyes, and aquiline features, he formed, along with Jefferson Davis and Henry Foote, the celestial, highly competitive trinity of political power in Mississippi. A transplanted New Yorker, he had embraced the southern way of life with the enthusiasm of a convert. Destined originally for the ministry, he abruptly abandoned the seminary at the age of twenty in 1819 and headed west to reinvent himself, coming to rest in Natchez, where in less than five years he had established a lucrative law practice, married into one of the wealthiest families in the state, and acquired a plantation worked by more than one hundred slaves: by 1850, he owned more than 450. Quitman not only defended slavery, he adored it. Slavery, he believed, was "a moral, social, and political good," and he hoped that slaves would eventually become "a permanent fixture, a hereditary heirloom" in every household.

An enthusiastic imperialist, he further believed that slavery both needed and deserved room to expand. He had led Mississippi volunteers to fight in the Texas War of Independence, and had taken the field again in the war against Mexico, where he had risen to the rank of general. He personally led his division in the capture of Chapultepec Castle during the assault on Mexico City. Although every member of his staff was either killed or wounded, Quitman himself, amazingly, survived unscathed—proof, he maintained, that "Providence seemed to turn the bullets from me." He regarded Clay's compromise as both a political disaster for the South and as a personal affront: he wanted to ship some of his own slaves to California, to establish a new plantation there, but would scarcely risk doing so unless the new state made slavery secure. He was already looking, as were other southern expansionists, beyond the Mexican Cession to the annexation of Cuba as the best possible strategy to avert the "social dangers" that menaced the South. "Her fate is ours," Quitman proclaimed.

Southern advocates of annexation suggested that one or more new slave states could easily be carved from the Caribbean island, adding two or four more senators to the proslavery bloc. Increasingly anxious that they would be cut off from the Pacific coast, southerners were looking toward the Caribbean as the core of a new commercial empire, a great cotton, tobacco, sugar, and coffee-producing union, incorporating "the boundless fertility of Cuba, and renovating the West Indian islands with the labor of the blacks of the southern states," as the *Democratic Review*, a mouthpiece for southern interests in the Democratic Party, put it. López's backers, Cuban sugar planters who feared that Spain might proclaim a general emancipation, and believed that either independence or annexation was the only way to protect their human property, lent credence to such dreams. Unless new slave states were found somewhere, editorialized the official *Texas State Gazette* in March, "the South would be compelled to secession, and perhaps a bloody war of defense." (American designs on Cuba stretched back at least to the 1820s. Even some northerners, including Stephen Douglas—who owned stock in steamship companies that traded with Cuba—regarded the extension of American power into the Caribbean as a natural right, and supported the acquisition of Cuba at little political cost: they could not be accused of seeking to "extend" slavery, since it was already legal there.)

Shrugging off his gubernatorial duties, Quitman traveled down the Mississippi by steamboat to López's headquarters at Bank's Arcade in New Orleans, a colonnaded confection on Magazine Street, where the two conspirators recruited volunteers for the "army of liberation." Some of these were serving members of the United States Army, others were veterans of the Mexican War, a few were idealists in the cause of Manifest Destiny, and still others had been recruited as far afield as Kentucky and through Quitman's connections in Mississippi. But the majority were hired from the throngs of unemployed young men who prowled the sultry streets of New Orleans, looking for adventure.

Weapons for the López expedition were generously supplied, for a price, by the state arsenals of Mississippi and Louisiana, and powder by compliant officers of the United States arsenal at New Orleans. The expedition was financed by Cuban émigrés and New Orleans businessmen, including the owner of one of the city's leading newspapers, the *Daily Delta*, and by the sale of Cuban bonds for 10 cents on the dollar, to be redeemed at full value once López had secured the island. López officially claimed that he was organizing a company to travel to California to mine gold, but his real purpose was an open secret. Newspapers from New York to New Orleans reported rumors of preparation for the invasion, as did federal officials—and the alert Spanish consul at New Orleans. Determined to block slavery's southern ambitions as well as its western ones, President Taylor ordered federal warships to sea to intercept the invasion before it made landfall.

At the end of April, two chartered steamboats left New Orleans carrying 550 American filibusters, and a cargo of guns for the Cuban rebels who were expected to meet them. López planned to command the invasion in person. Once López had achieved a secure beachhead, Quitman would follow with reinforcements and they would push on together to Havana. Easily eluding the U.S. ships that were meant to intercept them, López's force sailed south to the Yucatan, where his men were organized into three skeleton regiments and were put through two weeks of training by their officers. López himself left New Orleans on May 7 aboard his flagship, the *Creole*. At Yucatan, the invaders, reduced to about five hundred after desertions and sickness, reembarked on the *Creole*, and—now armed with Bowie knives, pistols, and rifles, and uniformed in red shirts, black caps, and striped trousers—set sail for Cuba and their rendezvous with destiny, as the idealistic among them believed.

On the night of May 18, a full moon shone over the Gulf of Mexico as López mustered his force on deck, where he finally informed them of their precise destination, the small city of Cárdenas on the north coast of Cuba, eighty-five miles east of Havana. He told them that they were "about to strike the first blow of a glorious revolution, the success of which would crown all with honor equal to that of their revolutionary fathers, with present rewards far greater." Cárdenas, he assured them, was undefended: they would be greeted as liberators and showered with flowers.

At 2:30 A.M., the Americans began pouring ashore, some heading for the local governor's office, others to secure the railway yards, where they planned to seize rolling stock for the journey to Havana. Things began to go wrong almost immediately. Instead of the friendly reception the filibusters had been led to expect, the Cubans balked at helping the Americans find their objectives, and were induced only at gunpoint to serve as guides. "A six-shooter pointed at their heads had a wonderful effect in brightening their ideas, and through the influence of such persuaders the requisite information was soon obtained," one American remarked. It quickly became clear that not only were there Spanish troops in the town, but that they had fight in them. Shouting "López and Liberty!" and

"Libertad de Cuba y Independencia!" the Americans raced through the streets—it was "a harum-scarum business," one Kentuckian recalled—losing men to sniper fire as they charged across the plaza. Until dawn, the Americans traded gunfire with Spanish regulars who were holed up in their barracks and the governor's office, as well as from armed locals. Every rooftop and window seemed to be defended by "some rascally shooting machine." At dawn, the Kentuckians stormed the barracks, and took the survivors prisoner. Not far away, López personally led another party of Americans in an assault on the governor's house, bayoneting its defenders as they rushed in.

Establishing his headquarters in the captured barracks, López issued a proclamation announcing to the people of Cárdenas that they had at last been liberated from Spanish despotism. Then he waited for the army of rebels that he had so confidently predicted. In fact, few if any Cubans joined the invaders, apart from a score of runaway slaves who tried to board the *Creole* in hope of being carried to safety in America; the filibusters, proslavery men all, threw off every one they managed to catch. Meanwhile, the Americans who had been sent to secure the rail yards discovered that in anticipation of an invasion—the Spanish consul in New Orleans had been sending regular reports on López's activities there—the colonial authorities had cut the line outside town: there would be no express to Havana for López's men. Convinced that they had won a great victory, many of the less disciplined Americans took up residence in the local *cantinas* and "drank a great deal of liquor of every description, most of which had a stupefying effect."

The bloodiest part of the invasion occurred at the end of the afternoon, when sixty Spanish lancers suddenly appeared, in a gallant but suicidal charge against a startled contingent of Kentuckians, who were both well armed and well led, and emptied almost every saddle to leave dying Spaniards and their horses shrieking in the dusty streets. Soon afterward, López learned to his dismay that as many as two thousand Spanish infantry were en route to Cárdenas, enough to easily overwhelm his own increasingly disorganized force. The Spanish governor of the island denounced the invaders as "miserable refuse" driven to America by the convulsions of Europe, and ordered any of them captured by his troops to be immediately put to death. To prevent a debacle, López ordered his men back onto the *Creole*, intending to land at a more promising point further down the coast, where he planned to call for Quitman and his reinforcements.

But López's miserable luck followed him to sea. Five miles offshore, the *Creole* ran aground on a reef. The Americans panicked, with good reason. Spanish warships were already hunting the *Creole*, and if they caught her everyone on board was likely to be executed. In an effort to refloat the ship, coal, ammunition, and even guns were thrown overboard, and a hundred of the filibusters ordered into small boats, to be rowed to a nearby islet. Around dawn on the 19th, the *Creole* finally managed to work its way off the reef. The marooned warriors reboarded and, with López in a frenzy of frustration, the *Creole* turned toward Florida, in what was about to prove a desperate race for survival. It was none too soon. Only by chance had the Spanish missed the *Creole* in the night. With daylight, however, the *Pizarro*, carrying two hundred seasoned grenadiers, easily discovered the *Creole*, and pursued it at top speed across the Florida Straits.

The *Creole* reached Key West just minutes ahead of her pursuers. The *Pizarro* followed her into the harbor, and was bringing her broadside to bear, when an American warship interposed herself: the Taylor administration may have been embarrassed by the expedition, but it was not about to let a foreign gunboat sink a vessel of any kind in an American harbor. To the chagrin of the Spaniards, the filibusters poured off the *Creole*, and disappeared into the streets and taverns of Key West before anyone could stop them. The only passengers from the *Creole* who were arrested were seven fugitive slaves who had managed to hide aboard the boat during her journey from Cárdenas. When they emerged in Key West, they were turned over to the district court, which in turn handed them to the Spanish consul for shipment back to Cuba and slavery. "*Libertad y Independencia!*" was not, of course, meant to apply to them.

Early rumors reaching the United States claimed that López had cut the Spanish to pieces, that shiploads of American Forty-niners in Havana harbor were about to storm the city, and that Barbados and Jamaica were in full revolt. When news came that the invasion was actually a failure, there was a surge of militant jingoism, at least in the South. "How many thousands of our bold and enterprising youth are there now ready to rush to the aid of their brethren in Cuba?" demanded the New Orleans *Daily Delta.* Southern critics of the administration howled at its interference with the raid. The invaders should have been protected by the navy, not harassed by it. In the Senate, David Yulee—whose father had made the family's fortune in Cuban sugar—chastised Taylor for trampling first on the Constitution, then on Cuba's desire for freedom, and finally on what he considered the right of Americans to invade their neighbors whenever they wished.

Yulee was but one of many proslavery men who boiled with frustration. Southerners who fumed at the apparent loss of California and feared the loss of New Mexico had now lost (at least for the time being) the lowest hanging territorial fruit in the Caribbean. Militarily, the invasion had been an abject fiasco. However, the inability of the Taylor administration to halt López's expedition starkly revealed the administration's weakness, particularly in the Deep South, where its influence was close to nil, even in the president's home state of Louisiana. Despite many warnings, the navy had proved unable to stop López's ships either from sailing or from reaching their destination. A sitting governor had baldly collaborated in the invasion of a country with which the United States was not at war. The state armories of two states and the officers of a federal arsenal had supplied the invaders with weapons. Members of the armed forces had openly enlisted with the filibusters. The raid was evidence, for those who cared to see, that in a creeping prelude to secession, the South was already crafting its own foreign policy, and its own dream of slavery-based expansion with no deference to the interests of the nation as a whole.

The ramifications of the invasion were immediately felt in the Senate, where John Davis of Massachusetts, already skeptical about the Omnibus, pointed an accusatory finger at the compromise's godfather. "Why this feverish desire for acquisition? What remedy have we for this, if annexation is to be continued by war and invasion? There is but one remedy, and that is to plant the frontier with a free population. I would ask the Senator from Kentucky how his compromise act would stop the progress of such events as this? What is there in it that is likely to curb this zeal for unlawful acquisition, which is the disease that we are contending with? Sir, I confess that I see nothing."

Clay, for once silent, had no answer.

CHAPTER 19

"A LEGISLATIVE SATURNALIA"

——————·◆·——————

Clay had hoped that his compromise package would be enacted back in January. It was now the end of May. Why couldn't his fellow senators see that there was simply no alternative? Think through the consequences of failure, he begged. Imagine the fury of the public if they quit now. "In that state of feeling of mutual exasperation and excitement, with a heated press, with heated parties, with heated lecturers, with heated men, how can you expect hereafter to come back to this theater of strife and contention calm and composed, to settle difficulties which six months of earnest and anxious labor have not enabled you to adjust?"

In one of the most memorable moments of the entire debate, Clay raised his left hand, and with his right ticked off his fingers, one by one: "Here are five wounds—one, two, three, four, five—bleeding and threatening the well-being, if not the existence of the body politic." There was California . . . the territories . . . the Texas boundary . . . the Fugitive Slave Bill . . . the slave trade in Washington. Clay then took a step— "a painful duty"—that he had avoided for months: he directly attacked the president. True, their relations had never been more than cordial, but he was still the national leader of Clay's own Whig Party. "What is the plan of the president?" Clay asked. "Is it to heal all these wounds? No such thing. It is only to heal one of the five, and to leave the other four to bleed more profusely than ever, by the sole admission of California, even if it should produce death itself."

Clay had hoped, he said, for some kind of help from the president in healing the nation's wounds. But instead Taylor clung stubbornly to his own "particular scheme," which promised only to make things much worse. Taylor's plan was no plan at all, but a recipe for continuing crisis. The president ignored the issue of runaway slaves, as well as that of the slave trade in the capital; worse yet, he left the burning problems of territorial government and the Texas boundary untouched, apparently, Clay remarked, "to cure themselves by some law of nature, or some self-remedy, in the success of which I cannot perceive any ground of the least confidence." These were harsh words indeed, enough so, he hoped, to pry loose a few votes from among the president's lukewarm supporters.

Turning to address the South, Clay summoned up one of his best performances yet. He knew that he needed more southern votes, and that they could come only from among the ranks of the prickly and suspicious radicals who had spurned his every overture. In his patented style— moderate but firm, provocative but sympathetic, realistic but generous— Clay begged to know how the South could say that it had gained nothing from the Omnibus. It was being handed just what it had demanded for years—the abandonment of the Wilmot Proviso. "The proviso is not in the bill," Clay reminded them. "The bill admits that if slavery is there, there it remains. The bill admits that if slavery is not there, there it is not. The bill is neither southern nor northern. It is equal; it is fair; it is a compromise, which any man, whether at the North or the South, who is desirous of healing the wounds of his country, may accept without dishonor or disgrace." Then, not mincing words, he urged the South to forget about Calhoun's notion of "equilibrium." The South could never keep pace with the North's rapid growth without overturning the basic structure of American government. But, he went on, pivoting to a tone of comforting reassurance, the South was in no danger with respect to "that great institution which exists there, and is cherished by so much solicitude." Slavery was perfectly secure, forever protected by the Constitution, by the fact that both houses of Congress had to concur in legislation that might threaten the South's interests, by the presidential veto, by the Supreme Court, and by "that sense of justice which appertains to enlightened man."

Then he challenged the South to question its assumptions. Was its "great interest . . . this institution of slavery" *really* so unique that it deserved all kinds of special protections? The fishing interest, the navigating interest, the manufacturing interest, the commercial interest—they were all "minority" interests, too. In short, every economic interest was a minority, "except that great and all-pervading interest of agriculture." Reconcile yourselves to the inevitable, he urged southerners. The South's power was inescapably fated to decline. Political "equilibrium" was a fantasy. But happily it was also unnecessary. The solution to the South's anxieties was already to hand. "If this measure of compromise goes to the country with all the high sanctions which it may carry—sanctions of both houses of Congress, and of the Executive, and of the great body of the American people—to a country bleeding at every pore—to a country imploring us to settle their difficulties, and give once more peace and happiness to them—I venture to say that the agitation will be at an end, though a few may croak and halloo as they please." It was another bravura performance. But what would be its effect on the men to whom it was directed?

Clay learned soon enough that he had delivered a dinner of rhetorical red meat to his nemesis, Tom Benton. The Missourian had remained relatively quiescent for several weeks. Spurred to action by Clay's eloquence, he sneered thunderously that the Committee of Thirteen had produced a "monster, and required us to worship what it is our duty to kill. I proceed to the destruction of this monster." With all his histrionics, Clay was merely manufacturing discontent, Benton sarcastically claimed, just as he had so often in the past, over the tariff, and over the national bank, and now slavery. "He treats us to the old dish of distress!" The Omnibus was a mere "farrago" of old bills. "No sooner are they jumbled together, and called a compromise, than the nation is filled with their perfume. People smell it all over the land, and like the inhalers of certain drugs, become frantic for the thing." Mocking Clay's arresting simile, he declared that he saw "none of those five gaping wounds" that Clay had enumerated. No one, not even "little Doctor Taylor," had provided such a "capacious plaster" as had Clay, with his "five old bills tacked together." Holding up his hand in imitation of Clay, Benton went on, "The senator and myself are alike, in this, that each of us has but five fingers on the left hand; and that may account for the limitation of the wounds. When the fingers gave out, they gave out; and if there had been more fingers, there might have been more wounds—as many as fingers—and toes also." Clay did not leave a record of his reaction, but he must have been livid.

Benton never knew when to stop. He went on to bombard the Senate with a lengthy account of slavery's history in the United States, and then with an interminable lesson in the geography of the newly acquired territories, larded with liberal quotations from the works of Alexander von Humboldt, Zebulon Pike, and other travelers, and with a potted history of Spanish settlement going back to the seventeenth century—followed by a paean to the glories of . . . *salt*! This was hinged, slightly, to his mention of the presence of valuable salt deposits near El Paso. "Mr. President, I am a salt man!" Benton crowed. "I have an almost mystical reverence for salt. It is the conservative principle of nature. The life of man and beast requires it. God has bestowed it; and let all keep it, to whom he has given it. No taxing, or taking any people's salt!"

Senators who were still listening then heard an assault on the very principle of compromise itself. Combining measures for the open purpose of forcing one to carry another was, in effect, to compel the friends of the stronger measure to take the weak one, too, for fear of losing the stronger one. The Omnibus was a monstrosity. Utah was stuffed in because it was linked to California, and Texas because it was linked to New Mexico. "And thus poor California is crammed and gorged until she is in about the condition that Jonah would have been in if he had swallowed the whale, instead of the whale swallowing him." Irritating though Benton's speechmaking might be, his analysis was fundamentally correct. There were many senators who were quite willing to support California's admission but who could not unite on the territorial questions. Some denied the power of Congress over slavery in the territories. Others granted the power, but rejected the expediency of exercising it. Others supported both the power and its exercise. Still others opposed installing any government in the territories.

The debate had turned into "a legislative saturnalia—a frolic," Benton scoffed, "where the amiable guests pummel each other," and "the great peace-maker"—this was Clay—was "stuck all over with arrows." It was time to end the comedy. "California is suffering for want of admission. New Mexico is suffering for want of protection. The public business is suffering for want of attention. The character of Congress is suffering for want of progress in business." The only way to put an end to all this was to postpone the whole "unmanageable mass" until its separate parts could rationally be dealt with singly.

Unfortunately for Benton, his overbearing style managed to alienate even those senators who fundamentally agreed with him. William Dayton of New Jersey, for one, dismissed his speech as a useless tirade. Benton, he said, "fancied long since that he saw disunion through the mists ahead, and forthwith he seized his club and has laid about him like Hercules ever since. He has kept up a great noise of battle [but] he has not even bruised the hydra's head."

After Calhoun's death, in April the governor of South Carolina appointed to replace him Franklin Elmore, a prominent banker and former congressman. A self-described "devoted disciple" of Calhoun, and a pillar of his state's power structure, the fifty-year-old Elmore, it was expected, would serve as another dependable advocate for states' rights and slavery. He took his seat, officially at least, on May 6. Plagued from the start by ill health, however, he played no role in that month's debate. On May 30, twenty-three days after his arrival, his stunned colleague from South Carolina, Andrew Butler, rose to announce that Elmore had suddenly dropped dead in his hotel room.

Elmore's fleeting presence in the Senate had no appreciable effect on the debate, beyond a discomfiting reminder that even senators were mortal. As May ticked away into June on the ornate clock that hung above the vice president's throne, and the first twinges of summer heat fed anxiety about the onset of the cholera season, the mood in Congress grew increasingly sour. "As for this compromise, I will vote for it because I wish to get the subject from before us," said Augustus C. Dodge of Iowa, a Democrat who generally followed the lead of Stephen Douglas. "I am sick, sore, and tired of it; and therefore, though this measure is one that does not please me in all its parts, I shall swallow it in order to get the subject out of the halls of Congress."

When David Yulee proposed a one-week recess in the wake of Elmore's death, to take up the winter carpets and prepare the Senate chamber for the warm summer weather—this was customary around this time of year—Clay snapped: "I am utterly opposed to it." The chamber hadn't been thoroughly cleaned for five or six months. But exhaustion made Clay imperious. More than a century and a half later, his petulance still fairly steams from the pages of the *Congressional Globe*: after six months of debate, "when the eye of every patriot and every friend of his country is intensely directed to this body," the Senate would dare to quit work for a week just to take up carpets! "For one," pronounced Clay, "I prefer these carpets to any others that can be put down." It was as if the carpets—filthy with the encrusted mud, tobacco juice, spittle, and heaven knows what else—had become for Clay a symbol of the Omnibus itself, to be kept intact and defended to the death. Clay would see that they stayed in place.

He was close to physical collapse. Just reaching the floor of the Senate each day was a struggle. He was so weak that increasingly, when he rose to speak he had to grip his walnut desk to hold himself steady, coughing so uncontrollably that he sometimes had to cut short his remarks. The pettiness of his fellow senators drove him to distraction. To his mind, much of the criticism that had been leveled against the Omnibus was not much more substantive than Yulee's fussing over the carpets. "This finding of fault, and, with the aid of a magnifying glass, discovering defects, descrying the little *animalculae* which move upon the surface of the matter, and which are indiscernible to the naked natural eye, is an easy task," Clay complained. Condescension did not help his cause.

Although he would not admit it publicly, Clay was losing confidence that the Omnibus would prevail. "The Administration, the Abolitionists, the Ultra Southern men, and the timid Whigs of the North are all combined against it," he wrote to his son Thomas. "Against such a combination, it would be wonderful if it should succeed."

The president's allies in the press attacked Clay as vain and dictatorial. In the Senate, the enemies of the Omnibus declared it a spectacular failure. "It has gone up in our political sky like some splendid specimen of pyrotechnic art, attracting by its show the gaze of the country far and wide; it may burst at its topmost height," New Jersey's Dayton scoffed. "If so, a deeper darkness, a more pervading gloom may for an instant follow." Amendments roared at the Omnibus from every side—twenty-eight of them in the month of June, most of them unfriendly. Abolitionists fired off amendments reasserting the Wilmot Proviso . . . southern radicals, amendments calling for the protection of slavery . . . Popular Sovereignty men, amendments to strike out the bill's ban on territorial governments legislating on slavery. Nearly all were shot down, as Clay piloted the Omnibus forward like a battered, leaking, but still (if barely) seaworthy warship.

On June 6th, Isaac Walker of Wisconsin, a stolid antislavery man, proposed an amendment making peonage illegal in the western territories, saying that his feelings "revolted" at the thought of men and women who were now American citizens being held in bondage "under the control of Mexicans." There were at this point at least hundreds, and probably several thousand, men, women, and children condemned to debt slavery in New Mexico. Most were Indians kidnapped in childhood and sold to Spanish-speaking farmers and ranchers, but at least some were of Mexican origin, and trapped in a form of servitude that extended from generation to generation. Several senators had obliquely cited peonage, with its pathetically low-cost labor, as the primary reason more costly black slavery would never take root in New Mexico.

Clay didn't want to get into this can of worms at all. "We have been six months, in some form or other, engaged in the consideration of African slavery, and as if we had not enough of that, peonage has sprung up," he grumbled. Most of what the senators claimed to know were mere travelers' tales, and didn't deserve to be taken seriously. He pleaded with Walker to withdraw his amendment.

William Seward, who had said comparatively little since his "higher law" speech, remarked that after months of struggling against *African* slavery, it was hardly beside the point at all to prevent the enslaving of *Indians*, or for that matter any other men. "We know this in regard to peon servitude—that it is SLAVERY, and that it is slavery that is created there either by law or by contract. If it is created by law, and without the consent and will of the slave, then it ought to be abolished."

At this, southern tempers instantly flared: any challenge to peonage must be a wedge to subvert slavery itself. If a peon had not been released from servitude, interjected Robert Hunter, with a figurative shrug, it could only be because of his own "recklessness" and "want of foresight." Peonage, added Jefferson Davis, was an inheritance from Mexican and Spanish law, and "one of those relations of personal property for which the federal government cannot legislate"—precisely the opposite of the position he took when abolitionists asserted that black slavery in New Mexico had already been abolished by Mexican law.

Stephen Douglas, whose reaction was, as usual, blunt and uninhibited, said that it was not so much peonage itself that bothered him, but the fact that American citizens, "the white man, the free man" could be ensnared in it. "If we are to restrict and limit the action of Territorial legislatures, our first duty should be to abolish this revolting system, by which white men, our own kindred, may be reduced to a system of slavery."

Walker's amendment was decisively defeated by a vote of 32 to 20, with Clay, Webster, and almost every conservative northerner siding with the solid South.

• • •

On the 14th, Yulee again pleaded for a recess for the carpets to be taken up and the chamber cleaned. "All these motions" came from senators who opposed the compromise, and were only interested in delay, and more delay, according to Clay. "To postpone, to delay, to impede, to procrastinate, has been the policy of the minority of this body." If there was anyone who needed rest, it was "the oldest member"—Clay himself. "Yet I would work on this carpet, or any other carpet, to accomplish the completion of this bill. Washington surrendered his sword in an uncarpeted room, and yet we must adjourn for three days, when the whole country is in a crisis to take up a carpet which I would prefer to the one which is proposed to substitute for it." There was a clear majority in favor of the Omnibus, he claimed. He hoped to pass it within a week—further delay was intolerable. There was no excuse for wasting three more days, or even one, merely to change a carpet. "Why, sir," Clay exclaimed, "I cannot afford to have a great many carpets, and I have been accustomed to a woolen carpet throughout the whole year; and the only change I have made this year was to procure a softer one, and the effect has been that I took cold by the means."

But this time, in the end, Clay relented. The carpets finally came up.

Clay's notion of concluding debate within the week was hopelessly optimistic, as indeed had been his every prediction since the start of the session. In the days that followed, with the chamber having been newly carpeted with summer-weight straw, four significant amendments to the Omnibus were adopted, three of them proposed by members of the hard-core proslavery bloc. The first, written by John Berrien of Georgia, one of the Deep South's grand old men, inserted language preventing a territorial government from "establishing or prohibiting African slavery," a locution which southerners believed could be interpreted to protect slave property where it existed in the territory. The second, proposed by Yulee, stated explicitly that constitutional guarantees, including as he believed the protection of slavery, applied to the territories. The third, sponsored by John Hale, extended the appellate power of the Supreme Court to the territories, making it possible—as the antislavery Hale desired—to challenge in court the right to carry slaves into the territories; however, since southerners had controlled the court through its entire history, they had little reason to object. The fourth amendment, crafted by Pierre Soulé of Louisiana, specified that future states created out of the territories be admitted to the Union with or without slavery, a provision that appeared to commit northerners to the admission of new slave states if they applied.

All the southern amendments passed thanks to crossover votes from cooperative northerners, several of whom defended themselves with sometimes tortured reasoning designed to assuage the anticipated wrath of antislavery voters back home. Stephen Douglas asserted that his vote for Soulé's amendment amounted to no more than a vote for Popular Sovereignty, the belief that people had a right to do as they pleased when they formed their constitution, no matter what "domestic regulations" they chose to make. Douglas's ally Augustus Dodge of Iowa added, addressing Soulé, "It is due to candor that I should tell him I am against his black boys—that is, I want none of them, nor anything to do with them." However, he added, as far as the settlement of New Mexico and Utah were concerned, "I defy the senator to come on with his constituents as fast as he pleases, and with his negroes too, and I tell him that, without congressional conditions or restrictions, I and my constituents will beat him in numbers and in influence; and, if not, we will go to the wall."

Webster's defense bordered on the pathetic. Spurned by his native New England, he lapped up the lush flattery slathered upon him by his new southern allies. "*Upon you*, the *safety* of the Country depends," wrote North Carolina senator Willie P. Mangum in a private note on April 11. "You may think this extravagance, I know it *to be sense*." Throughout the spring, Webster had continued to work behind the scenes to win support for the compromise despite the deepening feeling that enemies lay in wait for him everywhere. "There are a great many traps set, all round, & some spring guns," he gloomily replied. Although to others he spoke of his "steadiness of purpose," he as much as admitted that he didn't dare vote against Soulé's amendment for fear of being perceived by the South as secretly harboring a desire to enact the Wilmot Proviso in its place. The man who had once stood as the hero of antislavery New England saw "no occasion to make a provision against slavery now, or to reserve to ourselves the right of making such a provision hereafter." He rested on his unshakable conviction that "the law of nature"—here it was again, that mantra that so comforted him and Clay—barred slavery forever from the territories. "This is the foundation of all." He knew that his words displeased many of his onetime friends. "I leave consequences to themselves," he rumbled. "My object is peace. My object is reconciliation. I am against local ideas North and South, and against all narrow and local contests. I am an American." The galleries applauded. But the Godlike Daniel's rationalizations were wearing thin.

CHAPTER 20

A PACT WITH THE DEVIL

———·◆·———

"The territories." The words seemed plain enough. They rolled off tobacco-stained senatorial tongues day after day, week in and week out, month after month. "The territories" meant both Utah and New Mexico. But Utah was rarely mentioned, and when it was, it was mostly as an afterthought, a sort of geographical apostrophe. Prospects for a territorial bill had looked bright, John Bernhisel, who the Mormons of the Salt Lake settlement had despatched to make their case to Congress, had written hopefully to Brigham Young in April, "but a week or two may entirely blast the present prospect, for the aspect of things here changes about as often as a camelion [sic] changes his color." Remarked one senator, "We lose sight of Deseret entirely." It was New Mexico that was pushing the country to what Henry Clay repeatedly called "the crisis of the crisis." As early as January, the official *Texas State Gazette* had urged "patriots" to gird themselves for war, portraying Texas as an innocent victim whose "rights" had suffered outrage upon outrage—a euphemism for physical rape—by the "diseased sensibility" of northern aggression: "In the presence of these impending dangers, it behooves the South to gird up her loins and confront them." Texas, Sam Houston warned the Senate in June, "will submit to no aggression from any power under Heaven." To this, Tom Rusk added that although Texas would regret a "collision" with the federal authorities, "I greatly mistake the temper of the people of Texas if they would submit for a single moment to terms of degradation." This was more than bravado. They had the entire South behind them.

There had been innumerable proposals for quieting Texas's claims and defusing the crisis. All of them involved drawing and redrawing lines across the empty wastes that stretched away between the Red River and the Rio Grande. All this fiddling with borders by men comfortably ensconced in Washington was wonderfully abstract, rather like plotting charts of the heavens without the aid of a telescope, since the senators still knew little about the remote region they were arguing over. As recently as April, Webster could seriously ask, "What is New Mexico? Who is to say who her people are?" The senators were only now beginning to grasp just how dire the political situation in New Mexico had become.

Early in April—news from New Mexico took months to reach the East Coast—Robert Neighbors had arrived with his hard-riding party in Santa Fe, having traveled three hundred miles across a landscape scarred and wrinkled by erosion, past desolated villages where the bones of Mexican settlers slaughtered by Indians bleached in the sun. Fear pervaded Santa Fe's dusty lanes: fear of the war parties of Comanches, Apaches, Utes, and Navajos that swirled through the surrounding countryside, swooping down upon parties of travelers, ranchos, and even entire towns, carrying off children, and running off livestock in staggering numbers. The previous summer, Indians had killed forty-seven Americans and hundreds of Spanish-speaking villagers, destroyed 330 wagons, and stolen 6,500 animals along the Santa Fe Trail. Just since January the Apaches had run off an estimated twelve thousand sheep between Santa Fe and Las Vegas, killing their herdsmen, and taking many others captive. "There is hardly an American here that stirs abroad without being armed to the teeth, and under his pillow pistols and Bowie knives may always be found," one settler reported.

As far as Neighbors was concerned, the Indians could be dealt with in due time, Texas-style. At the moment, he had one goal: to dissolve New

Mexico's military government. He had left El Paso firmly under the control of men friendly to Texas, and he now expected at least the tacit cooperation of the military governor in Santa Fe, Colonel John Munroe, in establishing Texan rule over the rest of the territory. Neighbors, a big man, was forced to stoop deeply to pass through the diminutive door of the low-slung Governor's Palace, a symbolically apt foretaste of the humbling that lay in store for him. If Munroe was not quite all the federal government there was in New Mexico—there was Judge Joab Houghton, the leader of the antislavery faction in New Mexico, and a handful of other minor civilian officials—he was all that really mattered. Born in Scotland and raised in New York, Munroe had graduated from West Point, served in the War of 1812, battled Indians in Florida, and during the Mexican War commanded Zachary Taylor's artillery at Buena Vista, where his gunnery helped to deliver the future president his famous victory. They were men of a type, the saddle-weary young Texan and the sixty-year-old, bull-faced soldier: both unyielding of temperament, and hardened by life on the frontier and the omnipresent danger of violent death. Behind Munroe stood the uncertain might of the United States government, two thousand miles away in Washington; and behind Neighbors the slighter but considerably closer power of Texas, six hundred miles away in Austin. Neither man knew which would prevail.

Munroe—this "mere lieutenant colonel," in Clay's contemptuous words—was probably unaware of the vilification that was being heaped on him in Washington. Senators from the South and North alike, who knew nothing about him, accused him wildly of imposing a capricious personal dictatorship, of sheer incompetence, of carrying out some sinister program of the president's, of collaborating with the Texans, or of tyrannically stonewalling them. Munroe had, in fact, intimated to Neighbors a few weeks earlier that he would not interfere with the Texan's activities. But since then things had changed. President Taylor's agent, Lieutenant Colonel McCall, had arrived from the East with clear instructions—though they were not revealed to Neighbors—that the administration wanted New Mexico to advance toward statehood, and that it had no intention of acceding to Texan demands. Neighbors reminded Munroe, in a drawl that did nothing to conceal his stark message, that the 1845 treaty of annexation explicitly granted Texas the right to draw its own state boundaries, and that Santa Fe was "indisputably" included within them.

"Are you willing to acknowledge the jurisdiction of Texas, provided I hold the elections and qualify the proper civil officers?" Neighbors asked Munroe, indicating that he intended to start appointing Texan officials as he had done in El Paso.

"I am not prepared to say so," the soldier replied. Munroe informed Neighbors—by all accounts the exchange was polite, if a jolt to the overconfident Texan—that he recognized neither Neighbors nor Texas's claim to New Mexico, and that since the United States government had commissioned New Mexico's officials, he had no right to remove them. He would do nothing whatever to facilitate the Texan's mission.

Neighbors then told Munroe that if the army failed to facilitate his mission, Texas would extend its jurisdiction by proclamation anyway, and back it up by force of arms. Neighbors was not a political windbag. He meant what he said.

Neighbors next called on Houghton, who informed him that he would jail anyone who attempted to impose Texas law in his jurisdiction. Neighbors then discovered that it was virtually impossible for him even to publicize Texas's claims, since Houghton and his allies controlled New Mexico's single printing press. The only newspaper, the *Weekly Gazette*, whose editor, William G. Kephardt, had come to New Mexico as an agent of the American and Foreign Anti-Slavery Society, would certainly not offer any help. Neighbors protested in vain. Complaining to Texas governor Bell that "the masses are kept entirely uninformed or misinformed in regard to Texas," he called the Munroe-Houghton regime "more absolute and despotic than any other that exists on this continent." Doubtless he now regretted having tossed away those copies of the Texas constitution in order to lighten his load during the trek from San Antonio to El Paso. But they would have made little difference, since, no matter what politicians said in Washington or Austin, there was little public support north of El Paso for Texas's imperial schemes.

Although Neighbors found some friends among the merchants, teamsters, southern military officers, and lawyers who stood to gain from closer ties with Texas, Houghton's territorial court had already issued a proclamation in Spanish, urging the locals to actively resist Texas's "unjust usurpation," forcing Neighbors, to his chagrin, to cancel elections for Texas offices. Hispanics, in particular, feared that Texan occupation would mean the legalization of slavery, the degradation of free labor, and rule by the same freebooting Anglo frontiersmen who had pillaged the border country for the past decade. The Pueblo Indians, too, Neighbors complained, had "already been tampered with." However, there were enough Texans in Santa Fe to sow discord. Club-wielding teamsters broke up pro-statehood meetings. Armed ruffians assaulted Hispanic community leaders in broad daylight. The atmosphere grew dense with apprehension. Serious bloodshed was expected at any time.

Mass meetings nevertheless adopted resolutions calling for statehood, proclaiming, "We shall at all hazards vindicate the integrity of our Soil & just rights and bring to punishment those seditious persons if any there be who may be found aiding and supporting the Texas authorities." The largest of these, held with the obvious approval of the federal authorities—an army major presided, and Munroe's private secretary served as recorder— called for the election of delegates to a statehood convention. When the convention met in May, it not only firmly rejected Texas's claim to any part of New Mexico, but even declared New Mexico's boundary to lie as far east as Abilene—well within the generally accepted bounds of Texas. It also adopted a resounding resolution, probably written by Houghton, declaring that "wherever [slavery] has existed, it has proved a curse and a blight to the State upon which it has been inflicted—a moral, social, and political evil. The only manner in which this question now affects us is politically; and on the grounds of this character, with its general evil tendencies, we have unanimously agreed to reject it, forever." The South's nightmare was coming true.

By then, Neighbors was already on his way back to Texas. He considered his defeat no more than a temporary setback. He had already dispatched a courier ahead of him with a letter to Governor Bell, urging him to send a regiment of Rangers to enforce Texas law, "which can only be done by military force," he told Bell. The Texan leadership in Austin and its representatives in Washington might rail all they liked about "despotism" in the Governor's Palace at Santa Fe, but as Neighbors's letter made clear, popular will didn't come into it: Texas must have New Mexico. If it could be gotten no other way, the Texans would have it at the point of a gun.

Rumors had circulated for some time that President Taylor had already decided to call up volunteers to defend New Mexico. The War Department denied this, but in mid-June Lieutenant Alfred M. Pleasanton was called to the White House before departing for New Mexico. Taylor directed him to tell Munroe that no armed Texans were to be welcomed, and that if necessary the president himself would personally lead an army west before he relinquished even a foot of federal territory, declaring, "The whole business is infamous, and must be put down."

Munroe would obey whatever orders the president gave him, but he had barely a thousand men under his command scattered across a far-flung archipelago of Indian-fighting posts from the Gila River to the Rockies. As he gazed uneasily eastward, he doubtless wondered if his ill-paid, half-trained recruits would be a match for an army of "Texians" inured to Indian fighting, savage in battle, and intolerant of defeat. Would Americans fire on Americans? Would this be the beginning of civil war?

Henry Foote, for one, had little doubt that a general war was imminent. "I venture to declare that if this government shall ever shed one drop of Texan blood upon Texan soil," he told the Senate, "it will speedily be found that there is not one heroic son of the South who will not arm himself—and I trust that there will be hundreds of thousands of gallant and true-hearted men in the North, also, who will arm themselves if necessary—in defense of a patriotic, and persecuted, and oppressed people." Foote blamed Seward, of all people, for setting the country on the course to war. Ignoring Vice President Fillmore's attempt to rule him out of order, he claimed that Seward's "selfish and unnatural heart" was "panting" for war so that he might make himself "the chief executive of a new republic or empire" of the North. It's impossible to say if Foote actually believed such lurid claptrap. (He knew that he could get away with saying anything about the least popular man in the Senate, and that the mild-mannered New Yorker would never threaten him as Benton had.) But the fact that he could say such things in the Senate was evidence of the pervasive paranoia that had taken hold of the southern mind—even a Unionist southern mind—where it was enough simply to imagine the vilest intentions of a political opponent for many to accept it as virtual fact. "If one battle is ever fought in such a quarrel, the dissolution of the Union will be inevitable," Foote warned, now with no need to exaggerate. "If this question should be left unadjusted by Congress, who can doubt that it must be adjusted by the sword?"

Six hundred miles west of Washington, the specter of secession was swirling among the 176 delegates packed into the McKendree Methodist Church in Nashville. There the long anticipated Southern Convention, as it was formally called, had gathered on June 3 to fulfill Calhoun's cherished dream of creating a bloc of slave states that would be prepared, when the moment came, to declare its independence from the United States. "If the convention does not open the way to dissolution, I hope it shall never meet," former South Carolina governor James Hammond, one of its guiding spirits, had declared a few months earlier. Since then, however, the battle for compromise in the Senate, led by the slave-owning Henry Clay, and abetted by both the stridently proslavery Henry Foote, and by Daniel Webster, the icon of Yankee probity, had undermined radical assertions that the South's future in the Union was hopeless. Southern Whigs, at least, were now tilting decidedly in favor of compromise.

As historian William W. Freehling has put it, "The great southern middle remained anchored in Washington." Outside South Carolina, almost the entire proslavery establishment had aligned itself on the side of compromise. Only nine of the fifteen slave states sent delegates to Nashville. Texas sent only one, and Arkansas two; North Carolina, Louisiana, and the border slave states sent none at all. Many Tennessee Unionists, including the state's senior senator, John Bell, openly opposed the convention as inopportune, at best. But in a young bustling city that was proud of both its go-ahead style—embodied in its new Grecian state capitol, and the cables for the modern suspension bridge that workmen were stringing across the Cumberland River—citizens of all persuasions eagerly opened their homes to the delegates.

The convention's aim, it was officially declared, was not in fact to promote secession at all, but to preserve the Union "unimpaired"—that is, in accordance with proslavery interests. Recognizing that they were ahead of the curve of public opinion, and that they would weaken their cause by acting prematurely, even the South Carolinians strove to restrain themselves, at least while the convention was in session.

Still, there was plenty of fiery rhetoric. The galleries, which included many women, who enclosed the delegates on each side "like borders of flowers," thundered their applause after every speech. Fulminating orators urged the South to abandon the old party distinctions of Democrat and Whig, and unite instead on behalf of sectional rights. The vain and frosty Virginia patrician Beverly Tucker decried Clay's compromise as a pact with the devil—one that the heroic South would sign in blood, and the contemptible Yankees in invisible ink. Don't fear secession, he cried: the North would never dare to declare war, for it was too dependent on the South for its cotton, while a southern Confederacy could look forward happily to a "magnificent future" in which slavery would "endure until it shall have accomplished that to which it was appointed" by God. In the convention's concluding address, South Carolina's goateed Robert Barnwell Rhett, a former six-term congressman, loudly echoed Tucker's attack on the compromise, declaring that the only concession it offered the South, and a fraudulent one at that, was a proposed Fugitive Slave Law—which was already part of the Constitution. "Under the guise of a benefit the bill is useless as a remedy—and worse than useless in its usurpations," he exclaimed. (On his return to Charleston, Rhett embarrassed his more circumspect colleagues by calling for immediate secession.)

Given the widespread fears that had preceded the convention, most of the resolutions it adopted were relatively mild, and paralleled the positions that had been staked out by Jefferson Davis and his allies in Congress: Congress lacked constitutional authority to bar slavery anywhere; the territories were the common property of all the states; governments provided for the territories must recognize slaves as property; states had the right to ignore federal laws that imposed any restraint on carrying slaves into a territory. A few resolutions were primarily polemical, most glaringly one that turned logic inside out by declaring that the real "disunionists" were not those who were threatening secession but rather those who opposed the right of slaveholders to take their slaves into the territories, declaring, "The warfare against this right is a war upon the Constitution." As a concession, the delegates agreed that if "a dominant majority" refused to recognize slaveholders' constitutional rights, the territories should then be divided up in "an equitable partition" between the sections.

Considering its potential for mischief, the convention was seen by many relieved observers as a failure. The moderates, such as they were, had prevailed. Indirectly, then, Clay and the forces of compromise had achieved their first concrete victory: they had divided the South, and slowed the headlong rush to secession. Not that the disunionists had abandoned their principles: when the convention adjourned on June 11, the delegates voted to reconvene in November, by which time the compromisers in Washington would have shown what, if anything, they were really prepared to yield to the South.

Hammond, for one, felt that the convention had gone well indeed for the South Carolinians. Their goal had been to gain credibility with the rest of the South. "In this," he wrote in his diary, "we succeeded perfectly and won golden opinions and, what was better, laid the foundation for wielding hereafter great influence among the Southern States." Most important, leaders from across the South had taken their first firm step toward credible solidarity.

• • •

Thwarted, for the time being, in their attempt to force slavery into the territories by amendment, southern senators now launched a legislative assault on California. Its spearhead was the Senate's most exotic member, Pierre Soulé. The son of one of Napoleon's leading generals, he fled France in 1826 when he was implicated in schemes to overthrow the restored monarchy. He eventually made his way to New Orleans, where he arrived with empty pockets and a single shirt. Once he mastered English, he quickly rose to become one of the most sought-after attorneys in New Orleans. Though small of stature, he was imperious in both style and bearing, Frenchified in dress and speech, and—with his long hair, black flashing eyes, and ingratiating smile—said by many to be both the handsomest man in Congress and fully charged with "a deposit of vanity which is never exhausted." Although an ardent republican when it came to the freedoms of white men, he was a passionate defender of slavery for blacks, proclaiming that bondage of one sort or another was the norm for the vast majority of the world's population.

On June 24, Soulé demanded, in the form of an amendment to the Omnibus Bill, that all of California below the Missouri Compromise line be formed into a separate state, to be called "South California." The boundary that the Californians had proposed for themselves was "a scandalous subterfuge" that served only the "frantic cravings of a rapacious and intolerant free-soilism," he charged. Given California's vast size, unless her public lands, mines, and other resources were reserved to the federal government, Congress risked creating a virtual empire that possessed both the wealth and power to dominate the entire nation. "Are you prepared," he demanded of his fellow senators, "to receive her into the Union, unshorn of an atom of her monster dimensions," with the command of every outlet through which the territories west of the Rockies would "disgorge their products" to the Pacific? Imagine the California of the future with a population of 500,000, he urged, or one or two million—or even *three million* inhabitants. "How monstrous her importance if she should remain in the Union! How gigantic her power, if at any time she should decide to go out of it!" Gaze into the future, he cried, see the commerce and "the luxurious temptations" of "Hindoostan," China, and Japan in the grip of California alone. Were senators prepared to lay the foundation for an empire that might one day control the destiny of the United States itself?

A few days earlier, John Hale had also proposed that two or even three states be formed from California, prompting an exchange of snappy rejoinders between himself and Henry Foote: the two men by now knew each other's rhetorical moves so perfectly that they sometimes sounded like a pair of comic entertainers. Hale assumed that any subdivisions of California would automatically be free, and would thus counterbalance any new states carved from Texas. Henry Foote then moved to amend Hale's proposal by adding the words "with or without slavery," accusing Hale of attempting to introduce into the Omnibus "offensive passengers, who are likely to annoy the good people already on board. Now, what have I done?" he asked. "I propose to put another passenger in the omnibus, and a perfectly decent one, who may expel the offensive person." Hale retorted wittily: "I introduced a very respectable gentleman into the omnibus—one from a free state, and the Senator from Mississippi desires to introduce a negro in order to take care of him. I have found that they were not willing to let a free man get in the omnibus unless he took a negro with him." Hale ultimately withdrew his amendment.

In support of Soulé's amendment, Jefferson Davis urged that "South California" be shielded from the "hostile legislation" of the men of "North California." He believed, of course, that the inhabitants of any *state* had the right to decide for themselves if they wanted slavery or not. But this hardly meant that "every band of wandering men" who happened to get together and adopt a "so-called constitution" deserved to be taken seriously. What the Nashville Convention had strongly hinted at Davis took to its logical conclusion: anything less than the Missouri Compromise line constituted aggression against the South's right to its own outlet on the Pacific. "If the territory cannot be enjoyed in common," he said, "it should be divided." Davis meant, in essence, a de facto partition of the United States, a kind of shadow secession that would allow the South to carry out some form of self-determination below the Missouri Compromise line without any interference from the North.

Denying that he was a "disunionist," Davis then went on to preach disunion: "If we have got to the point where it is treason to the United States to protect the rights and interests of our constituents, I ask why should they be longer represented here? Why longer remain a part of the Union?" If southerners were no longer free men, but "crushed by the power of an unrestrained majority," the Union that he knew had already ceased to exist, "and the highest obligation of every man who has sworn to support that Constitution would be resistance to such usurpation." This was as close to a call for rebellion as had yet been uttered on the floor of the Senate. Others who felt the same way might very well "unfurl the flag of disunion," he casually remarked. "When thus fully warranted, [if] they want a standard-bearer, in default of a better I am at their command. This is part of my doctrine of allegiance to the people of Mississippi." With no ambiguity, Davis had just declared that he was prepared to lead the secession movement, to become, as it were, the president of a break-away southern nation.

Finally, on June 28, a vote was taken on Soulé's "South California" amendment. It was defeated by 36 to 19. It was further evidence, if more was needed, that although southern radicals lacked the votes to impose their expansionist agenda on the Senate, they remained unified enough to deny Henry Clay the bipartisan coalition that he needed to pass the Omnibus.

At the other end of Pennsylvania Avenue, the president was enduring what had surely been the worst months of his life as stoically as he had enemy fire on the bloody battlefields of Mexico. Privately, he boiled and brooded. Congress, he wrote to an associate in Louisiana, "has done little but quarrel about or discuss the unfortunate question of slavery, which has not been settled or adjusted, nor can I say when it will be." Democrats and Whigs alike hammered away at him in Congress. His policy for New Mexico and California, Henry Foote asserted, was "the most unstatesmanlike, yes, the most contemptible in all respects that was ever attempted to be advocated by any administration or any legislative body in Christendom!" Even the administration's own newspaper, the *Republic*, had insulted him by throwing its support to the compromise, while the *Daily Union*, a Democratic mouthpiece, denounced him as a man who "has not only recklessly repudiated the promises and pledges which he has made to the American people, but . . . has sinned against the virtues of gratitude and patriotism." For a proud and honest man who had devoted his life to hard service for his country, and was striving to honor the commitment to democracy that the nation had made to the inhabitants of the territories conquered from Mexico, this was close to insupportable. His motives, he felt, had been wildly misconstrued, his feelings outraged, and his reputation grossly impugned. But there was more, and it wasn't good.

Back in April, a scandal had detonated that was now, in late June, threatening to upend Taylor's presidency. This came in the form of a convoluted legal monstrosity known as the Galphin claim. Its roots lay almost eighty years in the past, in 1773, when the British government had agreed to pay off debts that southern Indian tribes owed to fur traders in return for yielding certain lands to the crown. With the coming of the Revolution, the crown refused to pay the claims of traders such as George Galphin, who had used his influence to prevent southern tribes from joining the British. After the war, the Georgia legislature approved Galphin's claim, but shunted responsibility for paying it onto the federal government. Galphin's heirs pursued the claim in federal courts for decades until, in 1848, Congress finally agreed to honor them. By this time, accrued interest had more than quintupled the settlement to almost $235,000—a fabulous sum for that day.

None of this had anything to do with the slavery debate in the Senate, or with Zachary Taylor. However, Taylor's secretary of war, George Crawford, had represented the heirs, and reaped a fortune in fees. Moreover, two other members of the cabinet, Treasury Secretary William Meredith and Attorney General Reverdy Johnson, were responsible for recommending the payout, which had made Crawford a rich man. All this provided ammunition for the administration's enemies in Congress. For months, the claim had become inextricably entangled with the slavery debate in the House of Representatives, where southerners defended the Georgian Crawford, northerners urged his dismissal, and southerners in turn then denounced the pressure against Crawford as a Yankee plot. A defter politician than Taylor would quickly have cleaned house, and fired all three members of the cabinet. But Taylor, always a good soldier, was loyal to his subordinates. He also didn't have a lot of friends to spare. Rumors were rife of a cabinet purge. But for months he sat athwart his pride as he had upon his steed at Buena Vista, saying little and doing nothing, waiting for the fuss to subside like the Mexican hordes, as public trust eroded around him.

Unknown to the public, Taylor was suffering from more personal worries as well. In May, floods had inundated one of his sugar plantations, destroying the harvest, spoiling quantities of felled timber that were supposed to be sawn and sold, and leaving scores of his slaves idle. "Something must be done or inevitable ruin must be the consequence," he wrote to his twenty-four-year-old son, Richard, who was managing affairs in Louisiana. Maybe it would be best to dispose of the whole plantation, "or if that can't be done the servants." (Taylor almost never referred to them as slaves.) "Misfortune on misfortunes have followed me in such rapid succession from floods and otherwise for the last six or eight years, I feel almost heartbroken and broken down." He was lifted from his funk, however, when Richard convinced him to buy a new plantation, and soon the president was firing off micromanaging letters advising his son to "bring no more hands than you can work with advantage" . . . "float as many logs out of the swamp as possible" . . . "keep the saw mill running day and night" . . . and lecturing him on "the great art of planting"—to wit, "a proper evolution of crops, sugar following corn and peas . . ." He wouldn't be surprised, he told Richard as an afterthought, if Congress was still sitting in September.

• • •

Daniel Webster also gloomily saw no end in sight. "We shall have a warm summer," he wrote to his son Fletcher. "The political atmosphere will be hot, however the natural [weather] may be." He was not optimistic. The success of the compromise bill depended on support from southern senators; by his count, if more than six rejected it, the bill would fail. Nor was he sanguine about eastern Whigs, who were also trending against the bill. Meanwhile, *truly important* public business such as a new tariff, which would benefit New England manufacturers, was languishing. To one supporter, he wrote in exasperation, "Will Massachusetts shut herself out from all the benefits she might receive from wise legislation on Congress, for the mere purpose of keeping up a senseless strife about such miserable abstract questions as slavery in New Mexico, or the law for redeeming fugitive slaves?" But he had committed himself, and he was not giving up. "I am for it, & shall fight it out," he told his son.

Meanwhile, the crisis in New Mexico was coming to a head. On June 27, Foote electrified the Senate when he reported that he had just learned that the New Mexicans were attempting to set up a state government. Whoever had instigated such a "vile scheme" was, he cried, "an insidious traitor to the public weal, an enemy to his country," whose perfidy should be branded with indelible infamy. (Foote could only mean the president, whom he had long accused of fomenting trouble.) Foote also reported that Robert Neighbors had returned to Texas to recruit a military force strong enough to enforce the "civil rights" of Texas against "the usurping violence of a lieutenant colonel of the United States army, acting with or without orders, as the case may be." He added, "We are about to be plunged into all the horrors of a civil war, unless Congress shall interfere, in season, and arrest the fatal course of events." Real war was suddenly in the air. Foote warned, "If a single drop of Texan blood shall be shed upon her own sacred soil, it will be the duty of every southern man, able to bear arms, to rush to the scene of strife, in order to put down usurpation and to maintain the cause of justice and of right." In short, if New Mexico was allowed to become a state, the Union was at an end.

In a letter circulated to the southern press, Congressman Volney Howard of Texas declared, "Every act of military government exercised [in Santa Fe] is a nullity. All acts of civil government exercised in Santa Fe by the military are gross usurpations of power, and tyrannical in the last degree. I know the people of Texas will resist, and resist to the knife." In Texas, mass meetings called for armed resistance. Texas governor Bell called for "immediate military action," declaring that Texas recognized no federal authority in New Mexico. On July 1, Bell issued a formal call for volunteers, mounted and armed, and ready to march on Santa Fe.

The *New York Journal of Commerce* reported that if the compromise bill were to be defeated, Texas would annex New Mexico outright, and if the United States interfered, the southern states would supply whatever aid Texas needed to resist. This was speculation, but it was not far from the truth, as the influential Congressman Alexander Stephens of Georgia made clear in an open letter. "I wish to say to you, lest you may be mistaken in the opinions of others, that the first federal gun that shall be fired against the people of Texas, without the authority of law, will be the signal for freemen from the Delaware to the Rio Grande to rally to the rescue. You may consider the 'gallant state of Texas' too weak for a contest with the army of the United States. But you should recollect that the cause of Texas, in such a conflict, will be the cause of the entire South. And whether you consider Santa Fe in danger or not, you may yet live to see that the fifteen states in this Union, with seven millions of people, 'who, knowing their rights, dare maintain them,' cannot easily be conquered!"

On July 1, in an effort to avert war, Stephens and Robert Toombs organized a committee of three congressmen to pressure President Taylor to swing his weight behind the compromise. Taylor turned them away: he would not abandon New Mexico. When Secretary of War Crawford— who was indebted to the Georgia congressmen for their support—refused to sign an explicit order to Colonel Munroe to resist any attempt by Texas to occupy New Mexico, the president declared that he would sign the order himself.

Stephens and Toombs met personally with Secretary of the Navy William Preston in front of the Treasury Building just east of the White House, and warned him that if federal troops were ordered to Santa Fe, the president would be impeached.

"Who will impeach him?" Preston asked.

"I will if nobody else does," Stephens grimly replied.

CHAPTER 21

"WAR, OPEN WAR"

———— •◆• ————

On July 2, Clay turned back yet another attempt to scuttle the Omnibus, when the southern radicals teamed up with the Senate's Free Soilers to press for adjournment of the session on August 1. This tactic, if successful, would have effectively killed the Omnibus until the next session of Congress. Then, if anyone still had the stomach for it, the whole process would have to start all over again. Attacked by moderates, who accused him of secretly collaborating with abolitionists, including even William Seward, Jefferson Davis denied that the Ultras of the two factions were caucusing together, but admitted that they had in fact met, though only "to say what they mean—to tell the country plainly, honestly what their purpose is." Beyond that, there was no "alliance" at all, he said, not very convincingly. Seward, for his part, had made it clear that he would do what he could to strike out every unpalatable feature of the bill as soon as it was proposed: "If we cannot break this bill down by a common opposition, I am willing to take it to pieces joint by joint, limb by limb."

Seward made no mention of the backroom confabulations with Davis when, on July 2, he rose to deliver his second major oration of the session. His "higher law" speech had made him famous: Horace Greeley had lionized him in the *American Whig Review*, while many tens of thousands of copies of the speech had been distributed across every northern state, including thousands translated into German for ethnic voters. "God bless you for the noble stand you have taken for Freedom and Philanthropy!" wrote one voter from Sinclearville, New York. "Stand firm! Falter not. The Slave Power trembles at thy noble moral daring. Millions of free hearts beat in unison with thine." The speech had seriously embarrassed the president, however, and although Taylor eventually forgave him, Seward's political friends urged him to tone down his rhetoric. He had also made an effort to humanize himself in the eyes of his enemies, inviting even Henry Foote to dinner, where he served him stewed terrapin, fried oysters, and roast duck, and listened patiently while the Mississippian ate his food and sneered at everything Seward stood for. In the Senate, Seward avoided controversial rhetoric even as he continued to work to undermine Clay's plan and to build support for Taylor's. At the end of June, he traveled home to Auburn, to his birds and gardens, and to work out his thoughts with his most trusted confidante, his beloved wife, Frances. He decided that he had been silent long enough.

Seward began with his usual clumsiness, straining at an eloquence for which he had neither the talent nor temperament, larding his deeply felt beliefs with gobs of Latin, mixed metaphors—likening the compromise in a single sentence to both the wedding of "confiding youth to querulous and wrangling age" and to a "struggling hind" fleeing "ravening hounds"—and slabs of frankly incomprehensible verbiage: "The same principle of dialectic philosophy which forbids multifariousness of issues and confusion of parties in the administration of justice, condemns incongruous combinations in legislation." But this time he made sure to declare his wholehearted support for Taylor's plan. The only real wound upon the body politic, he said, was the plight of California. "And this is the very one which, with exquisite surgery, the president proposes we shall heal immediately, and by itself, alone." California's only fault was that she refused "to let us buy and sell each other within her domain."

Gradually he picked up steam. The Omnibus threatened to convert New Mexico into a slave state: "Spare her!" he begged. Do not punish her for "the crime of loving liberty too well." If Congress thus left New

Mexico "a mutilated and lifeless thing," it would be like repeating the tragic partition of Poland. He put no faith in any supposed "natural law" that excluded slavery from New Mexico. "The discovery of a few flakes of gold, or of a few grains of silver, or even of a few clumps of coal in the unexplored recesses of New Mexico, would be followed by a new revelation of the will of the Almighty in regard to it," he dryly commented. He went on to defend the Wilmot Proviso in exceptionally forceful terms. "If it ever there was right at any time, in any place, under any circumstances, it is right always, and under all circumstances," he declared. "It can be renounced safely nowhere. Certainly New Mexico is not the region; nor is hers the soil, not hers the clime, where it should be renounced. If we surrender here, where we have all the [ad]vantage, where else shall we find ground on which to make resistance?"

So far, Seward had remained on well-trodden ground. Now he carried his indictment of slavery into new territory, accusing the Slave Power of imperial ambitions that threatened to hijack the nation's foreign policy. Americans had taken a breathing spell from annexation of territory "to divide the gain." But it was only a temporary pause. Doubtless "martial ambition" would soon hurry Americans on to new conquests. Slavery's ambitions in years past in Louisiana and Texas, and now in California and New Mexico, would soon be surpassed, he predicted, in the heartland of Mexico, in Cuba, and in the states of Central America, where the staple crops of the South flourished, mines of silver and gold beckoned, and "the climate disposes to indolence, indolence to luxury, and luxury to slavery." (No one listening to Seward could fail to think of the recent invasion in Cuba: though Narciso López was currently under indictment for breaking American neutrality law, he had been hailed as a hero on his return to New Orleans.) Soon new slave states would surround the Gulf of Mexico to form a "slave empire" based in New Orleans that "will domineer not only over the southern portion of the continent, but, through the Mississippi and its far-reaching tributaries," as far as the Rocky Mountains, he speculated. "Nothing seems to slavery impossible, after advantages already won."

Slavery and freedom were incompatible systems, Seward continued.

"Their antagonism is radical, and therefore perpetual," but the crisis could not be solved by cramming California, New Mexico, Utah, Texas, and a batch of other measures into "this unwieldy, rickety ark" of the Omnibus. As long as the question of the territories' sovereignty remained open, Congress and the nation would have to deal with the strife that was spawned by them. "You may slay the Wilmot proviso in the Senate Chamber, and bury it beneath the Capitol today; the dead corse, in complete steel, will haunt your legislative halls tomorrow," he predicted. Human rights, he said, in words familiar to the twenty-first century but rarely heard in the mid-nineteenth, were nonnegotiable. "The abstractions of human rights are the only permanent foundations of society. It is by referring to them that men determine what is *established* because it is RIGHT, in order to uphold it forever; and what is *right* only because it is *established*, in order that they may lawfully *change* it, in accordance with the increase of knowledge and the progress of reason."

Seward concluded with a plea to southerners, in whose own hands, he said, lay the power to peacefully solve the problem of slavery. Instead of scheming to invent an artificial "equilibrium" that had never existed, he called upon them "by some means, by all means of their own, and with our aid, without sudden change or violent action" to embrace emancipation and restore dignity to human labor. "They will thus anticipate only what must happen at some time," he said. "We shall then not merely endure each other, but we shall be reconciled together. The fingers of the Powers above would tune the harmony of such a peace."

His appeal, unfortunately but not unexpectedly, fell on deaf ears. However, with this speech Seward hoped not only to, perhaps, persuade men of the South to see beyond their short-term interests, but, more concretely, to regain the esteem of the administration, and that of his political friends in New York. This was a gentler Seward, no less committed to antislavery, but less strident and startling, and uttering no appeals to unsettling concepts such as a "higher law." Thurlow Weed, still recovering from the political headache that Seward's "higher law" speech had given him, assured Frances Seward that it was the greatest speech ever delivered in the Senate. Seward was encouraged to feel that his influence with the administration would grow: Taylor was rumored to finally be preparing an overhaul of his cabinet, and the New Yorker could expect to play an important role in shaping the new one. There were even those who whispered that the Whig nomination for the presidency in 1852 might be within his reach.

With good reason, everyone dreaded the onset of the cholera season, which, helped by the capital's appalling lack of sewage disposal, swept off scores, sometimes hundreds, of Washingtonians every year. Henry Clay was nearly prostrate with the heat, and retreated whenever he could to his friend Charles Calvert's home outside the city. Clay relished the laudatory letters that he continued to receive from across the country— "I regard the compromise bill as the rock of our salvation," wrote one admirer from Missouri—but the Omnibus still faced unyielding opposition. No end to "the distracting Slavery question" was in sight, he wrote to his long-suffering wife, Lucretia, at Ashland. "When and how it will be decided, God only knows. I hope for a decision, & a favorable decision in the Senate next week, but it is not certain. The breach between the Administration and me on that matter, is getting wider and wider." Taylor, Seward, and their friends, he felt, had completely lost touch with public feeling, and were "blindly rushing on their own ruin, if not the ruin of their Country." In the Senate, he accused the administration of waging "war, open war, undisguised war" against the Omnibus's proponents, and defiantly promised to defend it "against a thousand presidents, be they whom they may be."

The glacial pace of the debate continued to infuriate him. "A hundred times almost, during the progress of this bill, have I been quite ready to yield, and say, for one, I withdraw from all further efforts for the passage of this bill," he nagged the Senate. Seemingly insuperable difficulties "upon points of abstraction, upon points of no earthly practical consequence" were enough to discourage even the stoutest heart. Frustration fed Clay's autocratic tendencies. "Meet earlier, sit longer, meet every working day of the week!" he challenged his colleagues. When David Yulee proposed a month's adjournment, Clay growled, "I would as soon quit the field of battle at a moment when our arms were directed against a foreign enemy, and when it was my duty to expose my life to the utmost hazard." There was no adjournment. Senators resented the constant pressure, and increasingly told Clay so. "I am not willing to have these lectures, reproofs, or admonitions, delivered to us, and be driven here early and kept late, with no possible object except the purpose of producing apparent haste in the passage of this bill," John Hale protested.

The fate of the Omnibus was anyone's guess. Benton's arguments had taken a toll. The difficulty of winning a majority for a package that contained such "incongruous" measures was obvious. Most northern Whigs stood firmly with the president, and there were rumors that even several Democrats were about to switch to his side. "If you would have a compromise, in the first place, you must have a subject that is capable of being compromised!" exclaimed John Davis of Massachusetts. "You must have parties that want to enter into a compromise. And you must have parties who can and will be bound by the compromise. Has this bill any of these elements in it?" Undeterred, Clay continued to work desperately to round up supporters for the Omnibus, writing urgently to one friendly senator to hurry back to Washington from North Carolina: "We shall be hard run, if not defeated, without your vote." Webster rejoiced when Senator James Bradbury of Maine, a supporter, returned to Washington, then deflated when Bradbury confessed that his antislavery state legislature had ordered him to vote against any bill that failed to explicitly ban slavery from the West.

"I hardly dare say which way I think it will turn," Webster wrote to a friend in Massachusetts. "In the Senate yesterday, it was rather thought we had a majority." The compromisers labored under two great disadvantages, he confessed. The first was simply that Taylor had proven more stubborn than anyone had expected, and many members did not want to vote against the president's plan. "In the next place, Mr. Clay with all his talents, is not a good leader, for want of temper. He is irritable, impatient,

& occasionally overbearing; & drives people off." It was as damning an indictment as anyone had made against Clay, and it came from his closest ally.

John Bell of Tennessee was precisely the kind of man Clay and Webster were counting on. A slave-owning Whig unionist and self-described "son of the South," he could at the same time speak of the "magnificent results" of slavery, and of his dream vision of blacks civilized through slavery someday founding an empire of their own in the "measureless wilds" of South America, whence they might cross the Atlantic to Africa to tame, in turn, its savage inhabitants. Darkly, even forbiddingly handsome, with piercing eyes and a tight-lipped mouth that canted severely downward, he was an acknowledged leader of the southern moderates, and regarded as a man of integrity and impartiality. (In January, Bell had submitted his own compromise proposal, which would have created three new states from the territory that Texas claimed, two of them likely to be free, and the third slave, with the expectation that no additional slave states would ever be admitted to the Union.) Although Clay had worked hard to win Bell's support, he remained uncommitted. So far, he had scarcely spoken during the debate. Now, in a titanic throat-clearing oration that stretched over three days, Bell began to disburden himself of everything that he had been holding in.

"I fear there will be no peace, no permanent concord and harmony, whatever lulling influence the adoption of this measure might have," he declared. When the debate had begun under Clay's guidance, Bell had cherished high expectations. But the results had brought only deep disappointment. "When giants set their hands to a work, we expect something more than the product of ordinary mortals; something more than the expedient of a day," he said. A few months earlier, true leaders might have done almost anything, when every patriotic mind of the North and the South was roused and crying for a broad, just, and permanent settlement. But Clay had produced a mere "piece of political joinery." This must have cut Clay deeply, after his herculean struggle to craft a compromise. But

Clay would have to wait two more days to hear the rest of what Bell had to say.

On the Fourth of July, Congress enjoyed a respite of sorts from the debate on Capitol Hill. President Taylor began the day with a Sunday School recital. Then, as Washingtonians picnicked, paraded, and set off fireworks, he traveled by carriage to the marble stump of the Washington Monument, which stood on a hillock overlooking the fetid canal that traversed the future site of the National Mall. There a large audience of senators, congressmen, other luminaries, including Dolley Madison and Alexander Hamilton's aged widow, Elizabeth, gathered beneath a broiling sun to hear Henry Foote deliver his annual stemwinding holiday oration. A small, poorly shaded stand had been erected in front of the monument, occupied only by Foote and the president.

There was no way that the elderly Taylor could leave the stand, even temporarily, without calling attention to himself, which Taylor surmised, doubtless correctly, the volatile Foote would have taken as a personal insult. But Taylor's powers of physical endurance were legendary. So he sat, and sweated, as Foote plowed onward. "May sectional jealousy, fanatical rage, the accursed ambition for notoriety and power, the low appetite for place and its emoluments, and the spirit of political rivalry be banished forever from the council halls of the nation!" declared the Mississippian, who spoke for over two hours without a break. "Let justice, brotherly feeling, and true courtesy restrain the turbid current of angry and mischievous debate."

When George Washington Parke Custis, Martha Washington's grandson and self-appointed guardian of the first president's public memory, stepped to the platform to begin his own oration, Taylor motioned to Foote, and asked, "Why will you not always speak in this way?" Foote's reply went unrecorded.

Already suffering from a mild sunstroke, Taylor returned home to gorge himself on iced milk, cherries, and raw vegetables. Within hours, he was suffering from what was probably acute gastroenteritis, although his doctors diagnosed it as cholera, and dosed him with a mercury compound and opium, which, if anything, only made his symptoms worse. That evening, as a novel, high-intensity "Calcium Light" illuminated Pennsylvania Avenue from the Capitol to the White House, Vice President Fillmore, Benton, Webster, Foote, the new representatives from California, and many more of the capital's leading power brokers feasted gaily at the dinner table of former House speaker Robert Winthrop.

The next day, John Bell resumed his interrupted speech. The most critical question of all, he said, was whether the provisions of the Omnibus relating to New Mexico would quiet the country. "I fear they will not."

"I entertain no doubt at all that nine-tenths of the people of all the states will not only be satisfied but profoundly grateful to us for the adoption of this measure," piped up the irrepressible Foote, who was apparently unaffected by the previous day's heat.

"I wish I could entertain the same sentiments," Bell said with a sigh. He expected that the question would infect every election yet to come. Indeed, he feared that the bill would only exacerbate the danger that the nation faced. The nation stood upon a pivot that future historians would someday look back upon "and from it deduce the causes of our decline as a nation, or of increased prosperity and grandeur," he gloomily opined. The continued suspense was intolerable—worse than an open rupture, he said. Sectional selfishness had to be overcome. If the South was unprepared to yield, if it could not bring the North to agree to some kind of equitable settlement, he ventured, then perhaps it was time, after all, for the South to "manage our affairs in our own way." But in the end, like just enough other senators to deny Clay the majority he needed, Bell didn't really know what he would do. As unhappy as he was with the bill's shortcomings, he said that he might vote for it after all.

Seward's son Frederick, who was listening from the packed gallery, reported that the speech conveyed an impression of deep feeling and directionless uncertainty that left even Bell looking confused and unsatisfied. "On the first day of its delivery," wrote young Seward, "people in the galleries said, 'Bell is for it.' On the second day they said, 'Bell will vote against it.' On the third day that he 'cannot make up his mind.' "

On the final day of Bell's speech, President Taylor's sick chamber was invaded by yet another delegation of southern congressmen who warned him that unless he acted to protect the South, they would humiliate him over the miserable Galphin claim. The following day, they made good their threat by adding to the Galphin resolutions then on the floor an amendment censuring Taylor for his alleged "connection" with the claim. As if that wasn't enough for the ailing old man, the Democratic *Daily Union* demanded Taylor's impeachment "for usurping kingly powers and for trampling on the rights of a sovereign state"—that is, Texas. On July 6, Taylor signed a treaty with Britain, as his doctors continued to bleed him and blister him, and dose him with quinine and calomel. Somehow, he also managed to politely write to a Bostonian admirer, thanking him for sending him two "delicious salmon . . . which arrived most opportunely."

On Tuesday, July 9, Andrew Butler had been on the Senate floor for an hour, disingenuously bemoaning the widening chasm between the sections, which he had done more than most to foster, when a messenger entered the chamber and indicated to the vice president that he had something urgent to report. Fillmore came down from the dais, bent his silvery head to hear the whispered message, and suddenly went slack. The messenger then leaned low over Daniel Webster's desk. Webster signaled to Butler to pause, saying that he had a "solemn and mournful" announcement to make. Rising into the pregnant silence that followed, Webster declared solemnly that President Taylor's life could be measured in mere hours.

Earlier that morning, Webster had called at the White House to inquire about the president's condition. "I was informed that he had had a very bad night, but that at that moment he was more easy and more composed," Webster told the Senate. Hardly had Webster reached his seat in the Senate, he added, when he was informed by the messenger that the president's fever had suddenly returned with alarming symptoms.

Throngs of well-wishers flooded Lafayette Square and the streets surrounding the White House. A messenger stood posted at the main door to deliver bulletins. It was reported that the president had rallied, then at 1 P.M. that he was dead, then at 3:30 P.M. that the crisis had passed, and that he was out of danger. Bells rang, boys in the street lit bonfires and hallooed with joy. Then at 7 P.M. it was announced that the hero of Monterrey and Buena Vista was dying after all. Inside the White House, Mrs. Taylor fainted three times from exhaustion and anxiety. The president's secretary, Colonel Bliss, wept like a child. At 9 P.M., the president's vomiting ceased. A few minutes past 10 P.M., he prayed and asked for a glass of water. His last words were: "The storm in passing had swept away the trunk . . . I am about to die—I expect the summons soon—I have endeavored to discharge all my official duties faithfully—I regret nothing, but I am sorry that I am about to leave my friends." At 10:35 P.M. he died.

A thin rain fell on the president's funeral procession. Clay, Cass, Berrien, and Benton served as the president's pallbearers, marching alongside his coffin, which was followed by his beloved Old Whitey, the warhorse Taylor had ridden across the battlefields of Mexico, and which for the past seventeen months had grazed on the White House lawn to the amusement of the capital's cultivated class. Taylor's old rival, Winfield Scott, the commander of the army, sporting a towering plume of yellow feathers from his fore-and-aft headgear, led a two-mile-long parade of militia companies from Maryland, Virginia, and the capital, a detachment of cavalry and sharpshooters, artillerymen sent down from Fort McHenry, doddering veterans of the War of 1812, members of Congress, temperance societies, firemen, and more than a hundred carriages, passing an estimated crowd of 100,000 that lined the streets. In Congress laudatory speeches briefly replaced diatribes. "He is hereafter to belong to no party, to no section, but to the whole American family," declared Solomon Downs in the Senate, in a funeral oration whose encomiums for once seemed both apt and unusually poignant, for a man who had meant well and tried hard, but who had failed to decipher the runic language of politics.

The *Daily Union*, which had smeared Taylor for months, now proclaimed him a Hero and Patriot, whose name would "live as long as the name of the nation whose standard he so often bore to victory and to glory." But the *Charleston Mercury*, the preeminent organ of southern nationalism, dismissed the dead president with open contempt, and a grain of truth: "He had no natural aptitude for civil administration, no light of long experience to guide him, no love for the labors and the deep studies that form essential parts of the President's office, and no talent for the ruling of Cabinets."

The *Weekly Eagle* of Brattleboro, Vermont, was kinder. "His mind was above the narrow prejudices of district and class, and steadily aimed at the good of the nation as a whole. Having once made up his mind, [he] did not abandon his determination." It was a fair assessment.

CHAPTER 22

"ALL IS PARALYSIS"

———— •◆• ————

Of all the central players in the great drama of 1850, the most elusive is Millard Fillmore. Largely forgotten though he may now be by most Americans, he was far from a cipher in his own day. Henry Clay, reflecting the sentiments of many contemporaries, praised him as "able, enlightened, indefatigable, and patriotic." Physically, he was an impressive specimen: tall, muscular, broad-shouldered, radiant with health and heartiness. (Queen Victoria, who met him years later, would describe him as the handsomest man she had ever seen.) Temperamentally, he combined a sharp analytic mind with a warm and amiable nature, and shunned unnecessary confrontation. Like many men who had levered themselves far above humble roots, he put great store in dignity and good manners. To many, however, Fillmore seemed to be something less than the sum of all his excellent parts. In contrast to the confrontational Zachary Taylor, he seemed soft and pliable, his shrewdness too often suggesting lack of conviction, and his aversion to passionate causes a certain moral coldness. As one contemporary wrote of him, "He had the peculiar faculty of adapting himself to every position in which he served."

Behind Fillmore's pink-cheeked charm, there nonetheless lay a core of ambition as hard as the unyielding clay soil upon which he had spent his impoverished youth. In an era when many political careers—Henry

Clay's and William Henry Harrison's, to name two—were based on exaggerated, if not faked, log cabin origins, Fillmore was the real thing. Born in 1800 to a hard-luck sharecropper in western New York, he was bred from boyhood to backbreaking labor in a mostly losing struggle to keep his family's farm going. He didn't learn to spell until the age of seven, and at nineteen still had never seen a map or an atlas. Books, as they were for his equally disadvantaged contemporary Abraham Lincoln, were his escape hatch. Once he became literate, Fillmore read with a frightening ferocity. At the carding mill where he worked for a time, he propped a dictionary on his worktable, and looked up a word each time he passed by, and then fixed it in his memory while he changed rolls of wool. When, a few years later, he talked a local judge into taking him on as a law clerk, he was so grateful that he burst into tears. Through super-human perseverance, he eventually became one of the most sought after lawyers in Buffalo.

By 1848, Fillmore had been a presence in New York politics for most of twenty years. He first came to local prominence as an outspoken critic of the Masons during the anti-Masonic hysteria of the late 1820s and 1830s. New York's paramount power broker, Thurlow Weed, recognized his potential, and guided him through the state's brawling political arena to become, along with Seward, one of its leading Whigs. He served cred-itably in the House of Representatives, which elected him chairman of the powerful Ways and Means Committee, and as New York's comptrol-ler, the office from which he had been plucked to run for vice president in 1848. Although Fillmore's political base in western New York was a hotbed of Underground Railroad activity, he lent only the most minimal support to the antislavery movement. "God knows that I detest slavery, but it is an existing evil for which we are not responsible, and we must endure it," he remarked, a posture that was in tune with that of Yankee businessmen who profited from the southern cotton trade, and found Fillmore an easy man to support. Essentially, Fillmore saw slavery as a political problem rather than a moral one, and believed that the federal government had no authority to legislate either for or against it. He also believed that wholesale emancipation would lead to a bloodbath, which could be escaped only by the deportation of freed slaves to Africa, a process he supposed might take centuries.

Fillmore had naturally expected to assert considerable influence in the Taylor administration. Instead, he was humiliated to a degree that few men who have served in that notoriously unsatisfying job have ever been. It was obvious to everyone that his rival, Seward, had the president's ear, and that Fillmore was barely even welcome at the White House. "Where is Fillmore?" the *Albany Express* wondered, in May 1849. "He is nowhere." Apart from presiding, for the most part silently, over the Senate, he had nothing to do. To make matters worse, his wife, Abigail, loathed Washington, and remained mostly in New York. "How lonesome this room is in your absence," he wrote to her from his bachelor digs at the Willard Hotel in April 1850, sighing that he didn't even have anyone to play backgammon with. "I can hardly bear to sit down."

Fillmore was numbed at the news of Taylor's death. "I have no language to express the emotions of my heart," he told the cabinet. "The shock is so sudden and unexpected that I am overwhelmed." On July 10, looking profoundly exhausted, he took the oath of office in a gloomy little ceremony in the House chamber. It was only the second time that a vice president had been thrust into the nation's highest office as a result of the chief executive's death, and the first time in the midst of national crisis. He had barely slept, worrying that he might not be fitted for the job that was now his. Prayed one fearful Democrat, who in a letter to Fillmore wrote that he had never supported the Whigs, "May you be the instrument, in the hand of God, to save your country from ruin."

The physical condition of the White House made a vivid symbol for the country's plight. After thirty-five years of wear and tear—the mansion had been rebuilt after its destruction by the British in 1814—it was in a miserable state. Poor drainage left the cellars chronically waterlogged, "unfit even for the domestics," in the words of a Senate report. Fillmore was so disgusted that he took up temporary residence in Georgetown. Meanwhile, he was also flooded with whining, begging, and bullying letters from job seekers and no end of advice from the well meaning, the self-interested, and the ignorant: appoint more northerners to the cabinet . . . keep Taylor's men . . . get rid of them . . . make peace with Seward . . . good riddance to him. "Take Webster into your cabinet and see it damned from the outset," wrote one Whig who signed himself "A True Friend." "He is a prostitute in morals and sometimes one in politics. Loose in money matters, tainted with fraud, fixed in profligacy, he is a living ulcer and infection. Give us a pure cabinet, not for God's sake not whores like Webster." Fillmore ignored such innuendo and appointed Webster his secretary of state and senior adviser, depending on him to vet appointments and to help guide policy in almost every sphere. ("Black Dan," as some called him, never shy about taking money from wealthy businessmen, encouraged a group of them to provide a personal fund for him, so that he would not suffer financially by leaving the Senate and his law practice.)

Southerners initially feared that the new Yankee president would prove to be a pawn in the hands of Henry Clay. They were delighted when Fillmore's sudden accession to power proved a disaster for Seward and Weed. It "has suddenly dashed to pieces the brittle fabric of [Weed's] consciously and elaborately wrought personal plans," one New York Whig wrote confidentially to Fillmore. Weed and Seward, he added with undisguised glee, must now sink back "into the common Whig ranks, where they must serve as other good soldiers do." Weed threatened to ruin Fillmore unless he committed himself to Taylor's hard line against the Omnibus. But Fillmore, amiable as he was, could hardly forget or forgive Weed's abandonment of him in favor of Seward, or their ostracism of him in the seventeen months since Taylor's inauguration. The new president knew that he had the support of conservative Whigs, who were put off by Seward's radicalism and had never adapted to Taylor's stubbornness and frontier ways. Two days after Taylor's death, the influential Massachusetts Whig Edward Everett assured Fillmore that the country was in desperate need of "the political experience of an accomplished civilian," a rather elliptical way of saying that he was glad that the stubborn old soldier was gone. No one really knew what Fillmore would do. But he was more ready to wield power than many suspected. He would have to.

Texas threatened to explode at any moment. In Austin, opposition to the Omnibus was intense. In June, Texas governor Bell had written an exceptionally confrontational letter to Zachary Taylor, insultingly accusing the president of personally exerting a "hostile influence" by trying to deny Texas her justly won territory. Taylor had died before he was able to reply. Fillmore would have to decide quickly, and under terrible pressure, how to respond. Bell, who now considered war inevitable, sent an even more fiery letter to Texas's congressional delegation attacking federal policy in New Mexico as "wild, extravagant, and unauthorized," declaring that the time had come for "chivalry and daring" to play their part.

Congress remained frozen. "Here we are seven or eight months from the beginning of the session, and hardly able to keep the government alive," Webster declared on July 17, his last day in the Senate. He had often tried to damp down the sense of danger facing the country. But his parting words were ominous. "All is paralysis. We are brought nearly to a stand. We are all suspended upon this one topic, on this one idea, as if there were no objects in government, no uses in government, no duties in those who administer the government, but to settle one question." He had never known such a general "sickening" at the state of public affairs. "Men must live—to live they must work—to work they must be protected in their employment; and how are they to love, and work and educate their children, if in this way the business of society is stopped?" It was inconceivable to leave New Mexico without a government, he said, "with the highest degree of probability that there will arise collision, contest, and, for aught I know, bloodshed."

In that era of self-conscious pomp, when senators never removed their heavy broadcloth coats and neckpieces, the suffocating heat added exponentially to the accumulating political pressure. Anxiety, and physical and mental exhaustion, pushed the lawmakers to the edge of collapse, none more than Clay. Writing to a planter friend whose daughter was near death, he confessed the ineradicable grief he felt over his own dead children, which now, in the summer heat, seemed to swell even larger in his copious but weary heart. "My own experience in life has unhappily been that, in the dispensation of an inscrutable Providence, those cherished objects, on which the greatest amount of my affection was placed have, one by one, been taken from me. I have felt it nevertheless to be my duty to bow with resigned submission to irreversible decrees, and to trust that what has been ordered by an Allwise and Merciful God has been designed for the best, afflicting and incomprehensible as it may be to me." He added, "I have borne the seven months toil and arduous labor which have passed far better than I could have anticipated; but I begin to feel the debilitating effects of incessant and anxious exertion."

Trembling, soaked with perspiration, Clay rose on July 22 to deliver his final great oration. He held the floor for more than four hours, driving the arguments for compromise like an aged general mustering his troops for a final assault on a defiant bastion. He got off to an uncharacteristically rocky start, however. He had difficulty focusing, then snapped bitterly at one senator after another. He attacked John Hale for suggesting that he had participated in secret strategy sessions with certain unnamed senators: "May I ask to what keyhole he applied his ear or his eye—in what curtain he was ensconced?" He lambasted William Dayton of New Jersey for implying that the committee's members were a bunch of "quack" doctors. Robert Hunter, he charged, was guilty of petty-minded "fault-finding," and his Virginia colleague, James Mason, condemnable for daring to defend Hunter. At times Clay sounded as if he was lecturing a class of particularly obtuse students. "What is a compromise?" he wearily asked, as he had a hundred times before. "It is a work of mutual concession—an agreement in which there are reciprocal stipulations." Echoing the sarcastic refrain with which Tom Benton had for weeks mocked the Omnibus, he insisted a bit petulantly, "There is neither incongruity in the freight nor in the passengers on board our omnibus. We have no Africans or Abolitionists in our omnibus—no disunionists or Free-Soilers, no Jew or Gentile. Our passengers consist of Democrats and

Whigs," who had abandoned their customary antagonisms to confront the nation's crisis like men.

Clay, who throughout the debate had repeatedly declared himself a hater of slavery, now unexpectedly positioned himself as its apologist. With surprising venom, he went after staunchly antislavery John Davis for having earlier suggested that unless slavery was barred from New Mexico, the region could become a haven for the commercial "breeding" of slaves. (This was so offensive to delicate Southern ears that Davis had the record altered to state that he had said "traffic" in slaves rather than the "breeding" of them.) Such language, Clay exclaimed, might be fit "for the bar-rooms of crossroads taverns," but hardly for the august floor of the Senate. (Clay himself had in effect just called Hale a Peeping Tom, but no matter.) No slave owner even imagined such a thing as "breeding" human property for personal gain, Clay intoned. "He takes care of his slaves, he fosters them, and treats them often with the tenderness of his own children." They multiplied, he couldn't find work for them, and only then, alas, reluctantly and painfully, against his own wishes, might he be compelled to part with one in the market.

In contrast to virtuous slave owners, Clay painted a vicious portrait of the abolitionists, who, he charged, "would go into the temples of the holy God and drag from their sacred posts the ministers who are preaching his gospel for the comfort of mankind" and who, "if their power was equal to their malignity, would seize the sun of their great system of ours, drag it from the position in which it keeps in order the whole planetary bodies of the universe, and replunge the world in chaos and confusion to carry out their single idea." (Although there is little evidence that slaves were systematically bred for sale, the pathetic coffles that every member of Congress saw trekking past the Capitol, not to mention the disgrace of the local slave pens to which Clay himself had often alluded, exposed his rhetorical turn as just that.)

Clay then addressed the southern radicals with a more intellectually honest line of argument. He accused them of arbitrarily interpreting the Constitution to suit their own interests, and then crying, "All we want is the Constitution!" In other words, they had lost the ability to listen to anyone but themselves. Infallibility, he gently chided, is not the lot of mortal man. The radicals were also mistaken, he added, in believing that the Constitution inherently provided for the continuation of slavery: it did not. Finally, the South demanded the express recognition of a right to carry slaves anywhere south of the Missouri Compromise line should it be continued west to the Pacific. This, he said, exposed the fundamental and ultimately hopeless contradiction at the root of the radicals' position. "You cannot do it without an assumption of power upon the part of Congress to act upon the institution of slavery; and if they have the power in one way, they have the power to act upon it in the other way." Be realistic, he urged. The South's gains from passing the Omnibus were obvious: an end to the loathed Wilmot Proviso, a strengthened Fugitive Slave Law, and an end to the agitation for abolition in the District of Columbia. "What more can the South ask?"

The Omnibus might not be the only vehicle of compromise, Clay conceded, but it was the *best* one. "The omnibus is the vehicle of the people, of the mass of the people." Along with the Fugitive Slave Bill and the termination of the slave trade in the capital, which were to follow, it provided all that was necessary to bring peace to the country. Some said that the Omnibus was too heavily freighted, too full of "incongruous" matter. "It is not that the bill has too much in it," he said. "It has too little according to the wishes of its opponents; and I am very sorry that our omnibus cannot contain Mr. Wilmot, whose weight would break it down, I am afraid, if he were put there." (This was not a bad pun, considering the obese Wilmot's size, and it drew some laughter.)

Glancing meaningfully at the commander of the army, General Winfield Scott, who was seated in the chamber, Clay warned in grimmer tones than he had yet sounded that if the Omnibus were to be defeated, war was virtually inevitable—and not just one war, but two. First, war would begin between the peoples of New Mexico and Texas. "But Texas will not be alone; if a war breaks out between her and the troops of the United States on the upper Rio Grande, there are ardent, enthusiastic spirits of Arkansas, Mississippi, Louisiana, and Alabama, that will flock to the standard of Texas, contending, as they believe they will be contending, for slave territory. Who could say which side might prevail in such a fratricidal contest. The end of war is never seen in the beginning of war." Americans wanted no war, he declared. "The nation pants for repose, and entreats you to give it peace and tranquillity." The Omnibus would give it to them.

Gushing with perspiration, fighting his tubercular cough, grasping for his last reserve of diminishing energy, Clay then achieved one of his finest rhetorical moments of the debate. "I believe from the bottom of my soul that the measure is the reunion of this Union. I believe it is the dove of peace, which, taking its aerial flight from the dome of the Capitol, carries the glad tidings of assured peace and restored harmony to all the remotest extremities of this distracted land." He collapsed into his seat. Men and women wept. The old Kentuckian had sent his last verbal battalions over the enemy's walls.

In the course of his speech, Clay had complained that one of South Carolina's delegates to the Nashville Convention, the fire-eating editor of the *Charleston Mercury*, Robert Barnwell Rhett, had openly called for immediate disunion. Now Calhoun's successor, Robert W. Barnwell—despite the confusing similarity of their names, the two men were unrelated—rose to declare with irritating southern punctiliousness that Clay had been "disrespectful" to Rhett, although it was known to everyone that Rhett was the most uninhibited secessionist in the entire South, and so outspoken about it that he had been criticized by other radical South Carolinians for having revealed his hand too boldly and too early. However, Barnwell added pointedly, "It is true that this epithet 'disunionist' is likely soon to have very little terror in the South."

This was red meat for Clay. He replied stridently that calling for disunion was one thing, but "if he follows up that declaration by corresponding overt acts, he will be a traitor, and I hope he will meet the fate of a traitor."

The galleries thundered with applause. Clay flew onward, with a ferocity that boiled up like lava from his very core. "If Kentucky tomorrow unfurls the banner of resistance unjustly, I never will fight under that banner," he proclaimed. "When my state is right—when it has a cause for resistance—when tyranny, and wrong, and oppression insufferable arise—I will then share her fortunes; but if she summons me to the battlefield, or to support her in any cause which is unjust against the Union, never, *never*, will I engage with her in such a cause."

Barnwell starchily replied that when Clay referred to "traitors" history "may well prove that *they* are the *true men*." But the victory, the oratorical one at least, was Clay's.

CHAPTER 23

THE OMNIBUS OVERTURNED

——— ·•· ———

Clay's strategy was more than rhetorical. He had all along believed that the only real obstacle to the bill was President Taylor's stubborn hostility to it. With Taylor gone, the game had changed. Just after Taylor's death, in near-euphoria, he had extravagantly predicted in private that he would pass the Omnibus with forty votes. Since then, he had reduced his expectations, but he was still counting on a solid victory. He calculated that the votes he needed were more likely to be pried loose from among the more moderate southerners than from the antislavery opposition. (This explained Clay's smarmy defense of slave owners' feelings.) His most urgent goal was to stop the rush to war, and the cascade of secession that was sure to follow it. Clay and his friends decided that the best way to accomplish this was to turn over the drawing of the Texas–New Mexico boundary to a nonpartisan commission, thus pushing the entire question off the congressional agenda. Maine Democrat James Bradbury was delegated to introduce an amendment establishing such a commission. Having almost certainly won the approval of President Fillmore, with whom he boasted of having a "confidential" relationship, Clay had reason to feel confident that the plan would win the support of the two Texas senators. Houston, in particular, was eager for a compromise that would not "dishonor" Texas. If the Texans could be brought around, and the issue defused, other moderates would follow.

Houston rarely spoke. When he did, he was unimpressive, perhaps deliberately so. A Unionist of the deepest dye, he was hamstrung between his personal feelings and his official mission. "You may rely upon my fidelity to the *Union*,—always for the *federal union*, and the *union domestic!!!!*" he wrote in June to his wife, Margaret. "From union the country,—the people, have everything to realise, and hope, and from disunion, nothing but anarchy to expect." In the same spirit, two days after Taylor's death, he had written to Millard Fillmore, urging him to place himself at the head of "a great Union party" that transcended traditional partisan divisions. Still, Texas had sent him to the Senate to advance her cause. When he did speak, he tended to focus more on loyalty than on grievance. Texas expected "justice"; the military "usurpation" of New Mexico was an offense. But Texas—unlike, say, South Carolina he implied—had sown no discord, had never acted violently. She eyed the Constitution "with reverential deference." Wrong had been done to her: was there no one to sympathize with her, "no one to commiserate her disappointments"? The whole drift of the debate depressed him, as the Ultras of North and South combined, as he saw it, to cause as much "mischief" as they possibly could. To Margaret, he lamented, "We have some very bad men, and those who are guided by ambition, alone, without one feeling of Patriotism, or nobleness of soul." Mostly, he sat at his desk, morosely whittling ornate spoons and other knickknacks, leaving it to the more energetic Rusk to shoulder the main weight of making Texas's case.

On July 16, waving a map of Texas in his hand, Rusk accused the federal government of a litany of injustices, which he capped with the extreme, and baseless, charge of supplying Indian tribes with weapons that had been used to murder defenseless white women and children. Nothing was more inflammatory in a state where such real and (often) imagined depredations were felt to be a threat to every Texan's life and livelihood. And this was taking place, Rusk further alleged, implicitly addressing both Congress and the White House, "while you are seeking to take our territory from us, while you are raising armies in this country to force our land out of our possession." The federal government, he went on, had no legal right to attempt to establish a territorial government, much less a *state* government, in New Mexico. Texas had no conflict with New Mexico, since "there is no such organized community," he asserted. "Our controversy is with this government, goaded on by fanatics, fatally bent upon mischief." All through July, Rusk continued to pound the drum of war. He charged that the boundary commission was just a ploy to buy time. It was hardly "chivalrous" for the United States to threaten Texas "and then ask us, when we are looking each other in the eyes, to throw down our arms, to hoist the white flag, and beg peace of the United States."

The usual dueling amendments filled the torpid air. Complaining that the Omnibus would leave seventy thousand New Mexicans stuck inside Texas, Benton proposed setting Texas's western boundary at 102 degrees west longitude, just west of modern Lubbock and Amarillo. (In 1850, this entire region was open prairie, haunted by Comanche Indians.) The defeat of Benton's amendment was followed by a barrage of amendments by Henry Foote, who wanted to push New Mexico's southern boundary north to the 34th parallel, about halfway between El Paso and Albuquerque, and to split California from east to west seventy-five miles north of Los Angeles, at the 35th parallel, with its southern portion to become a new state named "Colorado."

Benton, meanwhile, indefatigable as ever, proposed an amendment that stipulated that the boundary commission should have no power to draw a line that did not exclude every portion of New Mexico, whether *east or west of the Rio Grande*—in effect, negating the whole point of a commission. When it went down to defeat, he proposed another amendment: this one specified that no one would be appointed to the commission who had already formed or expressed an opinion on the subject of the Texas border, thereby excluding just about anybody even remotely competent to be on such a commission. This amendment, too, was defeated, as Benton doubtless knew it would be.

To the Washington socialite Elizabeth Blair Lee, who lived across the street from the White House, the ongoing debate seemed like a duel to the political death between Clay and Benton, who seemed only to have swelled in "fire, courage, and strength" as the battle intensified. "They are the Richard and Saladin of the scene and it is not unlikely that the contest will end like that between the weighty battle-axe and the scimitar," she wrote to her husband, a naval officer. Although a close friend of the Bentons, Lee's esteem for Clay had steadily increased as the summer wore on. "Still Clay fights on as if he did not despair. The fertility and flexibility of his faculties in debate are really extraordinary, and show how much the mind can lift itself above the imbecility of the body." Encountering the Kentuckian in the Senate lobby, Lee expressed polite surprise at his unwilted vitality. "Why, the mistake is to suppose that I am an old man!" Clay replied genially. However heavy his burdens, he still knew how to flirt.

When the commission-establishing Bradbury amendment came to a vote on July 29, Clay felt that his day of victory had at long last arrived. Crowds of spectators packed into the narrow Senate gallery in anticipation of the dramatic climax. On the floor, Clay's men could be seen lining up their forces, while Hale, Clemens, and Benton—"persons who never agreed on anything before under the light of heaven," as Webster irritatedly put it—scurried around the chamber mustering the bill's enemies. To Clay's dismay, the amendment was defeated 28 to 28. He had won over a few new votes—but the Texans still remained beyond his grasp. Their price was steep: they wanted a guarantee that the commission would not subvert the Texan claim. Clay decided to give it to them. Benton saw what was coming. "The omnibus cannot drive, cannot get up and down the hills, and through the mud and mire, unless it has the Texas strength to carry it along," he remarked.

With Clay's approval, William Dawson of Georgia would offer an amendment to Bradbury's commission plan. (The use of this southern tool was hardly a coincidence, of course.) Dawson's amendment stated that New Mexico would not be allowed to exercise its authority east of the Rio Grande until the boundary commission had drawn a line that was acceptable to Congress—and to the Texas legislature. In other words, no boundary would be drawn that the Texans didn't like. This was a huge concession, and it took no account at all of the wishes of the New Mexicans. Clay, who may have written the Dawson amendment himself, nonetheless pronounced it to be one of "great fairness." With the Dawson proviso folded into it, the resuscitated Bradbury amendment was carried 30 to 28. The Texans were at last on board.

This should have been a moment of euphoria in Clay's camp. But Stephen Douglas was now unhappy. The Dawson proviso established the Rio Grande as Texas's de facto border, he observed. By banishing the territorial government from the entire eastern half of New Mexico—which included its capital, nearly all its settlements, and most of its arable land—the proviso implied the validity of the Texas claim, and encouraged both the Texans and their radical southern supporters to believe that the entire region would eventually be turned over to Texas. "When, I ask, will Texas ever agree to a boundary if she is to have the Rio Grande as her boundary up to the time she does agree to it?" Douglas demanded. "It is an invitation to Texas never to agree to a boundary. All that she will have to do is refuse to negotiate."

There was another problem, too. The amendment also stated that the legislative authority of the putative New Mexico Territory would encompass all the usual spheres consistent with the United States Constitution except "the primary disposal of the soil," which meant that the federal government was reserving control over public lands, and—this was what provoked Douglas and his friends—"prohibiting or establishing African slavery." Fundamentalist proponents of Popular Sovereignty such as Douglas insisted as an article of democratic faith that if men were competent to govern themselves, they had the right to legislate on whatever they wished. Several of the territories excluded banks, whiskey, and gambling tables. No one imagined that such prohibitions violated the Constitution. If they wanted to exclude slavery, that was their right, too. By denying them that right, the amendment set a precedent for federal "interference" in territorial government that Douglas and the northern Democrats found unacceptable.

Weighed down with the Dawson proviso, the Bradbury amendment was now in danger of losing its northern supporters. To placate them, Clay, at Douglas's urging, approved yet *another* amendment. This one would prune away the phrase regarding slavery. Their vehicle was Moses Norris, a craggy-faced New Hampshire Democrat who was famous, at least in his own state, for once having physically dragged a preacher from the pulpit of his local Baptist church for daring to preach abolitionism. (Paradoxically, he had also sheltered the black abolitionist Frederick Douglass overnight in his own home during a rainstorm, when no one else in town would take him in.) Although Clay and Foote defended this tweak in the amendment as an expression of the federal "nonintervention" that almost everyone claimed to support, southerners of all persuasions attacked it as a device that would permit territorial legislatures to ban slavery. Despite their opposition, Norris's amendment passed, and the offending words were removed. Clay remained optimistic. But there was trouble brewing. As one skeptical Yankee senator wrote to his wife, "What fastens one screw loosens another."

The heat on July 31 remained unforgiving. The temperature in the fetid and stinking streets of the capital was close to ninety degrees. Inside the densely packed Senate chamber, it was much hotter. Senators were reeling from discomfort. As if the atmosphere were not tense enough already, the day's session began with another tirade from Jefferson Davis, whose opposition to any form of compromise had only hardened as the weeks passed. Davis continued to call for nothing less than complete federal capitulation to the South's most radical demands. Much of what he now said was familiar, but it still rang with piercing menace. Northern aggression was "moving with an increased velocity." The rights of the minority were now "wholly controlled" by the will of an insolent majority. Irresponsible northern politicians were increasingly ready "to disregard, to destroy, to crush the instrument which their fathers created." Had the South not caved in to the Missouri Compromise thirty years earlier, he claimed, it would have kept control over the entire Louisiana Purchase as far north as the Canadian border, and "the policy of the Pacific country would probably have been through all time that of the slaveholding states." But the South, "in her generosity," had foolishly given away what was hers by right. Such was the sad past. But what of the future? Davis didn't fear conflict between federal troops and the "posse of citizens"— he was alluding to the army of battle-hardened Texas Rangers that was being raised by the state government—that was being recruited to invade New Mexico. No one would ever fight for the North in such a war, he scoffed. Turning to his fellow senators, he asked, "Is it you, or you, who will enlist in such a war? You must raise a foreign army; you must have a Swiss Guard when you attempt with sword and bayonet to enforce your laws upon the citizens of the United States." Nothing but corruption or madness would induce the federal government to embark on such a campaign. Would Congress ever give the South the justice it deserved? Stone-faced, he drawled, "I have despaired of ever finding it here."

Clay expected nothing less from Davis, or from the radicals who echoed his inflammatory sentiments. He was confident that he commanded a slim majority. But he was unprepared for what happened next.

James A. Pearce was a second-term Whig from Maryland. At forty-five, he had a round, fleshy face, dark curly hair and side-whiskers, along with a rather reticent, lawyerly manner that fostered neither deep friendships nor enmities. His career in the Senate had thus far been unremarkable. Although he felt strongly that the Texan claim to New Mexico had no legal basis, he had served as a staunch and loyal member of Clay's caucus. In short, he was one of the relatively few senators who gave the harried Clay no trouble at all. Now he shocked Clay, and just about everyone else, by moving to strike out the entire New Mexico section of the Omnibus, and then to reinsert all of it except the Dawson proviso, which he regarded as an intolerable capitulation to the Texans.

Later there were rumors that Pearce's motion was part of a secret strategy that he had contrived with President Fillmore to derail the Omnibus. Fillmore certainly liked Pearce, and had offered him the position of secretary of the interior; although Pearce declined, he had promised the president his "most cordial support" in the Senate. More likely, Pearce was acting on his own. Spurred by some combination of genuine conviction, physical exhaustion, the withering heat, and annoyance at Clay for having taken his vote for granted, he finally said exactly what he was thinking, with no heed to the consequences. The Texans, he said, in essence, couldn't be trusted: if there was a legal or geographical vacuum, they would fill it. The Dawson amendment "abandoned" to them everything east of the Rio Grande. Why, moreover, give a government to the emptiest part of New Mexico, while leaving the best and most populated part of it as prey for Texas? "It makes the bill cranky, lop-eared, crippled, deformed, and curtailed of its fair proportions," Pearce said. He had no wish to destroy the Omnibus as a whole, he emphasized: he merely wanted to restore its "fair proportions." With that in mind, once the Dawson proviso had been deleted, he said, he would immediately move to reinsert the original provisions of the bill—that is, the creation of the boundary commission, which he supported.

Clay was stunned. What on earth was Pearce doing? He begged Pearce to withdraw his motion. Without the Dawson proviso, the Texas votes would be lost, and along with them, Clay feared, his precarious majority. "Light was beginning to break upon us—land was beginning to be in sight once more—and is it possible upon slight and unimportant amendments that we shall now hazard the safety, the peace, if not the union of the country?" Clay cried. All the months of labor, all the sleepless nights, all the endless hours of debate, all the rancorous pleading, threatening, and wheedling—could it have all been for nothing? Was the Omnibus about to be overturned by a mere pebble in its path? Clay's friends swarmed around Pearce's seat, urging him to reconsider, but he was adamant.

Tom Rusk, equally flummoxed, expostulated that he felt like a man who had set out to fight a duel only to face an antagonist whose pistol misfired over and over, and finally just threw down his own gun in disgust. "He could be shot or shot at, but to be eternally snapped at was more than human nature could bear."

At this point David Yulee undertook a subtle but devastating parliamentary maneuver that took Pearce by surprise. Yulee politely asked the gentlemanly Marylander if he would be kind enough to divide his motion to allow senators to first vote on the deletion, and then afterward on the replacement.

"I have no objection," the unthinking Pearce replied. He clearly had no idea what Yulee was up to.

Benton got it right away. "We have all heard of a company of players—of that class of players in England who are called 'strolling players,'" he drawled, clearly relishing what was coming, as he offered up one of the more memorable and entertaining metaphors of the debate. It was said that one such company went out from London to perform *Hamlet*, he said, but when the play was about to begin the manager announced that the part of Hamlet would be left out. Asked why Hamlet had been left out, the manager replied, "Because the ghost was sick, and they couldn't play Hamlet without a ghost." At this, a wave of knowing laughter rolled through the Senate chamber. "This is the way we find ourselves," continued Benton. "Well, sir, our ghost has got sick—the ghost of the Omnibus—and I hope there will be light enough before long, with the help of the sun, of the chandelier, and of the intellectual illumination which will be received, to make the poor ghost fly from what he hates." Ostentatiously flaunting his geographical erudition, Benton then recited, map in hand, a list of all the towns on the east side of the Rio Grande that would be left without government, pausing several times for theatrical effect, placing his great finger on one place after another: "Can anybody tell me its name? I wait for an answer. No answer! Nobody ever heard of it? Its name is San Felipe . . . " Unless the Dawson proviso was wiped away, all of them would be left without government. Then he pointed dramatically to the west side of the river. There was nothing on the west to govern! "It is giving a government and leaving out the people!" he shouted. "It is the play of Hamlet—the part of Hamlet left out!" As far as he was concerned, the whole scheme should be discarded. "It is no compromise," he concluded caustically. "It is a humbug."

Pearce's amendment to strike out all the part of the bill that related to Texas and New Mexico easily passed, with Benton, Douglas, and many of the northern Democrats combining with most of the southern radicals against Clay and his most loyal allies. That done, Pearce then dutifully moved to replace everything that the first part of his amendment had deleted from the bill, except the Dawson proviso.

Now the real drama began. Yulee moved to delete from Pearce's amendment everything that related to Texas—to essentially cripple it by stripping away one of its central provisions. Only now did most of the senators begin to grasp what was happening: Yulee was out to kill the Omnibus.

A confusing flurry of motions filled the air. "It is proposed to insert certain matter in the bill," protested one befuddled senator. "Now, how do I know what it is?" Another begged, "What will be the limits of New Mexico? Does nobody know?" The enemies of the Omnibus scented blood. Its panicked partisans repeatedly called for adjournment, without success. "We are not in a condition to legislate," gasped Joseph Underwood of Kentucky, still loyal to Clay. Seward called for the yeas and nays on Yulee's motion. It passed easily by a vote of 29 to 23: Texas had now been knocked out of the Omnibus. For Clay, it was a stinging defeat.

The Omnibus was now so badly damaged that it really had become, as Benton had relentlessly charged all along, a congeries of "heterogenous elements." Successive votes struck out everything in the Omnibus that pertained to Texas, then to New Mexico, then finally to California, each by lopsided margins. Clay didn't wait for the outcome. He stalked alone from the chamber, looking to one observer like a man wandering through a ruin. All that was left in the gutted hulk of the Omnibus was Utah.

The men, both southern and northern, who for months had battled against Clay and the Omnibus, exploded in fits of ecstasy. The dour abolitionist Salmon Chase flung his arms around Pierre Soulé. Seward danced around like a little top. The humorless Jefferson Davis beamed. "Dayton shook his thick sides with sporadic spasms. Yulee looked solemn in solitary glory. Barnwell's spectacles twinkled; and Butler's gray hairs flourished more than ever," wrote a reporter for the New York *Express.* Benton trumpeted the defeat of his foes, not the least of them Henry Foote, who slumped in despair. "Their vehicle is all gone, all but one plank, and I wish to save that plank for them, by way of doing homage to their work," Benton roared. "The omnibus is overturned, and all the passengers spilled out but one. We have but Utah left—all gone but Utah!" Had Zachary Taylor lived, he would justly have considered the smashing of the Omnibus a triumph that vindicated the stubborn opposition for which he had been so cruelly pilloried.

There was still some fussing over Utah's southern boundary. Would it lie along the line of the Missouri Compromise at 36° 30′, as Jefferson Davis preferred? Or along some other parallel, as John Hale and the abolitionists wished, so as not to imply the North's acquiescence to the Missouri Compromise line. At Douglas's suggestion, the boundary was fixed at 37 degrees, where it remains today. After nine traumatic hours, the last fragment of the ruined Omnibus, the bill providing for the establishment of a territorial government for Utah, was read for the third and final time. It would be passed the next day with little opposition. The compromise "died of amendments," Elizabeth Blair Lee wrote to her husband. "[It] passed the Senate with no passengers in the omnibus save the Utah travellers. The Mormons alone got through living. The Christians all jumped out."

August 1 promised yet another midsummer steambath in Washington. In the Senate, everyone seemed hungover, either from the previous night's toasts to the demise of the Omnibus on the part of those who had destroyed it, or in a sort of cranky and depressed political daze among those who had fought long and hard for it, only to have victory snatched from their grasp at the last instant. The Omnibus may not have been quite so sure of immediate passage as they believed, but that was how they felt on that glum and sweat-sodden morning. Clay and his friends were unforgiving. Foote scourged the senators who had voted down the Omnibus as "shallow-minded, factious demagogues." Clay excoriated the "extremists" of both North and South for sabotaging the Omnibus, but he blamed the hapless James Pearce most of all, for betraying him by stupidly agreeing to Yulee's Machiavellian request to divide the two parts of his amendment.

Pearce tried to deny responsibility for what he had done, claiming that he had only meant to get rid of Dawson's amendment, "But being too obscure to be consulted and not having been consulted, this amendment was sprung on me, and I thought it my duty to oppose it in the best way I could." (Pearce later wrote to a friend, "The compromise bill was lost by Mr. Clay's own blunder, tho', like Napoleon, who never lost a battle, but charged every defeat on some subordinate, he has endeavored to make me the scapegoat falsely and unjustly, for which I will never forgive him.")

Clay ignored him. There was more at stake now than personal feelings. For months, Clay had told the American people that the Omnibus Bill offered the only hope of saving the Union. In the space of only a few hours, that hope had been dashed. The Union must prepare to fight for itself. "If blood is to be spilt, by whose fault is it to be spilt?" he asked. "It will be by the fault of those who choose to raise the standard of disunion, and endeavor to prostrate this government." Weak though his voice might now be, he declared, and feeble his arm, he would place both at the service of the Union.

Cheers roared through the gallery, as David Atchison, temporarily in the presiding officer's chair, hammered his gavel ineffectually for order.

When a semblance of calm had been restored, James Mason icily reminded Clay—as if he did not know—that almost every southern state had formally proclaimed that it would resist any exercise of federal power "in reference to this slave question." If Congress now dared to pass any law that excluded Virginians from taking their slaves anywhere they wanted south of the Missouri Compromise line, Virginia would take whatever measures were necessary "to preserve her own safety and her own welfare out of the Union." Clay had admitted that he would lend his aid "to the bayonets" of the federal government. At long last, Mason said, the South knew where Clay really stood: as its enemy.

Adding his angry South Carolina drawl to Mason's bare-knuckle attack, Andrew Butler dared the federal government to attempt to enforce its will on the South. What sons of any state from Virginia to Mississippi would ever be willing to cooperate in such a campaign against their homes? Clay himself had been born in Virginia, he noted, adding venomously, "I should like to see the recreant who could come with his sword against his native state." Butler, who believed with near-religious fervor in loyalty to state over nation, obviously intended to embarrass Clay, but Clay hurled the insinuation back at him with passion. "The Union is my country," he thundered. "The thirty states are my country; Kentucky is my country, and Virginia no more than any other state of this Union. But even if it were my own state—if my own state lawlessly, contrary to her duty, should raise the standard of disunion against the residue of the Union, I would go against her."

After this, Clay had nothing left to give. He was physically, mentally, and spiritually spent. Perhaps no other senator in American history up to that point—certainly none seventy-two years of age—had invested so much of himself in an issue of such vital urgency, and fought so hard for it, and failed. He had spoken scores of times and delivered a dozen major speeches, several of them hours in length, under conditions of discomfort and stress that would have brought low many a younger man. He was bruised, bloodied, and defeated. His enemies had prevailed. He knew that he had overreached. Even friends had criticized him for exercising "moral despotism," for his endless pressure and bullying, for cajoling them into postponing virtually all the Senate's other business in his relentless campaign to pass the Omnibus. And now it was dead. If any hope for compromise remained, it would have to be accomplished by others.

A few days later, depressed, ill, and desperate to breathe the restorative drafts of sea air, Clay abandoned Washington and headed north to Newport, Rhode Island. His lungs were ruined, his hands shaking, his voice failing, and he had had enough of applause and swooning maidens. But wherever he stopped crowds appeared as if out of nowhere, demanding a speech, and then another speech. To a pressing mob of adoring Philadelphians, he complained that Congress "after all these months have done nothing, absolutely nothing of moment." Then, catching himself, reaching down into himself for something that sounded hopeful, he added, "But we must never despair of the Republic. The best acts of that body are to come." In New York, he tried again to escape the multitudes that swarmed around the pier where his steamer docked. "I am fatigued and broken down," he told them, begging them to allow him to go to his stateroom and rest. "By and by, if God spares me," he promised, "I will return and see you all again; and as to my omnibus, you had better all get into it, and ride home as fast as you can." His admirers ignored his pleas, and the police were called to save him from being crushed.

CHAPTER 24

"A STEAM ENGINE IN BRITCHES"

——— •◆• ———

Into the gap left by Henry Clay stepped the Senate's deftest strategist, that "steam engine in britches," as he had been called, Stephen A. Douglas. In contrast to Clay, with his magnificent, sweeping orations, Douglas had thus far spoken only infrequently, though when he did it was always to the point, and in the practical realm of facts, where he always felt most comfortable. He would now take center stage. Without him, without his particular combination of talents, the compromise likely would have remained a political corpse: it was by no means clear to anyone that it could be resuscitated in any form. If Henry Clay couldn't do it, could anyone? What happened over the next few days and weeks transformed Douglas from a talented and boilingly ambitious, but essentially garden-variety, politician into a true national statesman to be reckoned with.

For months Douglas had waited patiently for Clay to work his magic. He had never really liked the Omnibus, but he had nevertheless thrown his prodigious energy behind Clay's effort to enact it. In a revealing letter to a friendly editor in Illinois, Charles Lanphier, Douglas offered a hardheaded analysis of what had gone wrong: "The Compromise Bill was defeated by a union between the Free Soils & disun[ion]ists & the administration of Genl'l Taylor. All the power & patronage of the Govt was brought to bear against us, & at last the allied forces were able to beat us." He added, "By combining the measures into one Bill the Committee had united the opponents of each measure instead of securing the friends of each." He expressed unvarnished disgust at Benton's obstructionism, for which, "In my opinion no justification—no excuse can be made," and went on to say, harshly but with considerable truth, "that if Mr Clay's name had not been associated with the Bills they would have passed long ago. The administration were jealous of him & hated him & the some democrats were weak enough to fear that the success of his Bill would make him President." Adding a reference to Shakespeare's gallant Prince Hal, he concluded, "But let it be said of old Hal that he fought a glorious & a patriotic battle."

Douglas boldly predicted that he would be able to pass the California statehood bill within days—a seemingly fantastical notion, given the standoff from which the Senate had yet to emerge. "We shall then take up the Bill for New Mexico & pass it just as I reported it four months ago," he told Lanphier, adding that he expected the bills to easily pass the House as well. Peacocklike egos were plentiful among the sixty broadcloth-swathed members of the Senate, but Douglas's strutting hubris seemed in a class of its own. If he failed, the past months of wrenching labor would go to waste, Congress would reveal itself as helplessly ineffectual, and its members would return home in disgrace to face desperate and frightened voters.

Now, however, he really went to work. With the Omnibus dead, he took stock of the voting patterns that had killed it. Nineteen northerners had joined with fourteen southerners to strike out everything that related to New Mexico, while only five Whigs joined with Clay to vote against it. David Yulee's sly and successful attack on the Pearce amendment had won sixteen northern and thirteen southern votes, with twelve northerners and sixteen southerners voting against it. Ten northerners and twenty-four southerners voted to strike out California. Feeding these and other numbers into his mental calculator, Douglas came to the conclusion that enough different combinations of votes existed to pass each of the measures separately. His strategy would differ significantly from Clay's. The

Kentuckian had struggled to enact the Omnibus by poaching individual votes from among the radicals to create a majority. Douglas would try to align shifting blocs of radicals of both sections with his core of Unionist supporters to pass each bill. His strategy would now depend less on grandiloquence than on tireless, mostly unrecorded negotiations, which were carried out as often as not over copious cups of wine in the Hole-in-the-Wall snack bar just off the Senate floor, where one senator after another might find himself in Douglas's persuasive bearlike embrace.

Unlike Clay, Douglas could also count on presidential support. The administration, less than a month old and still only half-formed, had no time for a honeymoon. Millard Fillmore would have to show what he was made of immediately. For six straight months, he had sat beneath the looming portrait of George Washington as the presiding officer of the Senate, observing the flotsam of pleas, threats, and tortured arguments that flooded through the chamber on the tidal wash of debate. As a result, probably no man in Washington had a more nuanced understanding of the issues at stake, as well as the tactics, personalities, and vulnerabilities of the battle-weary players. Fillmore and Douglas were convinced that the broad public wanted a compromise—South Carolina and parts of the cotton South were another story—and that Congress could continue to defy the voters' desires only at its own peril.

The Omnibus still lay a smoking ruin when, in the midst of the rancorous postmortems of August 1, Douglas introduced his bill calling for the admission of California into the Union. Here it was at last, the monster that the South had long feared: the new free state that would tip the balance in the Senate against slavery. Although Douglas initially hoped to push California through at a clip, he soon realized that hastiness would further inflame southerners whose support, or at least acquiescence, he hoped to win, unless he dealt first with the explosive problem of Texas, and in the process enabled them to come away with at least a few shreds of their ever touchy honor intact. John Berrien of Georgia, whose convoluted syntax made his speeches almost impossible to follow, warned in a moment of unusual clarity that "the admission of California with her present constitution and boundaries shall result in producing an excitement which it may be found impossible to control."

Once Douglas had settled on his course, the Senate suddenly began to move at what seemed like breathless speed, at least compared to its glacial pace of the past months. Fillmore lent his support, urging Congress to act quickly, warning that delay would lead to dire consequences. Douglas worked feverishly with James Pearce, who was desperate to redeem himself from the debacle he had instigated a few days earlier, and who on August 5 delivered a bill that the two men hoped would finally bring an end to the crisis in Texas. This plan laid out for the first time the shape that Texas has today: it proposed setting the state's northern border at 36° 30', and her western one in a line that ran south along 103° west longitude to 32° north latitude, where it turned abruptly west to the Rio Grande, which it reached just above El Paso. The boundary was frankly ludicrous, bestowing on Texas a form as illogical as a gerrymandered county, jutting hundreds of miles west and north across uninhabitable country, and leaving behind the spindly strip of land north of 36° 30' that would eventually become the western panhandle of Oklahoma.

Its virtue, however, at least so Douglas and Pearce hoped, was that the proposed boundary it drew lay far enough west to satisfy the Texans, far enough north to appease the South, and far enough south to accommodate New Mexico's northern defenders. The bill assigned Texas somewhat more land—about thirty thousand square miles—than it would have gotten under the Omnibus. However, it would have to agree to yield to the United States all the territory it claimed west of that line. As compensation, the federal government would give Texas $10 million in 5 percent stock—enough to pay off the state's groaning debt. Pearce reiterated that he personally considered the Texan claim to New Mexico legally worthless. However, he pragmatically concluded, "It cannot be denied that a feeling of great discontent prevails in Texas. It is useless to ask if there has been any justifying cause for this. The fact is so."

What did Texas's debt have to do with either slavery or the boundary question? The answer was nothing. But it provided federal leverage on the stubborn Texans. As an independent republic, Texas had pledged to pay off its bonds with income from customs duties. That income evaporated when Texas became a state, and the duties were taken over by the United States government. With no source of state income, apart from the sale of land, Texas could neither pay off its debts nor issue new bonds. Some kind of deal that would trade money for Texas's claim on New Mexico had been part of the compromise since January, when Clay had first proposed it. Many senators disagreed with this on principle, and had argued that the United States had no obligation at all to clean up after a state that couldn't manage its own finances. With the painful memory of the bloated Galphin claim fresh in everyone's minds, the prospect of another set of open-ended claims metastasizing in the courts was a powerful motivation to settle the Texas debt once and for all. (Behind the scenes, there was intense speculation in these Texas bonds. Their real value was anyone's guess. A few months earlier, they could be had for 5 cents on the dollar; by mid-August, they were worth ten times that. The greatest number were held by Daniel Webster's friend and benefactor the Washington banker William Corcoran, who would receive the largest single payout. Some bitter southerners, eager to excuse their opposition to the compromise, not to mention their overreaching, unreasonableness, and outright bullying, later alleged that the entire compromise was little more than a scam to reward venal investors.)

The Pearce bill was the carrot. Now came the stick. Webster proved his worth as an adviser by urging the president to reply forcefully to Texas's provocations, but using "as many soft words as we can to soothe the irritation." With Fillmore's assent, Webster wrote directly to Texas governor Bell, calmly defending the actions of Colonel Munroe, and stating that until the United States government was able to provide New Mexico with the free and democratic government that it had been promised after the Mexican War it was a matter of "absolute necessity" that military government should continue. Webster conceded only that the "constitution" the New Mexicans had written for themselves in June would be regarded by the administration merely as a *petition* for statehood, rather than a legal declaration of it.

The following day, August 6, Fillmore sent his own message to Congress. Webster may have contributed to it, but to give the president his due, anyone who thought that Fillmore lacked spine was now disabused. A weak man might well have capitulated to the Texans: Fillmore dug in his well-polished boots. The president declared unequivocally that New Mexico was federal territory, and that Texas enjoyed no rights or powers beyond her state limits. "If Texas militia march into any of the other States or into any Territory of the United States, there to execute or enforce any law of Texas, they become at that moment trespassers; they are no longer under the protection of any lawful authority, and are to be regarded merely as intruders," he declared. Should the laws of the United States be opposed or obstructed in any way, it was his duty as commander-in-chief to employ the armed forces as they were needed. The response to Fillmore's message, especially from northerners in Congress, was highly favorable; from Newport, Henry Clay sent a telegram offering the president his full support. The sleekly groomed Fillmore might not be the soldier that hard-edged Taylor had been, but his meaning was equally unmistakable: the United States was ready to go to war.

That same day, in his office at the War Department, General Winfield Scott, the acting secretary of war, penned a directive of the gravest import. It would be dispatched immediately to Colonel Munroe by special messenger. "You are hereby instructed, in the case of any military invasion of New Mexico from Texas, or by armed men from any other State or states for the purpose of overturning the order of civil government that may exist in New Mexico at the time, or of subjugating New Mexico to Texas, to interpose, as far as practicable, the troops under your command against any such act of violence," Scott ordered. Munroe was to use persuasion if possible. "But when necessary, and without losing any material advantage by delay, you will take all preliminary steps for defense and in the last resort resist with vigor."

The peacetime army had pathetically few men to spare. Before his death, President Taylor had ordered 750 fresh troops to New Mexico. Scott estimated that once they reached Santa Fe, taking account of attrition from desertion and disease—they would be marching straight through a cholera epidemic—Munroe would wind up with fewer than 1,400 men to defend all of New Mexico. He decided to order another five hundred regulars from the Seventh Infantry Regiment to head west from their base in Florida, where they had been fighting the Seminoles, but it would be many weeks before they got anywhere near Santa Fe. Scott also sent a message to the commander of federal troops in San Antonio, directing him to muster whatever troops were at hand, and interpose them, if possible, between Santa Fe and the invading Texans. "If attacked in the march, by the Texans, short of New Mexico, your troops will repel force by force," Scott ordered. Meanwhile, rumors—untrue, as it turned out, but plausible to many—raced through Washington that Texas already had thousands of men under arms, and that Tom Rusk was leaving for Austin to lead them.

No one had ever suggested that Stephen Douglas was guilty of either grace or delicacy, and whatever New England reserve he might once have possessed had long ago been replaced by the swagger of the frontier. However, he now set in motion a sort of legislative pas de deux, interweaving debate on both the California and Texas bills, with the hope that he could bring them both to a near-simultaneous and successful climax. Would his choreography actually work? No one knew. At least in its first act, the tussle over the Texas border, this was mostly a southern show that pitted such Unionists as the reinvigorated Henry Foote against ever truculent Jefferson Davis, David Yulee, and their cadre of radicals, who paid no more than sarcastic lip service to the Union, and were clearly praying for a debacle that would push the moderates toward secession. Davis, for one, was unrepentant. "If any portion of the defeat of [the Omnibus Bill] attaches to me, I feel highly honored," he exulted. "I glory in defeating it." They peppered Pearce with irritating procedural motions, quorum calls, and hostile amendments. James Mason proposed an amendment calling on the United States to "surrender to the constituted authorities of Texas" all territory that it occupied "within the limits of that state." John Davis of Massachusetts, on behalf of the antislavery men, moved to reduce

Texas's payment to $6 million. Three separate southern amendments proposed a new state in southern California that would create an opening for slavery. At this stage in the game, such amendments were primarily meant to demonstrate to the voters at home that their sponsors intended to go down fighting, and to fan the flames of grievance for the final break that they expected to come.

Only Yulee spoke at length, in a speech spread over two days. What he said was one of the most honest admissions of what slaveholders really wanted that had yet been delivered. It was only as a result of the South's generous concessions that the North had achieved its current power, Yulee asserted. Had the South not allowed slavery to be excluded above the Missouri Compromise line in 1820, the North could never have kept pace in either the number of free states, or in the House of Representatives. It had been nothing less than "madness" for the South to have given in to policies that had closed off to her "the avenues of colonization with her slave property." He then, quite literally, before the eyes of his fellow senators, invented a new human right to suit the interests of slavery, and a rationale for the proslavery imperialism that had fueled the recent attack on Cuba, and would be used to justify similar expeditions in Mexico and the Caribbean Basin in the decade to come. "The right of expansion or growth is one of the essential interests of every community," he proclaimed. "It is necessary to the happiness and prosperity of a community as it is to the comfort and existence of the individual man, that they should enjoy a free scope for their natural growth. I regard this as one of the great rights of a people, and I will denominate it the LIBERTY OF GROWTH. To all people it is important and useful; but to the slaveholding States of the South it is indispensable. This great liberty of growth—the free right to spread her settlements and extend her limits as the increase of population requires—is more essential to her, is a more imperious necessity, than to any other people that ever existed."

Other "overpopulated" countries that lacked vacant territory to colonize could dump their human surplus on other nations, Yulee continued, as Europe had upon the United States. This option was currently closed to southerners, since there was no slaveholding country to which they could emigrate with their slaves without "abandoning the enjoyment of popular government," and few places where they could emigrate with slaves on any terms at all. "If then they are confined to fixed limits, and without vacant territory to colonize, whenever the population of the slave-holding section becomes too great for subsistence or comfort, one of two results must follow," he continued. "Either the black race must be sent out free, as emigrants, at the cost of their value and an entire subversion of the structure and habits of our society, or the whites must, by an equally sure and progressive process, emigrate, leaving in the end of the graves of their sires to be trodden under the heel of the African." There were only two ways to avoid this unthinkable result. One was immediate abolition, and the deportation of the black race, which was obviously impractical because of the vast capital investment that slaves represented. The unacceptable alternative was to abandon any hope of expansion. "I repeat, then," said Yulee, "that the great liberty of growth is indispensable to our circumstances—is the condition of our existence. It is a liberty we cannot surrender."

Now it was obvious, he said, that the admission of California was about to deliver the North a majority in the Senate. While such an increase of power was not necessary to the North, it struck at the South's essential security. Could the North be trusted? Could it even *trust itself* to do right by the South? Hardly. He then called dramatically for a new Constitutional Convention "for the reforming of the compact of Union," to guarantee to the South "control of one of the legislative branches; and as the North is in admitted ascendancy in the popular branch, the South should be allowed a preponderance in this body." This chilling speech swayed no one. But it showed where the South was heading.

For another day or two, there was some haggling about the western-most corner of the boundary—"What is the precise latitude of El Paso nobody can say," Pearce asserted with a sigh—and a proposal by an Ohio Whig to carve a swath of territory out of Texas for displaced Indians. Pearce shot down this idea right away, arguing that the Indians were rapidly disappearing, as if by some mysterious natural process rather than systematic harassment and killing expeditions. "They are dwindling away, until, I suppose, at last, there will not remain one red man on the face of the continent—that is the inevitable destiny of the race," he pronounced. There was no reason to provide territory for people who would soon cease to exist. Several other senators complained that Pearce's plan was too generous to Texas, and had allotted her more land than she deserved. "The land is a thing that we can part with very well," Pearce wisely replied. "It will be no loss to us, and if it gratifies her, if it assists in the passage of this bill, it is well worth the giving away." He added, sounding rather like Clay, his former beau ideal, "This is not a bill to deal out exact rights or to determine titles, it is a bill of compromise—a bill of peace—a bill to reconcile conflicting opinions—a bill to stop agitation."

The real question was: what would the Texans do? Without their support, no compromise could work. Rusk was ferocious in defending Texas's claim; unlike Houston, he was also up for reelection. He was already suspect both at home and elsewhere in the South for being insufficiently extreme. "If you fail us, the South is gone—any compromise short of your full boundaries of Texas will undo us," one Virginian chided him. "Let us have no compromise—none—none whatever. I fear nothing so much as a compromise." Both Texas senators knew that federal troops were en route to New Mexico, that the president was firmly committed to resist an invasion, and that without the camouflage of the Omnibus Texas stood no chance of winning congressional recognition for its entire elephantine claim. Some Texans were also having second thoughts. "It is unpleasant to impoverish the state and tax our people with insupportable burthens to make war against the U.S. although it is as we all know on our soil," one uneasy constituent wrote to Rusk.

By August 9, if not earlier, Houston and Rusk had concluded that Pearce's plan was the best deal they were likely to get. Rusk, who spoke for both of them, put the best face on it that he could. Texas was anxious to "open the door" to emigrants, he told the Senate, to people her immense, rich, but sparsely populated domain. However, the state's crippling debt scared away prospective settlers, especially "men of property." Many Texans, he admitted, would probably see his vote as a betrayal. But he asserted, without any real evidence, that more than anything else the people of Texas wanted to wipe out their debt. "I would accept anything, so far as Texas is concerned, that she could honorably accept," he said.

When Douglas called for the bill's third reading, which in accordance with Senate tradition was tantamount to passage, his motion squeaked by with 27 in favor and 24 opposed: the Texans had tipped the balance. Several Whigs who had opposed compromise were absent, perhaps as a result of direct pressure from the president, or possibly because Fillmore had promised them sufficient dollops of patronage to outweigh principle. The final ballot, later that evening, was decisive, if anticlimactic. Douglas's coalition of northern and southern moderates—including sixteen Democrats and fourteen Whigs—decisively overwhelmed its opposition by a vote of 30 to 20, with Benton, Seward, and four other diehard antislavery men joining Jefferson Davis and his fire-eating followers on the losing side. Of these twenty, twelve were Democrats, six Whigs, and two Free Soilers. Perhaps the most surprising single vote was that of the fulminating Jeremiah Clemens of Alabama, who had contributed some of the most incendiary rhetoric heard in the debate, but was now found voting alongside the compromising majority. Clemens later protested that he was following the Texans' lead, though irate radicals charged that he was simply drunk.

Through a combination of personal magnetism, locomotive energy, an amazingly acute reading of the minds of his fellow senators North and South—and, yes, towering hubris—Douglas had wrought a miracle. He had achieved in just three days what Clay had failed to accomplish in seven months. Here was the steam engine at work indeed! He had crafted a feasible approach, which, if he could keep it going, finally held out real hope of dragging the country back step by step from the verge of dissolution. Robert Winthrop later provided a fitting coda to the conundrum that until only days earlier had seemed all but insoluble: "Upon this question we were brought at last to the alternative of drawing the line, or of drawing the sword. I confess to have believed that unless some measure of this sort were speedily adopted, we should not have a foot of free soil this side of the Rio Grande, without fighting for it. For my own part, I had rather that this boundary between sister States should be run by gold than by steel; by money than by blood; and that it should be marked upon the map of our Union in all time to come, in lines of any other color than red."

Hardly pausing for the Senate to catch its breath, three days after the passage of the Texas boundary act Douglas pushed on to California. On August 13, about the same time that Governor Bell was addressing the Texas legislature, Jefferson Davis, in his last, scathing speech on California statehood, urged the Senate to abstain from admitting California. Davis presumably had been polishing this speech, better crafted than most of his, for some time, in anticipation of what was now a foregone conclusion. Though he termed it a "solemn appeal," his tone, as always, was accusatory and self-righteous. He condemned the North's "lust for sectional domination," and its "reckless disregard" of the southern minority—this after seven months of excruciating negotiation. He dismissed northern appeals to the sanctity of the Union as sheer hypocrisy. What exactly was this supposed "crime" of disunion of which the South was accused? Was it treason to stand up against the real subversives—that is, the abolitionists—who were seeking to build upon its ruins a grotesque new country that rested not upon the Constitution, but on the will of the majority? If so, "then my heart is filled with such sedition and treason, and the reproach which it brings is esteemed as an honor."

In reply, Henry Foote, who was always frothing with zeal no matter what he had to say, cried, "Thank God I am no secessionist, no disunionist!" Scenting a shift in public opinion in the South, and contemplating a race for governor of Mississippi, Foote was becoming increasingly outspoken in his proclaimed loyalty to the Union. There was nothing in the bill to disgrace the South, he argued. Yes, he regretted California's expansive boundaries, he said, but he would never counsel resistance. Indeed, he was ready to fight anyone "who dared to raise his hand against the government." For Foote, this represented a remarkable journey from the ranting senator who, back in January, had himself threatened secession if California was admitted as a free state.

Fittingly perhaps, the last important speech before the final vote was delivered by Sam Houston. It was his best speech of the session, a heartfelt celebration of the Union. "I live very far south," he began. "I feel as a southern man, and I feel and think as my constituents do, that to be a southern man is to be a Union man." The Americans who had settled California were merely doing what came naturally to the Anglo-Saxon and the Anglo-American races. "Put a thousand Americans anywhere on the planet, and they will start to govern themselves," he exclaimed. "You cannot prevent it." If California was admitted, the slave states would become a minority, that was obvious. So be it. He could only hope that once that had happened, "the food of agitation will be taken away," and discord would end. "If we are men," he magnificently concluded, "let us meet the difficulties which have come upon us like men." Congress had talked long enough: the moment of decision had come. He would vote, he declared, for California statehood.

The vote, when it came, was the most rigidly sectional that had taken place so far, passing by a margin of 34 to 18. Among the slave state senators voting only five—Underwood of Kentucky, the two Delaware men, John Wales and Presley Spruance, Houston, and of course Benton—voted with the majority for admission. Foote, though he had made clear that he was ready to accept California's admission, for once voted with his southern colleagues, having been explicitly instructed to do so by the Mississippi legislature. All but four on the losing side were Democrats, and these four were from the South. Douglas's long struggle to bring government to California was finally over.

With brisk Yankee efficiency, and well aware that he was wise to exploit his momentum while he had it, Douglas then moved that the Senate take up the New Mexico bill, with the addition of an amendment providing that the act be temporarily suspended until Texas's legislature approved the disputed boundary. This time it was the northern men who were unhappy, since the bill failed to explicitly bar slavery from the new territory, shelving that entire issue for a future day. Douglas refused to be drawn into any philosophical defense of either his policies or strategy. When Salmon Chase complained that New Mexico had been "truncated," Douglas responded tersely that far from being "crowded into compressed limits" the new territory was receiving 223,000 square miles—"equal to the States of New York, Pennsylvania, Ohio, Indiana, and Illinois," of which 86,000 square miles lay east of the Rio Grande, an area double the size of New York state. "I think, therefore, that we have not dealt hardly by New Mexico in fixing her boundaries," he snapped.

There was little further debate. Senators were sick of the whole subject. "Nothing shall induce me to enter again into a discussion or an extended argument on this question, which has been so fully discussed when previous bills were before us," said Underwood, expressing what by this time was surely a widely shared sentiment. When Douglas brought the territorial bill up for a vote on August 15, it breezed through the Senate with a vote of 27 in favor to only 10 against, all of them Free Soil men. Douglas had his third victory, just two weeks after first bringing the Texas bill to the floor. His stamina, his perseverance, his patience had all been little short of superhuman.

CHAPTER 25

"BREAK YOUR MASTERS' LOCKS"

———— ·◆· ————

There was no denying that Stephen Douglas had scored a historic triumph in the Senate chamber. Whether it could really halt the rush to war was another question. Reports of the Senate vote would not reach Texas for at least another two weeks. They had to travel first by telegraph to New Orleans, where they would be printed in the local newspapers, which would be taken by steamship to Galveston, there reprinted in Texas papers, and finally carted overland in wagons and saddlebags to Austin. Governor Bell had already called a special session of the state legislature, which met on August 13, in a mood of warlike defiance. Robert Neighbors was on hand to offer to everyone who asked his views on New Mexico and, presumably, on how many troops would be needed to overrun the federal garrisons there. "Those who now deny our claim would continue to do so were it placed before them in characters written with a sunbeam," Bell arrestingly told the legislature. To wild bursts of applause, he asked for authorization to dispatch to Santa Fe "a military force sufficient to enable the civil authorities to execute the laws of the State in that part of the Territory, without reference to any anticipated action of the Federal Government": 1,600 men to defeat the federal forces in New Mexico, and another 1,300 to suppress dissent among the local population. In fact, Bell was really just asking for retroactive approval for what was already a fait accompli. In mid-July, he had written to the commanders of Ranger companies, inviting them to recruit volunteers—each equipped with a mule, a rifle, and two pistols—and to be ready to march by September 1.

How Texas would pay for the invasion was murky. The state treasury was empty. "Hot spirits" among the legislators called for a special war tax, issuing promises against the future sale of public lands, or plundering the state school budget. But few wanted to worry about money as war fever swept the state. "Why hesitate—why delay, to call upon the chivalry and patriotism of the State to rally once more around the flag of the single star and fly, when once the word is given, to the field of glorious battle?" demanded the *Clarksville Northern Standard*. Raucous public meetings all over Texas demanded that the "insurrection" in Santa Fe be put down by force, as the usual frontier mobs of adventurers, roughnecks, hired guns, and Indian killers rushed to sign up.

Secessionists across the South offered their support. S. S. Scott, a veteran of the Cuban invasion, promised to bring a hundred of the "choice spirits of Kentucky" along with him. "I sea that president filmore has thretened Texas with the army and navy of the United States," Presley Yates of Georgia wrote. "I will just say that if a Sovreign State has to be whiped out of her just rites by a set of lawless abolishinists the sooner they begin the sooner they will be convinced of their error. They mite get into a fite before they reach Texas I say stand up to the north and don't give an inch to the dogs for they would make slaves of us." Another Georgian promised to raise a one-hundred-man company there, and a Kentuckian that within six weeks of receiving a commission from Texas he could be at the city of Austin with a hundred men.

From Connecticut, Samuel Colt, the founder of the Colt Firearms Company, secretly wrote to Bell, offering to ship him a thousand brand-new government-issue pistols on short notice. Texas, he noted, had long been one of the company's best customers. "Texas has been of great service to me and you know what my sympathies are, and will be with her if there must be a collision with New Mexico." Colt knew that if the pistols were used, they would be used against federal troops. But business was business.

Across the desert in New Mexico, Colonel Munroe had his hands full. His thousand soldiers remained scattered around the territory, fighting Indians, while the local advocates for statehood were growing increasingly defiant. In June, they had approved a putative state constitution by a huge margin, and elected a governor, a would-be congressman, and a state legislature, which had in turn dispatched two hopefuls to Washington as United States senators—both of them former army paymasters—assuming that Congress would seat them when they arrived. This was all much more than Munroe, much less President Fillmore, was prepared for, especially in the face of imminent invasion. When Munroe forbade the newly elected officials to exercise civil power, and declared further appointments null and void, the irate legislators protested that "it is the indisputable right of the people in the absence of congressional legislation on the subject to organize a civil government and put it in immediate operation." This was a problem that the capable but overwhelmed and undermanned old soldier didn't need. But it worried him less than did the Texans, who for all he knew were already on the march.

In Washington, meanwhile, on August 19, the Senate began what should have been a volatile debate on the Fugitive Slave Bill that had first been introduced in January. Douglas judiciously disappeared during this phase of the debate, traveling to New York to settle a $4,000 debt. Although he might easily have delegated the matter to an agent, he decided to settle it in person, ensuring that he would offend none of his constituents by voting either for or against a bill that provoked strong feelings on both sides in Illinois. It was a particularly inopportune moment for Douglas to be advocating for the recapture of fugitive slaves: through his newspaper friends in Illinois, he was attempting to defend himself against accusations that he was a secret slave master who owned a large plantation in Louisiana. The plantation was in his wife's name, but the charges were essentially accurate. "It is true that my wife does own about 150 negroes & in Miss a cotton plantation," Douglas admitted to Charles Lanphier, whom he begged to write an editorial in his defense. "I do not wish it brought out before the public as the public have no business with my private affairs."

The bill called for a draconian overhaul of the toothless Fugitive Slave Law of 1793, which, when it was enforced at all was only done so haphazardly, according to the vagaries of local sheriffs and magistrates. Under the new law, federal commissioners would be appointed in northern counties to assist slave owners by ensuring that local officials carried out the law, and that recaptured slaves were protected against rescue by the abolitionists. Slave catchers would be empowered to use whatever "reasonable" force they deemed necessary to arrest a presumed fugitive, without the niceties of law as it applied to white people. The bill gave the federal commissioners the authority to draft anyone at hand to help restrain a fugitive, or to fight off rescuers. In essence, this would turn Yankees into slave catchers on their own soil. Anyone who obstructed a slave catcher, participated in a rescue, or abetted or concealed a fugitive, could be punished with a fine of up to $1,000, and up to six months in jail. Further, the bill created an incentive to arrest as many alleged fugitives as possible by rewarding the commissioner with a fee of $10 each time he certified a slave catcher's claim, but only $5 if he decided that sufficient evidence was lacking and ordered the prisoner released. Finally, the bill provided that if a fugitive was rescued from federal custody, his owner would have the right to sue the United States to recover the slave's value from the Treasury.

The bill's aim was to break the back of the Underground Railroad. Although paranoid slave owners credited the Underground with a deeper penetration of the South than it ever achieved, by 1850 it had extended its reach across the northern states as far west as Iowa, and was particularly effective in the border states of Pennsylvania, Ohio, and Indiana. At present, complained James Mason, alleging that Virginia was losing $100,000 a year in runaway slave property, it was virtually impossible to reclaim a fugitive once he had got away into a free state: "You may as well go down into the sea, and endeavor to recover from his native element a fish which had escaped from you."

The debate took place in a near-vacuum of reliable information. Everyone, North and South, seemed to agree that the northward hemorrhaging of slaves had to be addressed. But just how many fugitives were there? How many successfully reached the North? How many recaptured? How many abolitionists were helping them? How many of them had been arrested? Everyone was simply guessing. There was no official collection of data at all: no one, of course, was clocking in runaways as they crossed the Ohio River or the Pennsylvania state line. With the benefit of historical hindsight, however, based on anecdotal evidence and the fragmentary records of vigilance committees, perhaps one thousand or fewer fugitives each year succeeded in reaching the free states and Canada in the 1840s. Once settled in the North, fugitives simply lied to census takers, claiming to have been born not in Maryland or Tennessee but in, say, New Jersey or Ohio. Some abolitionists estimated that twenty thousand escaped slaves were living in the North and Canada, but the figure may well have been higher.

This factual vacuum lent an air of abstraction and unreality to the debate, such as it was among the heat-withered men in broadcloth who wanted only to go home. Seward, Hale, Hamlin, and nearly all the other passionate antislavery men had left town or were keeping mum under pressure from President Fillmore, who, though he had qualms about the bill, recognized it as a virtually nonnegotiable component of the compromise. In the America of 1850, fugitive slaves were helpless against not just the predatory vengeance of their former owners, but also against the pervasive apathy, if not outright hostility, of most of the Yankee politicians to whom they looked hopefully for succor. Most northern Whigs and Democrats alike, although they claimed to detest slavery, had no use for blacks, free or enslaved. There was also no way around the fact that the Constitution sanctioned the recapture of fugitive slaves. "The principle of the restitution of fugitive slaves is not objectionable unless the

Constitution is objectionable," Webster hectored. "If the Constitution is right in that respect, then the principle is right, and the law authorizing its exercise is right." Only the stuffy Salmon Chase of Ohio, seconded by the lukewarm William Dayton of New Jersey and the chilly Boston brahmin Robert Winthrop, who had replaced Webster, were left to articulate the antislavery position.

Only a single serious attempt was made to inject protection for fugitives' rights into the bill when Dayton proposed an amendment guaranteeing alleged fugitives a jury trial to protect them against kidnapping. For months, this principle had represented antislavery's best, if tenuous, chance to extract some kind of concession in a bill that offended even some of the northern men who were committed to voting for it. If it was approved, however, Dayton's provision would obviously negate the power of federal commissioners to expedite the delivery of captured fugitives to their masters, which was, after all, the whole point of the bill. But the fact that a lightweight like Dayton had been left to lead the fight suggested that the weightier men, such as Hale and Seward, had given up hope for it, and that this was little more than a symbolic gesture of defiance before the ship went down. Addressing the half-empty chamber, Dayton apologetically assured those senators who remained that he didn't want anyone to imagine that by advancing such a proposal he felt any personal sympathy for fugitive slaves. "They are a pest and an annoyance to us," he complained. "Our people are everywhere disposed to give them up according to law, but according to law only." It was not the most rousing endorsement for his own proposal.

South Carolina's white-maned and ready defender of slavery Andrew Butler scoffed that kidnapping was just an abolitionist fantasy—no one had ever heard of an instance of anyone pursuing a free man and claiming him as a slave. This was nonsense. In fact, blacks in many northern cities were at the mercy of professional slave hunters who worked in collaboration with local lawyers and officials. In border areas, the kidnapping of free blacks, often children, had long been a profitable business. The mother of the prominent black abolitionist Jermain Loguen—himself a fugitive slave—had been snatched from her home in Ohio by itinerant kidnappers, who sold her and other hapless children from the back of a wagon as they traveled through Tennessee. In another particularly well-documented case, Solomon Northrup, a free black musician, was lured all the way from upstate New York to Washington in 1845 by the promise of a job, imprisoned within sight of the Capitol, and sold into slavery in Louisiana.

What the senators were really talking about, however elliptically, was the much more common pursuit and arrest of fugitive slaves who lived peacefully, sometimes for many years, in northern states, where they had raised families, opened businesses, and were regarded by their neighbors as free. New Yorkers remembered the heartbreaking cases of seven-year-old Henry Scott, who was snatched from his classroom by a city police-man and a Virginia planter who claimed him as a slave, and Francis Smith, a waiter, who was preparing to be married when he was caught by slave hunters and shipped South, even though his fiancée begged to be allowed to purchase his freedom. Under the new bill, they would make even easier pickings. Abolitionists maintained that jury trial was a basic American right, and that—when it was held in the North, where the fugitive was arrested—it would allow the accused an opportunity to easily call witnesses on his or her behalf, which would put an end to flagrant kidnapping and, they hoped, stem some of the more egregious cases of re-capture. (In southern states, the burden of proof always fell on an alleged slave to prove that he was free, a crushing disadvantage to accused run-aways who had no money to hire a lawyer, no idea how courts worked, no friends willing to advocate for them, and had to confront the damning presumption that because they were black-skinned they were slaves no matter what they said.)

Mason argued that a jury trial would impose intolerable hardship on inconvenienced slave owners, even if it were to be held in their own com-munity, much less far away in the North. Every southerner, he said, knew that a master had to get rid of a troublesome slave as quickly as possible— it would be a gross burden to force him to keep a troublemaker on hand during what might prove a lengthy legal proceeding. "He cannot be put on the plantation to mix again with his associates," Mason explained, by way of enlightening his Yankee colleagues, who could hardly be expected to understand the fine points of slave management. "He has forfeited the confidence of his master, and to bring him home and turn him loose again amongst his fellows, would be to run great and serious risks; and in every point of view, therefore, it becomes necessary on the part of the owner speedily to dispose of and send him away. It is a right necessary to the enjoyment of the property which you have no power to restrain or qualify."

Shifting ground, Winthrop—even when he was saying the right thing, he sounded as if he were speaking to lesser mortals from a platform somewhere over their heads—came back with the observation that there seemed to him little difference between illegally kidnapping free blacks in the North and adhering to southern statutes—including South Carolina's—under which black seamen on northern ships could be seized and jailed while their ships were in port, with the cost of their imprisonment charged to the ship's captain. If he failed to pay, the sailor could then legally be sold into slavery for life. If he somehow managed to escape and make his way home to Massachusetts, he would now be considered a fugitive slave under South Carolina law, and be liable to be recaptured and dragged south again.

If there was any "higher law," shot back Butler, it was the law of self-protection, and it had no limits at all. He cited the case of a mulatto cook on a northern vessel, "who had learned his lesson in some school of fanaticism," and had concocted a plot to put the city of Charleston to flames, and its white inhabitants to the sword. The law regarding seamen was exactly what was needed, he said: its whole point was to inspire terror in "this class of persons."

The most substantive comment came from Salmon Chase, who attempted, without much success, to bring a moral focus to what had become a mostly legalistic and exceedingly dry (when it was not simply irrelevant) discussion. "If the most ordinary controversy involving a contested claim to twenty dollars must be decided by a jury, surely a controversy which involves the right of man to his liberty should have a similar trial," he said, warning that the bill would ultimately produce far more agitation than it calmed when a slave hunter began seizing peaceable men and women in northern states, where every legal presumption was in favor of freedom. "He is asked where is your warrant, and he produces none; where is your evidence of claim, and he offers none," declared Chase. "The language of his action is, 'my word stands for law; the laws of your State stand for nothing against my claim.' "

None of this mattered in the end. As expected, Dayton's amendment was blown away by a vote of 27 to 11. A limp attempt by Winthrop to move a resolution calling for the principle of habeas corpus to be recognized in cases of personal freedom was then crushed by the same lopsided margin.

The debate briefly flickered to life once more when several southern senators debated each other over the provision in the bill that allowed slave owners to sue the federal government for reimbursement if its commissioner failed in his duty to deliver a recaptured slave. This was a truly terrible idea. Not only was it deeply offensive to the North, it rested on the novel argument that the government should be made responsible financially for the enforcement of all provisions of the Constitution, and that if either states or individuals failed to carry out their duties, then the damaged party had a right to apply to the U.S. Treasury for compensation—"a principle which, once recognized, no man can tell where it will end," Dayton pointed out. The orthodox states' rights men hated it, too. While they liked the provision's coercive possibilities, they correctly saw that it created a new, dangerous, and unconstitutional opening for the federal government to impose its will on individual states. Nothing could be more anathema to the fundamentals of states' rights than that, and Jefferson Davis said so in no uncertain terms. Allowing the federal government any kind of power over slave property, fugitive or otherwise, would only play into the abolitionists' hands. Davis reminded his fellow Ultras that the South's security depended on the most rigid adherence to the terms of the Constitution. "If, for considerations of temporary or special advantage, we depart from it, we, the minority, will have abandoned our only reliable means of safety."

Mason, who had proposed the irritating Treasury provision, got the message. On the 23rd, he announced that he would withdraw it. This was followed by some desultory debate over a hopeless amendment, proposed by Chase, that would disallow application of the Fugitive Slave Bill in the territories. Then, suddenly bursting through the sultry lassitude of the chamber, David Yulee, in a volcanic rage, declared that he had almost no interest in the bill, since it was merely a "phantasmagorian" dream that would have no practical effect unless there was a wholesale transformation of public opinion in the North. "How is it possible that any law of Congress can reach the evil this bill proposes to correct when we have such evidence of the callousness of the northern community upon the subject as I have before me now?" he cried, shaking a copy of the day's newspaper for all to see. He had just read that a convention was "openly sitting in the State of New York, composed of white and black persons, with a black president and white and black officers and committees," congratulating its members upon their violations of the Constitution, and—impossible to believe!—actually devising ways and means to encourage the escape of slaves. Although scores of fugitives were sitting right there for all to see, "yet no public officer nor citizen of New York moves for their arrest, nor makes any attempt to restore them." There was still worse. The convention had even issued a proclamation calling on slaves to rob and murder their masters!

There had been abolitionist conventions before, many of them, in every northern state, since the 1830s. Even mainstream antislavery men regularly encouraged citizens to break the law on behalf of the suffering slave. Only a few days earlier, Seward, speaking to a rally in Ohio, had called upon his listeners "to extend a cordial welcome to the fugitive who lays his weary limbs at your door, and defend him as you would your household gods." But the men and women, white and black, who gathered for two days in the lakeside, white-clapboard town of Cazenovia, in the heart of New York's Burned Over District, were taking an exponential step that their many enemies barely yet grasped.

The convention met first at Cazenovia's Free Congregational Church, but so many people turned up, some two thousand in all, that they moved outside, where a wooden stage was cobbled together in a nearby apple orchard. Never before had so many fugitive slaves, fifty of them at least, exposed themselves so courageously in a public forum, daring the authorities to seize them. Not least, chairing the convention was the man who more than any other sent slave owners into dizzying paroxysms of rage, the most famous former slave in America: Frederick Douglass. Having escaped from slavery in Maryland in 1838, Douglass was all that slave owners claimed that blacks never could be. Once an illiterate laborer, he had educated himself and risen to become both the editor of his own antislavery newspaper, *The North Star*, and an orator of uncommon talent who mesmerized audiences with his "glowing logic, biting irony, melting appeals, and electrifying eloquence." At thirty-two, Douglass stood about six feet tall, and moved with surprising grace; light-skinned, with "crisped hair marked by a few silver threads," a square brow, aquiline nose, and compressed lips, he had a habit of twitching the muscles of the mouth when he became excited, as though a speech were breaking out of it in silent syllables.

The audience cheered, among other speakers, the "noble, portly, and dignified" Jermain Loguen, whose fiery oratory rivaled Douglass's own. They heard Charles B. Ray, the black leader of the Underground Railroad in New York City, the prominent women's rights advocate and Unitarian minister Samuel J. May, and the evangelical philanthropist Gerrit Smith, the leading financier of the abolitionist movement, and the real guiding spirit of the convention, who sheltered fugitive slaves in his home at Peterboro, a few miles from Cazenovia. Another highlight was the surprise appearance of the pretty Edmonson sisters, Mary and Emily, who were among the fugitives recaptured during the failed escape of the *Pearl* from Washington in 1848. The girls had been purchased by abolitionists from an Alexandria slave pen before they could be sold south, with money provided by Rev. Henry Ward Beecher of Brooklyn, who "sold" them at a consciousness-raising mock auction at his church. Dressed in prim plaid frocks and sunbonnets, they sang a mournful ballad called "I Hear the Voice of Lovejoy on Alton's Bloody Plains" commemorating the murder of the editor Elijah Lovejoy by an anti-abolitionist mob in 1837. There were lively debates: Should voters be advised to reject any candidate "who makes complexion a bar to either social or political equality"? (Yes.) Should they oppose candidates who agreed to obey laws that supported slavery? (Yes.) Should consumers boycott products such as cotton, rice, and sugar that were "wet with the tears and sweat, and red with the blood" of slaves? (Yes again.)

The convention's main order of business was the crafting of the letter that had so agitated David Yulee. This extraordinary screed was one of the most militant documents yet addressed directly to men and women in bondage, and represented a tectonic shift in the abolitionist movement away from pacifism and persuasion toward physical confrontation. "When the insurrection of the Southern slaves shall take place, as take place it will unless speedily prevented by voluntary emancipation, the great majority of the colored men of the North, however much to the grief of any of us, will be found by your side, with deep-stored and long-accumulated revenge in their hearts, and with death-dealing weapons in their hands," the letter fiercely proclaimed. Take off on your masters' fleetest horses, take his clothing and food, it urged, "break your masters' locks and take all their money . . . For you are prisoners of war in an enemy's country—and therefore, by all the rules of war, you have the fullest liberty to plunder, burn, kill, as you may have occasion to do to promote your escape."

"Why is there no law to suppress or punish these acts of war upon the constitutional obligations of the States, and upon the peace and safety of society in the southern states?" David Yulee demanded in response to the Cazenovia convention. Cazenovia was proof of everything that he and his friends had been warning of these many months. The horrifying sentiments expressed there were no longer the ravings of an insane fringe, but the tenets of an entire section that was bent on the destruction of the South's way of life, if need be through fire and sword. How could the South trust any promises of friendship from the North as long as such appalling gatherings were tolerated? "Let me not be told that, as a community, New York is not responsible," he shouted. "I deny it. As a community, she is responsible. I ask the good people of the northern States, if it is possible, while such things are permitted to occur within their jurisdiction, this Union can long continue?"

On August 23, the vote to engross the Fugitive Slave Bill for its third reading took place. It passed by a better than two-to-one margin, 27 to 12. All the negative votes were cast by northern Whigs, plus the Free Soiler Salmon Chase. The following day, the bill itself passed by a vote that was deliberately left unrecorded. Only when he learned that the bill was on the cusp of passage—he was at dinner at the posh Astor House, on Broadway, in New York, when the message reached him—did Stephen Douglas return to Washington, though he managed to fail to arrive until after the votes were taken. He was not alone in his judicious cowardice. Fifteen Northern senators who feared to face constituents liable to be outraged at a vote to approve the slave catchers' law abstained or avoided the votes. Passage of the Fugitive Slave Bill was thus as much a victory for northern racism as it was for the slaveholding South. It would have a more far-reaching impact on the nation's slavery crisis problem than any other facet of the compromise.

The last word in the debate, just before the final vote, was left to Daniel Dickinson of New York, the South's most obsequious northern friend in the Senate. Puffed with indignation, he rose to defend the good name of his state, declaring that the great mass of New Yorkers viewed the "atrocious proceedings" at Cazenovia with "unutterable scorn and contempt," and asserting that "the people of all parties of that State, except its half-demented and its madmen, look upon such exhibitions of folly and wickedness with loathing and disgust." This was the kind of speech that southerners wanted to hear from their Yankee colleagues. But it was deeply out of touch with the vast and inexorable shift in northern public opinion that was already taking place, and that the new Fugitive Slave Law would exponentially accelerate. The "dark tide" of abolitionism was at last ebbing, Dickinson reassured his southern friends. He couldn't have been more wrong. It was not his finger but that of Frederick Douglass that pointed to the future.

CHAPTER 26

"IT IS TIME WE SHOULD ACT"

———•◆•———

Euphoria was premature. Douglas's achievement in the Senate would remain stillborn unless it was repeated in the House of Representatives. There the political landscape was dramatically, dauntingly different. In contrast to the South's grossly disproportionate power in the Senate, the far more populous North commanded a decisive majority in the House, and had repeatedly inserted the poison pill of the Wilmot Proviso into territorial legislation. Many northern men had sworn to block any bill that would enlarge the boundaries of Texas, and they had the votes to make their threat stick. For its part, the South—with support from pro-compromise Democrats—had enough votes to block the free North's highest priority: the admission of California. Party alignments were hopelessly scrambled, loyalties in flux, and everyone maneuvering for position with an eye cocked to the rapidly approaching November elections. Northern men feared a backlash at the polls if they approved any bill that lacked the Wilmot Proviso, while southern moderates feared one if they approved any compromise that shortchanged their section's proclaimed "rights," and southern radicals feared one from voters who wanted to avoid war. Now, as Senate printers prepared the compromise bills—the Texas boundary, California statehood, creation of the territories of New Mexico and Utah, and the enactment of the new Fugitive Slave Law—for dispatch across the Capitol to the House, all that was certain was that northern and southern Ultras intended to collaborate as they had in the Senate to destroy the Texas boundary bill. " 'Look to the Senate,' was at one time the watchword, but 'Look to the House' is now the cry," the *New York Herald* reported.

Southerners' attempts to form a unified caucus against compromise had fizzled earlier in the month after a walkout by moderates such as H. W. Hilliard, an Alabama Whig, who felt they had little reason to oppose a settlement that Texas's own senators had accepted. Hilliard intended to give the bill his full support, he said—if he could be satisfied that the territory lopped from Texas would not be shackled to the Wilmot Proviso. Most significantly, a sea change had occurred within a key group of southern conservatives who had done much to set the whole machine of opposition in motion back in December: the Georgia triumvirate of Alexander Stephens, Robert Toombs, and House speaker Howell Cobb. Stephens, who just weeks earlier had been threatening disunion, was now telling Georgians that the compromise bills were "as good as they need to be for the South." He and his friends were scared: secession was no longer a mere catchword, it was an immediate possibility. Rumor had it that eight thousand Texan troops were on the March, while Governor Quitman of Mississippi had publicly offered to send his state militia to support the Texans when war broke out. States' rights hard-liners though they remained, they were realists enough to see that the South was not going to achieve either a guarantee for the protection of slavery in the territories or parity of power in the national government. A federal commitment not to intervene either for or against slavery was the best that they were likely to get.

It was in this volatile atmosphere that the Fillmore administration girded itself for battle. The administration's aggressiveness contrasted starkly with Zachary Taylor's politically passive and hopelessly maladroit approach. Fillmore and his generalissimo, Daniel Webster, who served almost as an unanointed prime minister for the administration during the remainder of the debate, made it abundantly clear that they wanted the compromise to pass, and that Whigs who opposed them would pay a price. Cabinet members were mobilized to cajole, browbeat, and, if necessary, bribe pliable Whig lawmakers from the northeastern states where Fillmore's personal influence was greatest. To assuage the South, a prominent Virginia politician, Alexander Stuart, was named secretary of the interior. James Wilson of New Hampshire, an outspoken proviso man, was promised a federal job in California and flipped overnight into an enthusiastic advocate of the compromise. Abraham Schermerhorn of Rochester, who was facing a strong renomination challenge from the party's Fillmore wing, was made to understand that his problems would end if he voted the right way on the compromise. New Yorkers, in particular, were warned that patronage appointments were contingent on their "cooperation." "The Administration hits back upon the progressive Whigs in New York through its papers and patronage and I come in for my full share of it," one outfoxed Seward man glumly remarked.

Meanwhile, Stephen Douglas and his Democratic allies in the House, under the command of bearded John McClernand of Illinois, planned for the brutal floor battles that the compromise was certain to face. The crux of their strategy hinged on combining the Texas, New Mexico, and Utah bills into a "little Omnibus." This would outflank antislavery Whigs who wanted to admit California and quiet the Texas border crisis but hoped to block the territorial bills, leaving Mexico's antislavery laws untouched across the region. Douglas's strategy would force southerners to accept the reduction of Texas, and northerners to accept New Mexico with popular sovereignty—with the risk that its inhabitants might someday vote to legalize slavery. The strategists had learned something from Pearce's fiasco in the Senate. The man they tapped to lead the assault was Linn Boyd, a laconic, strikingly handsome forty-nine-year-old Kentucky Democrat with a Roman nose, lofty forehead, and upswept mane of prematurely white hair, who in April, coincidentally, had married a relative of President Fillmore. He had served ably for more than a decade in the House. The job he was now called upon to perform would require almost superhuman self-possession, stubbornness, lightning reflexes, and a rare degree of parliamentary finesse.

Everything, however, hinged on the active collaboration of one man:

House speaker Cobb of Georgia, who participated actively in Douglas's strategy sessions. The bearlike Cobb was probably one of the most effective men of his era to hold the office of speaker: decisive, fiercely partisan, and unmatched at piloting the House through the labyrinthine bayous of congressional procedure. Of Cobb, remarked Congressman Horace Mann—one of the chamber's full-fledged abolitionists, and later to be nationally famous as an educator—slavery was his "politics and his patriotism, his political economy and his religion." But he was also a Unionist, if not an unadulterated one, who like Stephens and Toombs feared the rush toward secession. On July 17, he had addressed a public letter to Georgians, vigorously supporting the original Omnibus Bill as the only practical formula for compromise that he could see. Privately, to his wife, he expressed faith that "in the end we shall do what is right & proper," but he worried that the House was not really prepared to carry through the compromise. Conditions, he told her, "look more gloomy than at any time since this Congress was assembled."

Americans proudly believed Cobb's domain, the House chamber, to be the most elegant legislative hall in the world, and perhaps it was. Like the much smaller Senate chamber, it was semicircular in design, but rose fifty-seven feet from the floor to its magnificently domed and coffered ceiling. Members sat in arcs facing the speaker's dais, behind which loomed eight columns of mottled Potomac breccia surmounted by Corinthian capitals imported from Italy. From their entablature, directly over the speaker's chair, gazed down an eagle rampant, and above the eagle a sculpted figure of the spirit of Liberty. More Corinthian columns stood symmetrically spaced around the back of the chamber, supporting the main visitors' gallery, with seats for five hundred. A two-hundred-seat ladies' gallery also extended across the southern side of the chamber, behind the speaker's dais. Opposite the dais, between draped curtains, a clock ornately embellished with an allegorical image of History athwart the winged chariot of Time prominently, if not always successfully, encouraged the long-winded to speed up their remarks.

With its 230 members, the House required constant management. Ever since Henry Clay had shaped the office of the speaker into its modern form more than thirty years earlier, its occupant had wielded far more authority than the presiding officer of the Senate, enjoying near-dictatorial power to manipulate the course of debate by aggressively employing his right to issue rulings on points of order and by choosing whom to recognize when scores of members were simultaneously begging for the floor. The speaker, growled the oft-thwarted abolitionist Joshua Giddings of Ohio, "exerts more influence upon the destinies of the nation than any other member of the government except the President." In contrast to the nominally more formal Senate—admittedly, the past nine months in the Senate had scarcely been a model of decorum—the House members of the Thirty-first Congress had already made a name for themselves as a hotheaded and undisciplined lot. More than half were freshmen, many of them were unfamiliar with the House rules, and their manners shocked—and perhaps entertained—the female visitors who flocked to hear the debate. They typically sprawled with their boots atop their desks, observed the acerbic newswoman Jane Swisshelm, while "their language and gestures as they expectorated hither and thither were often as coarse as their positions." Some even amused themselves by flicking so many bits of paste at the opposition that the air overhead resembled "an inverted snowstorm." During debate, members idly wandered the floor, crowded around each other's desks, and engaged in nonstop conversations, a habit that added considerably to the general aggravation in a chamber that had awful acoustics, including an echo that made many speeches almost inaudible.

The battle began on August 29. Boyd rose to ask for the floor, and—in accordance with the prearranged plan—Cobb picked him out from among the shouting mob of members clamoring to be recognized. Boyd then moved to attach to the Texas boundary bill that had come from the Senate an amendment—it had been written by Douglas—establishing New Mexico and Utah as territories. Repeatedly in the days that followed, Cobb would clear the way for Boyd, gaveling down objections, while the Kentuckian tenaciously held the floor against any member who threatened to derail the forward progress of the bill.

Boyd was not known as an orator, but his brief opening statement

was a small masterpiece. "Sir, the path is beaten," he began, addressing
Cobb. "We have all investigated each and every proposition contained
in the bill or in the amendment." He was well aware, he said, that he
faced strong sentiment against combining "incongruous" measures as
the Senate's Committee of Thirteen had done in the Omnibus. "Piece by
piece it broke down," he admitted, "and there are many gentlemen here
who are unwilling, after it has been coopered up, to take passage in it."
By way of concession, he dropped Utah from his amendment, so that it
was composed of a simple, stark quid pro quo: a payoff of $10 million for
peace on the Rio Grande. His aim, he said, was to test the sense of the
House in relation to the establishment of territorial governments "on the
non-intervention principle," in which he "religiously" believed. The South
should have nothing to fear. "My people are slaveholders," he said. "They
never have asked, nor do they now ask anything from you in regard to
this institution—but they tell you to let it alone. We do not ask that the
Mexican laws shall be repealed, though I should like to see it done, to
satisfy the opinions and feelings of my Southern friends. But I say that
my constituents do not demand it, and I shall not. We have taken the
territory as it is. Let Congress hold its hands off." To ensure that no one
was left in doubt about where he stood, he declared, "I am for the Union.
I am for the Constitution as it is—I want no amendment to it." (He was
here brushing off the firebrands' demand for an amendment that would
give the South equal power in the federal government.) "I say I am for the
Union—not so much because it protects us from foreign aggression, as for
the more important reason that it protects us from one another."

　　Always economical with words, Boyd at this point decided to end
his prepared speech, saying that he had already said enough, but voices
begged him to continue, shouting, "Go on, Boyd, go on!"

　　"We have already been listening to speeches for nine long months,"
he at last said. "It is time we should act. I am astonished at the patience
with which our constituents have borne our procrastination. I think we
have talked enough—in God's name let us act. If the result of our action
should be that we cannot settle these questions upon the only principles

on which, as I have stated, I believe they can be settled, then I, for one, shall be in favor of an immediate adjournment. I should be pleased, in that event, to see every man of this House resign his commission into the hands of the people who gave it, and leave it to them to send here Representatives better disposed to do their duty and to save the Union. I have not another word to say."

Then the inevitable, and the expected, happened. Joseph Root of Ohio proposed adding the Wilmot Proviso to the bill, declaring that he wanted to "smoke out the doughfaces on both sides of the line"—that is, to find out who the pliable northerners were who would not stand on antislavery principle, as well as the southerners who might yield to compromise. Root's colorful expressions had often drawn friendly laughter even from those hostile to his free soil politics. But no one was laughing now.

McClernand, small, wiry, and taut as a bowstring, impatiently replied, "The time for action has arrived, and shall we not act?" Everything that could possibly be said about slavery in the territories had been said—the whole subject had been talked to death. "Slavery does not, nor can it, as I think, exist in Utah or New Mexico. The Wilmot proviso, therefore, in its application to those territories, is a humbug; and I say, sir, down with the humbugs and down with all mischievous humbuggers."

What followed was an extremely confused, slaloming succession of procedural maneuvers that tried the patience and skill of even the chamber's best players to the breaking point. (Unlike the Senate, the House did not permit unlimited debate, allowing it to be shut off relatively easily by moving "the previous question," which meant, essentially, bringing the pending question to an immediate vote.) At one point, a North Carolina congressman proposed to amend Root's amendment to state that any acts of Congress that barred slavery in any territory between the Mississippi River and the Pacific Ocean were null and void, but Cobb ruled it out of order because it did not specifically refer to New Mexico. Several times, Cobb actually allowed Boyd to fill in for him as speaker, while he rested, enabling the Kentuckian to rule on points of order affecting his own bill. More than once the bill came within a hair of being killed altogether.

On one occasion, it was about to go down by a single vote when Cobb cast his own vote to cause a tie, defeating the opposition's motion. On yet another occasion, three pro-compromise men dashed into the chamber just in time to forestall another imminent defeat.

Southerners attempted delay after delay with points of order, and demands to end debate, but Cobb repeatedly ruled them out of order. Roll call followed upon roll call. At times, members were treated to the extraordinary spectacle of northern and southern Ultras parading arm in arm in the aisles in a show of unity. The confusion in the chamber was often so extreme that Cobb halted the proceedings entirely, sending members back to their seats until order could be restored. But calm rarely lasted more than a few moments before deafening chaos once again reigned. When the House adjourned for the day on September 4, it seemed even to many seasoned observers who had only a hazy grasp of what was going on that the bill was "as dead as a herring," as the *New York Herald* reported.

The "little Omnibus" clung tenuously to life, however, thanks to Boyd's quick footwork, Cobb's reflexes, and the indefatigable Stephen Douglas, who seemed to be everywhere at once, advising Boyd, conferring with McClernand, and marshaling allies. (There was no House rule that precluded this sort of activity by a senator.) Douglas wrote to friends in Illinois the next morning, "The Ho of Reps yesterday killed off the Texas boundary Bill by 46 Majority, but the Bill will come to life again today." Fillmore's minions were also using every means at their disposal to wring a few more grumbling votes from their reluctant Whig following. "I am willing to become a convert to the doctrine of non-intervention, of non-action—and in good faith, too," declared one Whig defector, James Brooks of New York, who had until now been a reliable vote on behalf of the proviso. "I will vote for no Wilmot proviso, now or hereafter, on any matters before us. It was a bolt that had done its errand, that had discharged its duties, and the spent bolt now, that some men were for hurling, could only do mischief and create unnecessary alarm."

The dizzying procedural ballet continued on September 5. In the course of another long and confusing day, votes swung back and forth as the bill was first down, then up, then down again, seemingly defeated, then suddenly restored to life, then nearly strangled by crippling amendments, and then liberated from them in the most amazing act of prestidigitation of the debate. As the bill's sponsor, Boyd continued to hold the floor while members of all factions begged to be allowed to submit their amendments.

"I hope somebody else will have the privilege of offering an amendment besides the gentleman from Kentucky," cried one Virginian.

"My position is a very embarrassing one," Boyd replied, saying that he would personally have liked to see some of the amendments that were circulating adopted. "But I am perfectly satisfied, that if I throw this bill open to amendments, it will be destroyed by amendments. As friend to this bill, therefore, I cannot yield." He then called the previous question—that is, an immediate vote to end debate, to prevent further possibility of amendment, in an effort to move on to a final vote on the bill itself. Unfortunately for Boyd, this failed, which meant that he lost the floor, which in turn passed to a member of the opposition.

This was one of the House's rising young Whigs, John Wentworth of Illinois, known to everyone as "Long John" because of his great height, who owed his seat to Abraham Lincoln's not entirely willing retirement from Congress under pressure from party leaders. "I am as anxious to close this debate as any other man," Wentworth began.

"Don't make a speech!" begged a host of voices.

"Is it in order to commit the amendment with instructions?" Wentworth asked the speaker.

"Oh! No!" groaned voices throughout the chamber.

By this, Wentworth meant that he wanted to send Boyd's bill back to committee with the instructions of the House that it be rewritten to incorporate several amendments that he would now read. There were four of them, two each from the North and the South, a couple of which were literally handed to him scribbled on sheets of paper as he spoke. Wentworth himself was one of the strongest antislavery voices in the House.

Collectively, however, his proposals represented the main attack on the compromise by the allied forces of the northern antislavery faction and the southern Ultras. Begging for quiet, Wentworth first read the two northern amendments: the first, predictably, would apply the Wilmot Proviso to all the territory acquired from Mexico lying east of California; the second would move the border of Texas back to the 102nd meridian of longitude. Of the southern amendments, the first originated with Volney Howard of Texas and would strike out the bill's provision that no more than $5 million in stock should be issued until the state's existing creditors were paid. The second, written by Winfield Featherston of Mississippi, stated that the federal government would recognize Texas's right to whatever territory it had claimed at the time of its independence in 1836—in other words, all of New Mexico east of the Rio Grande. Were the bill to be sent back to committee stuck with impossibly contradictory "instructions" such as these, that would have been the end of it.

What happened next was Howell Cobb's most brilliant series of parliamentary strokes. When, on a point of order, William Duer, a loyal Fillmore Whig from New York, asked if the several measures could be divided, and thus ruled on separately, Cobb ruled that they could, based on the principle that a proposition could be divided only if it embraced subjects so distinct from one another that each could stand independently. With Cobb's ruling sustained by the House, Featherston's amendment was separated, and then crushingly voted down 128 to 71.

Samuel Inge, an Alabama radical, struggling to make himself heard over the din, then called for a second division of Wentworth's motion, in accordance with Cobb's ruling, presumably to pull out the unpalatable Wilmot Proviso.

Cobb now reversed himself. According to House rules, he said, only a *new* motion could be divided. That was the case when Wentworth had first introduced the question—all of half an hour earlier. Since then, several votes had taken place, and having thoroughly examined the question, Cobb now decided—"It is to be regretted"—that his earlier ruling no longer held: the question could no longer be divided. The only motion that he would allow was one to send Wentworth's motion to committee with the remaining "instructions" intact. This was outrageous, but Cobb got away with it.

"The decision of the chair is directly in conflict with the decision announced a little while ago!" Inge quite correctly expostulated.

What all this meant was that southerners would have to vote explicitly for the Wilmot Proviso if they wanted to send Wentworth's "instructions" to committee. This, even for tactical reasons, they would never do.

"There is some mistake," Wentworth began, trying to be heard over the Niagara of protests. "I certainly should not have offered the instructions—"

"Objection!" a host of voices cried.

"I must insist on my right to withdraw them," Wentworth declared.

Cobb curtly told him he had no such right.

To the chagrin of the compromise's opponents—Wentworth's sweat-soaked face was said to have glowed with rage—Cobb's ruling was sustained by a vote of 101 to 86. Wentworth's motion, along with its cargo of amendments, was then rejected by a vote of 121 to 80.

Robert Toombs then proposed to add to Boyd's bill a seemingly innocuous amendment bearing on the organization of the New Mexico Territory. It stated simply: "No citizen of the United States shall be deprived of his life, liberty, or property, in said Territory, except by the judgment of his peers, and the law of the land; and that the Constitution of the United States, and such statutes thereof as may not be locally inapplicable, and the common law, as it existed in the British colonies of America until the 4th day of July 1776, shall be the exclusive laws of said Territory upon the subject of African slavery, until altered by the proper authority." This was more than legalistic gobbledygook: it was a stealth bomb. Basically, what Toombs was doing was replacing the antislavery laws that New Mexico had inherited from Mexico with colonial common law dating from a time when slavery was legal in all the colonies—thus establishing slavery in New Mexico with one clever legal stroke. Northerners recognized what Toombs was up to, however. Their response was also ingenious. One moved to divide Toombs's motion at the semicolon after the word "land," and vote on the two parts separately. The House adopted the first, harmless, clause by a voice vote, and then crushed the second one by a vote of 134 to 64. With the second clause gone, the amendment now implied that a slave owner who settled in New Mexico could be deprived of his property by the "laws of the land," if those laws happened to include abolition statutes. This was hardly what the checkmated Toombs had in mind.

The next morning, September 6, much of the Senate—including Henry Clay, who had returned refreshed from his sojourn at Newport—packed into the House chamber alongside their colleagues, anticipating as just about everyone in Washington did that the debate was about to come to its climax. No one was more eager for its end than Cobb, who had lost forty pounds since the session began. The level of noise was again deafening, as lobbyists for the Texas bondholders and any number of unauthorized visitors crowded densely around the desks of congressmen, paying no attention to Cobb's repeated attempts to order them off the floor.

After an extended period of parliamentary wrangling, Cobb, ignoring scores of other members begging for his attention, called on Volney Howard of Texas. The Mississippi-bred Howard had been the only member of his state's delegation to strongly oppose the compromise, steadfastly defending Texas's claims to New Mexico as "identical with her independence." However, almost unnoticed, he had quietly evolved toward support of the boundary bill, although these past several days he had continued to fight its financial provision because he felt that it would deliver a windfall to speculators. (The lobbyists who were badgering his colleagues in front of his very eyes vividly illustrated his point.)

The day before, in a close vote, the enemies of the compromise had mustered enough votes to deny it a third reading, i.e., passage. Now, Howard moved for reconsideration of that motion. He had intended to propose another amendment, he said, "But as the friends of the bill prefer the bill as it is to my vote, I shall not press the amendment upon the House. I shall content myself with demanding the previous question," that is, an immediate vote. As the coalition of Ultras, South and North, gathered defensively in what amounted to their last ditch, in hope of snatching an unlikely victory from the jaws of likely defeat, the House voted by 108 to 98 to grant the bill its reading.

As the clerk began the roll call on final passage of the bill itself, utter silence for once blanketed the House. Noise grew steadily as he progressed down the long list of names: "Booth, Bowdon, Bowie, Bowlin, Boyd . . ." Soon members by the score, unable to contain themselves any longer, were out of their seats and milling in the aisles. Motions to clear the galleries were made and ignored. The tumult only increased. "Hoagland, Holladay, Holmes, Howard . . ." When the Texan Howard voted "aye," applause roared across the floor and galleries alike. At 2:45 P.M., Cobb, fighting back tears, announced that the "little Omnibus" had passed, by a vote of 108 to 97.

The entire hall was now in an uproar. "The announcement of the result was received with manifestations of applause of various kinds," the *Congressional Globe* reported in its inimitably neutral prose, "the most peculiar and attractive of which was a sort of unpremeditated allegro whistle, which the Reporter does not remember to have heard before, (certainly never in the House of Representatives). The other tokens of glorification were of a less musical order." Cobb tried helplessly to regain control. Cries of "order" were met with cries of "let them stamp—it's all right."

Senators, congressmen, and onlookers alike burst into tears. Clay flung his long arms around Lewis Cass's rotund hulk, and hugged him. "The 'Wilmot' is dead—Seward & Co crushed to atoms & the peace of the Country and the 'Union' of the States preserved," Linn Boyd wrote to his wife, who was visiting her family in Pennsylvania. Horace Mann wrote bitterly to *his* wife, "The North is again disgracefully beaten." Among the victorious majority were twenty-two northern Whigs who had publicly given their word that they would never vote to approve the creation of new territories without the Wilmot Proviso, but who had surrendered to pressure from the administration, if not to honest fear that continued stubbornness would lead to the nation's collapse. Had they stuck to their commitment, the compromise could never have passed. As for the phlegmatic Cobb, well, it was all part of the job. That evening he wrote to *his* wife in Georgia, "Another hard day's work—but unlike its predecessors it has not been wholly unprofitable."

The "little Omnibus" had done its political job. The next day, the California statehood bill cruised through without significant debate by a lopsided vote of 150 to 58. Next in line, later that day, came the bill establishing a territorial government for Utah, which Boyd had dropped from his bill as a palliative to members who resisted "incongruous measures" in a single bill. However, the fire-eaters were unwilling to let the Utah bill through without throwing at least a rock or two at it as it passed. Alluding to the "gross wrong and outrage" that the slave states had allegedly already endured, "The only chance remaining to the South is that in that isolated desert portion of the Great Basin, which has been abandoned, from its worthlessness, to the Mormons," declared James Seddon of Virginia. "I wish now to test whether there is really to be, on the part of the South, the privilege of participation in its enjoyment." He proposed to amend the bill by adding a provision that Utah's territorial legislature be explicitly prohibited from barring the emigration of citizens bringing with them "any kind of property recognized as such in any of the States of the Union."

Seddon's amendment was remarkable less for its desperate and symbolic attempt to shoehorn slavery somehow, somewhere, into the West, than for Robert Toombs's harsh response. Toombs, who had voted for the compromise, saw no "outrage" at all in it. Indeed, he said, "If there have been aggressions perpetrated against the South, she has done the mischief herself; she has only herself to blame. It is by her own hands, and by the hands of her sons, that the wrong has been done."

"Is it no wrong that the only laboring class in the world excluded for months past and forever henceforth from participation in the fertile resources and exhaustless mineral treasures of that vast region, is the laboring class of one-half of the owners?" the startled Seddon demanded.

Replied Toombs, the compromise had not been forced on Seddon and his radical friends by the North, but by the South itself. The North by a majority of twelve, he pointed out, had voted against the "little Omnibus," while the South by a majority of twenty-three had supported it. Driving his dagger in deeper, he added that eight of Virginia's own congressmen had voted for the bill. So apparently even Virginia's own sons had "forced" the compromise upon poor Seddon.

Seddon's amendment was easily voted down, 85 to 52, and shortly afterward the Utah bill itself passed, 97 to 85. But the nasty exchange revealed the depth of the fissure that had opened between Southern compromisers and defiant sectional nationalists, and that would rapidly widen in the months to come. It was but one of many signs that the apparent peace that had been achieved by the compromise might really prove to be a means to new and unanticipated political wars.

On September 11, California's two representatives—Edward Gilbert and G. W. Wright—were sworn in and allowed to take their seats. And on the 12th, with only the most perfunctory debate, the House passed the Fugitive Slave Bill by 109 to 75. On this, the most proslavery measure of all those that comprised the compromise, thirty-six members of the House abstained or failed to vote, most of them northerners. Supporting the bill were thirty-one Northerners. "In the face of the world, [they] take back their own declarations, a thousand times uttered," wrote a disgusted Horace Mann. "It is amazing; it is heart-sickening. The slave-holders have overthrown principles, and put them to rout as Napoleon did armies."

No one in Washington had ever seen such sheer joy at the passage of a law before. That night bonfires blazed, bells rang, and a hundred cannon boomed in honor of California and Utah. Throngs of merrymakers shouting "the Union is saved!" cruised the capital's dusty streets as skyrockets arched overhead, and the Marine Band marched along Pennsylvania Avenue playing "The Star Spangled Banner," "Yankee Doodle," and "Hail, Columbia." Serenaders roamed the city in search of the men who had wrought the compromise, calling for Houston, Rusk, Boyd, Cobb, and Clay. Stephen Douglas, never at a loss for words, delivered an impromptu oration "with a glow of enthusiasm which made the welkin ring with applause, of the spirit of reconciliation which had carried the day," declaring to all, "We are united from shore to shore, and while the mighty West remained as the connecting link between the North and the South, there could be no disunion." When the serenaders appeared at Daniel Webster's home on E Street, he came out onto his stoop and, as friends flanked him with candles, jovially misquoted Shakespeare, declaiming, "Now is the summer—no! Now is the winter of our discontent made glorious summer by this sun of York!" One drunk radical in front of the National Hotel announced that he wanted to hear no more about southern chivalry and honor, and asked every man to give him a kick in the backside, which he promised to redistribute to his friends. Men who had been at each other's throats for months marveled at the joy on each other's faces, and assured each other that from now on everything would be different, that the rivalry of the sections was a thing of the past. Millard Fillmore exulted, "The long agony is over." Except perhaps for Henry Foote, who, having severely overindulged himself, wound up the next day prostrate with diarrhea.

CHAPTER 27

TRIUMPHS

——— •◆• ———

Washington might celebrate, but the Union's fate still depended on what Texas would do. On September 9, Houston, Rusk, Secretary of State Webster, and Attorney General John Crittenden collectively telegraphed the ranking federal employee at New Orleans, the customs officer, and directed him to dispatch an urgent announcement of Congress's action by steamer, and then overland, to Texas. No one in Washington knew what kind of reception the news would face. For all anyone knew the Texas legislature had already declared war and sent an army marching on Santa Fe. Indeed, when the legislature met in special session on August 26, it was amid a viral statewide clamor for war. On the session's first day, it passed a bill calling for three thousand volunteers. (The rumor that eight thousand Texans were already in the field was pure fiction.) Almost immediately, however, enthusiasm for an immediate attack began to give way to second thoughts. Early reports of the Pearce bill's progress through the Senate gave many legislators pause; others, who had expected to get New Mexico without a fight, were taken aback by President Fillmore's unanticipated resolve. Many also realized that a winter campaign across the desert would be foolhardy. Texans could hardly forget the disgrace of the 1841 expedition, which had been captured wholesale when it stumbled starving and ragged into New Mexico, and even Robert Neighbors and his party had almost been overwhelmed by freak snowstorms. After vigorous debate, the legislature trimmed the expedition's size to two thousand and then delayed its departure to at least February. Then, as more details of the compromise percolated through the state capital, the bill was dropped altogether, in favor of a nonbinding plebiscite on war to be held later in the autumn.

Across the state, mass meetings and much of the press continued to issue bloodthirsty pronouncements. Declared the *Texas State Gazette,* "War to the knife is now our motto, if it be necessary." Outside the state, radicals also continued to dismiss compromise as heresy to the religion of states' rights. Mississippi governor Quitman, who was about to be hauled into a federal court for his part in the failed invasion of Cuba, stumped his state denouncing compromise as a fraud, and calling for a state convention to "annul the Federal compact." Both Quitman and South Carolina governor Whitemarsh Seabrook promised men and money if Texas continued to defy the federal authorities.

Yet, amid the warmongering, perceptible hints of a sea change in Texan opinion began to appear. Tom Rusk was renominated for the Senate, though perhaps more in spite of his support for the compromise than because of it. Then, significantly, former Texas governor George Wood, writing from Washington, where he was serving as a special agent for the state, strongly urged Texas to take the federal government's offer. "We got the best bill possible to be had," he wrote to Governor Bell's confidant, Washington D. Miller. The boundary would be settled, the state's creditors would be paid, and Texas would still acquire a vast unencumbered public domain. If Texas rejected the agreement, however, "the battle is to be fought again next Congress. If not fought on the plains of Santa Fe." Moreover, he added, "We will have thrown upon us a large foreign population antagonistic in their habits institutions education and . . . only held in subjection by a standing military force which must be kept at the expense of the State." Richard S. Hunt, the editor of the *Bonham Advertiser,* put it even more bluntly in a letter to Rusk: New Mexico was worthless. Wrote Hunt, "If its sale can bring us $10,000,000 or $0 we cannot be too soon rid of it."

•   •   •

As blissfully optimistic Washingtonians nursed their hangovers on the morning of September 8, to many the compromise seemed already complete. "Harmony is secured. Patriots rejoice!" trilled one editorialist, typical of many. "Lovers of the Union, throw up your hats! The occupation of agitators and disunionists at the North and at the South is gone." But the great national "adjustment" was not yet done. There was one last legislative act to play. Henry Clay's proposal to terminate the slave trade in Washington remained unconsummated. As the House debate was reaching its climax, once more the weary cast of senators assembled to take a turn on the stage, delivering their concluding lines, reprising with a last, fading flush of passion their oft stated arguments, attempting as best they could to sound as if they had never uttered them before. For the last time, the sonorous vocal chords of Clay and Benton would resonate across the floor of the Senate, counterpointed by the piping chorus of new men who were already shouldering the frayed mantles of their leadership.

Clay, who was desperate to return home to Lexington to his racehorses and his estate, "where I desire to be more than I ever did in my life," he wrote to his son Thomas, had taken center stage again on September 3 to orchestrate this final act. His bill's first section prohibited owners or their agents from bringing a slave into the District of Columbia for sale, or to be deposited in a slave "depot" for export to another market. The second made illegal the establishment of new slave pens within the district. More than any of the other compromise measures, this bill was truly Clay's own, incorporating his distaste for the slave trade with his pragmatic belief that without such a bill the compromise would fail to pacify the country. The South had gotten the recharged Fugitive Slave Law that it wanted. Now, Clay believed, it must give a mite in return. (In practical terms, this really was a mite, since in anticipation of just such legislation as this most of the slave trade had already relocated across the Potomac to Alexandria—"healing the wound by plunging deeper into it the knife that made it," Seward had sarcastically commented when the same issue had been debated back in July.)

Almost everyone assumed that Clay's bill would pass without great difficulty. He urged senators to "hasten to a decision"—there was no need to dwell endlessly on the subject. But slavery's defenders did not intend to give up without a fight. Yield on this issue, and worse would follow, warned raven-maned Robert Hunter of Virginia. Termination of the slave trade would be but the first step toward the abolition of slavery itself in Washington, since, logically, "If it be wrong to sell a slave from one State to another, it is wrong to sell from one man to another." No one would suggest that Congress had the power to prohibit the sale of, say, cotton fabric in the District. So how could it presume to ban the sale of another commodity, which merely happened to be human beings. Clay's bill was based on mere sentiment, on the insupportable notion that there was something wrong with the slave trade. Too much mischief had already been done by "sentimental legislation," Hunter claimed. What was wrong with the slave trade? With a free trade in slaves, whenever profits from slave labor sank too low, the master simply sold his slaves to another part of the country where they were in demand. "The slave who goes away"—Hunter made it sound as if slaves were free agents, ordinary emigrants—"not only benefits himself, but those he leaves behind," by re-ducing competition among his fellow slaves and by attracting investment capital (his purchase price) from his out-of-state buyer. It was a marvelous arrangement. "Where will you find three and a half millions of negroes so happy, or so advanced, morally and physically, as the slaves of North America?" he asked.

To this, Clay replied, "Well, sir, my opinion is that all just legislation should be the result of both the head and of the heart," arguing that the bill was essential to satisfy both northern feeling and much southern feeling alike, "for I have shared in the horror at this slave trade in this District, and viewed it with as much detestation as any of those at the North who complain of it." As a parting shot, he begged the South to stop taking alarm at every slight perceived threat "lest it should touch the particular institution which they cherish so much." Honeyed though his words were, he was telling the South, ever so politely, to shut up and be satisfied with what they had already attained, before the rest of the coun-try completely lost its patience.

Maryland's James Pearce, as if he hadn't annoyed Clay enough already, then proposed an exceptionally aggressive amendment that was so manifestly unpalatable to the North that it would destroy the bill if it were adopted. Its first part mandated a jail term of two to ten years for enticing a slave to escape, and provided that anyone convicted of facilitating a successful escape be fined the value of the lost slave. (This portion of the amendment was so clumsily written, John Hale pointed out, that under it a man could be arrested and convicted simply for reading the Declaration of Independence aloud in the presence of a slave.) Finally, the amendment empowered local authorities to ban free blacks from settling within the District of Columbia, and to remove any already living there. This draconian provision meant that the eight thousand or so free blacks living in Washington could be expelled at any time, without notice. The mere mention of free blacks drew bristling disgust from several southern senators. "The District is already overrun with this class of population," complained John Bell of Tennessee. If Clay's bill passed, "instead of ten thousand, we shall see congregated here twenty, perhaps forty, perhaps a hundred thousand . . . and they are with a few exceptions, standing agitators—always ready to get up mobs and insurrections."

Debate paused for a week while the Senate shoveled away at the accumulated piles of neglected public business. Discussion of Clay's bill resumed on September 10. That day, without fanfare, the Senate was also treated to a scene whose high drama was lost on no one. With California's statehood now a settled fact, the two California senators who had been cooling their heels since the spring were finally officially seated. The saga that had begun with James Marshall's discovery of a few pebbles of gold in the American River had continued through the raucous statehood convention in Monterey, and culminated here in the Senate, now climaxed in the solemn march of four men in black broadcloth down the aisles of the chamber. Stephen Douglas presented the credentials of William Gwin, the Mississippi Calhounite–turned–Free Soiler, while the fire-eating Robert Barnwell—amazingly overcoming his personal disgust at the Pathfinder's antislavery views—walked John C. Frémont down the aisle in an elaborate act of courtesy that he considered due to a fellow native South Carolinian. In principle at least, the antislavery North for the first time now held a majority of the seats in the Senate.

By now the House had passed the "little Omnibus," and even the most adamant radicals realized that the end was at hand. Jefferson Davis, whose final, sharp-edge remarks were acerbic even for him, blamed the South's imminent defeat on the slave state senators who "desert us and go over to the enemy" by supporting one or another of the compromise measures and "are seized with such a wonderful sympathy for negro thieves." Clay's bill, as he saw it, was nothing less than an assault on all private property. "Where does this Government get the right to ask the citizen what he is going to do with his property, and where does it get the right to discriminate or decide, by his future intentions, on the right of possession and transit with such property?" he demanded. "What right has Congress to inquire for what purpose a man has brought his property here?" To deprive a businessman of the right to keep "a gang of slaves" at his own house, which for that matter looked "rather a boarding house in its aspect than a prison" was nothing less than an "act of inhumanity."

William Seward's last words were among his most eloquent of the entire debate and a fitting counterpoint to Davis's. He startled even some of his friends by proposing to substitute for Clay's bill a proposition for the immediate and complete *emancipation* of Washington's slaves. "I think it wrong to hold men in bondage at any time and under any circumstances," he said. "I think it right and just, therefore, to abolish slavery when we have the power, at any time, at all times, under any circumstances. If the present is not the right time, then there must be or there must have been some other time, and that must be a time that is already past, or time yet to come. Well, sir, slavery has existed here under the sanction of Congress for fifty years undisturbed. The right time, then, has not passed. It must, therefore, be a future time. Will gentlemen oblige me and the country by telling us how far down in the future the right time lies? The right time, if it be not now, will never come." It was no surprise to anyone, least of all Seward, that his amendment was rejected. Even fellow antislavery men felt that Seward's bill was "crude, ill-digested, and hastily considered." Its substance aside, no one could bear the prospect of another excruciating and prolonged debate. Said Dayton, "Let us make an end of this matter of slavery for the present at least; we have had, and the country, I am sure has had enough of it."

Clay, impatient for the end, complained of growing fatigue, and wished that he had stayed longer in the vivifying salt air of Newport. As if he had nothing else to preoccupy him, he worried about his indolent grandson Henry Clay III, who continued to amass demerits at West Point, and he felt compelled to spend precious time and energy personally lobbying both the president and Secretary of State Webster for a diplomatic appointment for the son of a friend. On September 12, however, Clay announced to the Senate with palpable joy that he had just learned that the House had passed the Fugitive Slave Bill by a large majority. "Our northern friends have behaved on that subject as well as some others, with liberality—some of them with great liberality," he crowed. All that remained now, he underscored yet again, was the slave trade bill. "When we go a hundred miles from this place to the North, the enormity of the slave trade here is the leading theme of conversation." Give the North *something*! If Pearce's amendments were forced onto the bill, both they and the bill would certainly fail: enemies of the amendments and the bill would combine to defeat them all. If anything should be done about free blacks, Clay added, in his most kindly manner, it "should be carefully done, and in a spirit of justice and humanity towards this unfortunate class." Suppose they were expelled from the District: what would become of them? "I could not, consistently with my feelings, vote under such circumstances for a proposition so harsh."

Clay got his way. Shortly after he spoke, by a solid though far from overwhelming majority, Pearce's amendments were voted down, with the assistance of the two new senators from California.

Nine months of debate, a thousand hours of argument, of threats, ripostes, anxiety, and soul-numbing weariness, were now finally coming to an end. On the morning of September 16, the Senate heard what were, in effect, the valedictory speeches of several of the men who had played leading roles in this monumental national conversation as it wound to a close. "The thing is now over, the votes have been taken, and the results will tell, what history will tell, that I was right in everything that I said," announced Benton, in the inimitably egoistic, twanging tones that had agitated and aggravated his fellow senators all spring and summer. Each piece of legislation had passed once they had all been separated, just as he had always demanded, Old Missouri announced. He then parsed every vote, noting which senators had voted for what bills, and how the majorities had been constructed, crowing, "I now say that the result has confirmed everything I said upon this floor."

Clay replied expansively, "The events of the past few weeks are not, in my opinion, a proper subject for individual triumph or for indulgence of a spirit of egotism. They are the triumphs of the country, the triumphs of the Union, the triumphs of harmony and concord in the midst of a distracted people. The question as to whether the measures should have been combined or separated was the merest question of form that ever occurred; and I venture to say that, if there had been no opposition"—he was needling Benton here—"to the combination, these measures would all have passed three or four months ago."

"I have a right to resist a measure, come from whom it may, and on this occasion, the result proves I was right," Benton fulminated, his appetite for rivalry unquenched, likening Clay to the Sun King, Louis XIV. "The result proves that we have lost four months about a matter which was unparliamentary, and which has failed, and the moment that it failed everything which was proposed was accomplished; at that moment the cats and dogs that had been tied together by their tails for months, scratching and biting, being loose again, every one of them ran off to his own hole and was quiet."

"As to tyranny and oppression, I have but a word to say," interjected Henry Foote, who had never yet managed to express himself in a single word. Sarcastic as ever, he launched a shotgun blast of insults that seemed to encompass abolitionists, Free Soilers, Seward, and naturally, above all, the alligator-skinned Benton. "If we have been the subjects of tyranny, if a domineering course has been at one time pursued here, and if we have borne it with patience for years, yes, sir, for almost thirty years entire, thank God! We may exclaim at last, 'BEHOLD THE TYRANT PROSTRATE IN THE DUST, AND ROME AGAIN IS FREE.' "

Stephen Douglas had more genuine reason for self-satisfaction than any senator. "If any man has a right to be proud of the success of these measures, it is the senator from Illinois," said Jefferson Davis—a surprisingly generous (if double-edged) assessment coming from the coldest, angriest man in the Senate, who had voted only for the Fugitive Slave Bill, and hated all the rest of it. Douglas, who was neither given to self-congratulation nor spendthrift with words (he was a Vermonter by birth, after all), was in a generous mood. "I do not deem it very profitable to stop to inquire whether it would have been better to have passed the several bills jointly or separately; the important point was to secure their passage," he said. "No man and no party has acquired a triumph, except the party friendly to the Union triumphing over abolitionism and disunion. The North has not surrendered to the South, nor has the South made any humiliating concessions to the North. Each section has maintained its honor and its rights, and both have met on the common ground of justice and compromise."

They—Clay, Benton, Davis, Douglas—for once, were all right.

A short time afterward, the last plank in what would be known ever after as the Compromise of 1850, passed by a vote of 33 to 19.

President Fillmore signed all the bills in quick succession, except for the Fugitive Slave Act, over which he hesitated—some said agonized—for two days. He had no fondness for slavery, though he had never expended any political capital to oppose it. He also expected to run for reelection in 1852, and had to consider whether he would lose more by offending the North or the South. (The opprobrium heaped upon Webster after he defended the bill in the Senate could not have been far from the president's mind.) In the end, he threw in his lot with southern sentiment and, encouraged by Webster and by Attorney General Crittenden, swallowed his inhibitions, draped himself in the Constitution, promised to enforce the law, and signed the bill on September 20. "God knows that I detest slavery," he later wrote to Webster, "but it is an existing evil, for which we are not responsible, and we must endure it, and give it such protection as is guaranteed by the Constitution, till we can get rid of it without destroying the last hope of free government in the world." He soon overcame his qualms. In a letter to Webster, he promised, "I shall not hesitate . . . to bring the whole force of the government to sustain the law."

Fillmore had reason for optimism. His presidency was off to a brilliant start. Just two and a half months after taking office, his team had achieved what Zachary Taylor, and James Polk before him, had failed to accomplish since the end of the Mexican War. California was now a state. Slavery in the western territories would be left to their future inhabitants when they approached statehood. A formula had been found to prevent war over New Mexico. Texas—he hoped, anyway—had been placated. The slaveholders had gotten their draconian new law. The North had been fobbed off with the termination of the slave trade in Washington. Along with countless ordinary Americans, Fillmore regarded the compromise as the final settlement of the nation's disagreements over slavery. Violent passions would subside. Friendliness between the sections would return. Furious slave owners would relax. Abolitionism would fade. The Underground Railroad would be briskly mopped up. There would be no civil war. The Union would survive and prosper. It was a pretty vision.

Meanwhile, Congress raced to clear up the litter of issues that had lain ignored or repeatedly postponed for the past months. There were questions about the collection of customs duties in California, the payment of Mexico's wartime indemnity to the United States, new hydrographical and topographical surveys to be funded, the allocation of bounty lands for veterans, a slew of appropriations bills for the diplomatic corps and for assorted Indian tribes, flogging in the navy—which northerners wished to see abolished, and southerners vigorously defended: "It would be utterly impracticable to have an efficient navy without this mode of punishment," Jefferson Davis asserted—allocations for a military road in Arkansas, construction of a new customs house in New Orleans, the appropriation of public lands to benefit the "indigent insane," and the perennial question of reimbursement of members for their travel to Washington. The Senate's numbers shrank daily as members left for home, among them Clay, who departed Washington on the 28th, wondering if he would live to see the capital again.

On September 30, the Senate's president pro tem, the courtly William King of Alabama, addressed the senators who still remained. "Our protracted session is about to close," he announced. "The causes which have led to its unusual extension were of a character well calculated to produce an excited state of feeling, and occasionally to lead to altercations of a very unpleasant character. Whether the actions of Congress will allay that excitement, restore harmony, and bring about a better state of feeling in the country, remains to be seen."

With those words, at precisely twelve noon, he proclaimed the Senate adjourned, ending its longest session ever. Congress had sat continuously for three hundred and two days.

CHAPTER 28

"A SCANDALOUS OUTRAGE"

————— ·◆· —————

T he nation rejoiced, most of it anyway. Fanaticism had been vanquished, chaos averted, the sore of slavery cauterized, national amity restored. Millard Fillmore announced in his first State of the Union address, in December, "We have been rescued from the wide and boundless agitation that surrounded us," and assured Americans that the compromise measures had achieved "a final settlement of the dangerous and exciting subjects which they embraced." State legislatures passed resolutions affirming support for the Compromise. Businessmen who had dreaded the disruption in commerce that sectional conflict would bring welcomed the settlement with euphoria. Stephen Douglas was justly hailed for bringing the Compromise to completion. But everyone knew that his success rested on Henry Clay's long struggle to convince both Congress and the American public that without a "comprehensive adjustment" the Union would die. When he returned home to Lexington on October 22, Clay was greeted by cheering crowds and a spectacular barbecue in his honor, where—as entire hogs and the haunches of oxen turned on spits, and whiskey flowed like water—he assured adoring Kentuckians that a new age had dawned. Later, in a speech to the state legislature, he declared his complete confidence that the Compromise would "pacify, tranquillize, and harmonize the country."

Not everyone was happy, of course. Abolitionists denounced Fillmore as "the tool and lickspittle of the Slave Power" for failing to veto the Fugitive Slave Law—the "Bloodhound Bill" they called it. Secessionists were also vitriolic. Former Georgia senator Herschel Johnson dismissed the Compromise as nothing but "a fecund box of nauseous nostrums," while Georgia's Columbus *Sentinel* howled, "We *despise the Union, and the North as we do hell itself.*" In Texas, a huge rally of irate citizens voted to pay for a slave collar to be made for the pro-Compromise editor of the *Clarksville Standard*, inscribed: "Born a slave to Houston and Rusk."

The first southern test of the Compromise took place in Georgia. Governor George Towns had called for the election of delegates to a state convention that many assumed would declare secession over the admission of California. Through the autumn, Alexander Stephens, Robert Toombs, and Howell Cobb defended the Compromise in a barnstorming campaign that was characterized as much by pistol waving and fisticuffs as it was by gentlemanly debates. On November 25, to the trio's relief, Georgians elected slates of pro-compromise delegates to the state convention by a two-to-one majority, halting the rush to secession in its tracks. (Although the delegates voted to approve the Compromise, they warned, significantly, that if the federal government failed to execute the Fugitive Slave Law or refused to admit another slave state to the Union, the road to secession would reopen.)

In Texas, too, public opinion pivoted toward compromise. The warmongering *Texas State Gazette* impotently fumed that once trustworthy allies were now advocating "humble submission to the despotic and unconstitutional pretensions of the Executive government at Washington." As the results slowly trickled in from the nonbinding statewide plebiscite that Governor Bell had ordered, it became clear that in all but the biggest slaveholding counties the voters had decisively rejected war and approved the Compromise. In mid-October, Bell ordered the Rangers to stack their arms, and on November 11 he informed the legislature that given the "improved auspices" he believed that it was time for Texas to yield to the popular desire for a peaceful settlement. Two weeks later, the legislature overrode its still militant minority and voted to take the $10 million payment and, grudgingly, accept the western border proposed by Congress.

News from Texas was glacially slow in reaching the rest of the South. However, the influence of the Georgia vote was soon felt wherever the secessionist movement had seemed poised for victory. Former South Carolina governor Hammond, for one, was disappointed by moderates who revealed themselves to be, in his opinion, all too willing to betray the interests of slavery for temporary peace. But he was a realist. He didn't even bother to attend the second session of the Nashville Convention, which, though packed with his fellow secessionists, was ignored by most respected statesmen, cold-shouldered by Tennesseans, and ended in a state of sour uncertainty. "I see clearly that the true crisis is not yet, and that he who husbands his strength now can expend it to much more effect a few years hence," Hammond confided to his diary. "The fruit is not ripe." Only South Carolina was politically ready to secede, but she would be foolhardy to undertake it alone. "But in all the cotton states this sentiment is spreading rapidly," he calculated, "and I think that, aided by the aggressiveness of the abolitionists, in a few years it will predominate so far that we will be sustained in open secession from the Union."

The most bitter southern test took place in Mississippi, where the intensity of secessionist sentiment was second only to that in South Carolina. For almost a year, through the autumn of 1851, Unionists battled states' rights radicals in a pair of contests that surpassed even Georgia's for savagery. Governor Quitman had considered declaring secession outright, but decided instead to call a state convention, which he hoped would deliver a popular mandate to propel the state out of the Union. Quitman, who was forced to resign when he was indicted on federal charges for his role in the López fiasco, was simultaneously running for reelection against none other than Mississippi's champion of compromise, Henry Foote, who came home from Washington to lead a fusion party of pro-compromise Democrats and Whigs. Quitman argued that the central issue was the survival of slavery, charging that but for the North's outrageous interference battalions of Mississippi slaves could already have been sent to California to mine gold for their masters, and asserting that unless drastic action were taken slavery would perish altogether.

Foote countered that the Compromise was a victory for the South. He flayed the dignified but inarticulate Quitman with scathing ad hominem attacks until, in July 1851, Quitman finally snapped—Foote so often had this effect on people—and punched the bantam orator in the middle of a debate, leaving him with a huge purple bruise on his face that he bore for a month. When the ballots were tallied in the election for delegates to the state convention, Foote's ticket swept the state with 57 percent of the vote. Quitman had been so badly weakened that the Democrats replaced him with Jefferson Davis, pitting the Senate's two rivals against each other in a head-to-head match for governor. Davis claimed absurdly that he was no "disunionist" even as he defended secession, which he called "the right of revolution," and extolled the "holy" cause of states' rights, only cautioning that Mississippi "ought to stand aloof, in readiness" until the time was right, and then, "when, eventually, other States should join her, let them fall in to the right and left to arrange with them for mutual cooperation." This campaign, too, ended in a victory for the Compromise and for Foote, although by a margin of fewer than one thousand votes. Davis, if anything, only enhanced his personal appeal as the avatar of embryonic southern nationhood. Wrote one undaunted Davis supporter, "I regard your future political sky as being without a cloud and of Italian azure, and that your course will be necessarily onwards and upwards, until you reach the Presidency."

In the North, no aspect of the Compromise had more far-reaching consequences than the Fugitive Slave Law. Its first victim, just days after Millard Fillmore signed it, was James Hamlet, a thirty-year-old man of mixed race who had fled from slavery in Maryland in 1848 and made his way to New York City, where he worked as a porter for the waterfront commercial firm of Tilton and Maloney. Since his escape, he had acquired a wife and children, become a member of the Methodist Church, and was regarded by all who knew him as "a steady, correct, and upright man."

On September 26, 1850, a stranger bearing official papers accosted him at work and led him through the congested lanes of lower Manhattan to City Hall, where in a second floor office he found himself face-to-face with Commissioner Alexander Gardiner, the federal agent charged with enforcing the Fugitive Slave Law, and two relatives of his former owners brandishing a power of attorney. Hamlet insisted that his mother was a free woman, and that he, too, was therefore free. But the law precluded his testimony, Gardiner told him. Without informing Hamlet's wife and family or any of his friends, much less a lawyer, he was handcuffed on the spot, taken downstairs and forced into a carriage, hurried to a steamboat, and dispatched to Baltimore, where in less than twenty-four hours he found himself lodged in a slave jail being readied for sale.

Hamlet was fortunate. In October, New York abolitionists purchased his freedom for $800, and he returned to a hero's welcome. Others were not so lucky. By midwinter, there had been at least sixty, and possibly many more, attempted arrests as far north as Chicago. Panicky blacks embarked on an exodus of biblical proportions, fleeing northern cities, as Frederick Douglass memorably put it, "as from an enemy's land—a doomed city." After a man and his wife were dragged from their beds, leaving the couple's ten-month-old baby behind, the black population of Columbia, Pennsylvania, a longtime safe haven for fugitives, dropped by 40 percent. Two hundred of the six hundred blacks living around Syracuse abandoned their homes and fled to Canada. Of the 114 members of a black Baptist church in Rochester, all but two left the country, and in Buffalo, 130 left from another Baptist church. An estimated three hundred fled from Pittsburgh, including nearly all the waiters in the city's hotels. By early 1851, some three thousand may have crossed into Canada, and as many as fifteen thousand would do so by the end of the decade. In *The North Star*, Douglass wrote furiously: "Wo to the poor panting fugitive! Wo to all that dare be his friends! Wo to all that refuse to help hunt him down, hold him fast and send him back to his bloody prison-house. Wo to all the just and merciful in the land."

Others defiantly remained in the United States. Urged to flee, Jermain Loguen, who had escaped from slavery in 1834, publicly challenged the law from his Syracuse pulpit, daring the government to arrest him. "What is life to me if I am to be a slave in Tennessee?" he thundered. "I will not, nor will I consent that, anybody else shall countenance the claims of a vulgar despot to my soul and body. I have received my freedom from Heaven, and with it came the command to defend my title to it. I don't respect this law—I don't fear it—I won't obey it! It outlaws me, and I outlaw it, and the men who attempt to enforce it on me. I will not live a slave, and if force is employed to re-enslave me, I shall make preparations to meet the crisis as becomes a man."

The Fugitive Slave Law was the single most intrusive assertion of federal authority enacted during the entire antebellum era, an irony that was lost on southern radicals who habitually condemned any measure that even faintly smacked of interference with their own "domestic institutions." Brutal recaptures shocked northern consciences. When horrified Yankees grasped that the law required them to collaborate with slave hunters no matter what their feelings about slavery, it spurred civil disobedience on a massive scale. Public meetings from Maine to Wisconsin denounced the law as unjust, unconstitutional, and unchristian. Hundreds, if not thousands, pledged publicly to break the law. Syracuse declared itself an open city for fugitives at a huge rally where the mayor stood shoulder to shoulder with the defiant Jermain Loguen. And in Zanesville, Ohio, radicalized whites resolved to "throw the arms of protection around our fugitive brethren and sisters, and that we will feed them and clothe them, conceal them and assist them in their escape from the Negro Hounds."

Just how far would the white man's democracy have to be curtailed in order to protect the slave system in the South, more and more Yankee voters were wondering. All over the South, the freedoms of speech, assembly, and the press were suspended when it came to anything even remotely perceived as a challenge to slavery. There, too, schools were systematically purged of politically "unreliable" teachers and pulpits of independent-minded clergymen, books deemed too threatening were regularly suppressed, and mainstream northern publications were barred from the mails because they might contain articles unfavorable to slavery. Innocent northern agents and merchants traveled south in fear of being mobbed, jailed, or worse if they were suspected of sowing abolitionist doctrines. A few years earlier, the governor of South Carolina had told his legislature that abolitionism could be "silenced in but one way—*Terror—Death.*" When the South demanded ever more loudly that the northern states quash abolitionist "agitation" on their own soil, was this what it had in mind?

Slave hunters met mounting resistance. Two Baltimore men attempting to arrest the fugitives William and Ellen Crafts were mobbed in Boston, besieged in their hotel rooms, and arrested for slander for calling Mrs. Crafts "a slave." In mid-October, when slave catchers with a federal warrant appeared in Wilkes-Barre, Pennsylvania, and attempted to impress a posse of citizens to join in, a local correspondent reported, "After repeated orders, not even a *loafer* obeyed." Many officials simply ignored the law. One Illinois magistrate, presented with an alleged fugitive on a writ of habeas corpus, decided on the spot that the law was unconstitutional, and discharged the man immediately. And in February 1851, the boldest challenge yet to the Fugitive Slave Law took place in Boston, when the biggest crowd of black men ever seen in the city burst into the federal courthouse and forcibly liberated Shadrach Minkins, a waiter who had been seized a few hours before.

The South watched and waited to see what President Fillmore would do, and whether the law, as secessionists had always warned, would prove a mere sham when it was tested. Fillmore had made his intentions abundantly clear the previous October, warning that he intended to bring the full force of the government to bear in enforcing the law whenever and wherever necessary. After a special cabinet meeting, under pressure from Webster, he condemned Minkins's rescue as "a scandalous outrage," and ordered civil and military officials of all ranks to cooperate in recapturing him. By this time, Minkins had already been dispatched to safety in Canada via the Underground Railroad. But if there was any single moment that can be said to have marked Fillmore's transformation from a northern man with clear, if mild, antislavery views into a compliant collaborator with the Slave Power, this was it.

Webster, even more than Fillmore, took an almost obsessively personal interest in the enforcement of the Fugitive Slave Law. The secretary of state was by this time a spent force; gripped by advanced alcoholism, he was seen to sway and stumble in public, and when he spoke he often exhibited a bile-filled nastiness that became harder and harder for his dwindling band of friends to excuse. All who dared to oppose the Fugitive Slave Law, he raved in a bellicose speech to Syracuse businessmen, "are traitors! traitors! traitors!" He still maintained an irrational hope that he might win the Whig nomination for president in 1852, even though he had no party organization and little mass support outside New England, and even there it was rapidly ebbing. He needed as much southern support as he could get. When yet another freedom seeker, Thomas Sims, was arrested in Boston six weeks after Minkins's escape, Webster made sure that he would not get away. At his personal order, Sims was surrounded by a guard of three hundred armed militia and police, and in the middle of the night marched to the harbor, where he was embarked for his return to slavery in Georgia from the same wharf where Bostonians dressed as Indians had dumped British tea into the harbor in the prelude to the American Revolution. To Webster, the relieved Fillmore wrote, "I congratulate you and the country upon the triumph of law in Boston. She has done nobly."

Throughout 1851, the administration's determination to enforce the law was brought home repeatedly with brute force. In September, at Christiana, Pennsylvania, a slave owner named Edward Gorsuch was shot dead by free black vigilantes when, with a posse of federal officers, he attempted to recapture two men who had run away from his Maryland farm. The night after this "tragedy," as conservative newspapers dubbed it, scores of deputies joined by gangs of proslavery ruffians from Maryland and United States Marines combed the countryside in search of anyone who was implicated in the confrontation, invading homes and arresting scores of antislavery men on the flimsiest of charges, or none at all. As one eyewitness put it, "blacks were hunted like partridges."

Despite such flagrant intimidation, juries almost without exception refused to convict citizens who helped fugitives to escape. Of the ten men arrested in connection with the Minkins rescue—including two of the fugitive's lawyers—none was convicted. And in Pennsylvania, prosecutors initially charged thirty-eight participants in the Christiana riot with "levying war" against the United States government, the largest indictment for treason in American history. But the only man actually brought to trial, a hapless white man who had appeared in the midst of the confrontation, was declared not guilty after just fifteen minutes of deliberation by the jury.

Northern resistance continued to harden throughout the decade. More than half the northern states passed aggressive new liberty laws designed to thwart the slave-catching statutes. In Massachusetts, any official who granted a certificate permitting the removal of a fugitive from the state was to be instantly and permanently barred from holding state office. In other states, officials who violated similar statutes were punished with anywhere from $500 and six months in jail in Pennsylvania, to a $2,000 fine and ten years in Vermont. Meanwhile, the Underground Railroad grew exponentially into the largest mass movement of civil disobedience since the American Revolution. New underground lines were opened by road, canal, sea, and by iron railway. Safe houses were established in towns where only a few years earlier abolitionists had been stoned and mobbed for daring even to speak in public. In addition to "conductors" such as Harriet Tubman, whose exploits became the stuff of legend, thousands of Americans, black and white, provided fugitives with food, clothing, and shelter, among them Senator William Seward and his wife, Frances, who lent help to freedom seekers—including Tubman—in Auburn, New York.

By delivering thousands of freedom seekers into northern towns that had never seen a slave before, the Underground radicalized ordinary Americans. They discovered that men and women who had seemed like pathetic abstractions in faraway Mississippi or South Carolina were people much like themselves, whose hopes and dreams were shackled even in the free North to the eternal fear of recapture. Wrote a traumatized New Yorker after watching the fugitive Jerry McHenry dragged by deputies bleeding through the streets of Syracuse, "I have just witnessed a scene that has frozen my heart's blood. I have seen the perdition of slavery enacted in Syracuse, in the heart of New York . . . I have heard his frantic wail, his scream of despair. O such a wail!"

Henry Clay's reaction to the rescue of Shadrach Minkins was revealing. He demanded to know whether "a government of white men was to be yielded to a government by blacks." The rescue, he wildly claimed, must have been organized by white men who "openly, by word and by print everywhere . . . stimulate these negroes to acts of violence." (In fact, the rescue had been led by a black businessman, Lewis Hayden, who had escaped from slavery in Clay's own hometown of Lexington in 1845.) His remarks exposed not only an embedded racism that he rarely expressed so bluntly, but also anxiety that the compromise to which he had devoted the last year of his life might unravel before his own eyes. Clay knew that his life was drawing to a close. He suffered violent nightly fits of coughing that left him perilously depleted; he no longer had the strength to ride; and his copious memory was rapidly slipping, embarrassing him in front of admirers, to whom it was obvious that his once awesome command of issues was a thing of the past. There were halfhearted attempts to draft him to run for president in 1852, but he knew that it would never be. In August 1851, he wrote to a friend that he had tried in vain "all the old women's remedies," but "the machine is nearly worn out." It hardly seemed to matter: "When many of the tyes to life are broken, and when the source of one taste and pleasure after another have been dried up, it is of little consequence whether one remains here below a few months more or less."

As much as Clay loved Ashland, with its meandering pathways and browsing livestock, in the end he loved Washington more. In November, he left again for the national capital, never to return home. He made his last appearance in the Senate on December 1, but was too ill to participate in the debate, and dragged himself back to the National Hotel only with difficulty. He rarely left his rooms after that. As his lungs disintegrated, he coughed without letup. In February 1852, he wrote to his son John Morrison Clay that he had "nearly emptied an apothecary's shop," to no avail. His voice shrank to nothing. He lost weight and appetite. More and more frequently he spit up blood. In letters home, he delicately attributed his problems to "bronchitas" or a "derangement of the stomach," but he must have known that he was in the final stages of tuberculosis.

On June 29, 1852, tightly gripping the hand of his son Thomas, Henry Clay died. In his will, he shared out his slaves among his heirs, stipulating that all who had been born after January 1, 1850, be freed at the age of twenty-eight if male, and twenty-five if female. Three years prior to their emancipation they were to begin collecting wages, in order to pay for their transportation to Liberia. To the end, he believed that colonization, "the greatest project of the existing age," was the only viable solution to the slavery problem, a project he supposed would take perhaps two hundred years to complete.

In communities across America, Clay was lauded as the greatest statesman of his age. Among those who eulogized him was a forty-three-year-old Illinois Whig, Abraham Lincoln, who had looked to Clay as his role model, but whose own hopes for a political career had fizzled after his single ineffectual term in the House of Representatives. "Those who would shiver into fragments the Union of these States; tear to tatters its now venerated constitution; and even burn the last copy of the Bible, rather than slavery should continue a single hour, together with all their more halting sympathizers, have received, and are receiving their just execration; and the name, and opinions, and influence of Mr. Clay, are fully, and as I trust, effectually and enduringly, arrayed against them," Lincoln rather tortuously declaimed, self-consciously mirroring Clay's implacable hostility to both abolitionism and disunion. "But I would also, if I could, array his name, opinions and influence against the opposite extreme—against a few, but an increasing number of men, who, for the sake of perpetuating slavery, are beginning to assail and to ridicule the white man's charter of freedom—the declaration that 'all men are created free and equal.' " It was not a particularly impressive speech. Few would pay much attention to it or, for the time being, the gaunt, awkward lawyer who delivered it.

Four months later, Daniel Webster died, the ruined shell of a once great man, felled by cirrhosis of the liver, an undiagnosed hematoma caused by a severe fall, and the cumulative damage wrought by years of dosing with arsenic for his chronic catarrh. His last months were darkened by his humiliating defeat at the Whig convention, where his puny forces were trampled by the enthusiastic legions committed to General Winfield Scott, who though Virginia-born was friendly to the now ascendant free soil wing of the party. Deeply wounded, Webster sank into a funk from which he never withdrew. Retiring to his home at Marshfield, his main pleasure was watching cattle graze in front of his house. On October 18, 1852, he resigned as secretary of state. Three days later, he began vomiting blood. Through the night of October 23, he cried out scraps of Scripture, begged for a few favorite lines of poetry, and intermittently asked for sips of brandy. In the middle of the night, he suddenly cried, "I still live!" They were his last words. He was seventy years old. The last of the Great Triumvirate was now gone. Andrew Butler of South Carolina spoke touchingly of the three as the ghosts of a time that had passed, luminaries that "differed from each other as one star differeth from another; but they were all stars of the first magnitude. Distance cannot destroy, nor can time diminish, the simple splendor of their light."

THE RECKONING

——— ·◆· ———

"The mere perishable body of Clay has gone, but the principles to which he devoted his life will survive and will continue to animate mankind while Liberty has a votary upon earth," a leading Kentucky Whig intoned after the Great Compromiser's death. The fact was, however, with Clay and Webster gone, with many of the party's southern members defecting to the state's rights movement, and many of its northern men disgusted by Fillmore's sponginess on slavery, the Whig Party was finished. Clay's pet charity, the American Colonization Society, was also destined for oblivion. This ineffectual but morally convenient monstrosity satisfied no one except those who, like Clay, needed the crutch of a nonsolution to the slavery problem to condemn slavery even while they continued to enjoy the fruits of it. Free black Americans were, as Frederick Douglass and others impatiently reiterated, not *Africans* but *Americans*, who wanted freedom in their own homeland, not exile in a strange continent. Clay's greatest single principle, his near-religious yet pragmatic faith in the power of men to discover shared interest through compromise and to retain their sense of honor in the process, also died with him. As the decade ticked away, the political culture polarized, and old loyalties crumbled. More and more often now, as the sectional divide over the future of slavery widened, ideological differences would be addressed with rifles and bowie knives, and soon enough with cannon and marching armies.

The Compromise of 1850 was a brilliant example of collaborative statecraft. But it was, as historian Sean Wilentz has aptly put it, an "evasive truce," a balancing act that delayed, but could not prevent, the bloody reckoning over slavery. The unraveling began in 1853, when Stephen Douglas proposed the organization of the vast Nebraska Territory, which encompassed the present states of Nebraska and Kansas as well as parts of the Dakotas, Colorado, and Wyoming. This was not just geographical housekeeping: immense wealth was at stake. Douglas, still chairman of the Committee on Territories, most of all wanted to lay out a route for the transcontinental railroad to run from Chicago to San Francisco. The "savage barrier"—that is, the Indians—must be pushed aside, and "the tide of emigration and civilization must be permitted to roll onward until it rushes through the passes of the mountains, and spreads over the plains," he declared in his full-throttle expansionist mode. Development of the railroad would mean fabulous profits for speculators and their political friends in Washington, among them Douglas himself. Bringing this to pass would require all the political skill the "Little Giant" possessed.

In 1852, the Democrats had won commanding majorities in both houses of Congress. They had also elected as president Franklin Pierce, who though from New Hampshire would cater accommodatingly to the demands of the South. (Fillmore, ambivalent about running for a second term, and hobbled by Seward's unforgiving opposition to his renomination, had lost the Whig nomination to Winfield Scott.) Territorial policy was controlled in the Senate by four hard-line proslavery Democrats, all of them veterans of the debates of 1850: the Virginians James Mason and Robert Hunter, chairmen of the Foreign Relations and Finance Committees, respectively; Andrew Butler of South Carolina, who chaired the Judiciary Committee; and the famously boozy and profane David Atchison of Missouri—who had sworn that he would let Nebraska "sink in hell" before allowing it to keep out slaves—presided over the Senate as its president pro tem. Adding to the lopsided proslavery tilt of the administration, Jefferson Davis now served as the influential secretary of war. In exchange for their support, Douglas agreed to a Faustian bargain. The proposed new territories of both Kansas and Nebraska lay north of the line defined by the Missouri Compromise of 1820, and were supposed to be closed to slavery. In accordance with the principle of Popular Sovereignty, however, Douglas now asserted that the Compromise of 1850 had made the earlier agreement "inoperative and void," and that settlers in each territory should be free to decide for themselves if they wanted to permit slavery or not. The Kansas-Nebraska bill, he said, merely proposed to carry into effect "the great fundamental principle upon which our republican institutions are predicated"—democracy pure and simple. This was stunningly disingenuous: no one in 1850 had claimed any such thing. But with the South's support, Douglas had the votes he needed. The Senate passed the Kansas-Nebraska bill 37 to 14, and the House by the narrower margin of 113 to 100. "I had the authority and power of a dictator throughout the controversy in both houses," Douglas boasted. "The speeches were nothing."

Nebraska lay far enough north that it was clearly destined to become a free state. Kansas, which bordered Texas, Arkansas, and Missouri (the future state of Oklahoma was still Indian territory) was another story entirely. Douglas had insisted that leaving slavery up to settlers would put an end to abolitionist agitation. Not only did Kansas prove him wrong, but it transformed what had been verbally brutal but bloodless combat in the halls of Congress into warfare on the prairies. Armed Missourians swarmed across the state line, egged on by Atchison in person, who swore to bring in enough proslavery gunmen "to kill every God damned abolitionist in the Territory." When word reached New York that free state settlers needed guns, and volunteers to use them, William Seward declared to a cheering Albany audience, "We will engage in competition for the virgin soil of Kansas, and God give the victory to the side that is stronger in numbers as it is in right." When elections for the territorial legislature were held in 1857, thousands of "border ruffians" swarmed in to vote illegally in a naked power grab, casting more than 1,800 proslavery votes in a county with only eleven cabins, and in another larding the voter lists with names copied from an old New York City directory.

The legislature, when it convened, barred abolitionists from holding office or serving on juries, and imposed a term of imprisonment for not less than five years on anyone who denied the existence of slavery in Kansas, opposed the right to own slaves, or circulated abolitionist literature. Guerrilla warfare between rival pro- and antislavery territorial governments continued for months, resulting in about two hundred extrajudicial killings. Although history most vividly remembers John Brown's murder of five proslavery men on Osawatomie Creek, the vast majority of the victims were antislavery men. Even Stephen Douglas finally had to admit that what had happened in Kansas was "a wicked fraud." In Chicago, unforgiving mobs shouted Douglas off speakers' platforms and burned him in effigy. "This Nebraska business," the black abolitionist Jermain Loguen wrote to Frederick Douglass, "is smashing up platforms and scattering partizans at a fine rate. The people are becoming ashamed to have any connection with the ungodly course that many of their Congressmen follow."

In the election of 1856, Democrats replaced the feeble Franklin Pierce with James Buchanan, one of the most experienced and least capable men ever to sit in the White House.

The election was notable also for the emergence of the Republican Party, founded just two years earlier as an amalgam of antislavery Democrats, abolitionists, Free Soilers, nativists, assorted reformers, and former Whigs, among them Abraham Lincoln, who was pried loose only with difficulty from his lifelong Whig allegiance, and William Seward, whose gimlet eye remained fixed on the presidency. For its nominee, the Republican convention—chaired by the redoubtable David Wilmot—cannily selected John C. Frémont, who had been absent from politics since the end of his short Senate term in 1853, and so remained unscarred by the sectional controversies of the mid-decade, and sent him off to campaign on a platform that equally denounced Mormon polygamy and slavery as twin relics of barbarism. Republicans marched in torchlight parades chanting "Free soil, Free speech, Free men, Frémont!" Seward, stumping for the ticket, decried the "ancient, eternal conflict" between freedom and "the system of slave labor, with unequal franchises secured by arbitrary, oppressive and tyrannical laws." Voters responded far beyond the new party's best hopes. Though defeated, Frémont won all of New England, plus New York, Ohio, Michigan, and Iowa, winning 114 electoral votes to Buchanan's 174. (Millard Fillmore, running as the candidate of the "Know Nothing" American Party, won only Maryland and its eight paltry electoral votes, putting a dismal end to what had been his once promising, if accidental, national career.) The election was, in short, a triumphant defeat for a party that now felt the wind of public opinion at its back.

Pennsylvanian by birth, Jacksonian by conviction, Buchanan—who was aptly nicknamed the "Old Public Functionary," or "OPF" for short—had served variously since the 1820s as a congressman, senator, cabinet member, and diplomat, and had for most of that time demonstrated a pronounced fondness for the interests of the South. (As a young congressman, he had once boasted that if the South were ever threatened with a slave rebellion, he would be among the first "to bundle on my knapsack" and march "in defense of their cause.") In his inaugural address, Buchanan declared that slavery was the business of neither Congress nor the president, but of the courts. Just two days later, the Supreme Court handed down the notorious Dred Scott decision. The case had been creeping through the courts since 1842. It arose when an army surgeon took the enslaved Scott first into Illinois and then into the Wisconsin Territory, and eventually returned with him to Missouri, where Scott, with the aid of abolitionist lawyers, sued for his freedom, arguing that since slavery was illegal in both Illinois and Wisconsin he automatically became free when he set foot there. A Missouri court agreed, but a federal court reversed the decision. Scott's lawyers then appealed to the Supreme Court, which ruled, by seven (five of them slave owners) to two, that as an "inferior class of beings" blacks had "no rights which the white man was bound to respect," that no negro slave or descendant of a slave could ever be a citizen of any state, and that neither Congress nor a territorial legislature had the power to exclude slavery from any United States territory.

This, in effect, nullified antislavery laws in virtually every northern state, and turned into national policy the angry question that Jefferson Davis had put to the Senate in September 1850: "Where," he then demanded, "does this Government get the right to ask the citizen what he is going to do with his property, and where does it get the right to discriminate or decide, by his future intentions, on the right of possession and transit with such property?" Government, the slaveholders' Supreme Court had decided, had no such right.

The Dred Scott decision naturally pleased the South, but it pushed still more northerners beyond their limit of endurance. Its inescapable meaning, observed Lincoln, when he sought the Republican nomination for the Senate from Illinois in 1858, was that "what Dred Scott's master might lawfully do with Dred Scott, in the free State of Illinois, every other master may lawfully do with any other one, or one thousand slaves, in Illinois, or in any other free state." Alluding to the Kansas-Nebraska Act, Lincoln said: "We are now far into the fifth year, since a policy was initiated with the avowed object, and confident promise, of putting an end to the slavery agitation." The promise had proved empty, and the nation's crisis more dangerous than ever. "A house divided against itself cannot stand," he famously declared, repeating the arresting phrase that Sam Houston had used during the debate of 1850. "This government cannot endure permanently half slave and half free." Although the house, the nation, would not collapse, he believed, it must cease to be divided. "It will become all one thing or all the other."

Another who attacked the Dred Scott decision was seventy-five-year-old Thomas Hart Benton, who in his last significant foray into national politics issued a densely reasoned 130-page argument supplemented by no fewer than sixty pages of appendices, in which—to distill this elephantine production to its essence—he asserted that the Supreme Court simply had no authority to rule on such "political subjects." In 1850, Benton's enemies in Missouri had defeated him for reelection to the Senate by targeting his deviation from the proslavery southern line. Two years later, he won election to the House of Representatives, where he continued to blister his opponents, including Stephen Douglas, when in 1854 he savaged the Kansas-Nebraska bill with a memorably baroque masterpiece of Bentonian prose: "The mare's nest had not then been found in which has been laid the marvelous egg out of which has been hatched the nondescript fowl, yclept [i.e., called] 'squatter sovereignty.' " Whatever he meant exactly, everyone knew that it was an attack on the extension of slavery, and all the more effective because it came from a southern man—albeit, the last one holding national office who dared to challenge the relentless demands of the Slave Power. Although Yankees lionized him—"No northern doughface with a cotton heart, He is the southern Nestor of the race," poetized a Boston wordsmith—Benton's outspokenness cost him his seat in the House after a single term.

In April 1858, just past his seventy-sixth birthday, he died after a prolonged and painful bout with cancer, reputedly denouncing to those gathered around him at his deathbed, in a strangled whisper, the incompetence of the Buchanan administration. The Washington *Union*, in its obituary, spoke feelingly of him as a man "of gigantic intellect, imposing presence, inflexible will, emphatic eloquence," and—rather an understatement—"angularity of manner." Benton was rude, tiresome, and uncooperative. But like Clay, Webster, and Calhoun, he had lived large, and to the end of his life never shirked from expressing the courage of his (so often contrarian) convictions.

If there was a moment in American politics that begged for creative politics—a fusion of vision and skill that could reverse the skid toward disunion, and reweave the national fabric in a new way—it was now. It should have been Stephen Douglas's moment. Yes, Popular Sovereignty had faltered; and the bloodshed in Kansas had damaged him. But as the ravaged decade stumbled toward a close, no other political man possessed his maturity, his national recognition, his leadership ability, his proven command of the legislative process, and his sheer *energy*. He was still only forty-five, and on the ascending curve of his political trajectory. In 1850, he had had a pitch-perfect instinct for what most northerners felt. The Compromise of that year had catapulted him to the presumptive leadership of the northern Democrats, and to an almost universal assumption that he was destined for the presidency. But his time had passed, although he didn't yet know it. The country needed more now than a legislative technician, however deft. Douglas, beneath the western folksiness, was a Yankee entrepreneur who treated politics essentially as a matter of human technology, an experimental endeavor that should be judged not by its intentions, much less its pretensions, but by its results. He was also, however, the unacknowledged heir to almost seventy years of political and moral evasion that stretched back to the first great compromise over slavery fatally embedded in the Constitution. Passionately democratic with respect to the rights of white men, he was deeply and irremediably racist when it came to blacks, and failed utterly to realize how the country would react once its conscience was aroused. Slavery, whose profits helped fuel his dramatic political ascent, and his self-indulgent life, also sealed his demise.

Stephen Douglas and Abraham Lincoln had known each other since the 1830s. They had argued cases in the same courtrooms, swapped stories in the same taverns, stumped for their parties' contending candidates in the same dusty crossroads towns. For nearly that entire period, Douglas was a rising star, and Lincoln a frustrated rival, an excellent lawyer everyone agreed, and a loyal Whig until his recent switch to the Republican Party, but a flop as a candidate. He was not then the haggard, hollow-eyed figure familiar from photographs of the Civil War era. At forty-nine, he was clean-shaven and virile, with chiseled cheekbones and a faint smile that hinted at the wry humor for which he was famous. Although he affected a homely awkwardness that put voters at their ease, he dressed in expensive broadcloth, and enjoyed a comfortable upper-middle-class life in a choice section of the state capital. When they met in their famous series of debates in the autumn of 1858 as candidates for the United States Senate, it was Douglas who was expected by virtually everyone to be the champion performer. Symbolizing their relative resources (and degrees of self-regard), Douglas cruised across the state in his own luxurious railway carriage followed by a flatcar carrying a cannon dubbed "Popular Sovereignty," which fired off a round whenever his train approached a town; Lincoln traveled unobtrusively by coach. (The debates were not a head-to-head contest for votes; neither Lincoln nor Douglas was on the ballot. Senators were chosen by state legislatures, as they would continue to be until 1913, which meant that the party holding the most seats in the State Assembly and Senate could automatically elect its candidate to the U.S. Senate.)

The two contenders met first on August 21 in Ottawa, west of Chicago. Douglas, who spoke first, accused Lincoln of being a closet abolitionist who, whatever he claimed, wanted to allow blacks "to vote on an equality with yourselves, and to make them eligible for office, to serve on juries, and adjudge your rights." Lincoln, who failed to marshal his arguments effectively, seemed stiff and embarrassed. The pro-Douglas *State Register* crowed, "The excoriation of Lincoln was so severe that the Republicans held their heads in shame."

At Freeport, six days later, Douglas kept Lincoln largely on the defensive. However, Lincoln managed to skillfully trap Douglas into a rhetorically fatal statement, indeed, a single word that devastated his hopes for higher office. He demanded to know if, in Douglas's opinion, Popular Sovereignty would permit settlers to exclude slavery from a new territory before it became a state. Douglas had already irritated the South by opposing the fraudulent pro-slavery constitution in Kansas; he didn't want to offend the South any further. If Douglas answered "no" then it would be obvious that Popular Sovereignty was impotent to stop the westward expansion of slavery, as Douglas still claimed it could. If Douglas answered "yes," he would satisfy his increasingly free soil Illinois base, but he would alienate the southern voters he would need when he ran for the presidency. Lincoln's tactical goal was to convince voters that Popular Sovereignty was a sham, to make clear that Douglas's laissez-faire attitude toward slavery would inevitably lead to more slave states, and to deeper entrenchment of the Slave Power in Washington. Douglas took Lincoln's bait: "Yes," he replied. Southerners had suspected Douglas of disloyalty on the expansion of slavery. Their fear had now been confirmed, and it would come back to haunt him.

The debaters met for the third time at Jonesboro on September 15, in the part of southern Illinois known as "Egypt" because of its proximity to the city of Cairo. Douglas harangued Lincoln once again for his alleged abolitionism, charging that he would not only give freed slaves citizenship, but even allow them to marry white women—the ultimate horror in many voters' minds, both North and South.

At Charleston, three days later, Lincoln played his own race card. The site of the debate, a fairground north of town, lay just a few miles north of the log cabin where Lincoln had spent his adolescence, when his father hired out young Abe's labor to farmers in the vicinity, a searing experience that hardened, and perhaps inspired, Lincoln's lifelong hostility to slavery. Although he opposed slavery, that didn't mean he believed in racial equality, he declared. "There is a physical difference between the white and black races which I believe will forever forbid the two races living together on terms of social and political equality. And inasmuch as they cannot so live, while they do remain together there must be the position of superior and inferior, and I as much as any other man am in favor of having the superior position assigned to the white race." *You can trust me*, Lincoln was reassuring voters, *I'm a racist, too.*

The debaters' next venue, Knox College, in the western Illinois city of Galesburg, was a bastion of abolitionism. Perhaps 25,000 men and women packed the rain-drenched campus beneath banners that proclaimed: "Douglas the Dead Dog—Lincoln the Living Lion," and "Greasy Mechanics for Lincoln." Douglas rehashed his usual defense of Popular Sovereignty, and then waded into Lincoln once again, declaring that the challenger's alleged belief in equality of the races was "a monstrous heresy." When Lincoln stepped forward a half-hour later, he seemed a man transformed. His high tenor voice rang out "as clear as a bell," one listener recalled. Without repudiating his crude remarks at Charleston, he challenged Douglas's racism on moral grounds. "I suppose that the real difference between Judge Douglas and his friends, and of the Republicans on the contrary, is that the Judge is not in favor of making any difference between slavery and liberty, and consequently every sentiment he utters discards the idea that there is anything wrong in slavery," Lincoln asserted. "Judge Douglas declares that if any community want slavery they have a right to have it. He can say that, logically, if he says there is no wrong in slavery. But if you admit that there is a wrong in it, he cannot logically say that anybody has a right to do wrong." Rhetorically, this was devastating. In the judgment of most observers, Lincoln won the debate.

At Quincy, a river port on the Mississippi, Lincoln returned to the assault that he had launched at Galesburg. Although the Negro could not expect social and political equality, like all Americans he enjoyed the same right to the freedoms of life, liberty, and the pursuit of happiness that were promised to all by the Declaration of Independence. "In the right to eat the bread without the leave of anybody else which his own hand earns, he is my equal and the equal of Judge Douglas, and the equal of every other man," he provocatively declared. Douglas, who seemed unsteady, and was ill with bronchitis, sounded desperate. He accused Lincoln of promoting mob violence, rebellion, and even genocide by confining slavery only to the states where it already existed—the very arguments that during the debate of 1850 southern radicals had hurled at any northerner who suggested that slavery must be contained. Without room for slavery to expand, the natural increase of the slave population would lead to catastrophe, Douglas unconvincingly claimed.

The next day, the two men walked down to the Mississippi River, boarded a riverboat, and steamed south to Alton for the final debate. From the speakers' platform that had been set up in the sloping, amphitheater-like city square, they gazed over busy docks piled high with bales, barrels, and crates, riverboats belching smoke from their lofty stacks, and the vast mile-wide expanse of the Mississippi, where the slave state of Missouri was visible across the water. Here Lincoln administered his oratorical coup de grâce. He hammered again on the basic immorality of slavery. "It should *be treated* as a wrong, and one of the methods for treating it as a wrong is *to make provision that it shall grow no larger*," he declared, his high-pitched voice growing shrill. Nothing else had ever so threatened Americans' liberty and prosperity as did slavery. "If this is true, how do you propose to improve the condition of things by enlarging slavery—by spreading it out and making it bigger?" He then went on to the powerful climax of the argument that he had been building since Galesburg: "It is the same spirit that says, 'You work and toil and earn bread, and I'll eat it.' No matter in what shape it comes, whether from the mouth of a king who seeks to bestride the people of his own nation and live by the fruit of their labor, or from one race of men as an apology for enslaving another race, it is the same tyrannical principle."

No mainstream politician had more succinctly articulated the moral dimension of slavery in terms that ordinary white Americans could understand. In doing so, Lincoln had also exposed the fatal flaw in Popular Sovereignty, which Douglas had spent the previous decade denying.

Lincoln may have been the rhetorical winner, but he lost the election. When the returns came in on election night, the voters returned a legislature with a Democratic majority, which, when it met in 1859, reelected Douglas over Lincoln to the U.S. Senate by 54 to 46. But news of the debates rippled far beyond Illinois, introducing Lincoln to a national audience, and transforming him into a contender for the presidency. Lincoln had also, finally, forced the issue of slavery out into the open. Despite his own racist remarks at Charleston, he rose above the conventional bigotry of his time to ask Americans to think more deeply about both race and human rights. He had nothing to gain by suggesting that blacks had rights, too. Abolitionists were never going to vote for Douglas in any case. Lincoln believed that there was a moral line that no amount of Popular Sovereignty could cross.

• • •

Stephen Douglas would achieve his long-standing ambition of winning the Democratic nomination for president in 1860. But by the time he got it, it was a prize of doubtful value. He could not win the election. As a national party, the Democrats were on their way over a cliff. Apart from Illinois, the Republicans had trounced them in the 1858 elections and taken control of the House of Representatives. The Democrats' northern wing now held only one-third as many seats in Congress as it had before the Kansas-Nebraska crisis, and just half as many as the party's southern wing.

At the end of April the Democrats held what was probably their worst convention of the nineteenth century, in Charleston. The atmosphere in the spacious hall of the South Carolina Institute crackled with suspicions, festering resentments, disintegrating loyalties, and on the part of a large majority of southern delegates, outright hatred toward Douglas, whom they never forgave for his words in the Freeport debate, or for his larger failure to throw his weight behind southern territorial demands. Douglas was the party's presumptive nominee: his supporters commanded a majority of the delegates, but not the two-thirds necessary to nominate. (The allocation of delegates was based on state populations rather than on actual voting patterns, giving the northern delegations disproportionate strength, even as their states had migrated toward the Republican Party.) The only hope for the Union, Douglas reiterated, as he had for more than a decade, was Popular Sovereignty. It was, in the end, his only Big Idea; he had no other. The South demanded that the party's platform include a national slave code that explicitly and unequivocally committed the federal government to protect slavery in the territories, a proposition that was unpalatable to northern voters.

William Lowndes Yancey of Alabama, one of the most aggressive fire-eaters of that ever overwrought tribe, upped the ante precipitously by demanding not just support for slavery itself, but a reopening of the overseas slave trade to supply the South's need to expand westward. "If slavery is right per se, if it is right to raise slaves for sale, does it not appear that it's right to import them?" Yancey demanded. "We want negroes cheap, and we want a sufficiency of them, so as to supply the cotton demand of the whole world." This was precisely the sort of thing that was driving northern Democrats out of the party, and Douglas's forces were adamant. "Gentlemen of the South, you mistake us—you mistake us—we will not do it," roared a Douglas delegate from Ohio, who was understood to be speaking for the Little Giant himself. When the convention rejected the radicals' platform, Yancey led eight southern delegations out of the hall. Charleston's secessionist women laid a rose on the chair of each delegate who departed.

With the convention in shambles, Douglas's forces voted to reassemble and try again to nominate their man in Baltimore in June. In the weeks that followed, the rump of the old Whig Party, calling itself the Constitutional Union Party, nominated John Bell of Tennessee on a platform of superlative vagueness: "The Constitution of the Country, The Union of the States, and The Enforcement of the Laws." The Republicans, meeting in Chicago, nominated Lincoln, who overcame an assortment of rivals, among them the redoubtable Seward, whose long-remembered appeal to a "higher law" in 1850 crippled his candidacy among the party's conservatives.

When the Democrats met again in Baltimore, Douglas's forces sufficiently controlled the rules and credentialing that his nomination was assured. Whether southern delegates would acquiesce was an open question, however, until the motion was made to proceed with nominations, and a delegate from Virginia rose solemnly and nervously to announce that his delegation was leaving the hall. They would not vote for Douglas no matter what concessions he offered. The Virginians were followed out of the convention hall by five southern delegations—South Carolina had boycotted the convention entirely, while Florida had shown up but declined to participate—plus the delegates from California and Oregon. Wrote Douglas's biographer Robert W. Johannsen, "As most of the delegates looked on in silence, the Democratic Party destroyed itself." Retiring to their own spur-of-the-moment convention a few blocks away, at

Maryland Institute Hall, the defectors nominated their own ticket, naming the vice president of the United States, John C. Breckinridge of Kentucky, as their candidate for president.

Douglas waged a physically punishing campaign, racing around the country by rail, even into the South, speaking without letup, declared himself unequivocally opposed to secession in a bravura display of the steaming, inexhaustible energy that had carried him from tree-stump speeches in the thrown-together hamlets of frontier Illinois to the United States Senate, and finally to this last churning contest for the presidency. To the last, Douglas behaved like a man certain of victory. In nearly thirty years of political life, he had never lost an election. But his long run of luck ran out on November 6, 1860. He won just 29 percent of the popular vote, 10 percent less than the victorious Lincoln, and a mere twelve electoral votes. He was beaten even by John Bell, and the ghost of the Whigs. Breckinridge swept the Deep South, in most of which the Republican Party was not even on the ballot. It was an omen of what was to come.

Defeat liberated something in Douglas. Opportunist and racist though he might be, he was unequivocally committed to the Union. To the last moment, he kept searching for a formula that would be acceptable to the South. Perhaps, he suggested, rather desperately, Mexico could be brought into the Union as a new slave state? He still clung, even now, with secession and war almost certainly in the offing, to his cherished belief that peace could be preserved by banishing the slavery question from the national agenda. "Nothing will do any good which does not take the slavery question out of Congress forever," he insisted to the New York financier August Belmont on Christmas Day. The way to do it, he told anyone who would listen, was by resuscitating Jefferson Davis's old plan from 1850—by means of a constitutional amendment that would extend the Missouri Compromise line to the Pacific, barring slavery explicitly north of the line, and permitting it to the south. He made clear, however, that no matter what transpired, he would stand by the new president. "I am ready to make any reasonable sacrifice of party tenets to save the country," he told Belmont. It was perhaps his finest moment.

Lincoln had repeatedly made clear that he did not intend to free any slaves, and that he cared more for the principle of white men's right to govern themselves than he did for the fate of all the blacks in Christendom. But the time for compromise was over. South Carolina seceded on December 20. "Experience has proved that slaveholding States cannot be safe in subjection to non-slaveholding States," South Carolinians declared, in an address explaining their action to the rest of the South. "United together, and we must be a great, free and prosperous people, whose renown must spread throughout the civilized world, and pass down, we trust, to the remotest ages. We ask you to join us in forming a Confederacy of Slaveholding States." Mississippi, Florida, Alabama, Georgia, and Louisiana followed in January. In 1850, Sam Houston could still sincerely insist, as he did during the Compromise debate, that nonslaveowning southern whites would never go to war to defend secession. "Go to the yeomanry, the hard-handed men of the country," Houston had cried. They would never risk their homes and security for disunion. "Never! Never will they do it, sir! I say the South will hug the Union to her heart as the last blessing of Heaven." In the winter of 1861, as one by one the states of the South peeled away from the Union and armed themselves for war, such former verities seemed outlandishly, even pathetically, quaint. Houston, serving yet again as governor as the tide of secessionist fever washed over Texas, resisted disunion to the last. "The Union is worth more than Mr. Lincoln, and if the battle is to be fought for the Constitution, let us fight it in the Union and for the sake of the Union," he pleaded, to no avail. Denounced, threatened, and demonized, Houston was overthrown by what was, in effect, a coup carried out by delegates to an extralegal Secession Convention, which on February 1, 1861, declared overwhelmingly for disunion, proclaimed the governor's office vacant, and named a secessionist in his place.

• • •

A few days later, Jefferson Davis departed his plantation to become president of the Confederate States of America. Slaves rowed him from Brierfield out into the Mississippi River to catch the steamboat to Vicksburg, whence he traveled by train to the temporary Confederate capital at Montgomery, Alabama. All along the way, he was saluted by enthusiastic crowds of men and women, salvos of artillery, and martial displays by local militias. The South's only hope, he declared to the mass rally that greeted him at the depot in Montgomery, was to make its enemies smell southern powder and feel southern steel. "Our separation from the Union is complete," he shouted, to tremendous applause. "NO COMPROMISE; NO RECONSTRUCTION CAN NOW BE ENTERTAINED."

On April 12, at four-thirty in the morning, a signal shell fired from a gun positioned on James Island in Charleston harbor sketched an elegant arc over the bay, and burst immediately above the red-brick walls of Fort Sumter. Within fifteen minutes, more batteries positioned on Sullivan's Island and Cumming Point went to work hurling shot at the fort, while Charlestonians thronged gaily to various points of observation to watch the show, and to enjoy the strange whirr of hurtling shells, as plumes of dust and clouds of smoke rose from the fort's walls into the dawn light. The war that had been postponed for so long had come.

Within a month after Fort Sumter's surrender, Virginia, Arkansas, Tennessee, and North Carolina had also left the Union. Stephen Douglas finally abandoned his last hope of reconciliation. He had strained for a decade to placate the South—he had gone to "the very extreme of magnanimity." In return, he moaned, the South had declared war. He could do nothing more: "There can be no neutrals in this war, *only patriots—or traitors.*" Douglas's considerable oratorical talents, not to mention his residual popularity among Democrats who remained ambivalent about war, would surely have proved an invaluable asset to the administration's war effort. But it would never be. His health ruined by stress, overwork, and dissolute living, he died on June 3, only forty-eight years old.

By now, many of the players in the drama of 1850 had passed from the scene, some from death or old age, some as the result of political defeat. But others remained. Seward, defeated in his hope of winning the Republican nomination in 1860, became Lincoln's secretary of state and his closest cabinet adviser. Millard Fillmore, after his reputation-wrecking flirtation with the Know Nothing movement, subsided into grumpy criticism of the war effort, and in the election of 1864 supported Lincoln's Democratic challenger, General George McClellan. John Hale remained a stalwart voice for antislavery in the Senate throughout the war, though at its end he would be embarrassed by the revelation that his daughter's favorite beau was a certain actor and Confederate spy named John Wilkes Booth. John C. Frémont served as the Federal military governor of Missouri, and then in command of an army in the Shenandoah Valley, where in 1862 he was trounced in one of Stonewall Jackson's most decisive victories. Douglas's right-hand man in the House of Representatives, John McClernand, rose to lead an army corps under William Tecumseh Sherman. Jefferson Davis would serve until 1865 as the first and only president of the Confederate States of America, with Alexander Stephens as his vice president. Howell Cobb and Robert Toombs saw battle as generals in the Confederate Army. Henry Foote, who opposed secession longer than most Mississippians, finally threw his support to the Confederacy and became a member of its Congress, where he proved as irritating to his colleagues and to Jefferson Davis as he had in the United States Senate. Sam Houston remained a Unionist to the end, dying ill and isolated in June 1863, having freed his dozen slaves in a last act of defiance against Texas's law against voluntary manumission.

On March 28, 1862, a column of 1,300 troopers from the 4th, 5th, and 6th Texas Mounted Volunteers entered a narrow defile known as Glorieta Pass, twenty miles east of Santa Fe, in the New Mexico Territory. They were a hardy bunch, most of them frontiersmen, Indian fighters, ex-Rangers, and Mexican War veterans. Dressed now in dusty and sweat-stained Confederate gray, they were about to initiate the westernmost battle of the Civil War. They had left San Antonio in October

1861, under the command of Brigadier General Henry Sibley following the road blazed by Robert Neighbors in the winter of 1850, first west to El Paso, then north along the Rio Grande, defeating a Federal force at Fort Craig, capturing Albuquerque, and then Santa Fe, over which they raised the flag of the Confederacy, fulfilling the Texan ambition of annexing the territory that unreconstructed Texan expansionists believed they had been cheated of by the Compromise of 1850.

Their immediate objective was Fort Union, the linchpin of defense on the Santa Fe Trail, seventy miles north of Glorieta Pass. If they were victorious, they hoped to capture Denver and its rich mining region, and then march west to invade Utah and California, thus bringing to completion the southern dream of a slave-based empire extending to the Pacific Ocean. At Glorieta Pass, the Confederates crashed into a scratch force of Colorado volunteers and Federal regulars under the command of a Denver attorney named John Slough. They came together in a stupendous landscape of sweeping red-rock bluffs, wind-chiseled crags, and piñon forest, fighting bushwhacker-style behind boulders and cottonwoods, falling and dying with the sweet scent of sage and mesquite in their nostrils. Although the numbers involved were small by the standards of eastern warfare, the action was sharp and bloody. The Confederates tried three times to storm the Union line, but were cut down by cannon positioned around the outbuildings of Pigeon's Ranch. The outnumbered Federals slowly withdrew up the Santa Fe Trail, forming a defensive line across the road. Meanwhile, however, a five-hundred-man Yankee force circled in a wide arc across the mesa that flanked the pass on the east, unseen by the main body of Confederates. While fighting raged in the pass, these men suddenly appeared in the Confederate rear, sliding and tumbling down the steep slopes of the canyon to destroy the entire Rebel supply train, sixty wagons in all, wiping out their supplies and ammunition, taking prisoners, and destroying at a single stroke what hope the Confederates had of marching any further north.

"It is with sorrow that I tell you of the death of so many of yours and my friends who have fallen in the two Battles we have fought in this worthless Territory," a defeated Confederate soldier wrote to his parents. What was left of the command, he concluded, "leavs tomorrow morning before light, and it is so dark that I must git." By the end of May, the Texans were gone from New Mexico, and with them the southern dream of a slave empire in the West.

Two weeks after the Confederate debacle at Glorieta Pass, just days after he received news of the appalling slaughter at Shiloh, the bloodiest battle of the war to date, Abraham Lincoln completed the unfinished moral business of the Compromise of 1850 by signing into law a piece of legislation couched in the typically bloodless language of Congress. "All persons held to service or labor within the District of Columbia by reason of African descent are hereby discharged and freed of and from all claim to such service or labor," the act declared, "and from and after the passage of this act neither slavery nor involuntary servitude, except for crime, whereof the party shall be duly convicted, shall hereafter exist in said District." In short, it declared the 3,100 slaves in the nation's capital free, in the first act of emancipation by the Federal government in the nation's history. The signing took place without fanfare, and with comparatively little attention from the press, which after all was largely preoccupied, as was the president, with the maneuvering of the republic's immense armies for their spring campaigns. But in its way the movement of Lincoln's pen across the page was no less bold an assault against the bulwarks of the rebellion than the shot hurled by the howitzers and field guns that pounded the armies of the Confederacy. In freeing the enslaved men and women of the District of Columbia, Lincoln, who had proclaimed when he took office as president that he did not intend to end slavery, took his first step toward broader emancipation.

Every black church in Washington held special services of prayer and thanksgiving. A supercilious white observer recalled, "The proceedings did not always conform to the established rites for public worship, as church members were singing, shouting, praying, weeping, or jumping, all without direction from the pulpit." But *The Christian Recorder,* the newspaper of the AME Church, captured the real spirit of the day: "All hail the day of emancipation here!" its correspondent wrote, throwing objectivity to the winds, and plunging into the volcanic joy that was erupting around him. "All hail the day of prospective emancipation everywhere! Aha! Thou rattle-snake, slavery! And art thou at last humbled in the dust? FREEDOM—ALL HAIL!"

Five months later, following the September bloodbath at Antietam, Lincoln announced the Emancipation Proclamation. It took effect on January 1, 1863, and declared free all slaves in every state that was in rebellion against the United States. Where Union armies marched, slaves in ever-swelling numbers dropped their tools and followed them into freedom.

For at least some ordinary soldiers, the remembered words of the debate of 1850 lingered on amid the carnage and fear of sudden death, distilling just what it was they were fighting for. Years later, in a letter to a Massachusetts senator, a former Union infantryman wrote that he had kept up his courage as he paced up and down as a sentinel in an exposed place by repeating over and over, "Liberty and Union now and forever, one and inseparable."

In 1902, Andrew J. Harlan, the last surviving member of the Thirty-first Congress, then eighty-seven, published his recollections of the great debate, in which he had participated as a member of the House from Indiana. After fifty-two years, his memory of Henry Clay "bounding up like a meteor," of Daniel Webster invoking the spirit of Nathan Hale, of the bored Sam Houston whittling wooden bears and snakes from pine boards while their colleagues pleaded, poetized, and harangued each other across the floor was still intense. "In this Congress," Harlan wrote, "there was but one great overshadowing question—that of slavery. Members were subjected to but one inquiry: 'Are you for the extension of slavery or against it?' I do not think anyone can form an adequate idea of the bitterness and intensity of partisan feeling that prevailed. It resembled nothing so much as a bundle of combustible material to which every spoken word was as a spark. Often this spoken word was dropped, and the great mass flared terribly and was smothered only by strenuous effort, but there was a consciousness that such a conflagration once lighted must sweep on and engulf the nation."

As pure theater, the debate was unsurpassed in American history. Indeed, as Senator William Dayton of New Jersey said of the debate, "It has gone up in our political sky like some splendid specimen of pyrotechnic art, attracting by its show the gaze of the country far and wide." It is not always easy to empathize with the men of 1850, much less with the opinions that they expressed. Many beliefs that were commonplace in the mid-nineteenth century, especially surrounding the issue of race, are deeply repellent today. Through the distorting lens of hindsight, we inevitably see the drama's central players very differently from the ways in which they were seen in their own time. Abolitionists such as Seward, Hale, and Chase were far in advance of their age in their enlightened concern for human rights, but were shamelessly pilloried then as madmen, subversives, or worse. As judged today, Calhoun, Davis, and their fellow radicals, meanwhile, seem perverse and twisted, though their opinions were then perfectly respectable in most of the South. And the two greatest statesmen of all, Clay and Webster, can too easily seem like mere hypocrites who failed to catch, or who willfully ignored, the great wave of human liberation that was gathering in their own backyards. They all lived in an age when the range of what was politically possible was, as it is in most eras, frustratingly narrow.

But within the cramped orbit of the possible, there were many displays of remarkable political courage: Clay's unflagging struggle to seek out common ground, Seward's lonely stand against slavery, President Taylor's clumsy but stalwart opposition to slavery's expansion, Webster's suicidal defiance of his New England constituency, and even the monumentally annoying Henry Foote's decision to defy his section's rush to secession by embracing compromise. Their courage mattered: compromise was not inevitable. Winners and losers alike collaborated to force the most painful issue Americans faced onto the national agenda. By doing so they saved the Union for a few crucial years.

Like Andrew Harlan, few who sat in either the Senate or the House during that epic debate doubted that the survival of the nation hung in the balance. Wrought in a political landscape more fraught with danger than any the country previously had faced, the Compromise was in many respects a brilliant if imperfect confection. It overcame the crippling paralysis that had gripped Congress, and showed that even in a fiercely partisan climate compromise and collaboration were possible, if politicians were willing to take risks, act creatively, and persevere. As aggrieved as southern radicals sounded, the Slave Power got more from the Compromise than it gave. True, the North won the admission of California as a free state, and a nominal majority in the Senate. And the nation as a whole was well served by the Texas boundary bill, which halted that state's rush to war and, legally at least, settled its claim to New Mexico. (The assumption of Texas's debt was also the first federal bailout of a state in American history.) However, the South obtained the harsh new Fugitive Slave Law that it had long sought, as well as the North's tacit abandonment of the hated Wilmot Proviso, which would have barred slavery from new territories. The bills to organize New Mexico and Utah were also clear southern victories, since by failing to explicitly prohibit slavery in those vast regions they tacitly opened the West to it. The District of Columbia bill terminated the slave trade there, but decisively squashed abolitionist hopes of putting an end to slavery itself in the nation's capital. "A shrewd defender of slavery," the historian Paul Finkelman has written, could expect the measure to "reduce the growth of antislavery sentiment by removing an aggravating practice that was always in the face of antislavery members without actually harming slavery."

In the course of the decade that followed, however, almost every one of these measures, which had been crafted with such ingenuity, weakened and buckled. California's Democratic senators voted consistently with the South, making the North's nominal majority meaningless. The Fugitive Slave Law became a dead letter across most of the North. The slave trade, expelled from Washington, merely moved across the Potomac to Virginia, where it continued to thrive. Peonage, which was slavery by another name, flourished on the "free" soil of California and in the New Mexico Territory.

For Indian peoples who had never asked to be ruled by the United States, the Compromise was an unmitigated catastrophe. Texans pushed steadily westward in a pitiless race war, driving the tribes before them, breaking up reservations, leaving hundreds if not thousands to perish from disease and starvation resulting from the destruction of their towns and food supply. Few whites attempted to stand in their way. (Robert Neighbors was shotgunned in the back and killed in 1859 for attempting to defend some of the few Indians left in the state.) In California, tribes were hunted down and butchered wholesale. Entrepreneurial whites "indentured" many of the survivors as agricultural slaves under laws based on southern slave codes that bound them to their masters, and punished anyone who attempted to "entice" them away. Before the Gold Rush, California's native population was at least 150,000. "You couldn't go amiss for them," Horace Bell, a Yankee emigrant, commented. "Mountain and valley, forest and plain, were covered with Indians." By 1860, there were only thirty thousand.

Despite all this, as an achievement of the art of politics, the Compromise must be judged a success, albeit a temporary one. Failure would have meant war, with its first shots fired at Santa Fe instead of Fort Sumter. Even if Texas had suffered an initial defeat, southerners were ready to rush to her aid. The North, if it had any stomach for war at all in 1850, would likely have lost. Large numbers of southerners had come to accept secession as politically reasonable, economically rational, and morally justified; few northerners, however, were prepared to fight a war for the Union, much less to end slavery. There was nothing in the North to compare with the flaming war fever that was epidemic in the newspapers of the Lower South, and the fiery letters that war-hungry men from South Carolina to Mississippi sent to the leaders of Texas, begging for a chance to fight for slavery. Had secession taken place peacefully in 1850, the South would have set a precedent that in time might well have splintered what remained of the United States still further. The United States might then have evolved into a congeries of states—a Pacific Republic, a federation of New England, another of the upper Midwest—competitive with one another, vulnerable to foreign interference, and perhaps chronically at war. A truncated United States would never have become a globe-striding power, or a beacon of liberty for the rest of the world, but more likely a second-tier state like Germany or France. And while an independent South might have continued paying lip service to the democracy of Jefferson and Jackson (for whites at least), in practice it would probably have evolved into a permanent model not of freedom but of tyranny resembling apartheid South Africa. That none of this happened, we owe to the compromisers of 1850.

It is tempting to suppose that another "comprehensive adjustment" might have staved off Civil War in 1861, that if Henry Clay had lived he might have somehow worked his old compromise magic once again. This is fantasy. Capable political men, including Stephen Douglas, tried to emulate Clay in 1861 and failed. There had always been only one practical, peaceful way to end slavery, but it was politically impossible. Gradual, compensated emancipation had long been advocated by some Whigs, including William Seward. Even *without* compensation, in the late eighteenth and early nineteenth centuries it had proved workable in the North, where slaves were admittedly fewer in number, but where the institution, especially in New York and New Jersey, was deeply entrenched. Purchasing, emancipating, and educating the nearly four million enslaved people of the South would have required an enormous public investment, but it would still have been far cheaper than the cost of the Civil War, in both blood and treasure. Slave owners, however, had no interest in disencumbering themselves of a form of wealth that reproduced itself every generation. Nor, sadly, were most northerners prepared to welcome a flood of free blacks into their communities, competing for their jobs, and challenging their own ideas about racial superiority.

The once common notion that slavery, if left alone, would have faded away naturally is also nonsense. Far from shrinking, the number of American slaves *quadrupled* in the years between 1800 and 1860. As

Jefferson Davis and other spokesmen for the South repeatedly made clear during the debate of 1850, slavery was not coincidental to the sectional crisis; it lay at the core of it. Slavery, they told their colleagues, and the nation, was nothing to apologize for, but rather to be celebrated as the foundation of southern prosperity and the engine of its future development. They believed in slavery: its steady expansion was part of their version of the American dream. Slavery, wrote William Henry Trescot, a South Carolinian who served as James Buchanan's assistant secretary of state, "informs all our habits of thought, lies at the basis of our political faith and of our social existence. In a word, for all that we are, we believe ourselves, under God, indebted to the institution of slavery—for a national existence, a well ordered liberty, a prosperous agriculture, an exulting commerce, a free people and a firm government." Nothing was made more clear by Jefferson Davis and his allies in the debate of 1850 than that slavery wanted still more *lebensraum* into which to expand, westward to the Pacific, and southward into the Caribbean Basin. "With Cuba and St. Domingo [the island of Hispaniola] we could control the productions of the tropics, and with them the commerce of the world," Congressman Albert Gallatin Brown of Mississippi declared in mid-decade. "I want Tamaulipas, Potosi, and one or two other Mexican states, and I want them all for the same reason—for the planting and spreading of slavery." So central was the annexation of Cuba for slavery to American foreign policy that in his last State of the Union address, Buchanan spent more time discussing his efforts to acquire it than he did the secession crisis in South Carolina.

During the decade that was purchased by the Compromise of 1850, the North's advantages in population, industrial production, and transportation steadily grew. By 1860, northerners outnumbered southerners by seven million people, nearly twice as many as in 1850, while northern states added almost twice as many miles of railroad, and built four times as many ships as the seceding states, and overwhelmed the value of goods manufactured in the South by a factor of eleven. But it took more to win the Civil War than factory output: it required will. In the course of the 1850s, as slavery continued to gnaw at the nation's political vitals, as the slave-owning South continued to demand more territory, more constitutional privileges than its shrinking proportion of the population warranted, and more control over the federal government, white Americans increasingly understood that the erosion of their own rights was tied to the fate of enslaved blacks, and that the continued enslavement of the federal government to the Slave Power meant diminishing freedom for all. Paradoxically, the compromise that was meant to tranquilize the nation and quiet antislavery agitation forever unintentionally but irrevocably lit the fires of liberty far and wide across the states of the North, awakening Americans to the thing that Stephen Douglas never cared about, that Henry Clay chose not to see, that Daniel Webster forgot: the moral dimension of slavery, and its corruption of the nation's entire body politic. The measure most hateful to black Americans helped transform white Americans into soldiers who would fight and die to liberate a people who only a few years earlier they feared and despised.

Before the debate, it was still possible to seriously suggest, as Zachary Taylor had done, that the United States give back to Mexico most of what it had conquered. By the time it ended, such talk had disappeared. The United States no longer aspired to an empire: it had one. The Compromise transformed "Manifest Destiny" from a slogan into a pacification policy for the Wild West, embodied in territorial governments, military installations, westbound wagon trains and railway lines, displaced and slaughtered Indians, and the diffusion of land-hungry Americans from the Missouri River to the Pacific. As historian Robert Kagan has written, the southern version of Manifest Destiny, in particular, became "a politician's trick, to talk of America's civilizing mission and the beneficent spread of its political institutions, when southerners insisted that among the blessings they would bring to newly absorbed peoples was slavery." The Mexican War taught Americans that their foreign wars would always be easy, their victories glorious, and their messy aftermaths simple to overcome with goodwill, incantatory appeals to democracy, and, sometimes, harsh repression. The Compromise enabled the United States to consolidate the continental power that it had seized in the Mexican War, and eventually to build upon its foundation an imperial career that would continue unabated through the rest of the nineteenth century and take new form in the twentieth.

ACKNOWLEDGMENTS

———— ·◆· ————

Throughout the writing of *America's Great Debate*, I benefitted from the constant encouragement of United States Senate Historian Donald A. Ritchie and his predecessor Richard Allan Baker, who patiently fielded countless queries, and shared with me both their rich insights into the workings and personalities of the antebellum Senate, and the resources of their office. They helped to make this a far better book than it might otherwise have been. Brian McLaughlin opened to me the doors of the Senate Library, while Senate Curator Diane Skvarla and assistant curator Amy Burton invited me to witness the restoration of the long lost portrait of Henry Clay by Phineas Staunton that now hangs in the Capitol. Emily Claire Howie of the Library of Congress was exceptionally helpful during the initial phase of my research, drawing my attention to many documents that I would never have found without her. The staff of the LOC's manuscript collection was once again unflagging in their efforts to answer my research inquiries. At a time when attacks against the federal government have grown feral, these individuals and departments represent sterling examples of public money well spent in the greater public interest.

Many colleagues and friends enriched this book in ways great and small, pointing me toward new sources, and challenging me both to deepen my thinking, and to rethink ill-planned lines of research before they led me into the deep weeds of irrelevance. At the risk of overlooking others, I owe particular thanks to Orville Vernon Burton, whose support has been unbounded, as well as to Kathleen Burke, Lydia Chavez, Rebecca Edwards, Paul Finkelman, Stanley Harrold, Graham Russell Gao Hodges, Jill Jonnes, Kate Clifford Larson, David Lipton, Randy K. Mills, Bernard Powers, Milton Sernett, and Emory Thomas. Conversations with Henry Clay biographer Robert V. Remini and Mark J. Stegmaier, whose meticulous *Texas, New Mexico, and the Compromise of 1850* provided an invaluable key to an unusually intricate phase of southwestern history, were more valuable to me than perhaps they knew.

Expert assistance from research libraries and archives at many institutions made my work immeasurably easier. Among these were the Filson Historical Society, in Louisville; the United States Military Academy at West Point; Harvard University's Houghton Library; the Princeton University Library; the Margaret I. King Library at the University of Kentucky; the Bancroft Library at the University of California Berkeley; the South Carolina Historical Society; the Texas State Library and Archives at Austin; the Center for American History and the Nettie Lee Benson Center at University of Texas, Austin; and the splendid new New Mexico State Records Center and Archives, at Santa Fe, where Samuel Sisneros spent much of his valuable time helping me make my way through many manuscript collections and other sources. Jennifer Haines of the Seward House Museum, in Auburn, NY, provided me with important documentation testifying to William Seward's assistance to fugitive slaves.

My good friend Maggie Rivas-Rodriguez of the University of Texas was a generous host to me in Austin, and along with her colleagues Dan Arellano and Emilio Zamora helped to illuminate for me the history of pre-independence Texas, the Texas Republic, and the early statehood period from a Latino point of view. In New Mexico, John "Pen" LaFarge was, as he has often been, both generous with his own keen insights and with introductions to others, in particular Tomas Jaehn of the Fray

Angelico Chavez History Library in Santa Fe, who ferreted out documents that I would surely have otherwise overlooked. Jerome V. Reel was an exceptionally charming companion during my visit to Clemson University and the home of John C. Calhoun. Bettis C. Rainsford and Tricia Price Glenn were kind hosts and guides during a day spent in Edgefield, South Carolina, which perhaps more than any other district of its size embodied the spirit and values of the antebellum Deep South.

Without the constant encouragement of my editor, Bob Bender, and my agent, Elyse Cheney, this book would have been no more than a mere gleam in its author's eye.

NOTES

The record of debates in the United States Senate and House of Representatives was published under the successive titles of the *Annals of Congress*, from 1789 to 1824; the *Register of Congressional Debates*, from 1824 to 1837; and the *Congressional Globe*, from 1833 to 1873. In the notes that follow, these have been abbreviated as *Annals*, *Register*, and *CG*. The sessions of Congress have similarly been abbreviated: 31/1, for instance, refers to the Thirty-first Congress, First Session.

PROLOGUE

Page

5 *"When my services":* CG, 31/1, App., p. 115ff.

8 *"as much the law":* Quoted in George C. Herring, *From Colony to Superpower*, p. 139.

8 *"wanton violation":* James K. Polk Papers, No. 47, Library of Congress.

8 *"Let our arms":* *Brooklyn Daily Eagle*, May 11, 1846.

9 *"Away, away":* John L. O'Sullivan, "Annexation," *United States Magazine and Democratic Review*, Vol. 17, July–August 1845.

9 *"More, more, more":* Quoted in Robert D. Sampson, *John L. O'Sullivan and His Times*, pp. 200–201.

9 *"The Mississippi, so lately":* James K. Polk statement to Congress, December 5, 1848. Online at www.presidency.ucsb.edu.

10 *"Of all the dangers":* Calvin Colton, ed., *The Life, Correspondence, and Speeches of Henry Clay*, Vol. 3, pp. 58–65.

10 *"all is wilderness":* Quoted in Robert V. Remini, *Daniel Webster*, p. 647.

10 *"I would not care"*: *The North Star*, June 15, 1849.

11 *"ignorance, vice, bigotry"*: Quoted in Richard Kluger, *Seizing Destiny*, pp. 444–45.

11 *"Nations and races"*: Quoted in Reginald Horsman, *Race and Manifest Destiny*, p. 137.

11 *Slavery was growing*: David L. Cohn, *The Life and Times of King Cotton*, pp. 116, 83.

11 *"Niggers and cotton"*: Quoted in ibid., p. 52.

12 *"The day that"*: Ross M. Lence, ed., *Union and Liberty*, p. 516.

12 *"A vague, indefinite"*: Ibid., p. 518.

12 *"morbid sympathy"*: Quoted in William W. Freehling, *The Road to Disunion*, p. 458.

13 *"a perfect firebrand"*: Adam Beatty to Thomas B. Stevenson, January 11, 1847, Adam Beatty Papers, Filson Historical Society, Louisville, Kentucky.

CHAPTER 1: "A FRENZY SEIZED MY SOUL"

Page

17 *Accounts of Marshall's first words*: Johann A. Sutter, *New Helvetia Diary*, April 1838, March 1844, May 1847, January–February 1848; Sutter, "Personal Reminiscences," pp. 1ff, 153–55, 160–62; Thomas O. Larkin to James Buchanan, April 12, 1844, Consular Letters, Vol. 1, Justin H. Smith Collection, Nettie Benson Center, University of Texas, Austin; *New York Herald*, June 27, 1849; *San Francisco Chronicle*, February 9, 1856; *Frank Leslie's Illustrated Newspaper*, July 10, 1880; David L. Bigler, *The Gold Discovery Journal of Azariah Smith*; Hubert H. Bancroft, *History of California*, pp. 26–41; Edward E. Dunbar, *The Romance of the Age*, pp. 106–7, 113–15; Erwin G. Gudde, *Bigler's Chronicle of the West*, p. 82ff; Theressa Gay, *James W. Marshall*, pp. 34–51, 126ff, 145ff, 161–62.

19 *"It appeared that"*: *Century Magazine*, Vol. 61, February 1891.

20 *General Stephen Kearny*: "Lt. William Helmsley Emory's Journal of General Stephen Watts Kearny's March to Santa Fe," *Niles's Weekly Register*, October 31, November 7, 14, 1846; Larkin to Buchanan, January 14, 1847, June 30, 1847, August 25, 1847, Consular Letters, Vol. 1, Nettie Benson Center; *The Californian*, August 29, 1846; Kluger, pp. 452–57; Hampton Sides, *Blood and Thunder*, pp. 33, 116–34; Joseph Wheelan, *Invading Mexico*, pp. 221–23.

21 "A frenzy seized": Quoted in Mary Crosley-Griffin, *Hangtown*, pp. 4–5.

22 "Male and female": *New York Herald*, January 1, 1849.

22 "What will this": Ibid., January 11, 1849.

22 "I am a friend": *CG* 30/2, p. 257.

23 "a dull, phlegmatic": Oliver Dyer, *Great Senators of the United States Forty Years Ago*, p. 45.

23 "Let them come": Quoted in Elbert B. Smith, *The Presidencies of Zachary Taylor and Millard Fillmore*, p. 37.

23 "I pity those": Sam Houston to Margaret Houston, February 8, 1849, in Madge Thornall Roberts, ed., *The Personal Correspondence of Sam Houston*, Vol. 3, p. 69.

24 "sleeping forty years": Quoted in Robert V. Remini, *Henry Clay*, p. 710.

24 "unnecessary and senseless": Zachary Taylor to R. C. Wood, October 12, 1847, Zachary Taylor Papers, Special Collections, King Library, University of Kentucky, Lexington.

24 "I am much satisfied": Taylor to J. W. Webb, Taylor Papers, University of Kentucky.

24 "It is now evident": Taylor to Wood, October 12, 1847, Taylor Papers, University of Kentucky.

25 "My opinions, even": Quoted in Brainerd Dyer, "Zachary Taylor and the Election of 1848," *The Pacific Historical Review*, June 1940.

26 "The salubrity of": *CG* 30/2, p. 4ff.

CHAPTER 2: ONE BOLD STROKE

Page

29 *From every state: New York Herald*, January 11, 24, 25, 1849; *New York Tribune*, April 2, June 22, 1849; *Daily Missouri Republican*, March 3, 8, 1849; *The National Era*, November 22, 1849; Malcom E. Barker, *San Francisco Memoirs, 1835–1851*, pp. 181–83, 189–94; Frank Soulé and John H. Gihon, *The Annals of San Francisco*, pp. 214–17.

30 "The discovery of": *CG* 28/2, p. 21.

30 "His legs are": Quoted in Allen C. Guelzo, *Lincoln and Douglas*, p. 7.

31 "Finding myself in": Quoted in Robert W. Johannsen, *Stephen A. Douglas*, p. 15.

31 *"On my way"*: Quoted in Guelzo, *Lincoln and Douglas*, p. 4.

32 *"The people of"*: Quoted in Johannsen, *Stephen A. Douglas*, p. 24.

32 *"I would exert"*: CG 28/2, pp. 95–97, 226–27.

33 *"We of the South"*: Lence, ed., *Union and Liberty*, pp. 559–60.

34 *The situation in California*: Soulé and Gihon, *The Annals of San Francisco*, pp. 211, 227–28; *Daily Missouri Republican*, March 3, 5, 1849; E. Gould Buffum, *Six Months in the Gold Mines*, pp. 65–67; Sutter, "Personal Reminiscences," p. 174ff; H. W. Brands, *The Age of Gold*, pp. 261–62.

34 *"Rarely a day"*: *New York Herald*, June 27, 1849.

34 *"It is as though"*: Ramón Gil Navarro, *The Gold Rush Diary of Ramón Gil Navarro*, p. 28.

34 *"There was nothing"*: James K. Polk, *Diary*, October 3, 1848, Library of Congress.

35 *"It is a fact"*: *Daily Missouri Republican*, March 3, 1849.

35 *"The whole of it"*: CG 30/2, p. 192.

35 *"I wish, sir"*: CG 30/2, p. 193.

CHAPTER 3: "ORDER! ORDER! ORDER!"

Page

36 *"one of the grossest"*: Quoted in Michael A. Morrison, *Slavery and the American West*, p. 100.

36 *"the most servile tool"*: Quoted in ibid., p. 43.

37 *Douglas was careful to obscure*: Stephen A. Douglas to Charles H. Lanphier, August 3, 1850, in Robert W. Johannsen, ed., *The Letters of Stephen A. Douglas*, pp. 189–91; Anita Clinton, "Stephen Arnold Douglas—His Mississippi Experience," *Journal of Mississippi History*, February 1944.

38 *"which, though slight"*: Dyer, *Great Senators of the United States Forty Years Ago*, p. 236.

38 *"the Marx of"*: Richard Hofstadter, *The American Political Tradition*, p. 87ff.

39 *medals were struck*: John Hoyt Williams, *Sam Houston*, p. 265.

39 *"full and equal right"*: Lence, ed., *Union and Liberty*, p. 521.

39 *"Small as they"*: Ibid., pp. 536–37.

39 *It was difficult*: Ibid., p. 513ff.

40 *the petitioners protested*: CG 30/2, p. 33.

40 *"Whereas," intoned Dix: CG* 30/2, pp. 309–10.

41 *"These resolutions are":* Ibid.

41 *"there will be": CG* 30/2, p. 312.

41 *Yulee's father, Moses:* Leonard Dinnerstein and Mary Dal Palsson, eds., *Jews in the South*, p. 52ff; Wickliffe C. Yulee, "Senator Yulee," *The Florida Historical Society Quarterly*, Vol. 2, April 1909.

41 *"gratuitous and wanton": CG* 30/2, p. 313.

42 *"The dangers to which": CG* 30/2, pp. 315–16.

42 *"It is not": CG* 30/2, pp. 314–15.

43 *Hopeful proposals: CG* 30/2, pp. 684–92.

45 *Foote and Cameron began:* Dyer, *Great Senators of the United States Forty Years Ago*, p. 140; Johannsen, *Stephen A. Douglas*, pp. 247–48.

46 *"Never in my life":* Quoted in Morrison, *Slavery and the American West*, p. 103.

46 *"like a monument": Brother Jonathan*, broadside, March 1849.

46 *His speech was awkward:* Online at avalon.law.edu.19th_/taylor.asp; Ben Perley Poore, *Perley's Reminiscences of Sixty Years in the National Metropolis*, Vol. 1, pp. 353–54; Smith, *The Presidencies of Zachary Taylor and Millard Fillmore*, pp. 49–51.

47 *"I think the Administration":* Quoted in Morrison, *Slavery and the American West*, p. 103.

47 *"is not considered":* Ibid., p. 106.

CHAPTER 4: "THAT DEMON QUESTION"

Page

49 *"ought to be":* Quoted in Morrison, *Slavery and the American West*, p. 104.

49 *"We are laying":* J. Ross Browne, *Report of the Debates in the Convention of California, on the Formation of the State Constitution, in September and October, 1849*, pp. 278, 434–35.

50 *"that demon question":* Ibid., pp. 418–19.

50 *"Never did we": The National Era*, November 22, 1849.

51 *"We will find":* Browne, *Report of the Debates in the Convention of California*, p. 200.

51 *"I feel a most":* Levin H. Coe to John C. Calhoun, August 20, 1849, in Clyde Wilson and Shirley Bright Cook, eds., *Papers of John C. Calhoun*, Vol. 27, p. 27.

51 *Slaves were already:* Browne, *Report of the Debates in the Convention of California*, pp. 146, 148; Rudolph M. Lapp, *Blacks in Gold Rush California*, pp. 27, 132, 65–66, 72; Leonard L. Richards, *The California Gold Rush and the Coming of the Civil War*, pp. 59, 68–69.

52 *"Free men of":* Browne, *Report of the Debates in the Convention of California*, p. 139.

52 *"What will be":* Ibid., pp. 140–41.

53 *"What is the":* Ibid., pp. 62–65.

54 *"You may say":* Ibid., p. 187.

54 *settlers in "Deseret":* *The National Era*, November 22, 1849.

55 *"This secures to us":* Browne, *Report of the Debates in the Convention of California*, p. 193.

55 *ineffectual John Sutter:* Sutter, "Personal Reminiscences," pp. 198–200.

56 *In November, Californians:* Richards, *The California Gold Rush and the Coming of the Civil War*, pp. 91–94.

56 *"Now that he":* *Texas State Gazette*, October 20, 1849.

CHAPTER 5: "ULTIMA THULE"

Page

57 *"the Ultima Thule":* Minutes of the New Mexico Bar Association, Sixth Annual Session, p. 29.

57 *"What is New Mexico?":* CG 31/1, App., p. 859ff.

57 *"ten acres to":* CG 31/1, pp. 790–92.

58 *"I doubt whether":* Quoted in Jane Lenz Elder and David J. Weber, *Trading in Santa Fe*, p. xix.

58 *"I can only":* George F. Ruxton, *Adventures in New Mexico and the Rocky Mountains*, p. 189ff.

59 *"How are ye":* Quoted in Ralph E. Twitchell, *The Leading Facts of New Mexico History*, Vol. 2, p. 262.

59 *With relative stability:* (New Orleans) *Daily Delta*, September 8, 1848.

59 *"egotism was as":* Dyer, *Great Senators of the United States Forty Years Ago*, p. 207.

59 *"a unique, robustious":* William N. Chambers, *Old Bullion Benton*, p. xi.

60 *"All the animal":* Dyer, *Great Senators of the United States Forty Years Ago*, pp. 196–97.

60 *"cold, hard, ruthless"*: Ibid., pp. 190–91.

60 *"Why, sir, if"*: Ibid., p. 201.

60 *"If there was"*: Quoted in Chambers, *Old Bullion Benton*, p. 345.

60 *"We respectfully but"*: CG 30/2, p. 33.

61 *"Has Congress any"*: CG 30/2, pp. 312–13, 309.

61 *"Our right to go"*: CG 30/2, p. 33.

61 *Texas's claim to:* Mark J. Stegmaier, *Texas, New Mexico, and the Compromise of 1850*, p. 5ff; William Campbell Binkley, *The Expansionist Movement in Texas*, p. 3ff; W. H. Timmons, "El Paso: The Formative Years," *The Southwestern Historical Quarterly*, Vol. 87, July 1983.

62 *"an Olympian display"*: Kluger, *Seizing Destiny*, p. 353.

62 *"as much the law"*: Quoted in Herring, *From Colony to Superpower*, p. 139.

63 *"Texas must be"*: Stephen F. Austin to Wily Martin, May 30, 1833. Online at www.tamu.edu/ccbn/dewitt/slaveryletters2.

63 *"Near 100 had"*: Quoted in Randolph B. Campbell, *An Empire for Slavery*, pp. 41, 45–46.

64 *"Once its glorious"*: Quoted in Binkley, *The Expansionist Movement in Texas*, p. 31.

64 *Typical reports formed:* J. W. Wilbarger, *Indian Depredations in Texas*, pp. 283, 275, 361–62, 281, 398, 365, 142, 269, 140; T. R. Fehrenbach, *Comanches*, pp. 212, 250–59, 285ff.

65 *"The chain and"*: Dorman H. Winfrey and Michael L. Tate, *The Indian Papers of Texas and the Southwest, 1825–1916*, Vol. 3, p. 78.

65 *"wild cannibals of"*: Quoted in Gary Clayton Anderson, *The Conquest of Texas*, p. 180.

65 *"tributary vassal"*: Charles Adams Gulick, Jr., ed., *The Papers of Mirabeau Buonaparte Lamar*, Vol. 2, pp. 319–22, 324–25.

65 *"cornucopia of the world"*: Quoted in Binkley, *The Expansionist Movement in Texas*, p. 44.

65 *Texas's finances:* Gary Anderson, *The Conquest of Texas*, pp. 196–97; George W. Kendall, *Narrative of the Texan Santa Fe Expedition*, p. 14ff.

65 *"Snakes, lizards, tortoises"*: Kendall, *Narrative of the Texan Santa Fe Expedition*, p. 369.

66 *asked Andrew Jackson:* Sam Houston to Andrew Jackson, February 16, 1844, December 12, 1844, in Donald Day and Harry H. Ullom, eds., *The Autobiography of Sam Houston*, pp. 201, 208.

67 *"The great importance"*: *The Liberator*, February 21, 1844.

67 *Annexation, Clay warned*: Melba Porter Hay, ed., *The Papers of Henry Clay*, Vol. 10, p. 18ff.

67 *In March 1845*: *CG* 28/2, pp. 362–63; Binkley, *The Expansionist Movement in Texas*, pp. 125–26, 166–67; Stegmaier, *Texas, New Mexico and the Compromise of 1850*, pp. 21–23.

67 *"to the end that"*: George T. Wood to James K. Polk, March 23, 1848, Santa Fe Papers, Texas State Library.

68 *"New Mexico does not"*: *Niles's Weekly Register*, Vol. 74, p. 224.

68 *professing "astonishment"*: Spruce Baird to John M. Washington, November 22, 1848, Santa Fe Papers, Texas State Library.

68 *"I shall continue"*: Washington to Baird, November 22, 1848, Santa Fe Papers, Texas State Library.

68 *"packs of human bloodhounds"*: Quoted in Wheelan, *Invading Mexico*, p. 293.

69 *"To yield to"*: Wood to Zachary Taylor, June 30, 1849, Santa Fe Papers, Texas State Library.

69 *"All proceedings not"*: "Proclamation," June 18, 1849, Santa Fe Papers, Texas State Library.

69 *"industry and enterprise"*: Quoted in George Archibald McCall, *New Mexico in 1850*, p. 22.

70 *"crisis of the crisis"*: *CG* 31/1, App., p. 567.

70 *"If you become"*: Online at www.furman.edu/~benson/docs/calhoun.htm.

71 *Calhoun was furious*: Stegmaier, *Texas, New Mexico, and the Compromise of 1850*, pp. 42–44.

CHAPTER 6: OLD HARRY

Page

72 *"Old Harry can"*: J. J. Wycoff to Sam'l Mairs, March 15, 1848, Special Collections, Filson Historical Society, Louisville.

72 *"high-toned chivalric dignity"*: Dyer, *Great Senators of the United States Forty Years Ago*, p. 219.

73 *"Tens of thousands"*: Allan Nevins, ed., *The Diary of Philip Hone, 1828–1851*, Vol. 2, p. 845.

73 *"and Informed her"*: Webb to Snell, March 15, 1848.

73 *"He, my master!"*: Dyer, *Great Senators of the United States Forty Years Ago*, pp. 233–35.

74 *"his imagination frequently"*: Carl Schurz, *Henry Clay*, Vol. 2, p. 410.

74 *Enemies damned him*: Remini, *Henry Clay*, pp. 14, 648ff.

74 *Clay claimed humbler*: Ibid., p. 1ff; David S. Heidler and Jeanne T. Heidler, *Henry Clay*, p. 3ff; J. Drew Harrington, "Henry Clay and the Classics," *The Filson Club Historical Quarterly*, Vol. 61, April 1987.

74 *"an orphan boy"*: Calvin Colton, ed., *Speeches of Henry Clay*, Vol. 2, p. 356.

75 *"I prefer the"*: *Annals* 11/2, pp. 579–80.

75 *"Who has not"*: Calvin Colton, ed., *The Works of Henry Clay* (Federal Edition), p. 202.

76 *"as something snatched"*: *Annals* 15/1, p. 1180.

76 *Clay was forced*: *Annals*, 15/2, pp. 1170–84; *Annals* 16/1, p. 986ff; Remini, *Henry Clay*, p. 177ff; Schurz, *Henry Clay*, Vol. 1, p. 173ff; Daniel W. Howe, *What Hath God Wrought*, p. 17ff.

77 *"set in motion"*: *Annals* 15/2, p. 1170.

77 *"fellow human beings"*: Quoted in Remini, *Henry Clay*, p. 27.

77 *he was harassed*: *The Liberator*, February 15, 1839.

77 *"kindl[ing] a fire"*: *Annals* 15/2, p. 1204.

78 *"If a dissolution"*: Ibid.

78 *One of Clay's*: *Annals* 16/1, pp. 1588–90.

79 *"outrage . . . an unprincipled artifice"*: Alfred Lightfoot, "Henry Clay and the Missouri Question," *Missouri Historical Review*, Vol. 61, January 1967.

79 *"The history of"*: Schurz, *Henry Clay*, Vol. 1, p. 181.

79 *"The words civil war"*: Calvin Colton, ed., *The Private Correspondence of Henry Clay*, p. 61.

80 *"have mercy"*: *Annals* 16/2, pp. 43–44.

80 *"the Great Pacificator"*: Schurz, *Henry Clay*, Vol. 1, p. 193.

80 *The aged Thomas Jefferson*: Thomas Jefferson, *Writings*, pp. 1434, 1447–50.

81 *On average, southern*: Leonard L. Richards, *The Slave Power*, pp. 48–49.

81 *"The slave power"*: Schurz, *Henry Clay*, Vol. 1, p. 195.

82 *"We are the serfs"*: Lence, ed., *Union and Liberty*, p. 320.

82 *a "disease"*: Ibid., p. 341.

82 *"to herself"*: Ibid., p. 361.

83 *"It is not possible"*: Colton, ed., *Speeches of Henry Clay*, Vol. 1, pp. 393, 403.

83 *"forthwith proceed to"*: Quoted in Remini, *Henry Clay*, p. 413.

83 *"Disunion by armed"*: Ibid., p. 414.

83 *"some years of"*: Quoted in Merrill D. Peterson, *The Great Triumvirate*, p. 230.

83 *"The difference between"*: *Register* 22/2, pp. 741–42.

CHAPTER 7: "WE HAVE ANOTHER EPIDEMIC"

Page

85 *"Ambition! I have"*: *Register* 22/2, pp. 741–42.

86 mere *"military chieftain"*: Henry Clay to Francis T. Brooke, January 28, 1825, in Harry L. Watson, *Andrew Jackson vs. Henry Clay*, p. 158.

87 *"Whigs knew each other"*: Quoted in Glyndon G. Van Deusen, *The Jacksonian Era*, p. 97.

87 *"I had rather"*: Quoted in David S. Heidler and Jeanne T. Heidler, *Henry Clay: The Essential American*, p. 300.

88 *"by a singular"*: Colton, ed., *Speeches of Henry Clay*, Vol. 2, p. 356.

88 *"That my nature"*: Dyer, *Great Senators of the United States Forty Years Ago*, pp. 244–45.

88 *"the soul quitting"*: Quoted in Remini, *Henry Clay*, p. 609.

88 When *Clay had first*: Harrington, "Henry Clay and the Classics"; Remini, *Henry Clay*, p. 625ff; Van Deusen, *The Jacksonian Era*, p. 183ff; (Washington) *Daily Intelligencer*, April 17, 1844.

89 *a Clay rally*: Leonard S. Kenworthy, "Henry Clay at Richmond in 1842," *Indiana Magazine of History*, Vol. 30, December 1934; Charles W. Osborn et al., "Henry Clay at Richmond: The Abolition Petition," *Indiana Quarterly Magazine of History*, Vol. 4, September 1908.

90 *"There is no doubt"*: Clay to Calvin Colton, October 26, 1844, in Hay, ed., *Papers of Henry Clay*, Vol. 10, p. 138.

90 *"Bad news needs"*: William H. Seward to Clay, November 7, 1844, in Hay, ed., *Papers of Henry Clay*, Vol. 10, pp. 141–42.

90 *"there would have"*: Quoted in Remini, *Henry Clay*, p. 668.

90 In an *intriguing*: Gary J. Kornblith, "Rethinking the Coming of the Civil War: A Counterfactual Exercise," *The Journal of American History*, June 2003.

91 Clay *tried again*: Remini, *Henry Clay*, pp. 689, 698ff; Schurz, *Henry Clay*, Vol. 2, pp. 290–92; Heidler and Heidler, *Henry Clay*, p. 419ff.

91 *"We should not"*: Richard Hewes to Orlando Brown, April 24, 1848, Orlando Brown Papers, Filson Historical Society, Louisville.

91 *"War unhinges society"*: In Hay, ed., *Papers of Henry Clay*, Vol. 10, p. 361ff.

92 *"I shall hardly"*: Clay to Thomas B. Stevenson, January 31, 1849, in ibid., p. 568.

92 *"bilious cholick"*: Clay to Lucretia Hart Clay, August 13, 1849, in ibid., p. 611.

92 *"In Kentucky, we"*: Clay to Mary S. Bayard, June 16, 1849, in ibid., p. 602.

92 *Cassius M. Clay: True American*, August 15, 1845, and "Annex," Cassius M. Clay Papers, Filson Historical Society, Louisville.

93 *"I should rejoice"*: In Hay, ed., *Papers of Henry Clay*, Vol. 10, p. 361ff.

93 *"inveigled away"*: Clay to James B. Clay, September 3, October 2, 1849; Clay to Lucretia Clay, September 5, 1849; Clay to L. Hodges, September 15, 1849, in ibid., pp. 614–16, 620.

93 *"If the principle"*: Clay to Richard Pindell, February 11, 1849, in ibid., pp. 574–80.

95 *"be like baling"*: Browne, *Report of the Debates in the Convention of California*, p. 146.

95 *"Henry Clay's true"*: Quoted in Merrill D. Peterson, *The Great Triumvirate: Webster, Clay, and Calhoun*, pp. 378–79.

96 *"thorough pro-slavery man"*: Harold D. Tallant, *Evil Necessity*, p. 148ff; Ivan E. McDougle, *Slavery in Kentucky*, pp. 123–24.

96 *"They quarreled about"*: John W. Finnell to Orlando Brown, dated 1849, Brown Papers, Filson Historical Society, Louisville.

97 *"The right of property"*: Quoted in Tallant, *Evil Necessity*, p. 155.

97 *Always disposed to:* Clay to Morton McMichael, April 17, 1849; Clay to Stevenson, June 18, 1849, in Hay, ed., *Papers of Henry Clay*, Vol. 10, pp. 588, 604.

97 *"I confess that"*: Clay to Robert S. Hamilton, October 2, 1849, in ibid., p. 621.

97 *"There is no"*: Quoted in Tallant, *Evil Necessity*, p. 158.

CHAPTER 8: THE CITY OF MAGNIFICENT INTENTIONS

Page

98 *"[I] shall go"*: Henry Clay to Joseph R. Underwood, February 11, 1849, in Hay, ed., *The Papers of Henry Clay*, Vol. 10, p. 569.

98 *"to be a calm"*: Clay to Mary S. Bayard, June 16, 1849, in ibid., p. 602.

98   *"some capital scheme"*: Thomas B. Stevenson to Adam Beatty, December 12, 1849, Adam Beatty Papers, Filson Historical Society, Louisville.

98   *"buoyant and elastic"*: Ibid.

98   *"For seven days"*: Sam Houston to Margaret Houston, December 3, 1848, in Day and Herbert, eds., *The Autobiography of Sam Houston*, p. 220.

99   *"pester him to death"*: Nevins, ed., *Diary of Philip Hone*, Vol. 2, p. 877.

99   *"I stand pledged"*: *Lexington Observer*, December 5, 1849.

99   *Physically drained, Clay*: Clay to Bayard, December 14, 1849; Clay to Susan Jacob Clay, December 15, 1849; Clay to Lucretia Hart Clay, January 2, 1850; Clay to Leslie Combs, January 22, 1850; Clay to Nicholas Dean, June 21, 1849; Clay to Thomas B. Stevenson, June 30, 1849, in Hay, ed., *Papers of Henry Clay*, Vol. 10, pp. 632–33, 642, 651, 605.

100 *city of "magnificent intentions"*: Charles Dickens, *American Notes*, pp. 125–30.

101 *"It increases the"*: Houston to Margaret Houston, February 25, 1849, in Roberts, ed., *Personal Correspondence of Sam Houston*, Vol. 3, p. 82.

101 *"As we got"*: George Bryant to Arodus Bryant, May 5, 1851, U.S. Senate Historical Office, tourism file; Isaac Bassett, Manuscript Memoir, U.S. Senate Library.

103 *"One could neither"*: Jane G. Swisshelm, *Half a Century*, pp. 128–29; Robert Remini, *Daniel Webster*, p. 307.

103 *regional center of slave trading*: Frederic Bancroft, *Slave Trading in the Old South*, p. 47ff; Stanley Harrold, *Subversives*, pp. 8, 52ff, 62ff; Constance M. Green, *Washington*, pp. 95–100.

105 *Congressman Abraham Lincoln*: Robert S. Pohl and John R. Wennersten, *Abraham Lincoln and the End of Slavery in the District of Columbia*, pp. 20–26.

106 *seemed to have "unhinged"*: R. Hewes to Orlando Brown, July 28, 1849, Orlando Brown Papers, Filson Historical Society, Louisville.

106 *"The feeling for"*: Clay to Leslie Combs, December 22, 1849, in Hay, ed., *Papers of Henry Clay*, Vol. 10, p. 635.

107 *"I fear for"*: Clay to Bayard, December 14, 1849, in ibid., p. 632; Richards, *The Slave Power*, p. 57.

108 *Voting began on*: CG 31/1, pp. 2–7.

108 *"There is no"*: Clay to James B. Clay, December 4, 1849, in Hay, ed., *Papers of Henry Clay*, Vol. 10, p. 629.

108 *in the tradition*: U.S. Senate Historian Donald Ritchie, email to author, July 12, 2010.

109 *"kindly, honest, farmer-like"*: George W. Julian, *Political Recollections, 1840 to 1872*, p. 82.

109 *"The people of"*: Quoted in Smith, *Presidencies of Zachary Taylor and Millard Fillmore*, p. 94.

109 *Taylor's address reviewed:* James D. Richardson, *A Compilation of the Messages and Papers of the Presidents*, Vol. 5, pp. 7–24; *31/1 Serial Set, Senate Executive Document 57*, pp. 46, 51–52.

110 *Cuba "cannot resist": New York Herald*, January 11, 1849.

110 *histrionic Narciso López:* Tom Chaffin, *Fatal Glory*, pp. 37–40, 63–65; James Morton Callahan, *Cuba and International Relations*, pp. 23ff, 178ff; Chester Stanley Urban, "New Orleans and the Cuban Question During the López Expeditions of 1849–1851," *The Louisiana Historical Quarterly*, Vol. 22, October 1939; *Texas State Gazette*, September 8, October 6, 1849.

111 *would "eventually drop"*: Quoted in Chaffin, *Fatal Glory*, p. 47.

CHAPTER 9: DEADLOCK

Page

114 *Balloting for the speaker: CG* 31/1, pp. 2–66.

114 *just "mock thunder"*: Ibid., App., p. 39.

115 *William J. Brown:* Julian, *Political Recollections*, pp. 74–75.

116 *Curiously, a number:* Ibid.

116 *"All that I" and ensuing debate: CG* 31/1, p. 21ff.

119 *Meade thereupon rushed: CG* 31/1, p. 27; Richards, *The California Gold Rush*, p. 96; Poore, *Perley's Reminiscences of Sixty Years in the National Metropolis*, Vol. 1, p. 361.

120 *Stephens and Toombs:* Thomas E. Schott, *Alexander H. Stephens of Georgia*, pp. 82–85, 102–8.

120 *"his eyes glowing"*: Poore, *Perley's Reminiscences of Sixty Years in the National Metropolis*, Vol. 1, p. 360.

120 *"I do not hesitate"*: Ibid.

121 *"It was so"*: Henry Clay to James B. Clay, December 29, 1849, in Hay, ed., *Papers of Henry Clay*, Vol. 10, p. 639.

122 *"Madness rules the"*: Nevins, ed., *Diary of Philip Hone*, Vol. 2, p. 880.

CHAPTER 10: THE GODLIKE DANIEL

Page

123 *"several gentlemen lost"*: Quoted in Smith, *The Presidencies of Zachary Taylor and Millard Fillmore*, p. 102.

123 *"If there be no"*: Clay to Thomas H. Clay, January 11, 1850, in Hay, ed., *Papers of Henry Clay*, Vol. 10, p. 646.

123 *"I have been thinking"*: Clay to James B. Clay, January 2, 1850, in ibid., p. 642.

124 *The opening days of the session*: CG 31/1, pp. 97, 117–23, 137, 159, 165–68, 178, 210–12, 233–36.

125 *"We do not intend"*: CG 31/1, App., p. 52.

126 *Human bondage*: Jefferson Davis to Samuel J. Cartwright, June 10, 1849, in William J. Cooper, Jr., ed., *Jefferson Davis: The Essential Writings*, pp. 62–64.

126 *"Davis is one"*: Quoted in William J. Cooper, Jr., *Jefferson Davis, American*, p. 167.

126 *No power known*: CG 31/1, p. 137.

127 *Butler's bill*: CG 31/1, App., p. 79.

127 *Mason of Virginia proposed*: CG 31/1, pp. 210, 233–35.

128 *in a letter*: Richardson, *Compilation of the Messages and Papers of the Presidents*, Vol. 5, pp. 26–31.

130 *"phenomenal in size"*: Dyer, *Great Senators of the United States Forty Years Ago*, pp. 251–53, 257, 263.

130 *"When my eyes"*: *Register* 21/1, p. 80.

131 *"It is not fit"*: Online at www.dartmouth.edu/~dwwebster/speeches/plymouth-oration.html.

131 *"mild influences of"*: Quoted in Remini, *Daniel Webster*, p. 664.

132 *"yet some physical"*: CG 31/1, p. 226.

132 *"No benefit can"*: CG 31/3, p. 227.

133 *"Oh! That word"*: CG 31/1, App., pp. 81–83.

CHAPTER 11: "A GREAT SOUL ON FIRE"

Page

134 *Clay was at last*: CG 31/1, pp. 244–46.

134 *"He spoke to"*: Dyer, *Great Senators of the United States Forty Years Ago*, pp. 222–31.

139 *There were scattered: CG* 31/1, p. 246ff.

139 *When Clay rose: CG* 31/1, App., pp. 115–26.

144 *"a spectacle of":* New York Herald, January 31, 1850.

144 *At a giant: Savannah Daily Republican*, March 5, 1850.

144 *"The fever of":* Nevins, ed., *Diary of Philip Hone*, Vol. 2, p. 885.

145 *"In no man":* The North Star, March 1, 1850.

145 "Compromise?" *roared: CG* 31/1, p. 371.

145 *"she derives ninety-nine": CG* 31/1, p. 372.

CHAPTER 12: "WOUNDED EAGLE"

Page

146 *Jefferson Davis delivered: CG* 31/1, App., pp. 149–57.

149 *"He who seeks": CG* 31/1, App., p. 287.

150 *Henry Foote suddenly: CG* 31/1, pp. 355–56.

150 *"On the contrary": Daily Alabama Journal*, February 20, 1850.

150 *"a high pressure":* Ibid.

151 *on Christmas Day:* Cooper, *Jefferson Davis, American*, pp. 208–9.

151 *"a pestiferous demagogue":* Nevins, ed., *Diary of Philip Hone*, Vol. 2, p. 889.

151 *"Clad in the": Daily Atlas*, January 30, 1850.

152 *Clay, Foote suspiciously: CG* 31/1, p. 368.

152 *"I know of":* Ibid.

153 "Public justice is": *CG* 31/1, p. 367.

153 *a "peculiar significance": CG* 31/1, p. 402.

153 *Clay gently chided: CG* 31/1, pp. 404–5.

153 *"Would it not": CG* 31/1, pp. 419–20.

154 *"commanding every highway":* Quoted in Waldo W. Braden, ed., *Oratory in the Old South, 1828–1860*, p. 169.

154 *a shadow of himself:* "Memorandum" by John Randolph Tucker, ca. February 1850, John C. Calhoun to H. V. Johnson, January 19, 1850, Calhoun to J. H. Hammond, February 16, 1850, in Wilson and Cook, eds., *Papers of John C. Calhoun*, Vol. 27, pp. 163–64, 166–68, 174–75.

155 *"You have spent":* Anna C. Clemson to Calhoun, February 18, 1850, in ibid., pp. 175–76.

155 *"I am exceedingly":* Calhoun to Anna Clemson, February 24, 1850, in ibid., p. 183.

156　*"an existing institution":* CG 31/1, pp. 398–99.

156　*"It seemed generally":* Pennsylvanian, March 6, 1850.

156　*"wounded eagle":* Quoted in John Wentworth, *Congressional Reminiscences,* pp. 22–23.

156　*The speech was:* CG 31/1, pp. 451–58.

157　*Chase pointed out:* CG 31/1, App., pp. 472–74.

157　*Calhoun acknowledged that:* CG 31/1, pp. 462, 519–20, 529; Lence, ed., *Union and Liberty,* pp. 276–79.

158　*"If you who":* CG 31/1, pp. 451–55.

CHAPTER 13: "SECESSION! PEACEABLE SECESSION!"

Page

159　*"to cast in":* CG 31/1, App., p. 97ff.

159　*"a magnificent barbarian":* Dyer, *Great Senators of the United States Forty Years Ago,* pp. 116–18.

160　*"They are bastards":* CG 31/1, App., p. 97ff.

160　*"Calhoun is mad":* Houston to Margaret Houston, December 26, 1848, in Roberts, *Personal Correspondence of Sam Houston,* Vol. 3, p. 33.

160　*"as so many":* Houston to Margaret Houston, Ibid., p. 83.

160　*"I have been charged":* CG 31/1, App., p. 97ff.

161　*"To speak plainly":* CG 31/1, pp. 519–20.

162　*"Things will cool":* Quoted in Robert F. Dalzell, *Daniel Webster and the Trial of American Nationalism,* p. 175.

162　*Representative James Doty:* CG 31/1, p. 375ff.

162　*"The evening was":* Ibid.

164　*"that if they":* Quoted in Smith, *The Presidencies of Zachary Taylor and Millard Fillmore,* p. 104.

164　*"We are on":* New York Herald, February 8, 1850.

164　*"look to secession":* Quoted in Herbert Darling Foster, "Webster's Seventh of March Speech and the Secession Movement," *The American Historical Review,* Vol. 27, January 1922.

165　*"A dismemberment of":* Quoted in ibid.

165　*"I am nearly":* Quoted in Dalzell, *Daniel Webster and the Trial of American Nationalism,* p. 176.

165 *"Your speech this"*: Quoted in Remini, *Daniel Webster*, p. 668.

165 *"I wish to speak"*: CG 31/1, pp. 476–83.

170 *"discreet, reflecting men"*: Nevins, ed., *Diary of Philip Hone*, Vol. 2, p. 888.

170 *An estimated ten thousand*: Alabama Daily Journal, March 13, 1850.

170 *Isaac Hill*: Cited in Foster, "Webster's Seventh of March Speech and the Secession Movement."

171 *"This speech is"*: Reprinted in *Alabama Daily Journal*, March 15, 1850.

171 *"The South prefer"*: Alabama Daily Journal, March 18, 1850.

171 *"emphatically a great"*: Reprinted in the *Alabama Daily Journal*, March 19, 1850.

171 *"overturn every Whig"*: Quoted in David D. Van Tassel, "Gentlemen of Property and Standing: Compromise Sentiment in Boston in 1850," *The New England Quarterly*, Vol. 23, September 1950.

171 *"perfidious and heartless"*: The North Star, April 12, 1850.

171 *"O, Daniel Webster"*: Aaron Foster to William H. Seward, April 22, 1850, Seward Papers, Library of Congress.

171 *Theodore Parker, one of Boston's*: Cited in Foster, "Webster's Seventh of March Speech and the Secession Movement."

171 *" 'Liberty! Liberty!' "*: Quoted in Peterson, *The Great Triumvirate*, p. 465.

172 *"All else is gone"*: The National Era, May 2, 1850.

172 *"As much as"*: Cassius Clay to Daniel Webster, March 20, 1850, Cassius Clay Correspondence, Special Collections, University of Kentucky, Lexington.

CHAPTER 14: "A HIGHER LAW"

Page

173 *the urbane Seward*: Frederick W. Seward, *William H. Seward: An Autobiography from 1801 to 1834*, pp. 19, 27–28, 528–29, 743–44; Frederick W. Seward, *Seward at Washington*, p. 105; Frederic Bancroft, *The Life of William H. Seward*, Vol. 2, pp. 70–72; Glyndon G. Van Deusen, *William Henry Seward*, pp. 65–67; George E. Baker, ed., *The Works of William H. Seward*, Vol. 1, pp. 390–92, 413–14, 492–95.

175 *"abstracted from"*: CG 31/1, App., p. 79.

175 *"If we ever"*: Seward, *Seward at Washington*, pp. 125, 130.

175 *"I am alone"*: Seward at Washington, p. 116.

176 *"Congress has no"*: Baker, ed., *Works of William H. Seward*, p. lxxxvi.

176 *"a covenant with death"*: Quoted in Henry Mayer, *All on Fire*, p. 313.

176 *"The world seems"*: Quoted in William O. Lynch, "Zachary Taylor as President," *The Journal of Southern History*, Vol. 4, August 1938.

177 *"of different metal"*: Seward, *Seward at Washington*, p. 115.

177 *"there is as yet"*: Ibid., p. 107.

177 *"We could put"*: Quoted in Robert J. Rayback, *Millard Fillmore*, p. 204.

177 *"a perfect Automaton"*: Wilson Lumpkin to John C. Calhoun, August 27, 1849, in Wilson and Cook, eds., *Papers of John C. Calhoun*, Vol. 27, p. 38.

177 *"It was able"*: Nevins, ed., *Diary of Philip Hone*, Vol. 2, p. 888.

178 *"No wonder if"*: CG 31/1, App., p. 261ff.

181 *"These principles destroy"*: CG 31/1, App., pp. 387–88.

181 *"The thing is"*: Seward, *Seward at Washington*, p. 129.

CHAPTER 15: "GOD DELIVER ME FROM SUCH FRIENDS"

Page

182 *"Don't talk to me"*: Wentworth, *Congressional Reminiscences*, p. 28.

182 *One evening*: Ibid.

183 *"I will vote"*: CG 31/1, p. 510.

183 *"There is a power"*: CG 31/1, pp. 211–12.

185 *"a studied suppression"*: Stephen A. Douglas to James W. Woodworth, March 5, 1850, in Johannsen, ed., *Letters of Stephen A. Douglas*, p. 187.

185 *This day, Douglas spoke*: CG 31/1, pp. 364–74.

185 *"This government was"*: Robert W. Johannsen, *The Lincoln-Douglas Debates of 1858*, p. 196.

189 *"Is each to"*: CG 31/1, pp. 529–30.

189 *If anyone still*: CG 31/1, p. 601; 31/1, App., pp. 172, 176, 288, 295, 375–82, 382–91.

CHAPTER 16: "HE IS NOT DEAD, SIR"

Page

191 *"I wish to give"*: CG 31/1, p. 602ff.

193 *"Indians, Mexicans, and"*: CG 31/1, pp. 395–96.

193 *"You abandoned your child":* CG 31/1, p. 400.

193 *congressional delegation:* Arthur Quinn, *The Rivals,* pp. 75–87; Richards, *The California Gold Rush and the Coming of the Civil War,* pp. 91–93; Lately Thomas, *Between Two Empires,* pp. 47–48.

194 *"war of extermination":* Quoted in Horsman, *Race and Manifest Destiny,* p. 279.

194 *On his arrival:* Thomas, *Between Two Empires,* p. 31.

195 *Bell, who supported:* CG 31/1, pp. 436–39; Joseph H. Parks, "John Bell and the Compromise of 1850," *The Journal of Southern History,* Vol. 9, August 1943.

196 *"Texas is too":* Quoted in W. H. Timmons, "El Paso: The Formative Years," *Southwestern Historical Quarterly,* Vol. 87, July 1983.

196 *"cut New Mexico":* Quoted in ibid.

197 *"fixed and settled":* CG 31/1, App., p. 233ff.

197 *Robert Simpson Neighbors:* Kenneth F. Neighbors, *Robert Simpson Neighbors and the Texas Frontier, 1836–1859,* pp. 5–18, 81–83.

198 *"We have trusted":* Texas State Gazette, December 29, 1849; Stegmaier, *Texas, New Mexico, and the Compromise of 1850,* pp. 54–55.

198 *"friendly disposition towards us":* Decree of Gov. Peter H. Bell, "To the Citizens of the Counties of Presidio, El Paso, Worth, and Santa Fe," January 5, 1850, *Appendix to the Journals of the Senate,* 3/2, State of Texas, pp. 69–72; Neighbors to Bell, January 8, 1850, Governor's Papers; *Texas State Gazette,* April 27, May 4, 1850; Kenneth F. Neighbors, "The Taylor-Neighbors Struggle over the Upper Rio Grande Region of Texas in 1850," *The Southwestern Historical Review,* Vol. 61, April 1958.

199 *amazingly named Dr. Wham:* Neighbors, *Robert Simpson Neighbors Correspondence, 1846–1847,* p. 69.

199 *the two slaves: Texas State Gazette,* May 4, 1850.

199 *El Paso, with:* Timmons, "El Paso: The Formative Years"; Charles A. Hoppin to Bell, January 3, 1850, Governor's Papers; Stegmaier, *Texas, New Mexico, and the Compromise of 1850,* pp. 66–68.

200 *"The election went":* Quoted in Neighbors, "The Taylor-Neighbors Struggle over the Upper Rio Grande Region of Texas in 1850."

200 *"a perfect Texan":* Neighbors to Bell, March 23, 1850, Executive Records, Texas State Library.

201 *Judge Joab Houghton:* Loomis Morton Ganaway, "New Mexico and the Sectional Controversy, 1846–1861," *New Mexico Historical Review,* Vol. 18, July

1943; Thomas S. Edrington, "Military Influence on the Texas–New Mexico Boundary Settlement," *New Mexico Historical Review*, Vol. 59, October 1984; Neighbors, "The Taylor-Neighbors Struggle over the Upper Rio Grande Region of Texas in 1850."

201 *"We shall then"*: Quoted in Stegmaier, *Texas, New Mexico, and the Compromise of 1850*, p. 74.

201 *"Should the people"*: George W. Crawford to George A. McCall, November 19, 1849, Santa Fe Papers, Texas State Library.

201 *"I found politics"*: McCall to W. S. Bliss, March 21, 1850, George A. McCall Papers, National Archives; McCall, *New Mexico in 1850*, pp. 64–70.

202 *"impassable on account"*: Neighbors to Bell, March 23, 1850, Executive Records, Texas State Library.

202 *"a bitter, unprincipled"*: Neighbors to Bell, April 14, 1850, *Appendix to the Journals of the Senate*, 3/2, State of Texas, p. 12.

203 *"a name without"*: Calhoun to Joseph A. Scoville, ca. March 25, 1850, in Wilson and Cook, eds., *Papers of John C. Calhoun*, Vol. 27, pp. 268–70.

203 *"The Union is doomed"*: Memorandum of James M. Mason, March 1850, in ibid., pp. 186–87.

203 *"He is gone!"*: *CG* 31/1, p. 624.

203 *"undaunted genius"*: *CG* 31/1, p. 625.

203 *"He is not dead"*: Quoted in Wentworth, *Congressional Reminiscences*, pp. 23–24.

204 *"the disgraceful spectacle"*: Quoted in John Niven, *John C. Calhoun and the Price of Union*, p. 345.

205 *"What have we done?"*: *CG* 31/1, p. 517.

205 *as everyone remembered*: *CG* 31/1, pp. 375–85.

205 *He quietly sent*: Schott, *Alexander H. Stephens of Georgia*, pp. 113–14; Johannsen, *Stephen A. Douglas*, p. 272.

206 *"We are just"*: *New York Herald*, April 15, 1850.

CHAPTER 17: "LET THE ASSASSIN FIRE!"

Page

207 *The spring brought*: Clay to Lucretia Clay, April 25, 1850, in Hay, ed., *Papers of Henry Clay*, Vol. 10, p. 709; Clay to Thomas B. Stevenson, April 3, 1850, in ibid., p. 694.

207 *"We are still"*: Clay to James B. Clay, March 13, 1850, in ibid., p. 687.

207 *"There is very"*: Clay to James Harlan, March 16, 1850, in ibid., p. 689.

208 *"eradicated the respect"*: Clay to Stevenson, April 25, 1850, in ibid., p. 710.

208 *he described himself:* CG 31/1, App., p. 591.

208 *outlandish rumors:* Smith, *The Presidencies of Zachary Taylor and Millard Fillmore*, p. 132.

209 *"There is no man"*: Quoted in Wentworth, *Congressional Reminiscences*, p. 50.

209 *"It was easy"*: Dyer, *Great Senators of the United States Forty Years Ago*, pp. 202–03, 206.

210 *"leaving the consequences"*: Thomas Hart Benton, *Thirty Years' View*, p. 742.

210 *the Missourian laid out:* CG 31/1, App., pp. 446–50.

211 *rules then in operation:* Gregory J. Wawro and Eric Schickler, *Filibuster*, pp. 9–17.

212 *the national census:* CG 31/1, pp. 672–77, 989–94, 1304.

215 *the open secret:* Drew Gilpin Faust, *James Henry Hammond and the Old South*, p. 87; Carol Bleser, *Secret and Sacred*, pp. 17–18.

216 *"I am against"*: CG 31/1, p. 450.

216 *"Nothing but a great"*: CG 31/1, p. 710.

217 *"I have nine"*: CG 31/1, p. 713.

217 *unseemly "insinuations"*: CG 31/1, p. 632; Anne M. Butler and Wendy Wolff, *United States Senate Election, Expulsion and Censure Cases, 1793–1990*, pp. 57–58.

218 *"He wants California"*: CG 31/1, p. 752.

218 *Benton mildly protested:* CG 31/1, pp. 753–57.

218 *"But if I cannot"*: CG 31/1, pp. 762–64.

219 *"There has been a cry"*: Ibid.

219 *Benton snapped: New York Tribune*, April 18, 1850; Isaac Bassett, Manuscript Memoir, U.S. Senate Library; James P. Coleman, "Two Irascible Antebellum Senators: George Poindexter and Henry S. Foote," *The Journal of Mississippi History*, Vol. 46, February 1944; John M. Bernhisel to Brigham Young, April 23, 1850, *BYU Studies*, Vol. 22, No. 3 (1982).

220 *"I have never"*: Quoted in Swisshelm, *Half a Century*, pp. 130–31.

221 *"Pistols in the Senate!"*: Nevins, ed., *Diary of Philip Hone*, Vol. 2, p. 892.

221 *In July, a committee:* Chambers, *Old Bullion Benton*, p. 363; Butler and Wolff, *United States Senate Election, Expulsion and Censure Cases, 1793–1990*, p. 58.

222 *"could make more"*: Quoted in Chambers, *Old Bullion Benton*, p. 279.

222 *In his attack:* CG 31/1, pp. 793–97.

222 *"When the senator":* CG 31/1, p. 798.

CHAPTER 18: FILIBUSTERS

Page

223 *"The North":* CG 31/1, App., p. 569.

223 *The plan he outlined:* CG 31/1, pp. 944–48.

224 *Utah was as usual:* Glen M. Leonard, "The Mormon Boundary Question in the 1849–50 Statehood Debates," *Journal of Mormon History*, Vol. 18, Spring 1992; *Utah: A Guide to the State*, pp. 62–64; George R. Stewart, *Names on the Land*, p. 262; Edward Everett to Daniel Webster, January 3, 1850, in Charles M. Wiltse and Michael J. Birkner, eds., *The Papers of Daniel Webster: Correspondence*, Vol. 7, p. 3.

224 *"I care not":* CG 31/1, App., p. 568.

224 *"Unless their morals":* CG 31/1, App., p. 811.

224 *"We propose to":* CG 31/1, p. 1005.

225 *"inoperative and invalid":* Ibid.

226 *"I have enlisted":* CG 31/1, p. 949ff.

226 *James Mason, a member:* Ibid.

226 *"which excludes":* Ibid.

226 *"be worse":* Ibid.

226 *"a slave pasture":* CG 31/1, p. 954.

226 *"I wish it was":* CG 31/1, App., p. 630ff.

227 *"The mystery is":* CG 31/1, App., p. 879ff.

227 *"I am in favor":* CG 31/1, p. 1005.

227 *"It is necessary":* Jefferson Davis to Franklin H. Elmore, April 13, 1850, in Cooper, ed., *Jefferson Davis: The Essential Writings*, p. 80.

228 *"willing to swallow":* Quoted in Thelma Jennings, *The Nashville Convention*, p. 100.

228 *"Wherever water is":* CG 31/1, App., p. 997ff.

228 *"I claim only":* CG 31/1, pp. 1115–16.

228 *"Proud in the":* Quoted in William C. Davis, *Jefferson Davis*, p. 200.

228 *The South's defense:* CG 31/1, pp. 943–44, 1006.

229 *a succession of amendments:* CG 31/1, p. 1083; App., pp. 787, 915–17.

229 *He also propounded:* CG 31/1, App., pp. 793–94.

229 *Until now, Foote reminded:* CG 31/1, App., pp. 579–85.

230 *"little short of treason":* CG 31/1, App., p. 585ff.

230 *Foote, who never:* CG 31/1, App., p. 589ff.

230 *David Yulee begged:* Ibid.; also CG 31/1, p. 1030.

231 *A dark game was afoot:* Chaffin, *Fatal Glory*, pp. 104–39; John McCardell, *The Idea of a Southern Nation*, p. 201ff; Robert E. May, *The Southern Dream of a Caribbean Empire, 1854–1861*, p. 1ff; Anderson C. Quisenberry, *López's Expeditions to Cuba, 1850–1851*, pp. 46–52; Sampson, *John L. O'Sullivan and His Times*, pp. 214–16; Antonio Rafael de la Cova, "The Kentucky Regiment That Invaded Cuba in 1850," *Register of the Kentucky Historical Society*, Vol. 105, Autumn 2007; Antonio Rafael de la Cova, "Filibusters and Freemasons: The Sworn Obligation," *Journal of the Early Republic*, Vol. 17, Spring 1997; *The Daily Picayune*, May 17, 20, 21, 26, 30, 31, June 1, 1850; *Texas State Gazette*, June 1, 15, 1850; *31/1 Serial Set, Senate Executive Document 57.*

231 *John Quitman:* Robert E. May, *John A. Quitman*, p. 1ff, 188ff, 230, 236–41; Robert E. May, "John A. Quitman and His Slaves: Reconciling Slave Resistance with the Proslavery Defense," *The Journal of Southern History*, Vol. 46, November 1980.

232 *"a moral, social":* Quitman to "Brother," March 11, 1823, in J. F. H. Claiborne, ed., *Life and Correspondence of John A. Quitman*, Vol. 1, pp. 81–82.

232 *"Her fate":* "Statement," Quitman Papers, Houghton Library, Harvard University.

232 *"the boundless fertility":* CG 31/1, App., p. 172.

233 *"the South would":* Texas State Gazette, March 9, 1850.

233 *American designs on:* Callahan, *Cuba and International Relations*, pp. 17, 23ff, 178ff, 195ff; Chaffin, *Fatal Glory*, pp. 22–23; *New York Herald*, January 11, 1849.

233 *Weapons for the López:* Urban, "New Orleans and the Cuban Question During the López Expeditions of 1849–1851," *The Louisiana Historical Quarterly*, Vol. 22, October 1939.

233 *the alert Spanish consul:* Don A. Calderón de la Barca to Secretary of State John M. Clayton, January 19, 1850, et al., *31/1 Serial Set, Senate Executive Document 57*, p. 19ff, Library of Congress.

233 *President Taylor ordered:* William Ballard Preston to Captain Josiah Tattnall, May 15, 1850, *31/1 Serial Set, Senate Executive Document 57*, pp. 54–55.

234 *"about to strike":* Quoted in Chaffin, *Fatal Glory,* pp. 129–30.

234 *"A six-shooter":* Quoted in de la Cova, "The Kentucky Regiment That Invaded Cuba in 1850."

235 *"a harum-scarum business":* Quoted in ibid.

235 *"some rascally":* True Delta, June 1, 1850.

235 *Meanwhile, the Americans:* New Orleans Times-Picayune, May 30, 1850.

236 *"miserable refuse":* The Daily Picayune, May 20, 1850.

236 *López's miserable luck:* The Daily Picayune, May 30, 1850; Samuel J. Douglas to Zachary Taylor, May 22, 1850, *31/1 Serial Set, Senate Executive Document 57,* p. 43.

237 *"How many thousands":* Daily Delta, May 26, 1850.

237 *In the Senate:* CG 31/1, pp. 1032–34.

238 *"Why this feverish":* CG 31/1, App., p. 884.

CHAPTER 19: "A LEGISLATIVE SATURNALIA"

Page

239 *"In that state":* CG 31/1, App., p. 612ff.

241 *Tom Benton:* CG 31/1, App., p. 676ff.

243 *"fancied long since":* CG 31/1, App., p. 818.

243 *Franklin Elmore:* CG 31/1, pp. 915, 1105–06; Bleser, *Secret and Sacred,* p. 314.

244 *"As for this":* CG 31/1, p. 1087.

244 *When David Yulee:* CG 31/1, pp. 1108, 1210–11.

244 *"This finding of":* CG 31/1, App., p. 612ff.

245 *Clay was losing confidence:* Clay to James Brown Clay, May 27, 1850; Clay to Thomas H. Clay, May 31, 1850; Clay to James O. Harrison, June 19, 1850, in Hay, ed., *Papers of Henry Clay,* Vol. 10, pp. 733, 736, 753.

245 *"It has gone up":* CG 31/1, App., p. 818.

245 *Isaac Walker:* CG 31/1, pp. 1141–44.

246 *"We have been":* Ibid.

246 *"We know this":* Ibid.

246 *southern tempers instantly flared:* Ibid.

246 *"the white man":* Ibid.

247 *Yulee again pleaded:* CG 31/1, pp. 1210–11, App., p. 862.

247 *"All these motions":* CG 31/1, pp. 1210–11.

247 *the days that followed: CG* 31/1, p. 1146, App., p. 897ff; Smith, *The Presidencies of Zachary Taylor and Millard Fillmore,* p. 148; Johannsen, *Stephen A. Douglas,* p. 289.

248 *Stephen Douglas asserted: CG* 31/1, App., p. 911.

248 *Augustus Dodge: CG* 31/1, App., p. 910.

248 "Upon you, *the": Willie P. Mangum to Webster, April 10, 1850, in Wiltse and Birkner, eds., *Papers of Daniel Webster: Correspondence,* Vol. 7, p. 65.

248 *"There are a":* Webster to Mangum, April 12, 1850, in ibid., p. 68.

249 *"no occasion to make": CG* 31/1, p. 1239.

CHAPTER 20: A PACT WITH THE DEVIL

Page

250 *"but a week":* John M. Bernhisel to Brigham Young, April 23, 1850, *BYU Studies,* Vol. 22, No. 3 (1982).

250 *"We lose sight of ": CG* 31/1, App., p. 967.

250 *"diseased sensibility": Texas State Gazette,* January 19, 1850.

250 *"will submit to": CG* 31/1, App., p. 866.

251 *"I greatly mistake": CG* 31/1, App., p. 792.

251 *There had been: CG* 31/1, pp. 859ff, 1154ff, App., pp. 854, 682; Timmons, "El Paso: The Formative Years," *Southwestern Historical Quarterly,* Vol. 87, July 1983.

251 *"What is New Mexico?": CG* 31/1, App., p. 859ff.

251 *"There is hardly":* Quoted in Twitchell, *The Leading Facts of New Mexico History,* Vol. 2, p. 285.

252 *he now expected:* Robert Neighbors to Peter H. Bell, June 4, 1850, *Appendix to the Journals of the Senate,* 3/2, State of Texas, pp. 7–10.

252 *Colonel John Munroe: Register of Graduates,* Special Collections, United States Military Academy; Edrington, "Military Influence on the Texas–New Mexico Boundary Settlement," *New Mexico Historical Review,* Vol. 59, October 1984.

252 *"mere lieutenant colonel": CG* 31/1, App., pp. 1009–10.

253 *"Are you willing":* Neighbors to Bell, June 4, 1850, *Appendix to the Journals of the Senate,* 3/2, State of Texas, pp. 7–10.

253 *"I am not prepared":* Ibid.

253 *"the masses are kept":* Ibid.

253 *"more absolute and despotic":* Neighbors to Bell, April 14, 1850, Executive Records, Texas State Library.

254 *issued a proclamation:* "Proclamation," March 13, 1850, *Appendix to the Journals of the Senate,* 3/2, State of Texas, p. 11.

254 *"already been tampered":* Neighbors to Bell, June 4, 1850, *Appendix to the Journals of the Senate,* 3/2, State of Texas, pp. 7–10.

254 *"We shall at all":* Quoted in Edrington, "Military Influence on the Texas–New Mexico Boundary Settlement."

254 *The largest of these:* Twitchell, *The Leading Facts of New Mexico History,* p. 271ff; "Proclamation," Col. John Munroe, April 23, 1850, *Appendix to the Journals of the Senate,* 3/2, State of Texas, pp. 13–14; Ganaway, "New Mexico and the Sectional Controversy, 1846–1861," *New Mexico Historical Review,* Vol. 18, July 1943.

255 *"which can only":* Neighbors to Bell, April 14, 1850, Executive Records, Texas State Library.

255 *"The whole business":* Quoted in Smith, *The Presidencies of Zachary Taylor and Millard Fillmore,* p. 153.

255 *"I venture to":* CG 31/1, App., pp. 862–63.

256 *the specter of secession:* Jennings, *The Nashville Convention,* pp. 135–55; Faust, *James Henry Hammond and the Old South,* pp. 297–99; Cooper, *Jefferson Davis, American,* pp. 212–13; Elizabeth R. Varon, *Disunion!,* pp. 224–25.

256 *"If the convention":* Quoted in William W. Freehling, *The Road to Disunion,* p. 481.

256 *"The great southern middle":* Freehling, *The Road to Disunion,* p. 481.

257 *"like borders of flowers":* Jennings, *The Nashville Convention,* p. 142.

257 *a "magnificent future":* Quoted in Freehling, *The Road to Disunion,* p. 485.

257 *"Under the guise":* Quoted in Jennings, *The Nashville Convention,* p. 149.

258 *"The warfare against":* Resolutions of the Nashville Convention, online at blueandgraytrail.com/event/Nashville_Convention; *Texian Advocate,* July 5, 1850.

258 *"In this," he wrote:* Bleser, *Secret and Sacred,* pp. 203–6.

259 *Pierre Soulé:* J. Preston Moore, "Pierre Soulé: Southern Expansionist and Promoter," *The Journal of Southern History,* Vol. 21, May 1955; Freeman, "The Early Career of Pierre Soulé," *The Louisiana Historical Quarterly,* Vol. 25, October 1942.

259 *Soulé demanded:* CG 31/1, App., pp. 960–68.

260 *A few days earlier: CG* 31/1, App., 911–14.

260 *Jefferson Davis urged: CG* 31/1, App., pp. 994–96.

261 *"has done little but":* Zachary Taylor to William Hill, May 9, 1850, Taylor Papers, Library of Congress.

261 *"the most unstatesmanlike": CG* 31/1, p. 664.

262 *"has not only":* Quoted in Smith, *The Presidencies of Zachary Taylor and Millard Fillmore*, p. 133.

262 *in April, a scandal:* Smith, *The Presidencies of Zachary Taylor and Millard Fillmore*, pp. 123–27; Allan Nevins, *Ordeal of the Union*, pp. 325–27.

263 *Taylor was suffering:* Taylor to Richard Taylor, May 5, 11, 12, 1850, Taylor Papers, Library of Congress.

264 *"We shall have":* Daniel Webster to Daniel F. Webster, June 12, 1850, in Wiltse and Birkner, eds., *Papers of Daniel Webster: Correspondence*, Vol. 7, p. 117.

264 *"Will Massachusetts":* Webster to Peter Harvey, June 2, 1850, in ibid., p. 107.

264 *"I am for it":* Webster to Daniel F. Webster, June 12, 1850, in ibid., p. 117.

264 *Foote electrified the Senate: CG* 31/1, App., p. 990.

265 *"Every act of":* Volney E. Howard, open letter to the press, April 4, 1850, *Appendix to the Journals of the Senate*, 3/2, State of Texas, pp. 34–42.

265 *mass meetings called: Texas State Gazette*, June 15, 1850; *Clarksville Northern Standard*, July 13, 1850; Neighbors, "The Taylor-Neighbors Struggle over the Upper Rio Grande Region of Texas in 1850," *Southwestern Historical Review*, Vol. 61, April 1958.

265 *"immediate military action":* Bell to Zachary Taylor, June 13, 15, 1850, *Appendix to the Journals of the Senate*, 3/2, State of Texas, pp. 42–50.

265 *Texas would annex: New York Journal of Commerce*, June 29, 1850.

265 *"I wish to say":* Quoted in Ralph E. Twitchell, *Old Santa Fe*, p. 318.

265 *a committee of three:* Smith, *The Presidencies of Zachary Taylor and Millard Fillmore*, p. 155; Myrta Lockett Avary, ed., *Recollections of Alexander H. Stephens*, p. 26.

CHAPTER 21: "WAR, OPEN WAR"

Page

267 *Jefferson Davis denied: CG* 31/1, App., pp. 997–1000.

267 *Seward, for his part: CG* 31/1, App., pp. 862–63.

268   *"God bless you"*: Worthy Putnam to Seward, March 29, 1850, Seward Papers, Library of Congress.

268   *Seward's political friends*: Van Deusen, *William Henry Seward*, pp. 121–33.

268   *Seward began with*: CG 31/1, App., pp. 1021–24.

271   *"I regard the compromise"*: J. W. Morrow to Henry Clay, June 15, 1850, in Hay, ed., *Papers of Henry Clay*, Vol. 10, p. 749.

271   *"When and how"*: Clay to Lucretia Clay, July 6, 1850, in ibid., p. 763.

271   *"war, open war"*: CG 31/1, App., p. 1088ff.

271   *"A hundred times"*: CG 31/1, App., p. 929.

271   *"Meet earlier"*: CG 31/1, pp. 1298–99.

272   *"I would as soon"*: CG 31/1, pp. 1329–30.

272   *"I am not willing"*: CG 31/1, p. 1299.

272   *there were rumors*: Avary, *Recollections of Alexander H. Stephens*, pp. 26–27; Smith, *The Presidencies of Zachary Taylor and Millard Fillmore*, p. 155.

272   *"If you would"*: CG 31/1, App., pp. 879–86.

272   *"We shall be hard"*: Clay to Willie P. Mangum, June 25, 1850, in Hay, ed., *Papers of Henry Clay*, Vol. 10, p. 756.

272   *"I hardly dare"*: Daniel Webster to Franklin Haven, July 4, 1850, in Wiltse and Birkner, eds., *Papers of Daniel Webster: Correspondence*, Vol. 7, p. 121.

273   *at the same time*: CG 31/1, pp. 436, 796, App., p. 1104ff; Parks, "John Bell and the Compromise of 1850," *The Journal of Southern History*, Vol. 9, August 1943.

273   *"I fear there"*: CG 31/1, App., p. 1088ff.

274   *On the Fourth*: Poore, *Perley's Reminiscences of Sixty Years in the National Metropolis*, pp. 376–79; Wentworth, *Congressional Reminiscences*, pp. 9–10; *National Intelligencer*, July 6, 1850.

274   *"Why will you"*: Quoted in Smith, *The Presidencies of Zachary Taylor and Millard Fillmore*, p. 156.

275   *John Bell resumed*: CG 31/1, App., p. 1094ff.

275   *"On the first"*: Seward, *Seward at Washington*, p. 80.

276   *"for usurping kingly"*: Quoted in Smith, *The Presidencies of Zachary Taylor and Millard Fillmore*, p. 157.

276   *two "delicious salmon"*: Zachary Taylor to H. S. Hanor, July 5, 1850, Taylor Papers, University of Kentucky.

276   *"I was informed"*: CG 31/1, pp. 1362–63.

277 *Throngs of well-wishers: Baltimore Sun*, July 13, 1850.

277 *"The storm in"*: Ibid.

277 *president's funeral procession: Daily Union*, July 16, 1850.

277 *"He is hereafter"*: CG 31/1, p. 1363.

278 *proclaimed him a Hero: Daily Union*, July 7, 10, 1850.

278 *"He had no": Charleston Mercury*, July 11, 1850.

278 *"His mind was": Weekly Eagle*, July 11, 1850.

CHAPTER 22: "ALL IS PARALYSIS"

Page

279 *"able, enlightened"*: Henry Clay to James Lynch et al., September 20, 1848, in Hay, ed., *Papers of Henry Clay*, Vol. 10, pp. 544–45.

279 *Like many men:* Frank H. Severance, ed., *Millard Fillmore Papers*, Vol. 1, pp. 1–16; Rayback, *Millard Fillmore*, pp. 6, 101–2, 201–4; Smith, *The Presidencies of Zachary Taylor and Millard Fillmore*, p. 162ff; *The National Era*, July 18, 1850.

279 *"He had the peculiar"*: Quoted in Rayback, *Millard Fillmore*, p. 177.

280 *"God knows that"*: Millard Fillmore to Daniel Webster, October 23, 1850, in Wiltse and Birkner, eds., *Papers of Daniel Webster: Correspondence*, Vol. 7, pp. 162–64.

280 *Fillmore saw slavery:* Suppressed portion of Fillmore's 1852 message to Congress, in Severance, *Millard Fillmore Papers*, Vol. 1, pp. 313–24; Zachary Taylor to J. W. Webb, September 24, 1848, Presidents Papers, Filson Historical Society, Louisville; Rayback, *Millard Fillmore*, pp. 174, 187, 368–69.

281 *"Where is Fillmore?"*: Quoted in Smith, *The Presidencies of Zachary Taylor and Millard Fillmore*, p. 160.

281 *"How lonesome this"*: Ibid.

281 *"I have no"*: Severance, *Millard Fillmore Papers*, p. 329.

281 *"May you be"*: B. B. French to Fillmore, July 16, 1850, Fillmore Papers, Library of Congress.

281 *"unfit even for"*: CG 31/1, p. 1473.

282 *"Take Webster into"*: "True Friend" to Fillmore, July 16, 1850, Fillmore Papers, Library of Congress.

282 *"Black Dan"*: Rayback, *Millard Fillmore*, pp. 241–46.

282 It *"has suddenly"*: D. D. Barnard to Fillmore, July 10, 1850, Fillmore Papers, Library of Congress.

282 *"the political experience"*: Edward Everett to Fillmore, July 11, 1850, Fillmore Papers, Library of Congress.

283 *an exceptionally confrontational letter*: Peter H. Bell to Zachary Taylor, June 15, 1850, Executive Record Book, Texas State Library.

283 *"wild, extravagant"*: Bell to Texas congressional delegation, June 13, 1850, Executive Record Book, Texas State Library.

283 *"Here we are"*: CG 31/1, App., p. 1266ff.

284 *"My own experience"*: Clay to William N. Mercer, July 21, 1850, in Hay, ed. *Papers of Henry Clay*, Vol. 10, p. 771.

284 *his final great oration*: CG 31/1, App., p. 1404ff.

287 *"It is true"*: CG 31/1, App., p. 1414.

288 *Barnwell starchily replied*: Ibid.

CHAPTER 23: THE OMNIBUS OVERTURNED

Page

289 *extravagantly predicted*: Elizabeth Blair Lee to Samuel P. Lee, July 12, 1850, Blair and Lee Family Papers, Princeton University Library.

289 *he boasted of*: Henry Clay to Thomas H. Clay, August 6, 1850, in Hay, ed., *Papers of Henry Clay*, Vol. 10, p. 791.

290 *"You may rely"*: Sam Houston to Margaret Houston, June 3, 1850, in Roberts, ed., *Personal Correspondence of Sam Houston*, Vol. 3, pp. 206–7.

290 *"a great Union party"*: Quoted in Donald Braider, *Solitary Star*, p. 263.

290 *Texas expected "justice"*: CG 31/1, App., p. 1478.

290 *"We have some"*: Sam Houston to Margaret Houston, July 18, 1850, in Roberts, ed., *Personal Correspondence of Sam Houston*, p. 230.

290 *Rusk accused*: CG 31/1, App., pp. 1420–22, 1429, 1435–37, 1440; *Appendix to the Journals of the Senate*, 3/2, State of Texas, pp. 84–102.

291 *Benton proposed*: CG 31/1, App., pp. 1266, 1430, 1433, 1455.

292 *"fire, courage, and strength"*: Elizabeth Blair Lee to Samuel P. Lee, July 29, 1850, Blair and Lee Family Papers, Princeton University Library.

292 *"persons who never"*: CG 31/1, App., p. 1462.

292 *Dawson's amendment*: CG 31/1, App., pp. 1463–70.

293 *Douglas demanded: CG* 31/1, pp. 1114–15, App., pp. 1458, 1470; Johannsen, *Stephen A. Douglas*, pp. 291–92.

294 *Paradoxically, he had:* Frederick Douglass, *Autobiographies*, p. 892.

294 *"What fastens one":* Quoted in Stegmaier, *Texas, New Mexico, and the Compromise of 1850*, p. 193.

294 *Davis continued to call: CG* 31/1, App., pp. 1470–72.

295 *James A. Pearce:* Millard Fillmore to James A. Pearce, July 19, 1850, and Pearce to Fillmore, July 19, 21, 1850, Fillmore Papers, Library of Congress; Rayback, *Millard Fillmore*, pp. 249–50.

296 *"It makes the bill": CG* 31/1, App., p. 1473.

296 *Clay was stunned: CG* 31/1, App., p. 1474ff.

296 *"He could be shot":* Ibid.

296 *David Yulee:* Ibid.

297 *"I have no":* Ibid.

297 *Benton got it: CG* 31/1, App., pp. 1476–78.

298 *Now the real drama: CG* 31/1, App., pp. 1479–83.

298 *He stalked alone:* Remini, *Henry Clay*, p. 757.

298 *The men, both:* New York *Express,* August 2, 1850; Nevins, *Ordeal of the Union*, p. 340.

298 *"Their vehicle is": CG* 31/1, App., p. 1484.

299 *There was still: CG* 31/1, App., p. 1485.

299 *"died of amendments":* Elizabeth Blair Lee to Samuel P. Lee, August 1, 1850, Blair and Lee Family Papers, Princeton University Library.

299 *Clay and his friends: CG* 31/1, App., pp. 1486–87, 1491–93.

300 *"But being too": CG* 31/1, App., p. 1488.

300 *"The compromise bill":* Online at www.nabbhistory.Salisbury.edu.

300 *"If blood is": CG* 31/1, App., p. 1488.

300 *James Mason icily:* Ibid.

301 *"I should like to": CG* 31/1, App., pp. 1490–91.

301 *"The Union is":* Ibid.

301 *Clay abandoned Washington:* Hay, ed., *Papers of Henry Clay*, Vol. 10, pp. 790–91, n.; *New York Tribune,* August 6, 1850; Nevins, ed., *Diary of Philip Hone*, p. 900.

CHAPTER 24: "A STEAM ENGINE IN BRITCHES"

Page

303 *"The Compromise Bill":* Stephen A. Douglas to Charles H. Lanphier, August 3, 1850, in Johannsen, *Letters of Stephen A. Douglas*, pp. 294–96.

304 *His strategy would:* Smith, *The Presidencies of Zachary Taylor and Millard Fillmore*, pp. 179–81.

305 *Douglas introduced his bill:* CG 31/1, p. 1502.

305 *"the admission of California":* CG 31/1, App., p. 1498.

306 *This plan laid:* CG 31/1, pp. 1500–01.

306 *"It cannot be":* CG 31/1, App., pp. 1540–43.

307 *William Corcoran:* Holman Hamilton, *Prologue to Conflict*, pp. 126–28.

307 *"as many soft":* Daniel Webster to Millard Fillmore, July 30, 1850, Fillmore Papers, Library of Congress.

307 *matter of "absolute necessity":* Webster to Peter H. Bell, August 8, 1850, Santa Fe Papers, Texas State Library.

308 *"If Texas militia":* Richardson, *Compilation of the Messages and Papers of the Presidents*, Vol. 5, pp. 67–73; *The National Era*, August 15, 1850.

308 *"You are hereby":* Quoted in Edrington, "Military Influences on the Texas–New Mexico Boundary Settlement," *New Mexico Historical Review*, Vol. 59, October 1984.

308 *The peacetime army:* Stegmaier, *Texas, New Mexico, and the Compromise of 1850*, pp. 221–31; *Texas State Gazette*, September 7, 1850.

309 *"If attacked in":* Quoted in Stegmaier, *Texas, New Mexico, and the Compromise of 1850*, p. 235.

309 *"If any portion":* CG 31/1, App., p. 1509.

309 *They peppered Pearce:* CG 31/1, pp. 1544, 1554–55, 1561ff, App., pp. 1510, 1561ff, 1570; Hamilton, p. 135ff.

310 *Only Yulee spoke:* CG 31/1, App., pp. 1158–68.

311 *"What is the precise":* CG 31/1, App., p. 1564.

312 *"They are dwindling":* CG 31/1, App., pp. 1566–67.

312 *"The land is":* Ibid.

312 *"If you fail us":* "A Virginian" to Thomas H. Rusk, August 8, 1850, Rusk Papers, Center for American History, University of Texas, Austin.

312 *"It is unpleasant":* Isaac Parker to Rusk, August 20, 1850, Rusk Papers, University of Texas.

312 *By August 9:* Stegmaier, *Texas, New Mexico, and the Compromise of 1850,* pp. 205–7.

312 *Rusk, who spoke: CG* 31/1, App., pp. 1576–77.

313 *When Douglas called: CG* 31/1, p. 1555, App., p. 1581; Hamilton, *Prologue to Conflict,* p. 135ff; Stegmaier, *Texas, New Mexico, and the Compromise of 1850,* pp. 219–20.

313 *"Upon this question": CG* 31/1, App., p. 1560.

314 *Davis, in his last: CG* 31/1, App., pp. 1533–44.

314 *"Thank God I": CG* 31/1, App., p. 1521.

315 *"I live very far": CG* 31/1, App., pp. 1535–37.

315 *The vote, when: CG* 31/1, p. 1573.

315 *This time it was: CG* 31/1, pp. 1583, 1589, App., p. 1560ff.

316 *"Nothing shall induce": CG* 31/1, App., p. 1556.

CHAPTER 25: "BREAK YOUR MASTERS' LOCKS"

Page

317 *"Those who now":* Peter H. Bell to Texas Legislature, August 13, 1850, Executive Record Book, Texas State Library; Washington D. Miller to Thomas J. Rusk, August 23, 1850, Rusk Papers, Center for American History, University of Texas.

318 *In mid-July:* Bell, circular letter, July 16, 1850, Executive Records, Texas State Library.

318 *"Hot spirits":* Isaac Parker to Rusk, August 20, 1850, Rusk Papers, University of Texas; James H. Raymond to Bell, August 10, 1850, *Appendix to the Journals of the Senate,* 3/2, State of Texas, p. 51.

318 *"Why hesitate": Clarksville Northern Standard,* July 27, 1850.

318 *Raucous public meetings: The National Era,* July 25, 1850; *Texas State Gazette,* June 15, 1850; Neighbors, "The Taylor-Neighbors Struggle over the Upper Rio Grande Region of Texas in 1850," *The Southwestern Historical Review,* Vol. 61, April 1958.

318 *"choice spirits of Kentucky":* S. S. Scott to G. McCrary, July 31, 1850, Rusk Papers, University of Texas.

318 *"I sea that":* Presley Yates to Rusk, August 28, 1850, Rusk Papers, University of Texas.

318 *Another Georgian promised:* E. M. Smith to Bell, September 12, 1850, Rusk Papers, University of Texas.

318 *"Texas has been"*: Samuel Colt to Bell, July 26, 1850, Rusk Papers, University of Texas.

319 *"it is the indisputable"*: Quoted in Twitchell, *The Leading Facts of New Mexico History*, Vol. 2, pp. 275–76.

319 *Douglas judiciously disappeared*: Johannsen, *Stephen A. Douglas*, p. 296.

320 *"It is true"*: Stephen Douglas to Charles H. Lanphier, September 5, 1850, in Johannsen, ed., *The Letters of Stephen A. Douglas*, pp. 189–90.

320 *The bill*: CG 31/1, App., pp. 1582–84.

321 *"You may as well"*: CG 31/1, App., p. 1604.

321 *one thousand or fewer*: Fergus M. Bordewich, *Bound for Canaan*, pp. 408–9, 436–37.

321 *Some abolitionists estimated*: Ibid., pp. 379–80; *The North Star*, September 5, 1850.

321 *"The principle of"*: CG 31/1, App., p. 1266ff.

322 *"They are a pest"*: CG 31/1, App., p. 1584.

322 *Andrew Butler scoffed*: CG 31/1, App., p. 1585.

322 *blacks in many northern cities*: First Annual Report of the New York Committee of Vigilance, p. 50ff.

322 *The mother of*: Jermain W. Loguen, *The Rev. J. W. Loguen, as A Slave and as A Freeman*, pp. 12–14.

323 *Henry Scott*: First Annual Report of the New York Committee of Vigilance, p. 50ff.

323 *Mason argued that*: CG 31/1, App., pp. 1610–11.

324 *Shifting ground, Winthrop*: CG 31/1, App., p. 1586.

324 *shot back Butler*: CG 31/1, App., p. 1587.

324 *"If the most"*: Ibid.

325 *The debate briefly flickered*: CG 31/1, App., pp. 1592–97.

326 *"If, for considerations"*: CG 31/1, App., p. 1614.

326 *David Yulee, in*: CG 31/1, App., pp. 1622–23.

326 *"to extend a"*: Quoted in CG 31/1, App., p. 1592.

327 *The convention met*: The North Star, September 5, October 3, 1850; *The Liberator*, September 6, 27, October 20, 1850; Hugh C. Humphreys, " 'Agitate! Agitate! Agitate!' The Great Fugitive Slave Law Convention and Its Rare Daguerrotype," *Madison County Heritage*, No. 19, 1994; Milton C. Sernett, *North Star Country*, pp. 129–32; Harrold, *Subversives*, pp. 147–48, 156–59.

328 *"Why is there"*: *CG* 31/1, App., pp. 1622–23.

329 *On August 23:* *CG* 31/1, App., p. 1630; Lynda Lasswell Crist, ed., *The Papers of Jefferson Davis,* Vol. 4, pp. 197–99; Hamilton, *Prologue to Conflict,* pp. 138–41.

329 *Only when he learned:* Johannsen, *Stephen A. Douglas,* p. 296.

329 *the "atrocious proceedings":* *CG* 31/1, App., p. 1630.

CHAPTER 26: "IT IS TIME WE SHOULD ACT"

Page

332 *" 'Look to the Senate' ":* *New York Herald,* September 6, 1850.

332 *H. W. Hilliard:* *CG* 31/1, App., pp. 1191–93.

332 *"as good as they":* *CG* 31/1, App., p. 1208; Schott, *Alexander H. Stephens of Georgia,* pp. 123–26.

333 *To assuage the South:* Michael F. Holt, *The Rise and Fall of the American Whig Party,* p. 542.

333 *"The Administration hits":* Quoted in ibid., p. 539.

333 *Douglas's strategy:* Holman Hamilton, "Kentucky's Linn Boyd and the Dramatic Days of 1850," *The Register of the Kentucky Historical Society,* Vol. 55, July 1957; Stephen A. Douglas to George Walker and Charles H. Lanphier, September 5, 1850, in Johannsen, ed., *Letters of Stephen A. Douglas,* p. 194; Stegmaier, *Texas, New Mexico, and the Compromise of 1850,* pp. 174–75; Holt, *The Rise and Fall of the American Whig Party,* pp. 538–43.

334 *"politics and his patriotism":* Mary Tyler Peabody Mann, *Life of Horace Mann,* p. 283.

334 *"in the end":* Quoted in Hamilton, *Prologue to Conflict,* p. 155.

335 *"exerts more influence":* Quoted in Nevins, *Ordeal of the Union,* p. 170.

335 *"their language and":* Swisshelm, *Half a Century,* pp. 128–29.

335 *"an inverted snowstorm":* Quoted in Hamilton, *Prologue to Conflict,* p. 154.

335 *Boyd then moved:* *CG* 31/1, pp. 1683, 1696–97.

337 *"smoke out the":* *CG* 31/1, p. 1700.

337 *"The time for action":* Ibid.

337 *What followed was:* *CG* 31/1, pp. 1736ff, 1747–50.

338 *"as dead as":* *New York Herald,* September 5, 1850.

338 *"The Ho of Reps":* Douglas to Walker and Lanphier, September 5, 1850, in Johannsen, ed., *Letters of Stephen A. Douglas,* p. 194.

338 *"I am willing"*: CG 31/1, p. 1701.

338 *dizzying procedural ballet*: CG 31/1, pp. 1751–58.

342 *The next morning*: CG 31/1, pp. 1762–64.

342 *After an extended*: CG 31/1, pp. 205–9; Stegmaier, *Texas, New Mexico, and the Compromise of 1850*, pp. 275, 290–91.

342 *"But as the friends"*: CG 31/1, p. 1764.

343 *At 2:45 P.M.*: Ibid.; Hamilton, *Prologue to Conflict*, p. 159.

343 *"The announcement of"*: CG 31/1, p. 1764.

343 *Senators, congressmen*: Hamilton, "Kentucky's Linn Boyd and the Dramatic Days of 1850."

343 *"The North is"*: Horace Mann to Mary Mann, September 6, 1850, Mann Papers, Library of Congress.

344 *"Another hard day's"*: Hamilton, "Kentucky's Linn Boyd and the Dramatic Days of 1850."

344 *The next day*: CG 31/1, pp. 1769–74.

345 *And on the 12th*: CG 31/1, p. 1807.

345 *"In the face of"*: Horace Mann to Rev. S. J. May, in Mann, *Life of Horace Mann*, pp. 331–32.

345 *No one in Washington*: Poore, *Perley's Reminiscences of Sixty Years in the National Metropolis*, pp. 384–85; *New York Herald*, September 8, 10, 1850; *New York Tribune*, September 10, 1850; *New York Post*, September 10, 1850; Hamilton, *Prologue to Conflict*, p. 160; Nevins, *Ordeal of the Union*, p. 343; Holt, *The Rise and Fall of the American Whig Party*, p. 543; Johannsen, *Stephen A. Douglas*, p. 298.

CHAPTER 27: TRIUMPHS

Page

347 *what Texas would do*: Stegmaier, *Texas, New Mexico, and the Compromise of 1850*, pp. 249ff, 297–98.

348 *mass meetings*: *Texas State Gazette*, September 7, 1850.

348 *"War to the knife"*: Ibid., September 21, 1850.

348 *Outside the state*: May, *John A. Quitman*, pp. 240–46; *Mississippi Free Trader*, September 7, 1850; *The Raleigh Register*, September 7, 1850.

348 *"We got the best"*: George T. Wood to Washington D. Miller, undated September, Executive Records, Texas State Library.

348 *"If its sale":* Richard S. Hunt to Thomas H. Rusk, September 17, 1850, Rusk Papers, Center for American History, University of Texas.

349 *"Harmony is secured": Frankfort Commonwealth,* September 10, 1850.

349 *"where I desire":* Henry Clay to Thomas H. Clay, September 6, 1850, in Hay, ed., *Papers of Henry Clay,* Vol. 10, p. 806.

349 *His bill's first section: CG* 31/1, p. 1743.

349 *"healing the wound": CG* 31/1, App., p. 1024.

349 *"hasten to a decision": CG* 31/1, App., p. 1647.

350 *Robert Hunter: CG* 31/1, App., pp. 1630–33.

350 *"Well, sir, my": CG* 31/1, App., pp. 1633–34.

351 *This portion of: CG* 31/1, App., p. 1666.

351 *"The District is": CG* 31/1, App., p. 1669.

352 *who "desert us": CG* 31/1, App., p. 1673.

352 *Seward's last words: CG* 31/1, App., pp. 1642, 1648–49.

352 *Even fellow antislavery: CG* 31/1, App., pp. 1643, 1646, 1647, 1651.

353 *Clay, impatient:* Clay to Thomas H. Clay, September 6, 1850, in Hay, ed., *Papers of Henry Clay,* Vol. 10, p. 806; Clay to Henry Clay, Jr., September 10, and October 22, 1850, in ibid., pp. 807, 823; Clay to Richard H. Bayard, September 13, 18, 1850, in ibid., pp. 811, 815.

353 *"Our northern friends": CG* 31/1, App., pp. 1664–66, 1673–74.

354 *"The thing is now": CG* 31/1, App., p. 1829.

354 *Clay replied:* Ibid.

354 *"I have a right":* Ibid.

354 *"As to tyranny":* Ibid.

355 *"If any man": CG* 31/1, App., p. 1830.

355 *"I do not deem":* Ibid.

356 *"God knows that":* Millard Fillmore to Daniel Webster, October 23, 1850, in Severance, ed., *Millard Fillmore Papers,* Vol. 1, p. 333.

356 *"I shall not":* Fillmore to Webster, October 28, 1850, in ibid., p. 336.

356 *"It would be utterly": CG* 31/1, App., p. 2057.

357 *"Our protracted session": CG* 31/1, p. 2072.

CHAPTER 28: "A SCANDALOUS OUTRAGE"

Page

358 *"We have been":* Online at millercenter.org/scripps/archive/speeches.

358 *"pacify, tranquillize":* Speech to the General Assembly of Kentucky, November 15, 1850, in Hay, ed., *Papers of Henry Clay*, Vol. 10, pp. 828–31.

359 *Abolitionists denounced Fillmore: The Liberator*, October 4, 1850; *The New Hampshire Statesman*, September 27, 1850.

359 *"a fecund box":* Quoted in Schott, *Alexander H. Stephens of Georgia*, p. 126.

359 *"We* despise the": Quoted in ibid., p. 127.

359 *a slave collar:* Stegmaier, *Texas, New Mexico, and the Compromise of 1850*, p. 310.

359 *"humble submission to": Texas State Gazette*, September 21, 1850.

359 *In mid-October:* Stegmaier, *Texas, New Mexico, and the Compromise of 1850*, pp. 312–13; Binkley, *The Expansionist Movement in Texas*, pp. 216–17.

360 *"I see clearly":* Bleser, *Secret and Sacred*, pp. 205–6.

360 *The most bitter:* May, *John A. Quitman*, pp. 242ff, 261ff; Cooper, *Jefferson Davis, American*, p. 218ff.

361 *Davis claimed absurdly:* Speech at Fayette, September 11, 1851, in Cooper, ed., *Jefferson Davis: The Essential Writings*, p. 95ff.

361 *"I regard your":* Quoted in Cooper, *Jefferson Davis, American*, p. 239.

361 *Its first victim: The Fugitive Slave Bill: Its History and Unconstitutionality, with an Account of the Seizure and Enslavement of James Hamlet and His Subsequent Restoration to Liberty; The North Star*, October 3, 24, 1850; *The National Era*, October 10, 1850; Wilbur H. Siebert, *The Underground Railroad from Slavery to Freedom*, p. 269.

362 *By midwinter: Voice of the Fugitive*, January 1, February 26, 1851; *Frederick Douglass' Paper*, November 13, 1851; *Columbia Spy*, January 15, March 8, April 26, 1851; Bordewich, *Bound for Canaan*, pp. 323–24; Siebert, *The Underground Railroad from Slavery to Freedom*, pp. 194, 299, 317–18.

362 *"as from an":* Douglass, *Autobiographies*, p. 279.

362 *"Wo to the poor": The North Star*, October 3, 1850.

363 *"What is life":* Loguen, *The Rev. J. W. Loguen, as A Slave, and as A Freeman*, pp. 391–93.

363 *Public meetings from: The North Star*, October 24, 31, 1850; *The National Era*, September 26, October 10, 21, December 19, 1850.

363 *"throw the arms"*: The North Star, December 5, 1850.

364 *"silenced in but"*: Quoted in Faust, *James Henry Hammond and the Old South*, p. 161.

364 *Slave hunters met*: The Liberator, December 6, 1850, February 21, 1851; *The National Era*, October 31, 1850, February 2, 26, 27, 1851; *Voice of the Fugitive*, February 26, December 3, 1851; Gary Collison, *Shadrach Minkins*, p. 112ff.

364 *Fillmore had made*: Millard Fillmore to Daniel Webster, October 28, 1850, in Severance, ed., *Millard Fillmore Papers*, Vol. 1, p. 336; Webster to Fillmore, October 29, 1850, in Wiltse and Birkner, eds., *Papers of Daniel Webster: Correspondence*, Vol. 7, p. 173.

364 *"a scandalous outrage"*: Fillmore, "Proclamation," February 18, 1851, in Wiltse and Birkner, eds., *Papers of Daniel Webster: Correspondence*, Vol. 7, pp. 206–7.

365 *"traitors! traitors! traitors!"*: Frederick Douglass' Paper, October 16, 1851.

365 *freedom seeker, Thomas Sims*: Remini, *Daniel Webster*, p. 723ff; Webster to Fillmore, April 13, 1851, in Wiltse and Birkner, eds., *Papers of Daniel Webster: Correspondence*, Vol. 7, pp. 232–33.

365 *"I congratulate you"*: Fillmore to Webster, April 16, 1851, in Wiltse and Birkner, eds., *Papers of Daniel Webster: Correspondence*, Vol. 7, p. 237.

365 *at Christiana, Pennsylvania*: Lancaster Intelligencer and Journal, September 16, 23, 1851; William Parker, "The Freedman's Story," *Atlantic Monthly*, February and March 1866.

366 *among them Senator*: emails to author from Brian Fleming, Special Collections, University of Rochester Library, Rochester, New York, February 19, 2010; and Jennifer Haines, Education Director, Seward House Museum, Auburn, NY, June 11, 2011.

367 *"I have just"*: Voice of the Fugitive, October 8, 1851.

367 *Henry Clay's reaction*: CG 32/1, App., p. 293ff; *The Liberator*, February 21, 1851.

367 *"all the old"*: Henry Clay to William N. Mercer, August 1, 1851, in Hay, ed., *Papers of Henry Clay*, Vol. 10, pp. 907–8.

368 *had "nearly emptied"*: Clay to John Morrison Clay, February 28, 1852, in ibid., p. 956.

368 *In letters home*: Clay to Lucretia H. Clay, December 9, 18, 1851, January 4, 12, March 22, 1852, and others, in ibid., pp. 936, 938, 943, 947, 961; Clay to James Brown Clay, May 9, 1851, in ibid., p. 889; Clay to Thomas H. Clay, April 21, 1852, in ibid., p. 965.

368 *In his will:* "Last Will and Testament," in ibid., pp. 900–904.

368 *"the greatest project":* "Speech to the Annual Meeting of the American Colonization Society," January 21, 1851, in ibid., pp. 844ff.

368 *"Those who would":* Online at millercenter.org/scripps/archive/speeches.

369 *Daniel Webster died:* Remini, *Daniel Webster*, p. 753ff; Dalzell, *Daniel Webster and the Trial of American Nationalism*, pp. 301–4.

369 *"differed from each":* CG 32/2, pp. 53–54.

EPILOGUE: THE RECKONING

Page

370 *"The mere perishable":* Untitled ms., June 1853, Adam Beatty Papers, Filson Historical Society, Louisville.

371 *an "evasive truce":* Sean Wilentz, *The Rise of American Democracy*, p. 637.

371 *"the tide of emigration":* Stephen A. Douglas to J. H. Crane et al., December 17, 1853, in Johannsen, ed., *Letters of Stephen A. Douglas*, pp. 268–71.

371 *"sink in hell":* Quoted in Douglas R. Egerton, *Year of Meteors*, p. 21.

372 *"the great fundamental":* Douglas to Concord (New Hampshire) *State Capitol Reporter*, February 14, 1854, in Johannsen, ed., *Letters of Stephen A. Douglas*, pp. 284–85.

372 *"I had the authority":* Quoted in Walter A. McDougall, *Throes of Democracy*, p. 333.

372 *"to kill every":* Quoted in Egerton, *Year of Meteors*, p. 25.

372 *"We will engage":* The National Era, July 10, 1856.

372 *When elections for:* Bordewich, *Bound for Canaan*, pp. 406, 416.

373 *"a wicked fraud":* Douglas to John W. Forney et al., February 6, 1858, in Johannsen, ed., *Letters of Stephen A. Douglas*, p. 408.

373 *"This Nebraska business":* Frederick Douglass' Paper, March 7, 1854.

374 *"ancient, eternal conflict":* Quoted in John M. Taylor, *William Henry Seward*, p. 104.

374 *"to bundle on":* Unpublished paper, W. U. Hensel, "The Attitude of James Buchanan, a Citizen of Lancaster County, Towards the Institution of Slavery in the United States," Lancaster (Pennsylvania) Historical Society.

374 *Dred Scott decision:* Online at caselaw.lp.findlaw.com.

375 *"Where," he then demanded:* CG 31/1, App., p. 1641.

375 *"what Dred Scott's master"*: Johannsen, *The Lincoln-Douglas Debates of 1858*, pp. 14–17.

375 *Another who attacked:* Chambers, *Old Bullion Benton*, p. 433.

376 *"The mare's nest"*: Quoted in ibid., pp. 401–2.

376 *"No northern doughface"*: Quoted in ibid., p. 403.

376 *"of gigantic intellect"*: Quoted in ibid., p. 436ff.

378 *famous series of debates:* Johannsen, *The Lincoln-Douglas Debates of 1858*, pp. 37ff, 75ff, 116ff, 162ff, 206ff, 245ff, 286ff.

382 *The only hope:* Douglas to William A. Richardson, June 20, 1860, in Johannsen, ed., *Letters of Stephen A. Douglas*, p. 492.

382 *"If slavery is"*: Quoted in Egerton, *Year of Meteors*, p. 74.

383 *"Gentlemen of the South"*: Quoted in Johannsen, *Stephen A. Douglas*, p. 754.

383 *"As most of"*: Johannsen, *Stephen A. Douglas*, p. 771.

384 *"I am ready"*: Douglas to August Belmont, December 25, 1860, in Johannsen, ed., *Letters of Stephen A. Douglas*, p. 505; Douglas to Charles H. Lanphier, December 25, 1860 in ibid.

385 *"Experience has proved"*: *Charleston Mercury*, December 25, 1860.

385 *"Go to the yeomanry"*: CG 31/1, App., p. 1540.

385 *"The Union is worth"*: Quoted in James L. Haley, *Passionate Nation*, p. 292.

386 *A few days later:* William J. Cooper, ed., *Jefferson Davis: The Essential Writings*, pp. 196–97; Cooper, *Jefferson Davis, American*, pp. 352–53.

386 *On April 12: Charleston Mercury*, April 12, 1861.

386 *"the very extreme"*: Douglas to Belmont, December 25, 1860, in Johannsen, ed., *Letters of Stephen A. Douglas*, p. 505.

386 *"There can be no"*: Quoted in Johannsen, *Stephen A. Douglas*, p. 868.

387 *Glorieta Pass: The War of the Rebellion*, Series 1, Vol. 9, pp. 530–45; Don E. Alberts, "The Battle of Glorieta and the Union Victory in the Far West," *Hallowed Ground*, Winter 2007.

388 *"It is with sorrow"*: E. R. Boles to "Dear father," April 25, 1862, Fray Angélico Chávez History Library, Santa Fe.

389 *Abraham Lincoln completed:* Pohl and Wennersten, *Abraham Lincoln and the End of Slavery in the District of Columbia*, pp. 63–68; Mary Tremain, *Slavery in the District of Columbia*, pp. 94–95; Green, *Washington*, pp. 272–76; Harrold, *Subversives*, pp. 234–39.

389 *"The proceedings did not"*: Quoted in Pohl and Wennersten, *Abraham Lincoln and the End of Slavery in the District of Columbia*, pp. 83–84.

389 *"All hail the day"*: The Christian Recorder, April 26, 1862.

390 *a former Union infantryman*: Quoted in Foster, "Webster's Seventh of March Speech and the Secession Movement," *The American Historical Review*, Vol. 27, January 1922.

390 *Andrew J. Harlan*: A. J. Harlan, "Last Survivor of a Great Congress," *National Magazine*, Vol. 15, March 1902.

391 *"It has gone up"*: CG 31/1, App., p. 818.

392 *"A shrewd defender"*: Finkelman, *Millard Fillmore*, p. 2111.

393 *Neighbors was shotgunned*: Anderson, *The Conquest of Texas*, pp. 325–26.

393 *In California*: James J. Rawls, *Indians of California*, pp. 83–84, 172; Russell Thornton, *American Indian Holocaust and Survival*, pp. 48–49; Bordewich, *Killing the White Man's Indian*, pp. 50–51.

395 *"informs all our habits"*: Pamphlet, William H. Trescot, *The Position and Course of the South.*

395 *"With Cuba"*: Quoted in Robert Kagan, *Dangerous Nation*, p. 231.

395 *the North's advantages*: Foster, "Webster's Seventh of March Speech and the Secession Movement."

396 *"a politician's trick"*: Kagan, *Dangerous Nation*, p. 233.

SELECTED BIBLIOGRAPHY

BOOKS

Abel, Annie Heloise, ed. *The Official Correspondence of James S. Calhoun.* Washington, D.C.: U.S. Government Printing Office, 1915.

Adams, Henry. *The Education of Henry Adams.* New York: Modern Library, 1931.

Allen, William C. *History of the United States Capitol: A Chronicle of Design, Construction, and Politics.* Honolulu: University Press of the Pacific, 2005.

Ambrose, Stephen E. *Halleck: Lincoln's Chief of Staff.* Baton Rouge: Louisiana State University Press, 1990.

Anderson, Gary Clayton. *The Conquest of Texas: Ethnic Cleansing in the Promised Land, 1820–1875.* Norman: University of Oklahoma Press, 2005.

Annals of Congress. Online at www.memory.loc.gov.

Appendix to the Journals of the Senate, of the Third Legislature, State of Texas, Second Session. Austin: W. H. Cushney, 1850.

Avary, Myrta Lockett, ed. *Recollections of Alexander H. Stephens.* New York: Doubleday, Page, 1910.

Baker, George E., ed. *The Works of William H. Seward*, Vol. 1. New York: Redfield, 1853.

Bancroft, Frederic. *The Life of William H. Seward*, Vol. 2. New York: Harper & Bros., 1900.

———. *Slave Trading in the Old South.* New York: Frederick Ungar, 1959.

Bancroft, Hubert H. *History of California.* San Francisco: History Company, 1888.

Barker, Malcom E. *San Francisco Memoirs, 1835–1851: Eyewitness Accounts of the Birth of a City.* San Francisco: Londonborn, 1994.

Benton, Thomas Hart. *Thirty Years' View: A History of the Working of the American Government for Thirty Years, from 1820 to 1850*, Vol. 2. New York: D. Appleton, 1856.

Berlin, Ira. *Many Thousands Gone: The First Two Centuries of Slavery in America.* Cambridge: Harvard University Press, 1998.

Bieber, Ralph P. *Southern Trails to California in 1849.* Philadelphia: Porcupine, 1974.

Bigelow, John. *Memoir of the Life and Public Services of John Charles Frémont.* New York: Derby & Jackson, 1856.

Bigler, David L. *The Gold Discovery Journal of Azariah Smith.* Logan: Utah State University Press, 1996.

Binkley, William Campbell. *The Expansionist Movement in Texas.* Berkeley: University of California Press, 1925.

Bleser, Carol. *Secret and Sacred: The Diaries of James Henry Hammond, a Southern Slaveholder.* New York: Oxford University Press, 1988.

Bordewich, Fergus M. *Bound for Canaan: The Underground Railroad and the War for the Soul of America.* New York: Amistad, 2005.

———. *Killing the White Man's Indian: Reinventing Native Americans at the End of the Twentieth Century.* New York: Anchor, 1996.

Braden, Waldo W., ed. *Oratory in the Old South, 1828–1860.* Baton Rouge: Louisiana State University Press, 1970.

Braider, Donald. *Solitary Star: A Biography of Sam Houston.* New York: G. P. Putnam's Sons, 1974.

Brands, H. W. *The Age of Gold: The California Gold Rush and the New American Dream.* New York: Anchor, 2003.

Brown, James S. Excerpt from *California Gold: An Authentic History of the First Find.* Oakland: Pacific Press, 1894.

Browne, J. Ross. *Report of the Debates in the Convention of California, on the Formation of the State Constitution, in September and October, 1849.* Washington: John T. Towers, 1850.

Buffum, E. Gould. *Six Months in the Gold Mines.* Los Angeles: Ward Ritchie, 1959.

Burin, Eric. *Slavery and the Peculiar Solution: A History of the American Colonization Society.* Gainesville: University Press of Florida, 2005.

Bushong, William B. *Glenn Brown's History of the United States Capital.* Washington, D.C.: U.S. Government Printing Office, 1998.

Butler, Anne M., and Wendy Wolff. *United States Senate Election, Expulsion and Censure Cases, 1793–1990.* Washington, D.C.: U.S. Government Printing Office, 1995.

Callahan, James Morton. *Cuba and International Relations: A Historical Study in American Diplomacy.* Baltimore: Johns Hopkins Press, 1899.

Campbell, Randolph B. *An Empire for Slavery: The Peculiar Institution in Texas, 1821–1865.* Baton Rouge: Louisiana State University Press, 1989.

Campbell, Stanley W. *The Slave Catchers.* Chapel Hill: University of North Carolina Press, 1970.

Chaffin, Tom. *Fatal Glory: Narciso López and the First Clandestine U.S. War Against Cuba.* Charlottesville: University Press of Virginia, 1996.

Chambers, William Nisbet. *Old Bullion Benton: Senator from the New West.* Boston: Atlantic Monthly Press, 1956.

Chávez, Ernesto. *The U.S. War with Mexico: A Brief History with Documents.* Boston: Bedford/St. Martin's, 2008.

Claiborne, J. F. H., ed. *Life and Correspondence of John A. Quitman*, Vol. 1. New York: Harper & Bros., 1860.

Clarke, Dwight L., ed. *The Original Journals of Henry Smith Turner: With Stephen Watts Kearny to New Mexico and California, 1846–1847.* Norman: University of Oklahoma Press, 1966.

Cohn, David L. *The Life and Times of King Cotton.* New York: Oxford University Press, 1956.

Collison, Gary. *Shadrach Minkins: From Fugitive Slave to Citizen.* Cambridge: Harvard University Press, 1997.

Colton, Calvin, ed. *The Life, Correspondence, and Speeches of Henry Clay.* Vol. 3. New York: A. S. Barnes, 1857.

———, ed. *Speeches of Henry Clay,* Vols. 1, 2. New York: A. S. Barnes, 1857.

———, ed. *The Private Correspondence of Henry Clay.* New York: A. S. Barnes, 1855.

———, ed. *The Works of Henry Clay* (Federal Edition). New York: Putnam, 1904.

Congressional Globe. Online at www.memory.loc.gov.

Cook, Sherburne F. *The Conflict Between the California Indian and White Civilization.* Berkeley: University of California Press, 1976.

Cooper, William J., Jr. *Jefferson Davis, American.* New York: Vintage, 2000.

———, ed. *Jefferson Davis: The Essential Writings.* New York: Modern Library, 2003.

Crallé, Richard K., ed. *The Works of John C. Calhoun.* Columbia: A. S. Johnson, 1851.

Crist, Lynda Lasswell, ed. *The Papers of Jefferson Davis,* Vol. 4, *1849–1852.* Baton Rouge: Louisiana State University Press, 1983.

Cross, Whitney R. *The Burned-Over District: The Social and Intellectual History of Enthusiastic Religion in Western New York, 1800–1850.* New York: Harper Torchbooks, 1965.

Currie, David P. *The Constitution in Congress: Descent into the Maelstrom, 1829–1861.* Chicago: University of Chicago Press, 2005.

Curtis, George Ticknor. *Life of Daniel Webster,* Vols. 1 and 2. New York: Appleton, 1872.

Dalzell, Robert F. *Daniel Webster and the Trial of American Nationalism.* Boston: Houghton Mifflin, 1972.

Davis, William C. *Jefferson Davis: The Man and His Hour.* Baton Rouge: Louisiana State University Press, 1996.

Day, Donald, and Harry Herbert Ullom, eds. *The Autobiography of Sam Houston.* Norman: University of Oklahoma Press, 1954.

Dickens, Charles. *American Notes.* New York: Penguin, 2000.

Dillon, Merton L. *The Abolitionists: The Growth of a Dissenting Minority.* DeKalb: Northern Illinois University Press, 1974.

———. *Slavery Attacked: Southern Slaves and Their Allies, 1619–1865.* Baton Rouge: Louisiana State University Press, 1990.

Dillon, Richard. *Captain John Sutter: Sacramento Valley's Sainted Sinner*. Santa Cruz, Calif.: Western Tanager, 1981.

Dinnerstein, Leonard, and Mary Dal Palsson, eds. *Jews in the South*. Baton Rouge: Louisiana State University Press, 1973.

Dippie, Brian W. *The Vanishing American: White Attitudes and U.S. Indian Policy*. Middletown, Conn.: Wesleyan University Press, 1982.

Douglass, Frederick. *Autobiographies*. New York: Library of America, 1984.

Dunbar, Edward E. *The Romance of the Age; or, The Discovery of Gold in California*. New York: D. Appleton, 1867.

Dyer, Oliver. *Great Senators of the United States Forty Years Ago*. New York: Robert Bonner's Sons, 1889.

Egerton, Douglas R. *Year of Meteors: Stephen Douglas, Abraham Lincoln, and the Election That Brought on the Civil War*. New York: Bloomsbury, 2010.

Eisenhower, John S. D. *Zachary Taylor*. New York: Times Books, 2008.

Elder, Jane Lenz, and David J. Weber. *Trading in Santa Fe: James M. Kingsbury's Correspondence with James Josiah Webb, 1853–1861*. Dallas: Southern Methodist University Press, 1996.

Falconer, Thomas. *Letters and Notes on the Texan Santa Fe Expedition, 1841–1842*. New York: Dauber & Pine, 1930.

Faust, Drew Gilpin, ed. *The Ideology of Slavery: Proslavery Thought in the Antebellum South, 1830–1860*. Baton Rouge: Louisiana State University Press, 1981.

———. *James Henry Hammond and the Old South: A Design for Mastery*. Baton Rouge: Louisiana State University Press, 1982.

Fehrenbach, T. R. *Comanches: The Destruction of a People*. New York: Knopf, 1974.

Fehrenbacher, Don E., ed. *Abraham Lincoln: Speeches and Writings, 1832–1858*, New York: Library of America, 1989.

Finkelman, Paul. *Defending Slavery: Proslavery Thought in the Old South*. Boston: Bedford/St.Martin's, 2003.

———. *Millard Fillmore*. New York: Times Books, 2011.

———, ed. *Fugitive Slaves*. New York: Garland, 1989.

Fischer, David Hackett. *Liberty and Freedom: A Visual History of America's Founding Ideas*. New York: Oxford University Press, 2005.

Fogel, Robert William, and Stanley L. Engerman. *Time on the Cross*. New York: Norton, 1989.

Franklin, John Hope, and Loren Schweninger. *Runaway Slaves: Rebels on the Plantation*. New York: Oxford University Press, 1999.

Freehling, William W. *The Road to Disunion: Secessionists at Bay, 1776–1854*. New York: Oxford University Press, 1990.

Frémont, John Charles. *Memoirs of My Life*. Chicago: Belfort, Clark, 1887.

Furgurson, Ernest B. *Freedom Rising: Washington in the Civil War*. New York: Vintage, 2004.

Gay, Theressa. *James W. Marshall: The Discoverer of California Gold*. Georgetown, Calif.: Talisman, 1967.

Green, Constance M. *Washington: Village and Capital, 1800–1871*. Princeton: Princeton University Press, 1962.

Gudde, Erwin G. *Bigler's Chronicle of the West*. Berkeley: University of California Press, 1962.

Guelzo, Allen C. *Lincoln and Douglas: The Debates That Defined America*. New York: Simon & Schuster, 2008.

Gulick, Charles Adams, Jr., ed. *The Papers of Mirabeau Buonaparte Lamar*, Vol. 2. Austin: A. C. Baldwin & Sons, 1922.

Haley, James L. *Passionate Nation: The Epic History of Texas*. New York: Free Press, 2006.

Hamilton, Holman. *Prologue to Conflict: The Crisis and Compromise of 1850*. New York: Norton, 1964.

Harrold, Stanley. *The Abolitionists and the South, 1831–1861*. Lexington: University Press of Kentucky, 1995.

———. *Subversives: Antislavery Community in Washington, D.C., 1828–1865*. Baton Rouge: Louisiana State University Press, 2003.

Hay, Melba Porter, ed. *The Papers of Henry Clay*, Vol. 10. Lexington: University Press of Kentucky, 1991.

Haynes, George H. *The Senate of the United States*, Vols. 1 and 2. Boston: Houghton Mifflin, 1938.

Heidler, David S., and Jeanne T. Heidler. *Henry Clay: The Essential American*. New York: Random House, 2010.

Heizer, Robert F., ed. *The Destruction of California Indians*. Lincoln: University of Nebraska Press, 1974.

Henderson, Timothy J. *A Glorious Defeat: Mexico and Its War with the United States*. New York: Hill & Wang, 2007.

Herring, George C. *From Colony to Superpower: U.S. Foreign Relations Since 1776*. New York: Oxford University Press, 2008.

Hofstadter, Richard. *The American Political Tradition*. New York: Vintage, 1989.

Holliday, J. S. *The World Rushed In: The California Gold Rush Experience*. New York: Touchstone, 1981.

Holt, Michael F. *The Fate of Their Country: Politicians, Slavery Extension, and the Coming of the Civil War*. New York: Hill & Wang, 2004.

———. *The Political Crisis of the 1850s*. New York: Norton, 1978.

———. *The Rise and Fall of the American Whig Party: Jacksonian Politics and the Onset of the Civil War*. New York: Oxford University Press, 1999.

Horsman, Reginald. *Josiah Nott of Mobile: Southerner, Physician, and Racial Theorist*. Baton Rouge: Louisiana State University Press, 1987.

———. *Race and Manifest Destiny*. Cambridge: Harvard University Press, 1981.

Howe, Daniel Walker. *What Hath God Wrought: The Transformation of America, 1815–1848*. New York: Oxford University Press, 2007.

Huston, James. *Stephen A. Douglas and the Dilemmas of Democratic Equality*. Lanham, Md.: Rowman & Littlefield, 2007.

Jefferson, Thomas. *Writings*. New York: Library of America, 1984.

Jennings, Thelma. *The Nashville Convention: Southern Movement for Unity*. Memphis: Memphis State University Press, 1980.

Johannsen, Robert W., ed. *The Letters of Stephen A. Douglas*. Urbana: University of Illinois Press, 1961.

———. *The Lincoln-Douglas Debates of 1858.* New York: Oxford University Press, 2008.

———. *Stephen A. Douglas.* Urbana: University of Illinois Press, 1973.

———. *To the Halls of the Montezumas: The Mexican War in the American Imagination.* New York: Oxford University Press, 1985.

Julian, George W. *Political Recollections, 1840–1872.* Chicago: Jansen, McClurg and Co., 1884.

Kagan, Robert. *Dangerous Nation: America's Foreign Policy from Its Earliest Days to the Dawn of the Twentieth Century.* New York: Vintage, 2006.

Kendall, George Wilkins. *Narrative of the Texan Santa Fe Expedition.* New York: Harper & Bros., 1850.

Klein, Philip Shriver. *President James Buchanan.* Norwalk: Easton, 1962.

Kluger, Richard. *Seizing Destiny: The Relentless Expansion of American Territory.* New York: Vintage, 2007.

Kolchin, Peter. *American Slavery, 1619–1877.* New York: Hill & Wang, 1995.

Lapp, Rudolph M. *Blacks in Gold Rush California.* New Haven: Yale University Press, 1977.

Lence, Ross M., ed. *Union and Liberty: The Political Philosophy of John C. Calhoun.* Indianapolis: Liberty Fund, 1992.

Libura, Krystyna M., Luis Gerardo Morales Moreno, and Jesús Velasco Márquez. *Echoes of the Mexican-American War.* Toronto: Groundwood, 2004.

Loewen, James W., and Edward H. Sebesta. *The Confederate and Neo-Confederate Reader.* Jackson: University Press of Mississippi, 2010.

Loguen, Jermain W. *The Rev. J. W. Loguen, as A Slave and as A Freeman.* Syracuse: J. G. K. Truair, 1859.

Lothop, Thornton Kirkland. *William Henry Seward.* Boston: Houghton Mifflin, 1899.

Mann, Mary Tyler Peabody. *Life of Horace Mann.* Boston: Lee & Shepard, 1904.

Mannix, Daniel P., and Malcolm Cowley. *Black Cargoes: A History of the Atlantic Slave Trade.* New York: Viking Compass, 1962.

Marszalek, John F. *Commander of All Lincoln's Armies: A Life of General Henry W. Halleck.* Cambridge: Harvard University Press, 2004.

Martin, Asa Earl. *The Anti-Slavery Movement in Kentucky Prior to 1850.* Louisville: Standard Printing Co., 1918.

May, Robert A. *John A. Quitman: Old South Crusader.* Baton Rouge: Louisiana State University Press, 1994.

———. *The Southern Dream of a Caribbean Empire, 1854–1861.* Gainesville: University Press of Florida, 2002.

Mayer, Henry. *All on Fire: William Lloyd Garrison and the Abolition of Slavery.* New York: St. Martin's, 1998.

McCall, George Archibald. Robert W. Frazer, ed. *New Mexico in 1850: A Military View.* Norman: University of Oklahoma Press, 1968.

McCardell, John. *The Idea of a Southern Nation: Southern Nationalists and Southern Nationalism.* New York: Norton, 1979.

McDougall, Marion G. *Fugitive Slaves (1619–1865).* Boston: Ginn & Co., 1891.

McDougall, Walter A. *Throes of Democracy: The American Civil War Era, 1829–1877.* New York: HarperCollins, 2008.

McDougle, Ivan E. *Slavery in Kentucky, 1792–1865.* Lancaster: New Era, 1918.

McFeely, William S. *Frederick Douglass.* New York: Norton, 1991.

Merk, Frederick. *Manifest Destiny and Mission in American History.* New York: Vintage, 1966.

Merrill, Walter M., ed. *The Letters of William Lloyd Garrison,* Vol. 3, *No Union with Slaveholders, 1841–1849.* Cambridge: Harvard University Press, 1973.

Miller, William Lee. *Arguing About Slavery: The Great Battle in the United States Congress.* New York: Knopf, 1996.

Morris, Roy, Jr. *The Long Pursuit: Abraham Lincoln's Thirty-Year Struggle with Stephen Douglas for the Heart and Soul of America.* New York: HarperCollins, 2008.

Morrison, Michael A. *Slavery and the American West: The Eclipse of Manifest Destiny and the Coming of the Civil War.* Chapel Hill: University of North Carolina Press, 1997.

Navarro, Ramón Gil. *The Gold Rush Diary of Ramón Gil Navarro.* Lincoln: University of Nebraska Press, 2000.

Neighbors, Kenneth F. *Robert Simpson Neighbors and the Texas Frontier, 1836–1859.* Waco: Texian Press, 1975.

Allan Nevins, ed., *The Diary of Philip Hone, 1828–1851*, vol. 2. New York: Dodd, Mead, 1927.

———. *Ordeal of the Union: Fruits of Manifest Destiny, 1847–1852.* New York: Scribner's, 1947.

Niven, John. *John C. Calhoun and the Price of Union.* Baton Rouge: Louisiana State University Press, 1988.

———. *Salmon P. Chase.* New York: Oxford University Press, 1995.

Nugent, Walter. *Habits of Empire: A History of American Expansion.* New York: Knopf, 2008.

Nye, Russel B. *Fettered Freedom: Civil Liberties and the Slavery Controversy.* East Lansing: Michigan State University Press, 1949.

Olmsted, Frederick Law. *A Journey Through Texas.* New York: Dix, Edwards, 1857.

Paskoff, Paul F., and Daniel J. Wilson. *The Cause of the South: Selections from De Bow's Review, 1846–1867.* Baton Rouge: Louisiana State University Press, 1982.

Peterson, Merrill D. *The Great Triumvirate: Webster, Clay and Calhoun.* New York: Oxford University Press, 1987.

Pohl, Robert S., and John R. Wennersten. *Abraham Lincoln and the End of Slavery in the District of Columbia.* Washington: Eastern Branch Books, 2009.

Poore, Ben Perley. *Perley's Reminiscences of Sixty Years in the National Metropolis,* Vol 1. Philadelphia: Hubbard Brothers, 1886.

Quinn, Arthur. *The Rivals: William Gwin, David Broderick, and the Birth of California.* New York: Crown, 1994.

Quisenberry, Anderson C. *López's Expeditions to Cuba, 1850–1851.* Louisville: John P. Morton, 1906.

Ramsay, Jack C., Jr. *Thunder Beyond the Brazos: Mirabeau B. Lamar, A Biography.* Austin: Eakin, 1985.

Rawls, James J. *Indians of California: The Changing Image.* Norman: University of Oklahoma Press, 1984.

Rayback, Robert J. *Millard Fillmore: Biography of a President.* Norwalk, Conn.: Easton, 1959.

Register of Debates in Congress. Online at www.memory.loc.gov.

Reinders, Robert C. *End of an Era: New Orleans, 1850–1860.* Gretna, La.: Pelican, 1998.

Remini, Robert V. *At the Edge of the Precipice: Henry Clay and the Compromise That Saved the Union.* New York: Basic Books, 2010.

———. *Daniel Webster: The Man and His Time.* New York: Norton, 1997.

———. *Henry Clay: Spokesman for the Union.* New York: Norton, 1991.

Reynolds, David S. *John Brown Abolitionist.* New York: Knopf, 2005.

———. *Waking Giant: America in the Age of Jackson.* New York: HarperCollins, 2008.

Richards, Leonard L. *The California Gold Rush and the Coming of the Civil War.* New York: Knopf, 2007.

———. *The Slave Power: The Free North and Southern Domination, 1780–1860.* Baton Rouge: Louisiana State University Press, 2000.

Richardson, James D. *A Compilation of the Messages and Papers of the Presidents*, Vols. 5 and 6. New York: Bureau of National Literature, 1897.

Ricks, Mary Kay. *Escape on the Pearl: The Heroic Bid for Freedom on the Underground Railroad.* New York: William Morrow, 2007.

Roberts, Madge Thornall, ed. *The Personal Correspondence of Sam Houston*, Vols. 1, 2, 3, 1848–1852. Denton: University of North Texas Press, 1996–1999.

Ruxton, George F. *Adventures in New Mexico and the Rocky Mountains.* Glorieta, N. M.: Rio Grande Press, 1973.

Sampson, Robert D. *John L. O'Sullivan and His Times.* Kent, Ohio: Kent State University Press, 2003.

Schlesinger, Arthur M. *The Age of Jackson.* New York: Little, Brown, 1945.

Schott, Thomas E. *Alexander H. Stephens of Georgia: A Biography*. Baton Rouge: Louisiana State University Press, 1988.

Schurz, Carl. *Henry Clay*, Vols. 1 and 2. Boston: Houghton Mifflin, 1899.

Sears, Lorenzo. *The History of Oratory*. Chicago: S. C. Griggs, 1896.

Seigenthaler, John. *James K. Polk*. New York: Times Books, 2003.

Serial Set, Thirty-first Congress, Senate Executive Document 57. Library of Congress.

Sernett, Milton C. *North Star Country: Upstate New York and the Crusade for African American Freedom*. Syracuse: Syracuse University Press, 2002.

Severance, Frank H., ed. *Millard Fillmore Papers*, Vol. 1. Buffalo: Buffalo Historical Society, 1907.

Seward, Frederick W. *Seward at Washington*. New York: Derby & Miller, 1891.

———. *William H. Seward: An Autobiography from 1801 to 1834*. New York: Derby & Miller, 1891.

Sherman, William T. *Memoirs*. New York: Barnes & Noble, 2005.

Sides, Hampton. *Blood and Thunder: The Epic Story of Kit Carson and the Conquest of the American West*. New York: Anchor, 2006.

Siebert, Wilbur H. *The Underground Railroad from Slavery to Freedom*. New York: Macmillan, 1898.

Silbey, Joel H. *Storm over Texas: The Annexation Controversy and the Road to Civil War*. New York: Oxford University Press, 2005.

Slaughter, Thomas P. *Bloody Dawn: The Christiana Riot and Racial Violence in the Antebellum North*. New York: Oxford University Press, 1991.

Smith, Elbert B. *The Presidencies of Zachary Taylor and Millard Fillmore*. Lawrence: University Press of Kansas, 1988.

Soulé, Frank, and John H. Gihon. *The Annals of San Francisco*. New York: D. Appleton, 1855.

Stampp, Kenneth. *The Peculiar Institution: Slavery in the Ante-Bellum South*. New York: Vintage, 1956.

Starr, Kevin. *Americans and the California Dream, 1850–1915.* New York: Oxford University Press, 1973.

Stefanson, Anders. *Manifest Destiny: American Expansion and the Empire of Right.* New York: Hill & Wang, 1996.

Stegmaier, Mark J. *Texas, New Mexico, and the Compromise of 1850.* Kent, Ohio: Kent State University Press, 1996.

Stewart, George R. *Names on the Land: A Historical Account of Place-Naming in the United States.* New York: New York Review Books, 2008.

Swisshelm, Jane G. *Half a Century.* Chicago: Jansen, McClurg, 1880.

Tallant, Harold D. *Evil Necessity: Slavery and Political Culture in Antebellum Kentucky.* Lexington: University Press of Kentucky, 2003.

Taylor, John M. *William Henry Seward: Lincoln's Right Hand.* Washington: Brassey's, 1991.

Thomas, John L., ed. *Slavery Attacked: The Abolitionist Crusade.* Englewood Cliffs, N. J.: Prentice Hall, 1965.

Thomas, Lately. *Between Two Empires: The Life Story of California's First Senator, William McKendree Gwin.* Boston: Houghton Mifflin, 1969.

Thornton, Russell. *American Indian Holocaust and Survival: A Population History Since 1492.* Norman: University of Oklahoma Press, 1987.

Trafzer, Clifford E., and Joel R. Hyer, eds. *"Exterminate Them": Written Accounts of the Murder, Rape and Slavery of Native Americans During the California Gold Rush, 1848–1868.* East Lansing: Michigan State University Press, 1999.

Tremain, Mary. *Slavery in the District of Columbia.* New York: G. P. Putnam's Sons, 1892.

Twitchell, Ralph Emerson. *The Leading Facts of New Mexico History,* Vol. 2. Albuquerque: Horn & Wallace, 1963.

———. *The Military Occupation of the Territory of New Mexico from 1846 to 1851.* Santa Fe: Sunstone, 2007.

———. *Old Santa Fe: The Story of Santa Fe's Ancient Capital.* Chicago: Rio Grande Press, 1963.

Utah: A Guide to the State. New York: Hastings House, 1940.

Van Deusen, Glyndon G. *The Jacksonian Era*. New York: Harper Torchbooks, 1959.

———. *William Henry Seward*. New York: Oxford University Press, 1967.

Varon, Elizabeth R. *Disunion! The Coming of the American Civil War*. Chapel Hill: University of North Carolina Press, 2008.

The War of the Rebellion: A Compilation of the Official Records of the Union and Confederate Armies, January–September 1862, Series 1, Vol. 9. Washington, D.C.: U.S. Government Printing Office.

Watson, Harry L. *Andrew Jackson vs. Henry Clay: Democracy and Development in Antebellum America*. Boston: Bedford/St. Martin's, 1998.

Waugh, John C. *On the Brink of Civil War: The Compromise of 1850 and How It Changed the Course of American History*. Wilmington: SR Books, 2003.

Wawro, Gregory J., and Eric Schickler. *Filibuster: Obstruction and Lawmaking in the U.S. Senate*. Princeton: Princeton University Press, 2006.

Wentworth, John. *Congressional Reminiscences*. Chicago: Fergus Printing Company, 1882.

Wheelan, Joseph. *Invading Mexico: America's Continental Dream and the Mexican War, 1846–1848*. New York: Carroll & Graf, 2007.

Whitlock, Flint. *Distant Bugles, Distant Drums: The Union Response to the Confederate Invasion of New Mexico*. Boulder: University Press of Colorado, 2006.

Wilbarger, J. W. *Indian Depredations in Texas*. Austin: Hutchings Printing House, 1889.

Wilentz, Sean. *The Rise of American Democracy: Jefferson to Lincoln*. New York: Norton, 2005.

Williams, John Hoyt. *Sam Houston: A Biography of the Father of Texas*. New York: Simon & Schuster, 1993.

Wilson, Clyde, and Shirley Bright Cook, eds. *The Papers of John C. Calhoun*, Vol. 27. Columbia: University of South Carolina Press, 2003.

Wiltse, Charles M., and Michael J. Birkner, eds. *The Papers of Daniel Webster: Correspondence*, Vol. 7, 1850–1852. Hanover: University Press of New England, 1986.

Winfrey, Dorman H., and Michael L. Tate. *The Indian Papers of Texas and the Southwest, 1825–1916*, Vols. 3 and 5. Austin: Texas State Historical Association, 1995.

Zarefsky, David. *Lincoln, Douglas and Slavery in the Crucible of Public Debate*. Chicago: University of Chicago Press, 1993.

ARTICLES, REPORTS, PAMPHLETS, AND BROADSIDES

"Address to the Non-Slaveholders of Kentucky." Pamphlet read to a meeting of the mechanics and laboring men of Louisville, April 10, 1849. Special Collections, Filson Historical Society, Louisville, Kentucky.

Alberts, Don E. "The Battle of Glorieta and the Union Victory in the Far West." *Hallowed Ground*, Winter 2007.

Anderson, Oliver. "To the Voters of Fayette County." Broadside, June 12, 1849. Special Collections, Filson Historical Society, Louisville, Kentucky.

Anonymous. *The Fugitive Slave Bill: Its History and Unconstitutionality, with an Account of the Seizure and Enslavement of James Hamlet and His Subsequent Restoration to Liberty.* Pamphlet. New York: William Harned, 1850.

Bassett, Isaac. Manuscript Memoir. United States Senate Library.

Bowditch, William I. *Cass and Taylor on the Slavery Question*. Pamphlet. Boston: Damrell & Moore, 1848.

Brother Jonathan. Broadside published for the inauguration of Zachary Taylor, March 1849.

Captain Sutter's Account of the First Discovery of the Gold. Lettersheet. San Francisco: Britton & Rey, 1854.

Cartwright, James F. "John M. Bernhisel letter to Brigham Young." *BYU Journal*, Vol. 22, No. 3 (1982).

Clark, T. D. "The Slave Trade Between Kentucky and the Cotton Kingdom." *The Mississippi Valley Historical Review*, Vol. 21, Dec. 1934.

Clinton, Anita. "Stephen Arnold Douglas—His Mississippi Experience." *Journal of Mississippi History*, Vol. 50, Summer 1988.

Coleman, James P. "Two Irascible Antebellum Senators: George Poindexter and Henry S. Foote." *The Journal of Mississippi History*, Vol. 46, February 1944.

Corts, Paul R. "Randolph vs. Clay: A Duel of Words and Bullets." *The Filson Club Historical Quarterly*, Vol. 43, No. 2, April 1969.

Crapol, Edward P. "John Tyler and the Pursuit of Manifest Destiny." *Journal of the Early Republic*, Vol. 17, Autumn 1997.

Crosley-Griffin, Mary. *Hangtown (Tales of Old Placerville)*. Universal City, Calif.: Crosley Books, 1994.

de la Cova, Antonio Rafael. "Filibusters and Freemasons: The Sworn Obligation." *Journal of the Early Republic*, Vol. 17, Spring 1997.

———. "The Kentucky Regiment That Invaded Cuba in 1850." *Register of the Kentucky Historical Society*, Vol. 105, Autumn 2007.

Dyer, Brainerd. "Zachary Taylor and the Election of 1848." *The Pacific Historical Review*, Vol. 9, June 1940.

Edrington, Thomas S. "Military Influence on the Texas–New Mexico Boundary Settlement." *New Mexico Historical Review*, Vol. 59, October 1984.

Emory, William Helmsley. "Lt. William Helmsley Emory's Journal of General Stephen Watts Kearny's March to Santa Fe." *Niles's Weekly Register*, Vol. 71, October 31, 7, 14, 1846.

First Report of the New York Committee of Vigilance, for the Year 1837. New York: Piercy & Reed, 1837.

Foster, Herbert Darling. "Webster's Seventh of March Speech and the Secession Movement." *The American Historical Review*, Vol. 27, January 1922.

Freeman, Arthur. "The Early Career of Pierre Soulé." *The Louisiana Historical Quarterly*, Vol. 25, October 1942.

Fuller, John D. P. "The Slavery Question and the Movement to Acquire Mexico." *The Mississippi Valley Historical Review*, Vol. 21, June 1934.

Ganaway, Loomis Morton. "New Mexico and the Sectional Controversy, 1846–1861." *New Mexico Historical Review*, Vol. 18, July 1943.

Garnett, Muscoe R. H. *The Union, Past and Future: How It Works, and How to Save It.* Charleston, S.C.: Walker & James, 1850.

Gillespie, Charles B. "Marshall's Own Account of the Gold Discovery." *Century Magazine*, Vol. 41, February 1891.

González, John Edmond. "Henry Stuart Foote: A Forgotten Unionist of the Fifties." *The Southern Quarterly*, Vol. 1, January 1963.

Hall, Wade. "Henry Clay, Livestock Breeder." *The Filson Club Historical Quarterly*, Vol. 59, April 1985.

Hamilton, Holman. "Democratic Senate Leadership and the Compromise of 1850." *The Mississippi Valley Historical Review*, Vol. 41, December 1954.

———. "Kentucky's Linn Boyd and the Dramatic Days of 1850." *The Register of the Kentucky Historical Society*, Vol. 55, July 1957.

Harlan, A. J. "Last Survivor of a Great Congress." *National Magazine*, Vol. 15, March 1902.

Harrington, J. Drew. "Henry Clay and the Classics." *The Filson Club Historical Quarterly*, Vol. 61, April 1987.

Hendricks, Rickey L. "Henry Clay and Jacksonian Indian Policy." *The Filson Club Historical Quarterly*, Vol. 60, April 1986.

Hittell, Theodore H. "The Gold Discovery." Excerpted from *History of California*, Vol. 2. San Francisco: N. J. Stone, 1897. Online at www.sfmuseum.net/hist6/impact.

Humphreys, Hugh C. " 'Agitate! Agitate! Agitate!' The Great Fugitive Slave Law Convention and Its Rare Daguerreotype." *Madison County Heritage*, No. 19, 1994.

Johannsen, Robert W. "Stephen A. Douglas and the South." *The Journal of Southern History*, Vol. 33, February 1967.

Jones, Thomas B. "Henry Clay and Continental Expansion." *The Register of the Kentucky Historical Society*, Vol. 73, July 1975.

Julian, George W. "Some Reminiscences of the Thirty-first Congress." *The International Review*, Vol. 40, August 1881.

Kenworthy, Leonard S. "Henry Clay at Richmond in 1842." *Indiana Magazine of History*, Vol. 30, December 1934.

Knupfer, Peter B. "Henry Clay's Constitutional Unionism." *The Register of the Kentucky Historical Society*, Vol. 89, Winter 1991.

Kornblith, Gary J. "Rethinking the Coming of the Civil War: A Counterfactual Exercise." *The Journal of American History*, June 2003.

Leonard, Glen M. "The Mormon Boundary Question in the 1849–50 Statehood Debates." *Journal of Mormon History*, Vol. 18, Spring 1992.

Lightfoot, Alfred. "Henry Clay and the Missouri Question." *Missouri Historical Review*, Vol. 61, No. 2, January 1967.

Lynch, William O. "Zachary Taylor as President." *The Journal of Southern History*, Vol. 4, August 1938.

Martin, John M. "The Senatorial Career of Jeremiah Clemens, 1849–1853." *The Alabama Historical Quarterly*, Vol. 43, Fall 1981.

May, Robert E. "John A. Quitman and His Slaves: Reconciling Slave Resistance with the Proslavery Defense." *The Journal of Southern History*, Vol. 46, November 1980.

Milton, Page. "The Emancipation of the Slaves of the District of Columbia." *Records of the Columbia Historical Society*, Vol. 16, 1913.

Minutes of the New Mexico Bar Association, Sixth Annual Session. Santa Fe: New Mexican Printing Co., 1891.

Moore, J. Preston. "Pierre Soulé: Southern Expansionist and Promoter." *The Journal of Southern History*, Vol. 21, May 1955.

Munroe, John. *Proclamación*, May 28, 1850. Territorial Governors Collection, New Mexico State Archives.

Neighbors, Kenneth F. "The Taylor-Neighbors Struggle over the Upper Rio Grande Region of Texas in 1850." *The Southwestern Historical Review*, Vol. 61, April 1958.

Nugent, Walter. "The American Habit of Empire, and The Cases of Polk and Bush." *Western Historical Quarterly*, Vol. 38, No. 1, Spring 2007.

Osborn, Charles W., Charles F. Coffin, and William H. Coffin. "Henry Clay at Richmond: The Abolition Petition." *Indiana Quarterly Magazine of History*, Vol. 4, September 1908.

O'Sullivan, John L. "Annexation." *United States Magazine and Democratic Review*, Vol. 17, July–August 1845.

Parker, William. "The Freedman's Story." *Atlantic Monthly*, February and March 1866.

Parks, Joseph H. "John Bell and the Compromise of 1850." *The Journal of Southern History*, Vol. 9, August 1943.

The People of St. Louis to the People of the United States. Broadside, 1849. Adam Beatty Papers, Filson Historical Society, Louisville, Kentucky.

Seager, Robert. "Henry Clay and the Politics of Compromise and Non-Compromise." *The Register of the Kentucky Historical Society*, Vol. 85, Winter 1987.

Stephenson, Nathaniel Wright. "California and the Compromise of 1850." *The Pacific Historical Review*, Vol. 4, June 1935.

Sutter, Johann A. "New Helvetia Diary of Events from 1845–8 by Swasey, Bidwell, Looker & Sutter." Manuscript. Bancroft Library, University of California, Berkeley.

———. "Personal Reminiscences." Manuscript. Bancroft Library, University of California, Berkeley.

Timmons, W. H. "El Paso: The Formative Years." *Southwestern Historical Quarterly*, Vol. 87, July 1983.

Trescot, William. *The Position and Course of the South.* Charleston: Walker & James, 1860.

Troutman, Richard L. "The Emancipation of Slaves by Henry Clay, A Document." *The Journal of Negro History*, Vol. 40, April 1955.

Urban, Chester Stanley. "New Orleans and the Cuban Question During the López Expeditions of 1849–1851." *The Louisiana Historical Quarterly*, Vol. 22, October 1939.

Van Deburg, William L. "Henry Clay, The Right of Petition, and Slavery in the Nation's Capital." *The Register of the Kentucky Historical Society*, Vol. 68, April 1970.

Van Tassel, David D. "Gentlemen of Property and Standing: Compromise Sentiment in Boston in 1850." *The New England Quarterly*, Vol. 23, September 1950.

Vigil, Donaciano. *Triunfo De Los Principios Contra La Torpeza!* Broadside, January 25, 1847. Territorial Governors Collection, New Mexico State Archives, Santa Fe.

Yulee, C. Wickliffe. "Senator Yulee." *The Florida Historical Society Quarterly*, Vol. 2, April 1909.

INDEX